GIRLS WHO BITE BACK

WITCHES, MUTANTS, SLAYERS AND FREAKS

Edited by

EMILY POHL-WEARY

SUMACH PRESS

NATIONAL LIBRARY OF CANADA CATALOGUING IN PUBLICATION

Girls who bite back: witches, mutants, slayers and freaks/
    edited by Emily Pohl-Weary.

ISBN 1-894549-33-3

1. Women in popular culture. 2. Violence in popular culture.
3. Women heroes — Fiction. I. Pohl-Weary, Emily

NX650.H43G57 2004   305.42   C2004-900663-0

Visit the on-line *Girls Who Bite Back* discussion forum:
www.girlswhobiteback.com

Edited by Lisa Rundle
Copy-edited by Deb Viets
Cover & Design by Elizabeth Martin
Cover image by Shary Boyle

*Sumach Press acknowledges the support of the Canada Council for the Arts
and the Ontario Arts Council for our publishing program. We acknowledge
the financial support of the Government of Canada through the Book Publishing
Industry Development Program (BPIDP) for our publishing activities.*

ONTARIO ARTS COUNCIL
CONSEIL DES ARTS DE L'ONTARIO

Printed and bound in Canada

Published by

SUMACH PRESS

1415 Bathurst Street, Suite 202
Toronto ON Canada
M5R 3H8
sumachpress@on.aibn.com
www.sumachpress.com

FOR THE FREAKS

"Diary of a Broom Girl" by Mariko Tamaki, from the forthcoming publication *Fake ID* (tentative title), to be published by Women's Press. Reprinted by permission of Women's Press.

"Myths" by Kij Johnson first appeared in "Underground," published by Dark Horse Comics, Inc. Text and Illustrations for Underground R & ©1993 Andrew Vachss and Dark Horse Comics, Inc. All rights reserved.

"Stinky Girl," by Hiromi Goto, was previously anthologized in *Due West*, ed. Aritha van Herk, Fall 1996, co-published by Coteau Books, NeWest Press and Turnstone Press. The story is also forthcoming in a collection of short stories by Goto entitled *Hopeful Monsters*, Spring 2004, Arsenal Pulp Press.

"Cinematic Super-Babes are Breakin' My Heart: It's hard to go all the way with the new breed of lady killers when they just won't let go of that man," by Lisa Rundle, is an expanded version of a column that originally appeared in *Herizons: Women's News and Feminist Views*, Fall 2003.

"A Manifesto for the Bitten: The Cyborg, The Vampire, The Alien and Me," by Sophie Levy, is reprinted from *Kiss Machine #4*.

"Medusa: Super Mom," by Sheila Butler, is reprinted from *Kiss Machine #6*.

CONTENTS

ACKNOWLEDGEMENTS

I'm thankful to the remarkable women behind the scenes at Sumach Press: Liz Martin, Lois Pike, Rhea Tregebov, Noelle Allen and especially Lisa Rundle. It was a pleasure working with them from start to finish.

The contributors exceeded my expectations and displayed superhuman strength in the face of my endless revisions. Particular thanks go to cover artist Shary Boyle for her commitment to this project and her inspirational power.

The women at the Virginia Kidd Agency helped cover my ass. Writer Emily Schultz suggested I do an anthology in the first place. Do-it-yourself role model Jim Munroe supported this project in all his usual helpful ways. I am also very grateful to live in a country with the political will to fund the arts.

My extended family gives me love (and stuff to write about — ha ha). *Como siempre, unos besos grandes para mis queridos hermanitos.*

And finally, without Jesse Hirsh in my life, I would not be able to do the things I do. He's like my own personal superhero.

THE MUTANT GENERATION
Shaping Stronger and Wiser Superheroines

Emily Pohl-Weary

I have a superpower. It's the ability to morph from indie press activist to pop culture junkie in the blink of an eye. After being dormant for decades, my skill manifested three years ago. I blame that skinny blonde vampire slayer. With super-strength on her side, she pranced through dark streets and graveyards, snuffing demons who came after her in the shape of football players, fraternity boys, scientist zombies, her mom's boyfriend and even the town's mayor. In short, she won my heart.

The creators of Buffy — and the rest of pop culture's range of super-women — understand that at some point in our lives, we all wish for the ability to fly past traffic jams or will our bosses to do our bidding. Deep down, we covet absolute power so that everything can be done our way: no arguments or negotiations necessary. Think how easy life would be!

In reality, however, it's more useful to take public transit or quit our jobs; it's better to change the frustrating dynamics with our lovers than it is to fantasize about killing them. But sometimes we're stuck in crappy situations and our only option is to escape into fantasy. There's absolutely nothing wrong with taking a couple of hours off from reality. It'll be there when we get back.

Consider this: I used to be allergic to all forms of corporate media. For about five years, I only watched art films and independent videos. I was the type of person who cringed self-righteously when friends referenced *The Simpsons*. I loathed the daily papers filled with so-called objective news written by strangers who were accountable to no one

AMY CHOY, 17

Fave superheroines:
I wasn't really exposed to the whole superhero comics and TV shows when I was young, but I can recall myself watching *Batman* and *X-Men* occasionally. If I have to choose, I think I'd pick Poison Ivy. She was awesome because she just kicked ass and didn't give a damn about what other people thought.

Fave comic:
Again, never really read comics when I was younger, but I guess *X-Men*, just because they had so many different people with different backgrounds, pasts, powers, and they all rocked in their own ways.

Fave TV show:
Ooh, that's really tough. *Buffy the Vampire Slayer* is one of them, of course (though not necessarily Buffy herself, she irks me sometimes), but that's only for English shows. If I can choose other types (i.e. Japanese anime), I'd say *Inuyasha*.

except their employers. I realized that every time I read the paper in the morning, I started the day in a foul mood. So I quit cold turkey. The quest for alternative media became my obsession. I started making zines and proselytizing the wonders of local media.

Fundamentally, I'm still the same person today — pick any article in the front section of a daily and there's a fifty/fifty chance it will make me want to riot. I still only read the arts section on a regular basis (I know, I'm *such* a girl) because a single glimpse of whatever war's splashed across the front page will profoundly disturb me. But when it comes to cultural consumption, everything has changed.

Buffy Summers and her loyal Scooby Gang were definitely my undoing. I watched her stake a vampire for the first time only because a friend pestered me relentlessly. But when I finally sat still long enough to let an episode sink in, I was mesmerized. The privileged, preppy girls in Buffy's world looked just like the ones who had gone to my high school. They were tidy, self-absorbed and white. They, too, flirted with each other's boy-friends and were capable of murder if they thought it would make them popular.

Meanwhile, in the centre of it all, there was broody, troubled (pretty) little Buffy sneaking out at night to stake vamps in the graveyard. She led a double life, like me! In high school, I was pretty and vapid, wore pink miniskirts, teased my curled bangs and dated the football quarterback. After school, I went to anti-war demos with Mom, read Germaine Greer's *The Female Eunuch*, and cared for my whip-smart, bitchy, second-gen (at least) feminist grand-mother. Don't all teenage girls face some kind of similar dichotomy?

I get it. I know the politics. Most television shows are simply vessels that deliver audiences to advertisers. Powerful corporations spend billions to package girl power in the form of popular culture and its attendant merchandise. They sell our dreams back to us. Queen of the freaks Courtney Love summed up the state of affairs back in 1998, when, on her *Celebrity Skin* album, she belted out lyrics about how cultural producers incorporate and sell out little girls. And millions of teens bought that album. It becomes hard to distinguish what's genuine and what isn't when that much money's changing hands.

None of that stops me from getting excited because the most recent *Charlie's Angels* installment has hit the cinemas. I'm one of those weird people who actually reads episode spoilers! (You know, summaries for plot twists that haven't yet aired.) I troll the recesses of Web sites like Spoilersluts.com and wake up in the morning, excited about spending three hours in front of the boob tube between 7:00 and 10:00 p.m. A couple of years ago, I even made my friends reschedule my own birthday party because there was a new episode of *Buffy* on TV that night. Yeesh. I've turned into my own worst nightmare.

How could this happen? My parents didn't raise me to love television. Not even close. As a child, I was only allowed to watch a half hour of educational television per day — no guns, no nasty stereotypes and no ads disguised as children's programming — so that I wouldn't become desensitized to the real horrors that were happening everyday in this world. Cable was forbidden fruit I indulged in secretly at friends' houses. Like candy, I craved pop culture as fiercely as a package of cherry and lime Lik-M-Aid (ooh, dyed sugar!).

Is Buffy a feminist?
Well, a feminist is someone who fights for equality of the sexes in the society, right? Well, how could she be a feminist if she relies so heavily on men? She relies on Giles for guidance, she relies on Xander, Angel and Spike for emotional support, hell, she even relied on Riley to make her feel like a normal person. Besides, I don't really recall her ever actually coming straight out and saying something or doing something to that effect, so no, I don't really think so.

Can you think of any superheroes who aren't white?
Well the first one who popped into my mind was Storm. She's Black, she's female, and she has wicked powers.

What do you think about the fact that almost all the characters are white?
It's really annoying because there's such a large majority of people in the world who are *not* white. I guess it's the whole concept of beauty that's been

hammered into our heads by the society. If you're white, (preferably) blonde and blue-eyed, then congratulations! You're considered ideal. Does this remind anyone of Hitler, or is it just me?

What don't you like about the female heroines on TV right now? Many are blonde, some are ditzy, all are inhumanly beautiful and they either rely heavily on men or act super-masculine to make up for their gender.

JULIA POHL-MIRANDA, 17

Fave superheroines: In terms of "real-life" superheroes, I am impressed by women who beat the odds, fight back against racial, physical, sexual, psychological and emotional abuses. Quite a few women I know have been able to succeed in spite of huge problems that stand in their way. Comic-book heroes I like include Storm, Psyche/Mirage (from *New Mutants*), the Scarlet Witch, the

Once in a blue moon, I managed to sneak in an early Saturday-morning binge of crappy cartoons with a sprinkling of interesting female characters. I would curl up in the living room, pull my favourite red blankie around me, turn on the TV really quietly (so as not to wake the parents) and flip through the channels to find She-Ra the Princess of Power — essentially He-Man with tits and Farrah Fawcett-worthy blonde flips — or an episode of *Rocket Robin Hood* in which Maid Marian made an appearance. Sometimes Wonder Woman would exhibit derring-do on the long-running *Super Friends*, which paired up two ordinary teenagers with DC Comics' Justice League of America, but really it was Superman's show. Marvel's retort, *Spider-Man and His Friends*, had Firestar, a composite of a couple of characters from the printed comics. And there was the bizarre glam-rock band/superhero team called Jem and the Holograms: a great concept that ultimately fizzled.

But, sadly, the gender dynamic on most shows was closer to the wise-cracking *Smurfs,* that watery late-1970s childhood staple with one lonely Smurfette and hundreds of guy Smurfs. Sure she was the sensible one, but she didn't bother to show her face in every episode. She was probably too tired from tending to the needs of all those chipper, Machiavellian blue guys.

Some of the happiest memories of my childhood include trips to a local comic shop called Memory Lane, down the block from Honest Ed's emporium in Toronto. It was run by a man named George Henderson, one of my grandmother's odder friends, who had excessive facial hair, a twinkle in his eye and a desire to provide anyone who entered his shop with their most desired item. I believe he also made a comic called *Captain George's Whizz-bang,* likely named after *Captain Billy's Whiz Bang*, a popular magazine in the 1920s (hence the name of Diamond Dame's gang in my short story included in this collection, p. 227). At the time, my tastes were pedestrian. They ran to *Betty and Veronica*, *Richie Rich* and *Wonder Woman*. Captain George, as he liked people to call him, steered me toward more obscure titles like *The Mighty Isis*, *Shazam* and *She-Hulk*. The store closed down over a decade ago, but I still wonder whatever became of Captain G.

I outgrew comics, or maybe just lost interest when I couldn't find any really cool girl heroes who lasted more than a few issues. Then I found Nancy Drew. For about two years, I wanted to be her (minus the racism and classism, of course, but then I only recognized that years later). I devoured the complete set of old hard covers that my cousin shipped over from BC for my birthday. For months, I went around dreaming about owning the *Nancy Drew Sleuthing Guide*, till my parents took pity on me and bought a copy for my birthday. I read it from cover to cover, as if it were a novel, then set out to practise the techniques outlined in each chapter. I learned to decode secret messages, take fingerprints and analyze handwriting. I practised on my family. There is nothing like perfection to inspire admiration and Nancy had everything I would never have: tidy hair, wealth, a housekeeper, a fast car and a devoted lawyer father.

When my parents allowed me to buy my first bottle of hair dye (or perhaps simply ceased threatening to ground me) I picked — one guess — titian! I so desperately wanted to be Nancy that, at the age of thirteen, I started dyeing my hair strawberry blonde and kept it up for so long that I forgot my natural hair colour. Soon, I also learned to lie about it: "Sure, it's natural!" These days, it's a

Valkyries from Asgard (like Brunhilde, who's in *The Defenders*), Firestar and many more.

Fave comic:
I always really liked the *New Mutants*, the *New Defenders* and *Spider-Man*. I liked the *X-Men*, but I didn't have many of their comics, since I was a second generation recipient of our comic collection, and I did very little comic-purchasing of my own.

Fave TV show:
It has to be *Buffy* all the way, but I also like *Relic Hunter*, and I thought *Dark Angel* was okay.

Is Buffy a feminist?
I'd say so — she's strong (physically, psychologically, even emotionally usually), she stands up for what she believes in, and she doesn't let other people push her around.

Can you think of any superheroes who aren't white?
Storm, Jubilee, Psyche, Power Man, the Puma, Dagger of Cloak and Dagger, and Bobby from the *New Mutants*.

They are (respectively) African, half-Japanese, Cherokee, African-American, Aboriginal, African-American and Brazilian. There really aren't many.

What do you think about the fact that almost all the characters are white?
I think it's a poor sign for a country that claims to treat everyone equally.

What don't you like about the female heroines on TV right now?
They're all completely emotionally dependent. They all seem to need relationships in order to feel good about themselves. I don't mind characters having problems, but they shouldn't all revolve around their boyfriends or girlfriends …

TEMPEST BUIE-POPE, 16

Fave superheroines: My favourite is Heath from *Thieves and Kings*. But my favourite mainstream superhero is Jubilee. She rocks out: all

strange thing to look around at all the women on the subway and realize that nine out of ten of them dye their hair, too.

As women, we strive for perfection but settle for anything that's different from our natural state. In my case, I wanted to become the attractive slip of a girl who speeds around in her brand-new roadster, never has to do boring chores and solves crimes neatly in her pumps with just enough chutzpah to keep her life from middle-class boredom. She was an alien figure, far removed from the bustling, poverty-plagued neighbourhood in Toronto where I lived: one of the city's last refuges for new immigrants and outpatients from the Mental Health Centre.

After Nancy, I kind of gave up on girl heroes — I was never cut out to be a wholesome femme with half-a-brain, I realized — just in time for the joys of high school. In truth, she was as unattainable as the caricatures I'd idolized earlier in life. She wasn't normal. She was very good at everything she did, from dancing to golf to getting loose when her hands and feet were tied. I wasn't particularly good at anything, or so I thought, so I dreamt about being anyone — anything — outstanding. I guess the capacity to be a pop-culture addict was in me all along, it was just waiting for a kick-ass girl hero to come along and unleash it. Mutants and witches with secret lives fighting evildoers fit the bill. If I had super-strength and could turn invisible, for instance, I would rid the world of torturers, nuclear weapons manufacturers, greedy millionaires who pay their workers pennies, school yard bullies, silly gossiping rich girls and warmongers.

I can't count the number of times I've wished fleetingly that I could crush an enemy simply because they were being close-minded, obliterate the cops trailing me home with their high beams on because they thought I was a hooker, or throw some lecherous guy into a wall with a flick of the wrist because he grabbed my ass or made me feel unimportant. Absolute power is coveted most by the powerless, and in our culture, that includes girls. Boys love superheroes, too. In fact, they love them so much they're Marvel and DC's target audience. But at that age, girls have a desperate need to identify women who can overcome obstacles (see Walker, p. 209).

Very little is empowering about the teen years: there's the subservience to teachers at school, the painful tests meant to confuse, the mystifying body changes, the boys who leer at you on the street, the pressure to start "real life" or to delay it a few years by conforming to standards set by universities. So it's easy to see why girls would love today's empowered, independent females. But why, as we grow older, do many of us never leave behind our fascination with indestructible superchicks? The popularity of shows like *Xena: Warrior Princess*, *Charmed*, *Wonder Woman* and *Alias* is undeniable (see Stafford, p. 25). Maybe this is because we still have days when we feel particularly fragile, our self-confidence is low and we appreciate how hard it is to be real (see Smolkin, p. 111). No matter what our age, we continue to strive for control over our lives, bodies, destiny and fantasies.

Perhaps it's a bit of a paradox that silly caricatures of ourselves can provide so much empowerment. When it comes to corporate culture, we settle for the least offensive female characters. Usually that means some vapid but distinctive chick who chases around a dude for the duration of the film/novel/comic (see Rundle, p. 305). Pop culture sets forward a myriad of examples of

sarcastic and smartass, but she always pulls through and has kick-ass powers.

Fave comic:
I like the spinoffs of *Batman*. I always liked Batman, he was cool, but my favourite comic is definitely *Thieves and Kings*.

Fave TV show:
La Femme Nikita. It's a great show, and you can tune in at any time and not be lost. Plus Nikita's really cool.

Is Buffy a feminist?
Yes she is, because she's a kick-ass chick who does what she needs to do to get things done, generally without the help of a male. However, a lot of the time she tries to do it all on her own, which is irritating.

Can you think of any superheroes who aren't white?
Yes I can ... Oh, did you want me to list 'em? Storm, Jubilee, Spawn, the current Green Lantern, Forge, Psylocke (but she was a white chick trapped in a ninja's body), Bishop and the Wonder Twins.

What do you think about the fact that almost all the characters are white?
To be completely honest, it never really bothered me, because I identify with those who are white, seeing as I am white myself. However, I can see why that would be irritating to anyone with a different background than myself.

What don't you like about the female heroines on TV right now?
I don't like how a lot of them are portrayed, which is generally very hard, not very nice at all.

KASHFIA RAHMAN, 17

Fave superheroines: Storm — mostly because she has these unbelievable elemental powers and yet is so wise. She seems approachably human and at the same time like a "higher power."

Fave comic: Hmm. This is a tough one mostly because I read a lot of *Spider-Man, Batman, X-Men,* and, uh, *Garfield.* I like *X-Men* the best.

idealized women. Turn on the TV set for a couple of hours, and we're left with the impression that eternal youth is the most coveted superpower. Everyone wants to be young forever, right?

To withstand the bright lights and paparazzi, movie and TV stars have to be smoother and cleaner than we can ever be. They're also indestructible. Long after they die, they remain immortalized on film and in photos. Time stands still for Hollywood. And before that, starlets get plastic surgery, Botox (it's natural!) and go on no-starch diets till they're bags of bones held together by skin.

Flip through the channels some day and take note that all the women over the age of forty look fake, like they've been pieced together by some cruel Dr. Frankenstein who's using a glossy fashion mag model as his template. Who can we look up to as we age and pass beyond the *Buffy* years (see Kasturi, p. 236)? Will I forever be forced to escape into the minds of characters who are essentially carbon copies of Betty and Veronica, doomed to fight forever over a dopey red-headed boy?

Intellectually, I know that the real superheroes are all around me (see Bianchini, p. 101). They're the people who face and overcome insurmountable hurdles everyday — like being afraid to walk the street and being judged in the subway because the mass media has recently depicted all people with the same skin colour as terrorists or, not just recently, as job-stealing immigrants. When pop culture's vast ranks of idealized Western beauties offer up only a handful of heroines who aren't white, how do women of colour escape into entertainment (see Gill, p. 39)? Should we forget about manufactured heroines altogether and look to each other for inspiration and role-models (see Tamaki, p. 96)?

Perhaps maturing is not so much about leaving youthful obsessions behind, but about understanding the complex social structures that lead us to desire certain things (see Whittall, p. 300). Perhaps it's also about fulfilling our desires and envisioning new role models (see Villegas, p. 315). It's how we invent and change society. Everyone needs to step out of their lives at times and dream about things that are beyond the drudgery of the day-to-day.

Nothing makes me happier than hunkering down on the weekend with a good mystery novel — if the protagonist is female and intelligent — or a video game in which the female has a lead role (see Livingstone, p. 187). Today, unlike when I was younger, that's actually possible. I've been watching my seventeen-year-old sister grow up with role models like brainy Willow the witch and grounded, quirky Rory on *Gilmore Girls*. I think she's lucky. Sure it's Hollywood schmaltz, but at least they're not cheery bottle-blonde appendages or breast-enhancement surgery rejects. We often find ourselves watching silly movies together, cringing internally because of the horrid dialogue and ridiculous premises — such as the notion that a girl's life could ever possibly be all about some silly boy — and laughing at the good parts.

Women born in the early 1970s or later have grown up surrounded by fictional images of super-heroes, witches, slayers and freaks; we're the new mutant generation. With the paradoxical image of the Barbie assassin planted firmly my in mind, I decided to put together an anthology that would critique and celebrate these constructs of the imagination. Naturally, the first thing I did was confer with the most knowledgeable source of information I have about pop culture: my sister and her teenage

Fave TV show:
I'm thinking *Buffy* — there aren't any good ones left, if any at all exist anymore.

Is Buffy a feminist?
Buffy is a feminist because she does stand up for herself and doesn't let anyone push her around. If you think back to some of the episodes when she was with Riley and Angel, she used all her slayer strength and was eventually empowered by it.

Can you think of any superheroes who aren't white?
Some of the X-Men ... Umm ... Oh yeah, *Static Shock*. It's pretty new. The Teenage Mutant Ninja Turtles, who count even if they aren't even human, Steel, and Spawn (I think).

What do you think about the fact that almost all the characters are white?
I'm hoping that time has passed or is passing — the world is too diverse to put up with that. The creators either move with the times or face a lot of

What don't you like about the female heroines on TV right now?
I'm sorry — they still exist? *X-Men* barely exists anymore and they had the strongest female roles. Most of the ones I see are too pretty and let guys control their lives. *Alias* was pretty good, up to a point, but the heroine annoys me.

criticism and hopefully extinction.

friends. The four girls who allowed me to buy them ice cream while I picked their brains were Julia Pohl-Miranda (my sister), Kashfia Rahman, Tempest Buie-Pope and Amy Choy. They all come from different cultural backgrounds but they've grown into young women alongside Buffy and the spawn of prime-time knock-offs who capitalized on the Slayer's successes. I asked them what they think of today's TV shows, whether there are any kick-ass girl characters in the movies and comics and who they think are the best female superheroes. It was interesting to learn that they think many of the current female heroes have the same short-comings they did when I was young. (See the sidebars for some of their answers to my questions.)

Then I approached several writers and artists and told them I wanted to create a book I would have loved to read as a teenager and that my friends and I would like to read now. The response was incredible: they, too, mourned the lack of strong, intelligent girls in pop culture (see Vincent, p. 327). Some writers decided to critique existing characters (see Stinson, p. 290) and others invented new, better, more interesting superheroes (see MacDonald, p. 231). Regardless of how inspiration presented itself, the consensus among writers and artists was that no one had ever heard of a book like this before. We were going to delve into the paradox and revel in it, through critical and personal essays, fiction, art and hybrid forms.

The collection you have in your hands is the result of many months of feverish work and thought. The cultural essays include genre overviews, a manifesto for people who affiliate more with the aliens and vampires in pop culture than the humans (see Levy, p. 132), a powerful piece about mental illness and the creation of fantasy worlds (see Gobatto, p. 119) and even a do-it-yourself guide to being a superhero (see Stasko, p. 77).

Talented artists created powerful alter egos (see Griffiths, p. 311), spellbindingly supernatural girls and otherworldly witches (see Boyle, p. 277). There's a collage monologue that belies the consumerist concept of the tough but beautiful bitch (see Ahlers, p. 34). One artist's work subverts the mythological heroine Medusa (see Butler, p. 250) and two more look closer to home to find familiar instances of the paranormal (see Poletto, p. 92) and the superhero in all of us (see Tjia, p. 154). As befitting a collection about superheroes, the art is heavily influenced by cartoons. An urban superheroine and her two feline sidekicks go on a mission in a poor neighbourhood (see Blackett and Crump, p. 71). The female superhero is placed within the context of a war-hungry, media-saturated world (see Dawson, p. 223). And there's even an adventure recipe comic (see Ngui and Wojtyra, p. 345).

The short stories range from modern-day myths (see Goto, p. 56) to twists on the kinds of superheroes created by Marvel Comics (see Dellamonica, p. 158). There are girls who become superheroes in response to girlhood traumas (see Hopkinson, p. 254) and women whose inner magic makes itself known against their will (see Lai, p. 336). Writers spin universes filled with magic and transgendered antiheroines (see Heath Justice, p. 140) or girl-gangs who trade quasi-magical trance-pronouncements for food and spare change (see Johnson, p. 282). A real-life genetic scientist has contributed a fake report on the various mutations that would result in superpowers (see Bustos, p. 179).

Read on to find out how to become your wildest dreams and fight the world's most insidious enemies. Keep in mind: deep down under our drudging exteriors, there's a superheroine in all of us just waiting to emerge! Enjoy!

HOLY BUTT-KICKING BABE, BATMAN!

The Comic-Book Origins of TV's Superheroines

Nikki Stafford

Buffy, Xena and Sydney Bristow are all names that, two decades ago, would have been considered silly; certainly not monikers with the power to strike fear in the hearts of men. But today these names all convey the same clear message: women know how to take care of themselves and those around them. On the small screen, we've watched each of them deal with heartache and loss, use their anger against their enemies and refuse to sit back and wait for a man to come and save them.

But where did these women come from? This surge of strong female characters on television seemed to appear out of nowhere in the mid-1990s, but these characters (and their flaws) have roots that go back decades. It all started — as so many modern-day stories do — in the comic books.

The 1940s saw the beginning of superhero comics. Superman, Batman, Captain Marvel and Captain America were all created during what has been deemed the Golden Age of comics. Each hero was a loner with a secret identity that he used when he wasn't fighting crime. They all had super strengths, and it was always clear who was good and who was evil. And, good or bad, they were all men. This was the era of World War II and propaganda, a time when it was clear who was the enemy and who was an ally. The ideology of the age made its way into movies, literature and comic books.

Where the 1940s was an era characterized by unquestioned patriotism, the 1960s was a time of civil unrest, war protests and deep suspicion of authority in general and the American government in particular. It was during this period that Stan Lee and Jack Kirby came along and revolutionized the comic strip, sparking the Silver Age of comics and making Marvel Comics the forerunner. They created a new brand of superhero, one with dark secrets and deep character flaws. These heroes were more fleshed out, and they blurred the distinction between superhero and human being. They were forced to battle the evils of everyday life, not just evil supervillains. The Thing (one of the Fantastic Four) was a grotesque creature with a rocky orange hide who had to deal with people fearing his appearance, often going into deep depressions and fighting his own teammates. The X-Men were mutants who had separated themselves from society and were treated as outcasts and horrible things to be shunned and feared. Even those characters who turned evil were treated sympathetically, as readers watched the bullying and horrible treatment they received from non-mutant characters. The Hulk was a normal man whose bouts of rage turned him into a massive beast against his will, a reluctant and terrified Mr. Hyde. The most popular character of them all — Spider-Man — was a teenaged boy who, before being bitten by a radioactive spider, was already dealing with his fair share of adolescent problems, including his extreme shyness, his lack of dating skills and the fact that he was seen as a nerd and a social outcast.

In each case, this new version of the superhero did not involve heroes with magical powers but instead regular human beings who, through either an accident or mishap that was beyond their control, suddenly found themselves with new abilities and gifts. With the exception of the X-Men mutants, each character remembered a life where he was normal and nothing extraordinary ever happened to him. For the first time in comics, black and white dichotomies had been replaced with many shades of grey, and it was increasingly difficult to tell the heroes from the villains.

But what about the women? In this vast gaggle of outcasts and mutants, the only "good guys" who were actually gals were token members of a team, such as Sue Richards (a.k.a. Invisible Woman) in the *Fantastic Four*, or Marvel Girl (later called Jean Grey) in the *X-Men*. Part of the reason stems from the fact that the writers and artists working on the series were all male, as well as the fact that in the 1960s, despite the budding feminist movement, women were far from being seen as the equals of men.

There was one exception to this rule. Princess Diana of the Amazons, daughter of Queen Hippolyta (a.k.a. Wonder Woman) was the first major superheroine in the comic-book world. Created in 1941 by Dr. William Moulton Marston (under the pseudonym Charles Moulton), Wonder Woman was part of the Golden Age of Superheroes. She had otherworldly powers, magical accoutrements, and rarely faced any moments of genuine angst.

In the early comics, she lived with the Amazons on Paradise Island, completely oblivious to the world around her. Everything was peaceful in their world until an American World War II plane crashed there, and the pilot, Captain Steve Trevor, was found clinging to life. Diana fell madly in love with him and was chosen to accompany him back to the US to seek medical attention. She had already been imbued with Aphrodite's beauty, Hercules's strength, Athena's wisdom and Mercury's speed, but her Amazon sisters also give her bulletproof bracelets, an invisible plane and a lasso that forced any bound victim to tell the truth (an interesting nod to Dr. Marston's own life's work as the inventor of the lie detector). Like her male counterparts in the Golden Age of comics, Wonder Woman was born of the politics of her time. As the men went off to war in the early 1940s, the women had jobs on the home front, keeping the economy running while the men were away. Similarly, Wonder Woman had the groundbreaking role of superheroine at a time when men were the heroes.

Wonder Woman appeared on television in 1975, first as a television movie and then a regular series. Cathy Lee Crosby, a professional tennis player, played the part of Wonder Woman in the television movie, lending a decidedly athletic appearance to the character. In the series, Wonder Woman was portrayed by Lynda Carter, a former Miss USA beauty-pageant winner and acting unknown who lent an innocence and hourglass figure to the part. (Incidentally, while current television executives have made leaps forward in the name of tough women, they've also made a few steps backward in casting anorexic-looking twigs to play the part of the superheroines.) The *Wonder Woman* series maintained the original storyline, set in the 1940s, but later shifted its timeline to the late 1970s when the show was renewed in a different format. Wonder Woman was a powerful female heroine with a sizeable fan base, who seemed to spend every episode saving Captain Trevor. While the series tried to remain faithful to the comic book, there were a few key changes. In the books, Wonder Woman's weakness was being bound by a man. The Amazons believed that being tied up and captured by a man was the most degrading thing that could happen to a woman, and Wonder Woman's powers would disappear as a type of punishment. On the television show, however, her powers disappeared if her belt was removed. Her new weakness didn't exactly have the same resonance. Furthermore, in the comics, when Diana Prince was hiding her identity, she was still Wonder Woman under her clothes. However, in the television series, she lost all her powers when she wasn't wearing her outfit, which undermined the notion that she had the powers of an ancient Greek goddess.

While the television show was a precursor to the strong television females that would follow two decades later, *Wonder Woman* wouldn't fly today. Her outfit was ridiculous: it sported the patriotic red, white and blue of the American flag, complete with the stars. She was touted as an "all-American girl" even though she was from an island far away from the US. She was gaga over Captain Trevor. And, like her comic-book counterpart, she wasn't particularly deep and didn't have a mysterious past. While she was championed as a positive role model for women (by no less than Gloria Steinem) in 1971, 90 percent of the comic's readership was male. Where else could you see pictures of 38–20–38 sized women that weren't in porn magazines? Undoubtedly, the television show had a large male viewership as well.

After Wonder Woman there weren't a lot of strong female heroines on television, save the Bionic Woman. Just as it took twenty years for the Golden Age of comics to morph into the Silver Age, it took two decades for another important female heroine to hit the small screen. One of the most amazing female characters to ever appear on television appeared in 1995.

Primarily a kid's show set in ancient times with a lot of camp, *Hercules: The Legendary Journeys* chronicled the adventures of Herc and his sidekick, Iolaus, who roamed the countryside fighting evil gods and monsters. In their world you were either a friend or an enemy, and there was rarely anything in between.

Until Xena showed up.

Introduced as an evil warrior who slaughtered whole villages of people, Xena was a tortured villain, one who had become evil because of her own pain and loss. As a young woman, she had lived a peaceful life until a warlord attacked her village. Xena formed an army to try to save her friends and family, but her brother Lyceus was killed. Her mother and the other villagers shunned her for putting people in danger, and out of hurt and anger she formed another army that roamed the countryside killing people and destroying homes, doing the very thing that she had tried to stop. By the end of her three-episode arc on the series — where Xena recognized the error of her ways and set off on a path of atonement — fans loved this character so much that she was spun off into her own show, *Xena: Warrior Princess*, where she, too, would have a sidekick and would roam the countryside, having adventures. The main crux of her character, however, was that she had a cloud of shame hanging over her. She hated who she used to be and spent every day on a path to redemption, trying to atone for the sins of her past. In the series premiere, the character buried her sword and military accessories in a move to put her past behind her, but she soon realized that as a warrior she could be most helpful to people.

By the show's second season, *Xena* was ranking high on the pop-culture icon-o-meter. The title character was seen as a feminist hero, and much attention was cast on her companion, Gabrielle. Unlike sidekicks of the past, like Batman's Robin, Gabrielle was much more to Xena than a helper. She became a co-star of the show, not a secondary character. She was Xena's strength, her best friend and, many viewers believed, her lover. The show developed a strong lesbian following, and where the relationship between Batman and Robin had developed into more of a late-twentieth-century joke, the one between Gabrielle and Xena was deep and loving. The themes of friendship, working together and love became as important to Xena's redemption as her fighting skills. Many of the show's arcs followed the highs and horrible lows of their friendship.

The character of Xena was undeniably influenced by the comic books. Created by writer John Schulian and executive producer Rob Tapert (and developed by Tapert and producing partner Sam Raimi), Xena embodied the looks and strength of Wonder Woman, complete with the gifts of the Greek gods. As for character traits, she was closest to Batman (the most brooding character of the Golden Age of super-heroes, who spent every day and night avenging the deaths of his parents) in that she had a sadistic side that stemmed from her desire for vengeance against the death of her brother. But unlike the more wooden aspects of the comic-book characters, Xena was constantly putting herself on trial, questioning her own motives and worrying that she could succumb to the evil within her at any moment. And all too often, she did. Her path of penitence was always being thwarted by her own inhibitions (she was constantly tempted by Ares to come back to him as an agent of war; she often gave in to temptation and believed herself unworthy of forgiveness) and as a result, she tried to push those who loved her aside and continue on her journey alone.

Despite the show's campy feel, and the fact that it explored the emotional ups and downs of the characters with all the subtlety of a Wagnerian opera, *Xena* maintained a decidedly adult audience and sparked a new wave of strong female heroes on television.

In 1997, Buffy Summers, played by actress Sarah Michelle Gellar, joined the group. Originally a campy 1992 box office flop, *Buffy the Vampire Slayer* was given new life on television, where its creator, Joss Whedon, would have complete creative control. Like *Xena*, the show was marketed to youth, but soon gathered an adult demographic that allowed the writers to take the series down increasingly more grim and complex paths. In Buffy, Whedon created the most fleshed-out heroine to date — a young girl with a pre-ordained mission to rid the world of evil who didn't want to be a hero; she just wanted to be a teenage girl. The character preserved many character traits of the comic-book hero — she had a secret identity (or, was supposed to ... she didn't really do a very good job with the whole secrecy thing), she had a tumultuous emotional life that stemmed from her solitude, and her superhero origins were a mystery. (Interestingly, while many suggest that Xena was the obvious television precursor to Buffy, in character Xena more closely resembles Angel, Buffy's true love, the vampire with a soul. He once slaughtered and tortured many people and is spending eternity trying to redeem himself. He is dark and brooding. He is always on the verge of slipping back into his evil ways and needs the help of those around him to prevent him from doing so. And, like Xena, he had his own spin-off show.)

Buffy the Vampire Slayer diverged from comic-book tradition in radical ways. Buffy had a mentor, Giles, who watched over her and helped her along the way. For the first couple of seasons, she also had the Watcher's Council, which functioned similarly to Commissioner Gordon from *Batman*. The council was a conglomerate of stuffy Brits who told her what to do and when (although she didn't have the cool red phone). But as she got older, she sloughed them off and became her own woman, answering to no one. Eventually, even Giles left her to battle the forces of darkness on her own.

In many ways, Buffy had more in common with the Fantastic Four or X-Men than any of the solo heroes. She was accompanied throughout the seasons by a group of friends: Willow (by the end of the show, a seasoned and powerful witch), Xander (the most emotional member of the group, a clever twist on the more traditional idea of men having the physical strength and woman having the empathy), Oz (who discovers he's a werewolf when he hits puberty), Anya (a former vengeance demon who joined the gang to help them fight evil while trying to understand how to live as a human), Spike (a nasty vampire who became a love interest to Buffy, and in many ways, was more dangerous as such) and her sister Dawn (not really her sister, but a ball of energy that some monks put into the form of a human and ... actually, if you don't watch the show, this one requires too much explanation). The increased focus on these supporting players set this show apart from the comics and added a richness to the story that would have been lacking had it only focused on Buffy.

But Buffy's angst stemmed from the fact that she was part of a line of Slayers who died young, fought alone, and had no futures. When the series began, she was feisty, quick with the comebacks and believed she was immortal. By season six, when she had died, gone to heaven, and been brought back by her friends, she was sombre, depressed, aware of her mortality and far more serious. In other words, she had matured into an adult.

Just as the comic-book characters developed over time, with surprise twists being dropped along the way that drastically changed our outlook on the characters, so, too, did Buffy — the character and the series — change and grow over seven seasons. Viewers knew that she descended from a long line of Slayers, but we didn't know how the first Slayer was made, or how a new slayer was chosen. In true comic-book fashion, Whedon finally unveiled most of the secrets near the end of the series, where we discovered that Buffy — the Slayer, the heroine, the "good guy" — was originally created through evil, and was part of the very darkness that she sought to slay. The heroine who had forged a path for strong women had, in fact, been created by a group of men in ancient times who had taken a defenceless woman from the village, imbued her with the evil of a demon and forced her to be the Slayer; hence the reason why all Slayers are women. So the reality was, Slayers were as controlled by men as any other woman in history, perhaps even more so. Whedon also revealed that while we had come to believe that she was created and watched over by men, the Watchers, in fact, were being controlled by a group of women called the Guardians, who were far more powerful. It was a fitting end to a series that had gained so much ground in the name of the superheroine.

Buffy brought the female heroine full circle, as her character lived in the present day and struggled with lifelike problems, emotions and friends. Where the traditional superhero often dealt with the perils of loneliness (a subject explored again and again on *Buffy* because Buffy could never really be honest with normal guys her age) the series also ended with the hope of a world filled with heroines, who no longer lived alone, hiding behind a secret, but were proudly out in the open, fighting for a better world. In the series finale, with the help of Willow, Buffy turns all potential Slayers into actual Slayers, and creates a race of strong women, able to fight darkness, demons and plain old school bullies. No longer will women be hiding behind objects while the stronger men save the day; in the Buffyverse, women are the heroes who can stand up for themselves, and probably save a few men along the way. Joss Whedon was beginning his own tradition, one that we can only hope others will follow and develop.

Now that *Buffy* and *Xena* have both left the airwaves, the superhero of the moment appears to be Sydney Bristow, played by Jennifer Garner, on *Alias*. A strong woman with no special powers, created by J.J. Abrams, Sydney does possess the secret identity like Wonder Woman, the tortured past like Xena, an unwanted destiny like Buffy, and has the added misfortune of finding out her parents are her worst enemies. Her mother, whom she believed was dead, had, in fact, been a Russian spy who married her father (a member of the CIA) in order to obtain government secrets. Her mother actually emerged at the end of season one, holding a gun to Sydney's head, and then tried to coax Sydney to trust her. Syd's father, on the other hand, began as the bad guy (Syd believed that he had somehow orchestrated her mother's death), but became a sympathetic character for a short time before we discovered that he had committed an unforgivable act when Syd was a child. He had programmed her from a very young age to become a spy. Just as Buffy had been called forth as a slayer against her will, Sydney has become a secret agent because it was what her mind was engineered to do.

As she discovers the penalties of letting her loved ones in on her secret identity (her fiancé is killed when she reveals who she is to him), Sydney also begins to question those around her and realizes that, unlike Buffy, she can't trust or count on her friends. One by one, the people around her are revealed to be something other than what they seem, and her world falls apart. In the very first episode, she discovered that even *she* wasn't who she thought she was, and that she'd been working for a terrorist organization rather than the CIA.

Unlike the superwomen who preceded her, Sydney's strength and wisdom are entirely human. Sydney doesn't have super-strength bestowed upon her by a higher power, she is a human being trapped in a situation that she doesn't want to be part of. Like Buffy, she remembers a time when she was a normal girl, but has recently discovered that even those memories were false. As a human being who is confused, alone, has no superpowers and bruises easily, Sydney is the next — and most complex — generation of butt-kicking women on television.

The only thing left to do is have a superheroine created by a woman. Men created all four of these strong women heroes. Of course, the sympathy and fascination that these characters have generated among fans is as much attributable to the women who play them as their scripts, but one can only imagine how different that could be if Wonder Woman, Xena, Buffy and Sydney Bristow were all women who either worked alone or in a group, and men played supportive roles in their lives, either as the enemy or as part of a team that helps them out. A new ideology has been gradually created, one where the concept of a cowering damsel in distress seems ridiculous, and where powerless men are the norm. So who will follow? Where can the genre go from here? Will the traditional male heroes of the world eventually disappear? Will women have to rescue them from oblivion?

... AND THE MYTH THAT THINGS HAVE PROGRESSED

Sonja Ahlers

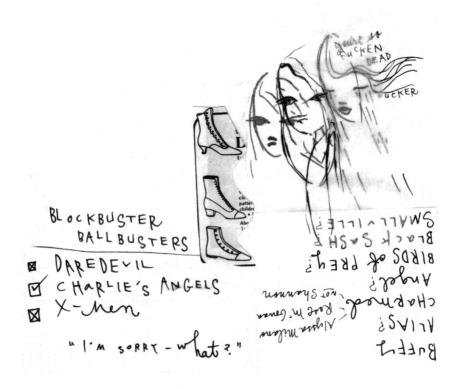

& THE MYTH THAT THINGS
HAVE PROGRESSED
& the myth that things
have progressed

& the myth that
things HAVE PROGRESSED.
& the myth that things
have progressed
& the myth that things
have progressed
& the myth that
things have progressed
& the MYTH THAT THINGS
HAVE PROGRESSED that things
& the myth & the
have progressed HAVE
THINGS
MYTH THAT SED & THE
PROGRES HAVE
MYTH THAT THINGS
PROGRESSED

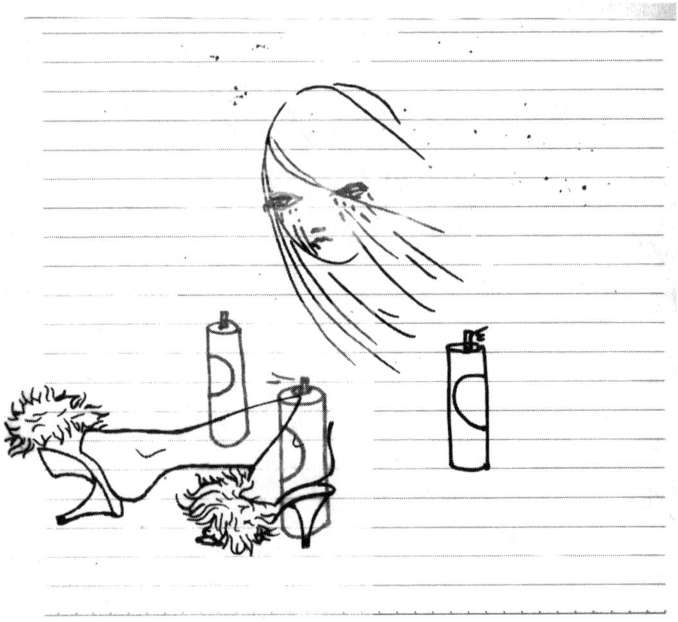

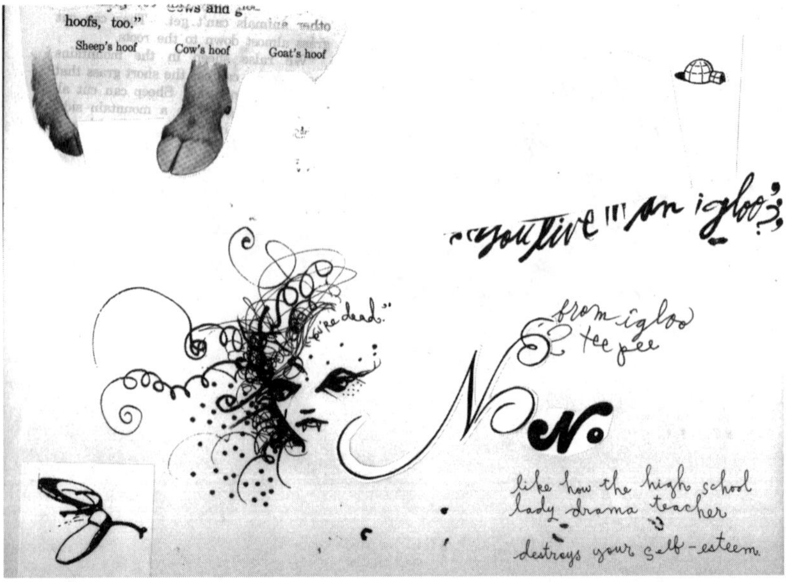
hoofs, too."
Sheep's hoof
Cow's hoof
Goat's hoof
"you live in an igloo?"
from igloo
to teepee
No. No.
like how the high school
lady drama teacher
destroys your self-esteem.

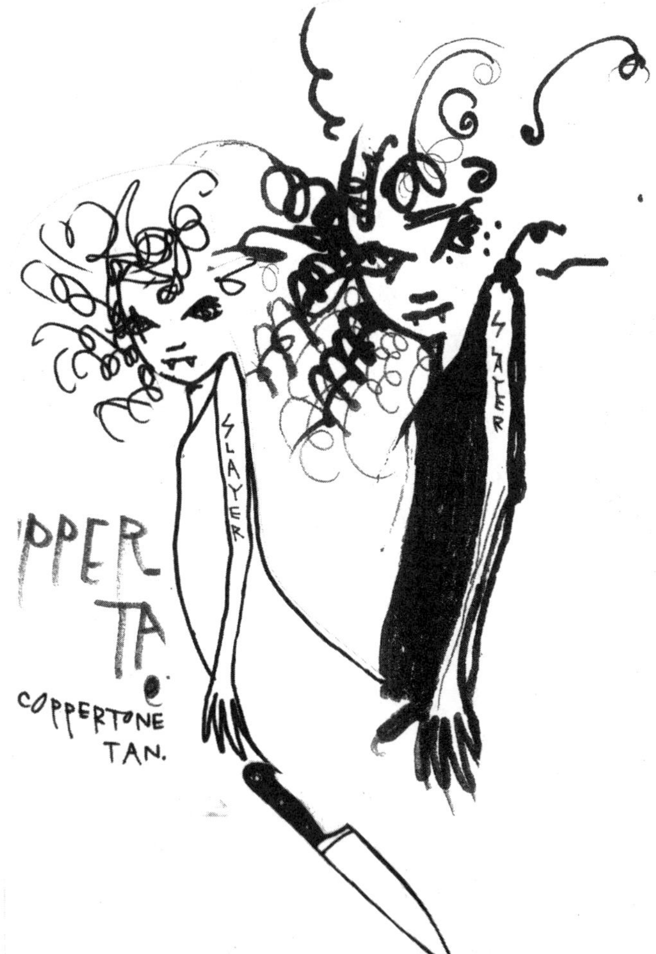
SLAYER
SLAYER
PPER
TA
COPPERTONE
TAN.

a machine gun
of a girl shooting
out the words SPEWING
Girl Power was the
stupidest thing
I ever say. CRINGE CENTRAL
MOLARS WITH FILLINGS CHEWING
ALUMINUM FOIL.
& another Super Bitch
is born TOTALLY TEDIOUS.
& I overheard overhead lighting
Tonya Harding etc.
say "I am into
the concept that
girls kick each other
down" like
"SOLIDARITY"
sisterhood
oneness.
Equals Survival of
the Shittiest.
Bitchiest
& it is all so VERY
HO HUM.

'CUZ THE BLACK CHICK ALWAYS GETS IT FIRST

DYNAMICS OF RACE IN *BUFFY THE VAMPIRE SLAYER*

Candra K. Gill

Since its premiere in 1997, *Buffy the Vampire Slayer* (*BtVS*) has been a feminist favourite. Whip-smart speculative fiction, it crossed horror, fantasy and drama with comedy in a show that both entertained and, often subtly, commented on the difficulties of coming into adulthood in America today. For seven seasons, the show followed Buffy Summers, a young woman living in fictional Sunnydale, California, who, while dealing with the everyday concerns of life, must also fulfill her role as the Chosen One: The Slayer.

There is only one Slayer at a time, and she protects the world from vampires and other supernatural ills. The Slayer is always an adolescent girl, and she is always called to her duty without notice. Others may know if a young woman is a potential slayer, but the only way to find out for certain who the next Slayer will be is to wait for the previous Slayer to die. When her predecessor dies, the new Slayer's true powers come to light. Since Sunnydale sits on a Hellmouth — a portal to hell — Buffy stays busy.

BtVS featured many regular characters over the years, but at the core were those Joss Whedon, the show's creator, called "the fearsome foursome"[1] — Buffy; Rupert Giles, her Watcher, whose job it was to teach Buffy what she needed to know about being a slayer and to record her exploits; Willow Rosenberg, Buffy's best friend, who was a bookish nerd in high school but eventually became a powerful witch; and Xander, another high school friend who, unlike Buffy and Willow, had no super-natural abilities, but played an important supportive role.

BtVS purposely recontextualized the image of women in a horror setting. In describing his conception of Buffy, Whedon says:

> I've always been a huge fan of horror movies, and I saw so many hor-ror movies where there was that blonde girl who would always get her-self killed. I started feeling bad for her — I thought, you know it's time she had a chance to, you know, "take back the night." And so the idea of Buffy came from just the very simple thought of a beautiful blonde girl walks into an alley, a monster attacks her, and she's not only ready for him, she trounces him.[2]

Several scholars have explored the way *BtVS* recontextualizes women in horror and action settings, particularly through the character of Buffy Summers. A characteristic analysis is that of Frances Early who argues that Buffy is a "transgressive woman warrior." Early cites Whedon's aca-demic background in film and in women's and gender studies. She quotes him saying he has "... always found strong women interesting because they are not overly represented in cinema" as evidence of his alignment with feminist ideas.[3]

In her study, Early writes, "As a feminist scholar, I appreciate the power of stories that bring women out of the shadows to centre stage and permit protagonists to be disruptive and to challenge patriarchal values and institutions in society."[4] She considers Buffy to be an "open image," a term she attributes to literary critic Sharon MacDonald, in contrast to a "closed image." Closed images are "analogous to symbols and ideals or stereotypes that appear fixed in the public consciousness" whereas open images "are inherently unsettling to the way things are."[5]

Of *BtVS*, Early writes:

> I would like to suggest that the woman warrior theme in Buffy — as presented through the mixed genre of fantasy/horror/adventure — rep-resents an attempt to demystify the closed image of the male warrior-hero not merely by parodying through comedic means this powerful stereotype but also by offering a subversive open image of a just war-rior.[6]

Buffy Summers is indeed a subversive warrior, and *BtVS* does recast women in horror settings, but for all its strong feminist imagery and its clever and complex dealings with issues people face through adolescence and early adulthood, the issue of racism has been conspicuously neg-lected in what fans of the show call the "Buffyverse" (the universe of

Buffy). It is important to place this discussion in terms of human-to-human racism, as there are several "races" represented on the show, most notably "demon" races. But when it comes to human characters, *BtVS* is an almost exclusively white show. Few recurring characters have been non-white, and no non-white characters have been featured in the title credits. It took *BtVS*'s spin-off series, *Angel,* to have a character of colour in the opening credits. On *Angel,* the character Charles Gunn appeared late in the first season and eventually became a regular during the second.

What is significant about *BtVS*'s treatment of race is how conventional it is. With few exceptions, the creators of *BtVS* have been content to perpetuate racial stereotypes or to ignore the issue of race altogether. In the African American community, for example, the perception is that in horror movies, if there is a Black character, particularly a Black male character, he or she will die before the film ends.[7] The first six seasons of *BtVS* did nothing to negate this belief: Black characters, or any other characters of colour for that matter, could expect to die by the end of an episode, or by the end of the season if they were lucky.

The people of colour who do appear in Sunnydale fit into two categories. The first: human characters who are actually human. The second, given the supernatural nature of the show, are characters who appear human, but who are not.

In the following sections, I will discuss the way race was handled in the first six seasons. Then, I will contrast this with the way the issue was developed in the seventh and last season.

THE FIRST SIX SEASONS:
BUSINESS AS USUAL

For the first six seasons of *BtVS*, people of colour in Sunnydale were portrayed in brief walk-on roles or in the background as non-speaking extras. The few non-white characters with substantial speaking roles could expect to die, be evil, be marginalized/exoticized, or all three.

The show's two-part pilot, called "Welcome to the Hellmouth" and "The Harvest," set the tone. There were very few non-white characters, and though some of them had speaking parts, they were mostly relegated to the background. In the first episode, a Black student at Sunnydale High School finds a dead body in her locker. In the second, a Black bouncer at the Bronze, the all-ages nightclub where Buffy and her friends often hang out, is killed by vampires who take over the club. And that's it. There were no significant non-white characters in the first season.

It was not until the second season's "Inca Mummy Girl" that a non-white character had a large guest role. Ampata was an exchange student from South America who turned out to be an Incan girl who had been sacrificed five hundred years before. When the audience first sees Ampata, she is a mummy in a museum that Buffy and her schoolmates visit. Ampata is freed from her imprisonment as a mummy when a seal is broken. To stay alive, Ampata has to suck the life from other people, which she does through kissing.

An Incan man violently defends her and argues that she should return to being a mummy. When he confronts Ampata and tells her that she has already died, he explains: "You are the chosen one. You must die. You have no choice."

Ampata kills him and sucks the life from him, saying: "Yes, I do." Calling Ampata "the chosen one" mirrors Buffy's position as the Slayer, a parallel Buffy notes at the end of the episode when she has defeated Ampata. Buffy kills Ampata to save Xander, with whom Ampata has gone to a school dance. Buffy refers to events in the first season's finale in which she died briefly. But unlike Buffy, of course, Ampata's sacrifice costs her life.

This episode is characteristic of the way indigenous cultures are represented on *BtVS*. They are relegated to museums and art galleries and are presented as lethal curiosities to be fought and overcome. Another example can be found in the third season episode called "Dead Man's Party," in which a Nigerian mask Buffy's mother brings home from her art gallery creates zombies that nearly destroy Buffy's home. The fourth season episode called "Pangs," discussed later in this paper, also fits this pattern.

Kent Ono, who has written about *BtVS* from a post-colonial point of view, has commented on Ampata's role and pointed out her marginalization from Buffy and her friends.[8] At first, she appears to assimilate into their culture. Buffy's mother even notes: "Two days in America and Ampata already seems like she belongs here. She's really fitting in." Ultimately, however, Ampata must be made a mummy once again in order to maintain Sunnydale's safety.

The second season also saw the appearances of Kendra the Vampire Slayer and the vampire Mr. Trick. Kendra first appears in "What's My Line: Part 1." She is a young Black woman who speaks with what sounds like a Caribbean accent. Where Kendra is from is never actually revealed, but the DVD commentary for that episode mentions that the vocal coach who worked with the actor placed the accent as an obscure Jamaican dialect.[9]

When Kendra first appears in Sunnydale, she is presented as a contrast to Buffy. While Buffy works hard to maintain her life outside of being a slayer, Kendra was given to her Watcher as a child so she could be trained for the possibility she would become The Slayer. Kendra has no life outside of Slaying. She is socially awkward, but extremely professional. By the time she leaves Sunnydale to return to her Watcher, in "What's My Line: Part 2," she has become more like Buffy, which is presented as a positive change. Kendra is able to joke and is even wearing one of Buffy's shirts when she leaves Sunnydale. Later, she returns for the episode "Becoming: Part 1," in which she is ambushed and killed by the vampire Drusilla.

Both Ono and Lynne Edwards, another writer who has explored the politics of race in *BtVS*, have commented on Kendra. Ono sees her as a challenge to Buffy's role as the lone Slayer,[10] while Edwards sees her death as a failed "quest for legitimacy."[11] Both situate her as Other in her relationship with Buffy. Kendra is marginalized, both in her relationship with Buffy and in her role as a slayer.

The appearance and demise of Mr. Trick, a Black vampire who was once a Black man, provide some of the few instances in the first six seasons where the writers of *BtVS* specifically comment on race. Mr. Trick arrives in Sunnydale in the episode, "Faith, Hope and Trick," working for an ancient vampire named Kakistos. Mr. Trick says about Sunnydale: "The town's got quaint, and the people — he called me 'Sir' — don't you miss that? Admittedly, not a haven for the brothers — strictly for the Caucasian persuasion in the 'Dale. But you gotta stand up and salute that death rate [...] and ain't nobody saying anything about it." With this statement, the writers acknowledge for the first time that Sunnydale is not at all racially diverse.

The death rate to which Mr. Trick refers is the amount of human deaths due to feeding vampires, demons and other supernatural causes. Ono suggests Mr. Trick is referring specifically to deaths of Black people here, but a close reading of the scene does not support this interpretation. Mr. Trick is simply telling his employer Kakistos about the town and why it is good for them, as vampires, to live there. He is suggesting that the fact that vampires can feed with impunity makes being there worthwhile, but that multiculturally, Sunnydale is lacking. It is worth noting that though Mr. Trick is a vampire, he maintains his Black identity.

The character Faith is also introduced in this episode. She is a white, working-class young woman who was called as a slayer as a result of Kendra's death. At the end of "Faith, Hope and Trick," Kakistos is killed by Buffy and Faith, who combine efforts, and Mr. Trick goes to work for Sunnydale's evil mayor. Twelve episodes later, in "Consequences," Mr. Trick is killed by Faith. Faith kills him to save Buffy. As Mr. Trick prepares to bite Buffy, he says, "I hear once you've tasted a slayer, you never want to go back," which is a riff on the saying, "Once you go Black, you never go back." Again, Mr. Trick makes a reference to race. This time, however, he dies.

Looking beyond Mr. Trick's quips, he is portrayed as intelligent and resourceful, but he also, significantly, works exclusively for white vampires and men. Unlike Buffy's other major vampire adversaries, such as The Master in the first season, or Spike and Drusilla in the second, Mr. Trick does not work for himself. And in the end, he does not last a full season (unlike, say, Spike, who becomes a regular character integrated into Buffy's core group).

While the third season briefly acknowledged race as an issue through Mr. Trick, the fourth season showed a return to characters of colour being relegated to minor roles and no acknowledgement of race. In the first episode of the season, "The Freshman," Olivia is introduced. She is a romantic interest for Giles, though little about her is ever revealed. Her character returns toward the middle of the season in "Hush," where we learn that she is visiting from England and that she knows Giles from his life before Sunnydale. The two are shown in bed together, but viewers know little else about their relationship other than that as a result of the events of "Hush," she comes to believe Giles's stories about the supernatural. Olivia is an incidental character who is given little background or significance to the arc of the show.

The fourth season also introduced the character Forrest, an African American man enlisted by The Initiative. The Initiative is a military operation that comes to Sunnydale to fight the supernatural forces there. Forrest is positioned in opposition to Buffy. He sees her as a threat, and repeatedly makes his feelings known. During this season, Buffy dates Riley, a soldier in The Initiative. As their relationship progresses, Riley begins to doubt what The Initiative does. Forrest sees Buffy as the cause of Riley's doubt and eventual desertion. He represents unquestioning military orthodoxy to which Buffy's independence is a threat. Forrest is eventually killed by Adam, a cyborg created by The Initiative as a weapon prototype. The military to which he is so loyal causes his demise. Because of the disproportionately large representation of Black people in the United States' Army, Forrest's death is all the more significant.[12]

That same season, "Pangs" deals with the effects of colonialism through the groundbreaking of a new cultural centre dedicated to the study of the Chumash, a Native American tribe indigenous to southern California. As a result of the digging, the spirit Hus is awakened. Hus kills several people in Sunnydale, including the director of the cultural centre and a priest, as revenge for his people's suffering. Buffy and Willow are conflicted about fighting Hus, as they acknowledge that his people were wronged and he has a right to be angry. The Thanksgiving holiday is used as a framework for a discussion about colonialism, culminating in an attack engineered by Hus on Giles's house as Buffy prepares a meal there.

What at first seems like a progressive handling of this theme actually perpetuates many stereotypes about America's indigenous peoples. In an article addressing "Pangs," Dominic Alessio points out several problems with the episode. First, Hus is portrayed as a violent warrior. Historically, however, the Chumash were a generally peaceful people.[13] Also, they are portrayed as having been wiped out — Hus is seen as the avenging spirit of a dead people. The problem is that the Chumash people still exist.[14] Alessio, while criticizing much of the stereotyping in the episode, gives credit to its writers for even addressing the issue.[15] He concludes that, "(...) the issue of race in [BtVS] remains one demon that Buffy can't deal with, one frontier that Buffy is incapable of crossing."[16] I find it particularly problematic that the discussion of the effects of colonialism is done exclusively by the white characters and there is no real voice given to the people about whom they speak.

Perhaps the most significant episodes in which race was a factor (albeit an unspoken one) were the episodes featuring Buffy's Slayer predecessors. The first such episode was the finale for the fourth season, "Restless," when "the fearsome foursome" are introduced to the First Slayer who stalks them in their dreams as punishment for invoking her spirit in the preceding episode. The First Slayer is a feral Black woman with a painted face and dreadlocks. She symbolically kills Willow, Xander and Giles in their dreams before encountering Buffy. Interestingly, Olivia appears in this episode — not in the real Sunnydale, but in the Sunnydale of Giles's subconscious during his dream. In this sequence, Giles is positioned as Buffy's father. Olivia is pregnant, pushes a pram and seems to be a part of this ad hoc family. Olivia isn't killed in the dream, but neither does she make any more appearances on the show.

When Buffy meets up with the First Slayer, she is told that what she and her friends have done is wrong. She is told this by the character Tara, Willow's girlfriend, who is serving as an interpreter. For some reason, despite, as Edwards points out, there having been a previous history of telepathic communication on the show, the First Slayer cannot speak directly to Buffy in anything but broken, guttural English.[17] In her confrontation with the First Slayer, Buffy challenges her and eventually saves her friends. Buffy makes her characteristic quips, one of which is about the First Slayer's hair and how unprofessional it is. While this is meant to be seen as an offhand comment, considering the challenges to wearing natural hairstyles Black women have often faced in the workplace, this statement is more than a joke and can be considered racist when looked at in some contexts. To the writers' credit, in making the First Slayer Black and, as we later learn, African, they are recognizing early human civilizations in Africa.

In the fifth season, we are introduced to two more Slayers in the episode "Fool for Love" — the two Slayers who were killed by the vampire Spike. At this point, Spike is incapable of attacking humans as The Initiative has implanted a behaviour modification chip in his head. Because of this chip, when Spike attacks a human he feels debilitating pain. Through a series of flashbacks, Spike tells Buffy the story of how he became a vampire and about the times he killed two of her predecessors. Both of the Slayers Spike kills are women of colour (one is Chinese, the other African American) and both of their deaths are sexualized.

The first is an unnamed young woman who encounters Spike in what looks like a Buddhist shrine in China during the Boxer Rebellion at the turn of the Twentieth Century. At one point, she has Spike pinned and is ready to kill him with an ornate, beautifully carved stake. A bomb goes off outside of the temple, knocking her down and giving Spike the chance to pin her. He kills her, drains her of blood and snaps her neck. Before she dies, she asks him in Chinese to tell her mother she is sorry. Spike replies that he does not speak Chinese.

After he kills this Slayer, Spike's sire and then lover, Drusilla, enters the shrine. He says, "You ever hear them say the blood of a slayer is a powerful aphrodisiac?" Drusilla then places one of Spike's fingers in her mouth, suggestively licking the blood off of it. They have passionate sex. After hearing the story, Buffy is disgusted, saying to Spike, "You got off on it?" Spike replies, "Well, yeah. I suppose you're telling me you don't."

The second story takes place in New York City in 1977, where Spike encounters a slayer we will later learn is named Nikki Wood. He says of his fight with her, "The first one was all business. But the second — well, she had a touch of your [Buffy's] style. She was cunning, resourceful. Oh, and did I mention, hot?" Spike and Nikki fight in a moving subway car, with each having the upper hand at some point. As he tells Buffy of his fight with Nikki, he and Buffy engage in a parallel sparring match. As the fights end, he is straddling Nikki, but kneeling before Buffy. He tells Buffy how he killed Nikki by snapping her neck.

After his stories, Spike, whose attraction to Buffy was revealed in a previous episode, finally tells her how he feels about her. Buffy rejects him, and as a result he decides to kill her, despite the excruciating pain that will ensue. Spike gets a gun and goes to Buffy's house. When he arrives, she is on her porch crying, completely unguarded. Instead of killing her, however, he puts the gun down, sits next to her and asks her what's wrong.

Spike's and Buffy's relationship is like this — problematic and violent, but also considerate and compassionate. The two develop a mutual respect, which plays a part in season seven.

That Spike would be cavalier toward the other Slayers he killed is not out of character. After all, he is a vampire, and the Slayer, whoever she is, is by nature his mortal enemy. What is notable about Spike and the way he treats Buffy in relation to his previous encounters with slayers is the compassion he shows for her. He falls in love with her. That he kills, and "gets off" on killing, two non-white Slayers and chooses to eventually voluntarily help Buffy in her mission as Slayer, has to be noted. Both Asian women and women of African descent have been historically sexualized and exoticized. That Spike takes the time to love Buffy but brutally kills the other two and eroticizes their deaths, marginalizes and devalues the women of colour who are slayers.[18]

In fairness, every Slayer before Buffy depicted on the show has been a woman of colour. It shows that the slayer legacy is not exclusive to white women. It is also significant that in both cases, the Slayer fighting Spike comes close to defeating him — it is only sudden reversals of fortune that lead to their deaths. However, with the exception of Buffy, the only Slayers who die onscreen — and therefore fail in their role as Slayers — are women of colour. And unlike Buffy, these Slayers are not (repeatedly!) resurrected.

SEASON SEVEN:
SUNNYDALE GETS SOME COLOUR

The seventh season of *BtVS* showed a marked difference in both the number of people of colour in Sunnydale and the way in which race and racism were approached. While still lacking in many respects, there was a definite improvement, if only in terms of numbers.

The increase in people of colour came after the show moved from the WB network to UPN. Also, in the last year, the shows that aired with *BtVS* in the United States changed. When it first went to UPN, *BtVS* was a lead-in to other speculative shows, including the short-lived *Haunted*. During its last months, *BtVS* ran before a show called *Abby*, which featured a primarily African American cast.

The plot of the seventh season revolved around the return of The First Evil (also called "The First"), a disembodied enemy who had made a brief appearance in the third season. The First decides to destroy the whole line of Slayers, which means killing every girl who is a potential slayer in the world. In response, Buffy and her friends start to gather all the potential Slayers to Sunnydale, where they can be protected. Ultimately, the final story arc of *BtVS* deals with the battle to defeat The First.

The seventh season featured an unprecedented number of people of colour as characters in Sunnydale. Many of the potential Slayers were women of colour, including Rona, an African American woman;

Kennedy, a Latina woman who eventually becomes romantically involved with Willow; and Chao-Ahn, a Chinese woman. Another regular character was introduced in the seventh season — the new principal of Sunnydale High School, an African American man named Robin Wood, who happens to be the son of the second Slayer Spike killed.

In addition to the regular characters, the seventh season featured many single-episode appearances by non-white characters and the return of significant past characters — the First Slayer and Nikki Wood. The *BtVS* writers make several references to race and racism throughout the season. In "Potential," after Rona has been mock-killed in a training exercise, she's asked why she "died." She replies: "'Cuz the Black chick always gets it first." In "The First Date," humorous allusions to cultural stereotypes and expectations are made through Giles's interaction with Chao-Ahn. There is a language barrier, so Giles in particular relies on assumptions that turn out to be erroneous and ethnocentric. It is played in such a way that Giles looks silly for doing this.

Also in "The First Date," Buffy, Xander and Willow each engage in romantic activities with people of colour (Buffy has a date with Robin Wood, Xander has a date with Lissa, played by African American R&B singer Ashanti, and Willow continues to develop her relationship with Kennedy). Factoring in Giles's relationship with Olivia, each of the "fearsome foursome" has interracially dated, though no discussion of this has taken place on the show. In this particular episode, much is made of the fact that Lissa turns out to be a demon who tries to kill Xander, but no one mentions at any point that Buffy, Xander and Willow are each seeing people of colour, nor is it mentioned that, with the exception of Willow and Kennedy, none of the potential relationships work out (this includes Giles and Olivia). This silence on the issue could be seen as a positive normalizing of interracial dating, which would be good. It does, however, seem strange that in a city where people can go days without seeing a non-white person, no one mentions that suddenly everyone's dating them.[19]

The most notable seventh-season episode when it comes to race and racism is "Get It Done." In this episode, the First Slayer appears to Buffy in a dream and talks to her. Apparently the First Slayer can suddenly communicate directly to Buffy in standard English instead of the stereotypical broken English she used previously.

The First Slayer tells Buffy "It's not enough!" The "it" to which she refers is the preparation to fight The First that the "fearsome foursome" and the potential Slayers are all engaged in. Through a mystical shadow box, Buffy is transported through a portal to the place and time of the First Slayer. When she goes through the portal, she encounters three men in non-specific traditional African garb, each carrying a staff. The men speak Kiswahili, but Buffy is able to understand them. They tell her that they have been waiting for her and that they "…can't give her knowledge […] only power."

When Buffy expresses doubt that the men are real, one of them hits her with his staff and knocks her out. When she awakens, she is chained to a rock. One of the men says, "We are at the Beginning. The Source of your strength. The well of the Slayer's power. This is why we brought you here." When Buffy protests, she is told that "The First Slayer did not talk so much." One of the men then takes a box, opens it, and as a black substance flows into the air, says, "Herein lies your greatest strength. The energy of the demon. Its spirit. Its heart." They reveal that this is the way the First Slayer got her power — by absorbing the demon's heart. Buffy balks, but is told, "It must become one with you" because she needs the strength to fight The First.

Buffy refuses to absorb the power, saying, "By making me less human?" The flowing, black essence of the demon starts to penetrate Buffy, trying to enter her through her nose. She screams, refusing it. It tries to enter her again, this time through her abdomen. Buffy says, "You think I came all this way to get knocked up by some demon dust? I can't fight this. I know that now. But you guys — you're just men — " she breaks her chains "— just the men who did this. To her. Whoever that girl was before she was the First Slayer."

One of the men says, "You do not understand," to which Buffy replies, "No, *you* don't understand! You violated that girl — made her kill for you because you're weak, you're pathetic, and you obviously have nothing to show me." She then starts to fight the men and knocks two of them down. She breaks one of the staffs of the fallen men and the essence of the demon disappears. She says, "I knew it. It's always the staff." The remaining man says, "We offered you power." Buffy says, "Tell me something I don't know." The man says, "As you wish," and gives Buffy a vision of the army she and the potential Slayers will have to defeat. At that moment, Buffy's friends succeed in their efforts to get Buffy back through the portal and she returns to Sunnydale.

The scenes that feature the makers of the First Slayer appear to be an exploration and condemnation of patriarchal power. The creation of the First Slayer is presented in terms of a violation, with the demon essence penetrating her. It is also clear that this was done against her will. By refusing the essence and physically overcoming the men who would have given it to her, Buffy challenges the patriarchy in language it can understand — through physical violence.

Another reading of this scene, however, is not as progressive. In having the physically slight, white female confront three Black men and accuse them of violation smacks of early twentieth-century rape narratives in which white women were depicted as the prey of Black men.

The continued problems of race in *BtVS* are encapsulated in the final episode, "Chosen." While people of colour are strongly represented in this episode, the resolution is racially problematic. In "Chosen," Buffy devises a plan to defeat The First once and for all. This plan involves using Willow's abilities as a witch to make each of the girls who is a potential Slayer become an actual Slayer. Buffy questions the tradition of a single Slayer, noting that the only reason there is one Slayer at a time is because the men who made the First Slayer created that rule. "They were powerful men," she says. "But this woman [pointing to Willow] is more powerful." The powerful men to whom she refers are specifically the men who made the First Slayer, the Black men who, in "Get it Done," are coded as rapists.

Willow is able to successfully awaken the Slayer within each of the potentials, both those fighting in Sunnydale and those around the world. In doing so, Willow taps into a great power that turns her hair white and causes her to glow. Willow's normal hair colour is red, but her hair changed colour in previous episodes as well. When she was overcome with evil in the sixth season episode, "Villains," her hair turned completely black. It stayed this way for three episodes, until the evil left her.

When Kennedy sees this final change, she says to Willow, "You're a goddess!" Thus, the climactic moment of empowerment when the potential Slayers all become actual Slayers is brought about by a white goddess standing in opposition to the will of Black male rapists.

Also, near the end of the final episode, the audience is led to believe that Robin Wood has died (to the point where Faith moves to close his eyes) before he stirs. This Black male character has lived, if just barely, through to the end of the show.

CONCLUSION:

BETTER ... BUT NOT QUITE THERE YET

In presenting Buffy as a sort of Everygirl (and later, woman), the creators of Buffy failed to acknowledge that not every girl would see herself in Buffy Summers (or Willow Rosenberg, Anya, Cordelia Chase, or any of the other women who have been regulars on Buffy). This leaves many fans of colour in a strange place.

Fans are aware of the shortcomings of the show and address them publicly. *Deadbrowalking*, a communal Web log subtitled, "The Principal Wood Death Watch," is a meeting place for fans of the show to approach the show as fans of colour and to discuss issues related to that fandom. The community information page states, "Given that he's an African American and has the Hellmouth in his office, we were convinced that Principal Wood is a man marked for Death (or some other unspeakable evil)." It also makes reference to the increase of people of colour on *BtVS* during the seventh season, facetiously mentioning, "[...] the implementation of court-ordered desegregation in Sunnydale and the resulting influx of people of color in the town [...]."[20]

There is reason to believe that the creators of *BtVS* pay some attention to fans of the show. The sixth season ended controversially with the death of Willow's girlfriend, Tara, and Willow's subsequent grief-driven rampage through Sunnydale, which resulted in her killing the man who killed Tara and attempting to destroy the world. Many fans who were invested in Willow and Tara's relationship felt betrayed by this storyline. Relationships on *BtVS* often ended tragically, so Tara's death was not so much the issue as the circumstances surrounding it. Many felt that killing Tara after she and Willow had sex onscreen perpetuated the stereotype that the punishment for having lesbian sex would be death. Willow's resulting rampage evoked the stereotype of lesbians as dangerous and homicidal.[21]

The seventh season saw the creators of the show addressing these criticisms. When Willow became involved with Kennedy and eventually started sleeping with her, neither of them died, and Willow became more powerful in a decidedly good way. While this does not change the implications of the Tara storyline, it does suggest that the writers are aware of fan response and were willing to address it in the show.

In that brief moment when it seemed as if Robin Wood had died in the finale, it is reasonable to suspect that the writers were giving a nod to the issue of the deaths of people of colour in horror and on their show. It was a welcome acknowledgement, though with the other issues presented in the final episode, it also inspired a mixed reaction.

It is important for feminist fandom to interrogate its favourites and inspect them for other biases and exclusions. Author and cultural critic Samuel R. Delany specifically challenges speculative fiction fandom to deal with its racism. In addressing fandom, Delany says, "How does one combat racism in science fiction, even in such a nascent form as it might be fibrillating, here and there? The best way is to build a certain social vigilance into the system." [22] Part of such vigilance is for us, as fans of shows, to be critical of those shows even as we enjoy them. We must become what Ono calls "resistant readers" [23] who challenge the racism (and other forms of oppression) in our favourites, even if the creators of those favourites often did not intend racism in their creations. We need to approach these works on multiple levels, so we can say, yes, *BtVS* was a great show with transgressive and recontextualized images, but it also ended up perpetuating some racial stereotypes even as it gestured toward critiquing them. Clearly, the Black chick still better watch her back.

*

NOTES

1. Laura Miller, "The man behind the Slayer," *Salon*, 20 May 2003, <http://www.salon. com/ent/tv/int/2003/05/20/whedon/print.html> (23 May 2003).

2. Joss Whedon, "Joss Whedon on 'Welcome to the Hellmouth' and 'The Harvest,'" *Buffy the Vampire Slayer: The Complete First Season on DVD*, Disc 1, Twentieth Century Fox Home Entertainment, Inc., 2001, DVD.

3. Frances H. Early. "Staking Her Claim: Buffy the Vampire Slayer as Transgressive Woman Warrior," *Journal of Popular Culture* 35.3 (2001): (11-27), 12.

4. Early, 12.

5. Early, 12.

6. Early, 18.

7. A popular-culture example of this can be found in the book *3 Black Chicks Review Flicks: A Film & Video Guide with Flava,* a movie guide written by three

African-American women. In it, they describe what they call "the Brotha Rule":

> "The Brotha Rule" is the same as the "Ensign Rule." You Trekkies out there know what I'm talking about (everyone else — just pretend you do). The only difference is that instead of the red shirt being sent to his/her demise, it's the brotha that gets to check out early. [...] If there is one Black man in the central part of the cast, he will die between 45 and 65 minutes of his first appearance. Most often, but not always, he will sacrifice himself for the life of the Caucasian main character.

> Kamal Larusuel-Ulbricht, Rose Cooper and Cassandra Henry, "Cheat Sheets: A Practical Guide to Understanding *3 Black Chicks*," *3 Black Chicks Review Flicks: A Film and Video Guide with Flava!* (New York: Amistad, 2002), xv.

8. Kent Ono, "To Be a Vampire on *Buffy the Vampire Slayer:* Race and ('Other') Socially Marginalizing Positions on Horror TV," *Fantasy Girls: Gender in the New Universe of Science Fiction and Fantasy Television*, ed. Elyce Rae Helford (Lanham, Maryland: Rowan & Littleford Publishers, Inc., 2000: 163–186), 174–177.

9. Marti Noxon, Commentary, "What's My Line Part 2," *Buffy the Vampire Slayer: The Complete Second Season on DVD*, Disc 3, Twentieth Century Fox Home Entertainment, Inc., 2002, DVD.

10. Ono, 174.

11. Lynne Edwards, "Slaying in Black and White: Kendra as Tragic Mulatta in *Buffy*," *Fighting the Forces: What's at Stake in Buffy the Vampire Slayer*, eds. Rhonda V. Wilcox and David Lavery (Lantham, Maryland: Rowan & Littleford Publishers, Inc., 2002: 85–97), 89.

12. The relationship of African Americans and other people of colour to the United States military is complicated. According to a recent article in the *Washington Post*, "38 percent of the [U.S.] military's 1.1 million enlistees are ethnic minorities, while they make up 29 percent of the general population. In the largest branch, the Army, the percentage of minorities approaches half of all enlistees, at 45 percent." The Initiative appears to be an Army unit. African Americans in particular are disproportionately represented in the Army. While only 12 percent of the general U.S. population, "African Americans alone account for nearly 30 percent of Army enlistees [...] Black women comprise nearly half of the Army's enlisted women." Darryl Fears, "Draft Bill Stirs Debate over the Military, Race and Equity," *Washington Post*, 4 February 2003, <http://www.washingtonpost.com/ ac2/wp-dyn/A21039-2003Feb3?language=printer> (4 June 2003).

13. Dominic Alessio, "Things are Different Now?: A Postcolonial Analysis of *Buffy the Vampire Slayer*," *The European Legacy* 6 (2001): 731–740, 733, 755.

14. Alessio, 735.

15. Alessio, 738.

16. Alessio, 738.

17. Edwards, 95.

18. These stories are being told by Spike. What he says may or may not be true, but his versions of the stories are all the viewers have.

19. The show made Robin Wood's interaction with Buffy complex, focusing on the parallels between Buffy's and Nikki's roles as Slayers. The episode "Lies My

Parents Told Me" shows Wood's relationship with his mother before she died. Throughout his childhood, his mother put being the Slayer first, telling him, "The mission is what matters." Wood tries to kill Spike as vengeance for Spike killing Nikki, but fails. When Buffy confronts Wood, angry that he has put his personal vendetta ahead of the fight to destroy The First, she repeats his mother's words, saying, "The mission is what matters."

20. *Deadbrowalking: The Principal Wood Deathwatch*, <http://www.livejournal.com/userinfo.bml?user=deadbrowalking> (20 May 2003).

21. Andy Mangels, "Lesbian sex=death?" *The Advocate*, 20 August 2002, 70–71.

22. Samuel R. Delany, "Racism and Science Fiction," *Dark Matter: A Century of Speculative Fiction from the African Diaspora*, ed. Sheree R. Thomas (New York: Aspect, 2000): 382–397, 396.

23. Ono, 163.

STINKY GIRL

Hiromi Goto

One is never certain when one becomes a stinky girl. I am almost positive I wasn't stinky when I slid out from between my mother's legs, fresh as blood and just as sweet. What could be stinkier, messier, grosser than that? one might be asked, but I'm certain I must have smelled rich like yeast and liver. Not the stink of I-don't-know-what that pervades me now.

Mother has just looked over my shoulder to see what I am trying to cover up with my hand and arm, while I meditatively write at the kitchen table.

"Jesus!" She rolls her eyes like a whale. "Jesus Christ!" she yells. "Don't talk about yourself as 'one'! One what, for God's sake? One asshole? One snivelling stinky girl?" She stomps off. Thank goodness. It's very difficult having a mother. It's even more difficult having a loud and coarse one.

Where was I? Oh, yes. I am not troubled by many things. My weight, my mother, my dead father's ghost and a pet dog that despises me do not bother me so very much. Well, perhaps on an off-day they might bring a few tears to my eyes, but no one will notice a fat stinky mall rat weeping. People generally believe that fatties secrete all sorts of noxious substances from their body. But regardless, the one bane of my life, the one cloud of doom that circumscribes my life is the odour of myself.

There's no trying to pinpoint it. The usual sniff under the armpits or cupping of palms in front of my mouth to catch the smell of my breath is like trying to scoop up an iceberg with a goldfish net. And it's not a simple condition of typical body odour. I mean, everybody has some natural scents and even the prettiest cover girls wear deodorant and perfume. It's not because I am fat that foul odours are trapped in the folds of my body. No, my problem is not a causal phenomenon and there are no simple answers.

Perhaps I am being misleading, calling myself a mall rat. It's true, I spend much of my time wandering in the subculture of gross material consumerism. I meander from store to store in the wake of my odour, but I seldom actually purchase anything I see inside the malls. Think, if you will, upon the word "rat." Instantly, you'll picture a sharp whiskered nose, beady black eyes, an unsavoury disposition, grubby hands with dirty nails, perhaps, and a waxy tail. You never actually think fat rat. No, what comes to mind is a more sneaky and thinner rodent. If I am a rat, think of, perhaps, the queen of all rats in the sewer of her dreams, being fed the most tender morsels of garbage flesh her minions bring her. Think of a well-fed rat with three mighty chins and smooth, smooth skin, pink and fine. No need for a fur covering when all your needs are met. A mighty rodent with more belly than breath, more girth than the diameter of the septic drains. If you think of such a rat, then I am that mighty beast.

Actually, I had always thought of myself more in terms of a vole or perhaps a wise fat toad, or maybe even a manatee, mistaken by superstitious sailors as a bewitching mermaid. But, no, Mother tells me I was born in the Year of the Rat and that is that. No choice there, I'm afraid, and I can't argue with what I can't remember. Mother isn't one for prolonged arguments and contemplative discussions. More often than not, all I'll get is a "Jesus Christ!" for all my intellectual and moral efforts. I hope I don't sound judgemental. Mother is a creature unto herself and there is no ground for arbitrary comparison. "Each to their own" is a common phrase, but not without a tidbit of truth.

Perhaps I mislead you by calling myself a stinky girl. I am not a girl in the commonly held chronological sense of time. I've existed outside my mother's body for three and thirty years. Some might even go so far as to say that I'm an emotionally crippled and mutually dependent member of a dysfunctional family. Let's not quibble. In the measure of myself, and my sense of who I am, I am definitely a girl. Albeit a stinky one.

When people see obesity, they are amazed. Fascinated. Attracted and repulsed simultaneously. Now if we could harness all the emotions my scale inspires, who knows how many homes we could heat, how many trains we could move? People always think there is a why to being grand, that there is some sort of glandular problem, an eating disorder, a symptom of some childhood trauma ... All I can say is, not to my knowledge. I have always been fat, and, if I must say so myself, I eat a lot less than my tiny mother. I wasn't adopted, either. Mother is always bringing up how painful her labour was to eject me from her body. How she had to be tied down and how she pushed and screamed and pushed and cursed for three days running. Perhaps that's the reason for her slightly antagonistic demeanour. She didn't have any more children after I was born, and I must say, this birthing thing sounds like a nasty business what with all the tying down and screaming.

Oh, yes. I do have siblings, but they are much older than I. Three sisters and a brother who became women and men long before their due. Cherry was born in the Year of the Rabbit, Ginger, the Year of the Dragon, Sushi, the Year of the Horse, and Bonus, the Year of the Sheep. Mother was feeling quite tired of the whole affair by the time her second-last child was born. Bonus was so named because he came out of her body with such ease, she couldn't believe her luck. There was a seventeen-year stretch with no other pregnancies and she must have thought that her cycles were finished. And what better way than to end on a bonus?

But Mother wasn't fated to an easy existence. She wasn't going to inhabit the autumn years of her life without considerable trials and tribulations. At the age of fifty-one, she became pregnant with me. Promptly thereafter, my father died and she was left in a trailer, huge and growing, her children all moved away. A tragic life, really, but I shouldn't romanticize. One is easily led toward a tragic conclusion, and one must fight the natural human tendency to dramatize the conditions of one's life. One must be level-headed. A fat girl especially. When one is fat, one is seldom seen as a stable and steadying force in an otherwise chaotic world. Fat people embody the disruptive forces in action and this inspires people to lay blame. Where else to point their fingers but at the fat girl in striped trousers?

Did I mention I am also coloured?

I can't remember my very first memory. No one can, of course. I must remember what others have told me before I can remember on my own. Of my living father I have no recollections, but his ghost is all too present in my daily life. I wouldn't be one to complain if he was a helpful and cheerful ghost, prone to telling me where there are hidden crocks of gold or if the weather will be fine for the picnic. But no. He is a dreadfully doleful one, following me around the small spaces in our trailer, leaning mournfully on my shoulder and telling me to watch my step *after* I've stepped in a pile of dog excrement. And such a pitiful apparition! All there is of him is his sad and sorry face. Just his head, bobbing around in the air, sometimes at the level of a man walking but, more often than not, down around the ankles, weaving heavily around one's steps. It's enough to make one want to kick him, but I am not one who is compelled to exhibit unseemly aggressive behaviour.

Mother, on the other hand, is not above a swift "kick in the can" as she calls it, or a sudden cuff to the back of the head. I would not be exaggerating if I said I had no idea how she can reach my buttocks, let alone high enough to cuff my head, for I am not only very fat, but big and tall. Well, tall might be misleading. It would make one imagine that height is greater than girth. Let there be no doubt as to my being rounder than I would ever be considered tall. However, I am at least two feet taller than my mother, who stands four foot eight. She is not a dwarf, and I am not a giant. But we are not normal in the commonly held sense of the word.

No, my mother is not a dwarf, but she is the centre of the universe. Well, at least the centre of this trailer park, and she leaves no doubt as to who "kicks the cabbage around this joint," as she is so fond of reminding me. It gives me quite a chuckle on occasion, because Father's ghost often looks much like a cabbage, rolling around the gritty floor of our trailer. And even though Mother cannot see him, she has booted his head many times, when she punctuates her sayings with savage kicks to what she can only see as empty air. It doesn't hurt him, of course, but it does seem uncomfortable. He rolls his sorry eyes as he is *tha-klunked, tha-klunked* across the kitchen.

"What are you sniggling at, Mall Rat?" Mother snaps at me.

"Nothing," I say, sniggling so hard that my body ripples like tides.

Mother kicks me in the can for lying and stomps off to her bedroom to smoke her cigars. I feel sorry for my father and right his head, brushing off some ghostly dust.

"See what happens when you inhabit this worldly prison? Why don't you float up to the heavens or at least a waiting room?" I scold. "There's nothing left for you here except kicks in the head and a daughter who doesn't want to hear your depressing talk of dog excrement and all the pains you still feel in your phantom body that isn't there."

"As if I'm here by choice!" he moans. "As if any ghost would choose to remain in this sorry purgatory of a trailer! Finally dead and I get the nice light show, the tunnel thing and a lovely floating body. I think that I might be hearing a chorus of singing mermaids when an unsympathetic voice utters, 'You have not finished doing time,' and I find my head bobbing in a yellow stained toilet bowl. It takes me a couple of minutes to figure out it's my own toilet bowl, in my old washroom, because I'd never seen the bathroom from that perspective before. Imagine my shock! What's a poor ghost to do? Oh woe, oh woe," he sobs. Because ghosts have ghostly licence to say things like that.

Frankly, his lamenting and "woeing" is terribly depressing and I have plenty of my own woes without having to deal with his. I might not give in to excessive displays of violence, but I am not above stuffing him in the flour bin to make my escape.

I suppose calling oneself a rat might seem gender-specific. "Rat," I'll say and instantly a man or a nasty boy is conjured up.

There are female rats as well, don't you know? His and hers rat towels. Rat breasts and rat wombs. Rat washrooms where you squat instead of peeing standing up. A girl can grow up to become a doctor or a lawyer, now. Why not a rat? Albeit a stinky one.

Yes, yes, the odour of my life. It is large as myth and uglier than truth.

There are many unpleasant scents as you twiddle twaddle through the grey felt tunnels of life. Actually, smells are what hinge the past to the clutter of memory. Nothing is comparable to the olfactory when it comes to distorting your life. To jar a missing thought. Or transmute into an obsession. The dog excrement smell that's trapped in the runnels of the bottom of a sneaker, following you around all day no matter how fast you flee. That high-pitched whine of dog shit, pardon my language. Mother is a terrible influence and one must always guard against common usage and base displays of aggression. Yes, there is nothing like stepping in a pile of doggy dung to ruin your entire day. It is especially bad when the dog is supposedly your own.

Mother found the dog in the trailer-park dumpster, and as it was close to my "sorry birthday," as she called it, she brought the dirt-coloured wall-eyed creature home as a gift for me. I was touched, really, because she had forgotten to give me a present for the last twenty-seven years and I had always wanted a dog as a devoted friend.

The dog started whining as soon as Mother dragged it into the trailer by the scruff of its mangy neck. It cringed against the floor, curling its lip back three times over. Then the dog started chasing itself, tried to catch up with its stumpy tail so it could eat itself out of existence. I was concerned.

"Mother, perhaps the dog has rabies."

"Arrghh." (This is the closest I can get in writing to the sound of my mother's laughter.) "Damn dog's not rabid, it's going crazy from your infernal stink. Lookit! It's hyperventilating! Aaaaaarrggghhh!"

The poor beast was frothing at the mouth, chest heaving, smearing itself into the kitchen linoleum. It gave a sudden convulsive shake, then fainted. It was the first time I had ever seen a dog faint. Needless to say, my "sorry birthday" was ruined. I actually thought the dog would die, or at least flee from my home as soon as it regained consciousness. But surprisingly, the animal stayed around. There is no accounting for dog sense. Perhaps it's a puerile addiction to horrible smells. Like after one has cut up some slightly going-off ocean fish and raises one's fishy fingers to one's nostrils throughout the day and night until the smell has been totally inhaled. Or sitting down in a chair and crossing an ankle over the knee, clutching the ankle with a hand, twisting so the bottom of the runner is facing upward. The nose descends to sniff, sniff, sniff again. There is an unborn addict in all of us, and it often reveals itself in the things we choose to smell.

I must admit, I cannot smell myself because I have smelled my scent into normality. I only know that I still emit a tremendous odour because my mother tells me so. Also, I have no friends, and people give me a wide berth when I take my trips to the mall. There is a certain look people cannot control when they smell an awful stink. The lips curl back, the nose wrinkles toward the forehead, trying to close itself. (Actually, if one thinks about it, the nostrils seem more greatly exposed when in this position than when at rest, but I needn't linger on that thought just now. Later, I'll ponder it at my leisure.) People cannot control this reaction. I have seen it the whole of my life and can interpret the fine sneer in the corner of an eye, a cheek twitching with the sudden sour bile rising from the bottom of the tongue.

Let me reassure you, I am not some obsessive fecal compulsive who is actually pleasured by foul odours. I am not in the league of people who get perverted thrills from the filth of metabolic processes. I bathe twice a day, despite the discomfort of squeezing my body into a tiny shower stall. Not to mention all the commotion Mother makes about how much hot water I use. I must say, though, that Mother would be wise to take greater care with her personal hygiene, what with her cigars and her general disregard for appearance and decorum.

In the summertime, I can bathe myself in my shower garden. I planted a hedge of caragana for some privacy and I only clip it in width, so it doesn't invade the yard. It stands over ten feet in height and inside the scratchy walls, when it is heady with yellow blossoms, I can stand beneath an icy stream of hose water and almost feel beautiful. Mother always threatens to burn my beautiful bush to the ground.

"It's like a damn scrub prison in here! We get no bloody sunlight in the yard. Nothing grows. Just mud and fungus, and you muck it up with water and wallow there like some kind of pig. Burn the thing to the ground," she smacks me with her words. But Mother isn't as cruel as her words may sometimes seem. She does not reveal her inner spirit to those who are looking; instead, she throws verbal daggers in order not to be seen. Regardless, I know she will never burn down my summer shower because, sometimes, I catch her standing inside the bower of caragana. When the days are summer long into night and the heat is unbearable, the humble yellow blossoms turn into brittle brown pods. The shells crack with tiny explosions of minute seeds that bounce and scatter on the parched ground. They roll to where my mother douses herself with icy water. I catch her when she thinks I'm still at the mall. I catch her hosing down her scrawny old woman body, a smile on her normally scowling face, and a cigar burning between her lips. I never let on that I see her in these moments. She is more vulnerable than I.

The dog decided to remain in the confines of our trailer, and it made me realize that one can never foretell the life choices that others will enact. That first day, Mother named the dog "Rabies," and dragged his floppy body outside. She hosed him off in the caragana shower and he came to, shook himself off like dogs will do, slunk into the kitchen and hunkered beneath the table.

Mother laughed once: "Aaarrrrgh," reached inside the refrigerator, and threw him the first thing her hand came in contact with. It was father's head. I had tucked him there to keep him from being underfoot, and he must have fallen asleep. The starving dog clamped down on an ear and gnawed with stumpy teeth. Father screamed in outrage.

"What you say, Stink-O? Speak up. Fat girls shouldn't whisper."

"Nothing, Mother. I think you tossed Rabies a cabbage. I'll just take it back and feed him something more suitable. Perhaps that beef knuckle we used to make soup yesterday."

"Suit yourself. But don't say 'perhaps.'" Mother stomped off "to sit on the can," as she calls it.

"A dog. Your mother fed me to a dog. Haven't I been tormented enough? When will this suffering end?" Father started weeping, the dog keening. I sighed. I am not one who gives in easily to the woes of this world. Sighing is an expression of defeat, or at least weakness that reveals a lack of toughness or that certain get-up-and-go attitude. But Father is a sorry shade, a cloud of perpetual doom and defeat. I don't even want to know what sort of man he was before he fell to this. It would only make a tragic comedy out of what was probably a pathetic life. I swooped down, scooped Father's head out from between Rabies' paws and set him on the table, right side up. I dug through the garbage for the dry soup bone and tossed it to the dog.

Yes, a fat girl can swoop. I am remarkably light on my feet, I almost float on the tips of my toes. Certainly, one may be fat and stinky, but it doesn't necessitate stumbling awkwardness. I never drag my feet and I never stomp fit to bring down the roof. It is Mother who is the stomper in this house and many a time I have whipped up the ladder to tap another layer of tarry paper on the rusty roof. I may be grand, stinky and hated by dogs, but I have a dancer's feet and the endurance of a rice-planter's thighs.

Did I mention that I'm also coloured? One is led to say "also" in a long list of things I am that are not commonly perceived as complimentary. One cannot say, "I'm coloured," and expect: "You know, I've always wanted to be coloured myself," as a standard reaction. Not that I would rather be a stinky, fat white girl. Perhaps mauve or plum. Plum ... now that's a colour!

A fat coloured rat girl has to look out for herself and never reveal her cards. Lucky for me, I must say I'm blessed with a certain amount of higher intelligence, a certain sensitivity that enables me to more than endure the trials of this existence. On my better days, I can leap and soar above the patchy roof of the trailer house. On my better days, the stars sing closer to my ears. I may be fat, I may stink larger than life, I may be a coloured mall rat in striped trousers, but I am coyly so.

Ah, yes, the mall. Now why would a clever girl like myself bother to habit such a gross manifestation of consumer greed? Is it some puerile addiction, a dysfunction I cannot control? Ahh, many a time I've pondered on this, but it is not as an active consumer that I return to the mall as I oft do. My forays there are part of an ongoing study of the plight of human existence in a modern colonized country. A mall is the microcosm, the centrifugal force in a cold country where much of the year is sub-zero in temperature. The mall reveals the dynamics of the surrounding inhabitants. Yes, the traits of the masses can be revealed in the Hudson's Bay department store and in the vast expanses of a Toys R Us, where hideously greedy children manipulate TV dinner divorcées into making purchases with the equivalent monetary value of feeding a small village for a week.

When I have fully understood the human mall condition, it will become a doorway to a higher level of existence. One must understand one's limitations, the shackles of social norms, in order to overcome them. And when I have accomplished this, I will cast aside my mantle of foul odour and float to the outer limits of time and space. Alas, one must always take care not to steep oneself too deeply in theoretical thought. It would only lead to the sin created by the Greeks and taught in every Western educational institution today: hubris, dreaded hubris.

Luckily for me, my father's pale and pathetic head is confined to the parameters of our trailer lot. Imagine what a hindrance he'd be in my pursuit of higher consciousness! I slip into my gymnast's slippers and chassé through my caragana bowers and out the tattered back gate. Father's head rolls down the walk after me as far as the last concrete slab, then teeters back and forth in what I assume is a head wave. Feeling extra generous, I throw back a kiss, and he levitates a few feet in pleasure. There is neither sight nor sound of Rabies, much to my father's relief.

"Arrrr! Stink-O! Pick me up a box of cigars. Don't cheap out on me and buy those candy-flavoured Colts, you hear?" Mother snarls from the tiny bathroom window. I blow kisses, five, six, seven and flutter down the sidewalk. Mother or her bowels growl from the dark recesses of our tinny home.

As I traipse between the rows of identical rectangular homes highlighted with large, colourful butterflies and plastic petunias, I hear the slamming of doors and the snap of windows closing. My odour precedes me. I never need an introduction; my signature prevails. Alas, a thought. If one smells a smell and was never taught to like it, would not one find it distasteful as a result of ignorance? Let me pursue the opposite line of thought. If one were taught as a very small child that roses were disgusting, that they were vile, noxious and ugly, to boot, would one not despise the very thought of their scent? It may be that I smell beautiful beyond the capacity of human recognition: the scent of angels and salamanders. There's just no one capable of appreciating the loveliness.

The mall. The mall. It is Saturday and the mall is a virtual hub of hustle and bustle. Infants cry and old women smoke. Unisex teens sprout rings from every inch of revealed skin and the mind boggles thinking about what's not revealed. Fake and real potatoes french fried into greasy sticks, stand-in-line Chinese food, trendy café au laits and iced coffees. It is crowded but I always have a wide path. A minimum ten-foot radius circumscribes my epicentre. No one dares come any closer, I'm afraid. Like a diver in a shark-protection cage. No, that's not quite right. Regardless.

I have a daily route I take and even if my eyes were put out, I could wind my way through the blind corners and dead-end halls of this mall. Like the tragic Shakespearean kings, I would prevail with an uncanny sense of despair and enlightenment. The merchants all know me by smell, and sometimes, a wave or a brief nod of a head is offered. There was a time when most of the merchants convened to put an end to my forays, to banish me from my chosen road of human contemplation. But legally there was nothing they could do as long as I bought an item now and again, like mother's cigars, or a soup bone from the butcher. They couldn't evict me for the way I smell, or how I looked in my striped trousers. There was a time when I could have been evicted for being coloured, but at the present time in history, in this geographical location, I am lawfully tolerated.

Alas, no one wants to be merely tolerated, like a whining child or an ugly dog. Such human arrogance. We dare to assume that some are meant to be merely tolerated while others are sought out to be idolized, glorified, even to have their dainty asses wiped. Have a care! I mustn't fall into the pit of baseness like my mother before me! The utter unfairness of it all is enough to make one want to bite one's own tongue off, a mute supplication to the evils of this world, but that's the other end of the stick. Father's end of misery and woe. It is my chosen path to seek another ...

I glide into Holy Smoke to pick out a box of cigars. If I wait until I have done my daily study of the machinations of mall existence, I may very well forget and Mother would be sorely vexed in a manner that would be audible for several square miles.

"Good afternoon." Adib nods politely, from behind his pastel handkerchief.

"Lovely." I breezily smile as I step up to the marble counter.

"A box of the usual for you?" he asks, backing up a pace and smiling behind the cover of his handkerchief to make up for his instinctual retreat.

"Please," I say, bobbing my head and leaning my arm against the cool grey rock slab that runs the length of the entire store. Men on stools on either side of me hop off, stuffing burning pipes in trouser pockets in their haste to escape me.

Adib sighs, even though he has his back to the mass exodus. He turns around with a box filled with cigars as thick as my thumb, individually wrapped and sealed with a red sticker. He has thrown five extra ones on top, so it will take that much longer before I have to return.

"Your generosity is so greatly appreciated." I bow, clicking my heels like some military personage and pay him with bills sweating wetly from the pocket of my striped pants.

Adib accepts them as graciously as a man extending a pair of tweezers can. No, I am not angered by his reticence to come into direct contact with me. Indeed, I find his manner refreshingly honest. He never hurls abuse like some are apt to do.

"My best to your mother." Adib hands me my change via the tweezers. "By the way," he adds, "you might want to take in the new children's play area in the western wing of the mall. I heard that it's quite the development."

"Why, thank you," I beam. Then frown. "But how is it that I am not acquainted with this wonder of childish bliss?"

Adib just shrugs, breathing shallowly from behind his lavender-scented hanky. I thank him again. Glissade en avant gracefully through the door and, toes pointed, leap excitedly to the west wing.

The sign reads: FRIENDZIES!

It's one of those obscure word conflations that means almost nothing at all. Like a joke told with a punchline from another, one realizes an attempt at humour has been made, but there is nothing to get. It does not bode well.

Grand-opening balloons, limp and wrinkled, dangle from pastel walls. Streamers trail limply from golden pillars and curl in the dust on the cold floor. There's a table with free coffee and donuts and Coke-flavoured pop made out of syrup. I walk up to the gate, disheartened, but must enter for study purposes. One must not let first impressions alter one's methodology, one's code of ethics.

"One adult please," I say, smiling courteously.

"Where's your kid?" a girl chews out with an unseemly quantity of gum.

I am amazed. She does not curl her nose in disgust at the stench that permeates my being. Her eyes do not water and she doesn't gape at my size.

"I have no children," I say. "I just want to see the newly constructed premises." How is it that she doesn't seem to notice? Perhaps her nose has been decimated from smoking or, perhaps, lines of cocaine.

"Ya can't go in without a kid, because adults go in free but a kid costs eight bucks." The girl tips forward on her stool to rest her chin in her hands, elbows splayed sloppily on the countertop before me.

"My goodness! Eight dollars for a child!" I am shocked. Who could afford to entertain their children here, and what could possibly be worth the price? "What if one were to tell you that the child is inside already, that one has only to come to join her?"

The young woman kicks a button with her foot and the gate swings open. "Don't forget to take off your shoes and keep valuables on your person," she intones, bored to insensibility.

She is from a generation where nothing seems to matter. She is so bored of the world and of herself that even my anomalous presence doesn't measure on her radar. Is there no hope for our next generation? Will the non-starving members of our species perish from ennui even before we've polluted our environment to the point of no return?

This turn of thought does nothing to advance my research. It only makes me weary. Ever weary. I adjust my mental clipboard and focus on the task at hand.

Plastic tubing runs crazily throughout the room, like a diseased mind twisting and turning back on itself with no end, no beginning. Plastic balls fill a pit of doom, three toddlers drown to the chorus of their parents' snap-shotting delight. Primary reds, blues and yellows clash horribly with khaki, lavender and peach. Children, fat children, skinny children and coloured children, pale from too much TV, run half-heartedly through the plastic pipes, their stocking feet pad-padding in the tubes above my head. They squeal listlessly from expectation rather than delight. A playground for children constructed from a culture of decay. There is enough plastic here to make Tupperware for a whole continent and I am too stunned to even drop my mouth in horrified dismay.

Mother would think that this is some kind of grandiose joke. She would laugh in her cigar-breath way, her ever-present stogie clenched between her molars in a manner that would make Clint Eastwood envious. Mother would enjoy this place to no end, but I am stricken. I am an urban rat, but I still recognize the forces of the sun, the moon, the patterns of wind that guide me. Albeit through a film of pollution. These tragic children who are taught to play in an artificial world can only follow the route to an artificial death. Their spirits will be trapped forever with a shelf-life of an eternity.

I wander, dazed, dismayed, my dancer's feet dragging heavily on the Astroturf. Some of the older, anemic children stop and stare, whisper to each other from behind covered mouths. I take no heed. I continue through the cultural maze of hyper-artificiality.

There is no hope, my mind mutters incessantly. My steps slow, motion is stilled, all joie de vivre leached through the bottom of my feet.

Stone.

A toddler topples backward out of a chute. A millisecond of silence. Then she bawls like the world has ended. Red, yellow and blue balls fly fitfully through the air. Children gulp from tubs of simulated Coke while waiting for their microwave-heated pizzas. A boy bends over and, splat!, vomits a soft pink mound of hotdogs.

Horrible humanity. How can I bear this? How can anyone bear it?

No! I must not waver from my calling. I will not follow the path of my father into woe and I won't encrust my airy spirit within a coarse mantle like my mother. It is not enough to simply stand on the outside and gape, albeit with a closed mouth. It is not enough that only I fully understand the human mall condition. What if I *am* to overcome the shackles of social norms and, thus, reach the outer limits of time and space? Do I want to survey the vista alone? I must join the epicentre of humanity.

I must enter the maze.

"Watch your fat can," I can hear my mother's raspy voice all around me. "Don't come crying to me. I'll only say 'I told you so' and kick you in the butt."

Mother, oh, Mother.

I circle the strange man-made maze, thinking to myself that a woman never would. I circle thrice before I spot a young child scurrying up a hot pink pipe like a rabbit with a watch. I squelch my body into the mouth of the tube, wishing for a ball of thread. Fat rat in a sewer pipe. The thought bubbles hysterically to the surface of my mind, but I kick it in the can just like my mother.

What is strangely interesting is that instead of getting stuck like an egg in the throat of an overly greedy snake, my body elongates. It spreads toward the ends. All I need to do is flutter my toes to initiate a forward motion.

I slide, glide smoothly through the twisting tubing. The only impediments are the large metal heads of bolts that are used to fasten the portions of pipe together. The friction of my clothing rubbing against the plastic raises such electricity that I am periodically zapped with great sparks and frazzle. Definitely a design flaw. Children in neighbouring tubes pad, pad, twirl down spiral slides. Their small muffled noises are only broken with intermittent zaps and small exclamations of pain.

I have never taken care of children, although I've cared about them in theory …

Something pokes the bottom of my foot. Of course, I cannot turn around to look. A barely discernible voice squeaks in protest and the single voice is joined with another, another. For in my contemplation I've ceased my inching progress and I've blocked the tube like a clot of fat in an artery. Their small mouse-like rustlings unsettle my philosophical and scientific musings. I flap my foot at them to go back the other way.

Then I notice, for the first time in my life, something that has always been with me. I am so completely encased in plastic that it cannot be diluted by outer forces.

I can smell myself.

The wonder! My odour is not smell, but sound ... It's the voices of mythic manatees, the cry of the phoenix, the whispers of kappa lovers beside a gurgling stream, the voice of the moon turning away from our gaze, the song of suns colliding. The sounds that emanate from my skin are so intense that mortal senses recoil, deflect beauty into ugliness as a way of coping. Unable to bear hearing such unearthly sounds, they transmute it into stench.

And my joy! Such incredible joy. The hairs on my arms stand electric, the static energy and my smell/sound mix with such dizzying intensity that the plastic surrounding me bursts apart, falls away from my being like an artificial cocoon.

I hover, twenty feet in the air.

The children who were stuck behind me tumble to the ground. They fall silently, too shocked to scream, but the pitch of sound that seeps from my skin intensifies, like beams of coloured light. The sound catches the children from their downward plummet and they bob, rise slowly up to where I float. I extend my hands and the children grab hold, hold each others' hands as well, smile with wonder.

"Oh my God!" someone finally gasps, from far beneath us. Another person screams. Fathers faint and an enterprising teenager grabs a camera from a supine parent and begins to snap pictures. None of it matters. This moment. Tears drip from my eyes and the liquid jewels float alongside us like diamonds in outer space. I burst out laughing and the children laugh too. I don't know what will happen tomorrow or the day that follows, but the possibilities are immense.

We float, the rest of the plastic pipes shimmer, buckle beneath our voices then burst into soft confetti.

The Parkdale 3

**MATTHEW BLACKETT
& MEAGAN CRUMP**

EVERY NIGHT, AS THE SUN SINKS
BEHIND THE APARTMENT BUILDINGS,
THE PARKDALE 3 HIT THE STREETS.

PARKDALE IS A NEIGHBOURHOOD JUST
WEST OF TORONTO'S DOWNTOWN CORE. IT
WAS ORIGINALLY A SUBURB FOR THE WEALTHY
BACK IN THE MID-1800S.

ABOUT 50 YEARS AGO THE COMMUNITY SLID INTO DISREPUTE.
IT BECAME A HAVEN FOR THE DISENFRANCHISED, AND HAS BEEN
RATED THE LEAST LIVABLE PART OF THE CITY BY A SNOOTY
LOCAL LIFESTYLE MAGAZINE.

BUT IT HAS ALSO BEEN THE HOME TO THOUSANDS OF
ARTISTS, ACTIVISTS, AND REGULAR CITY DWELLERS WHO
DON'T WANT BOUTIQUE CAFES OR SLICKER-THAN-SLICK SHOE
STORES.

AND IT'S NOT ALWAYS THE HOOKERS AND DRUG PUSHERS
WHO CAUSE PROBLEMS ...

TONIGHT, SOME OF OUR OPERATIVES HAVE ALERTED US, VIA THE PARKDALE 3 EMERGENCY CALL, TO ONE SUCH MATTER REQUIRING OUR ATTENTION...

AN IMMENSE CONDO DEVELOPMENT IS CURRENTLY SELLING EXPENSIVE UNITS. DESPITE NOT OWNING THE LAND IN QUESTION, NOT HAVING CONDUCTED ANY FORM OF COMMUNITY IMPACT STUDY, AND NOT HAVING HAD THEIR REZONING APPLICATION APPROVED.

HIGH RENT
a new community

MORE IMPORTANTLY, THE DEVELOPMENT IS SMACK IN THE MIDDLE OF A COMMUNITY THAT DESPERATELY NEEDS AFFORDABLE HOUSING. WE FIND THIS, AND THEIR TACTLESS MARKETING, UNCONSCIONABLE.

SO WE DECIDE TO PERFORM A LITTLE IMPACT STUDY OF OUR OWN...

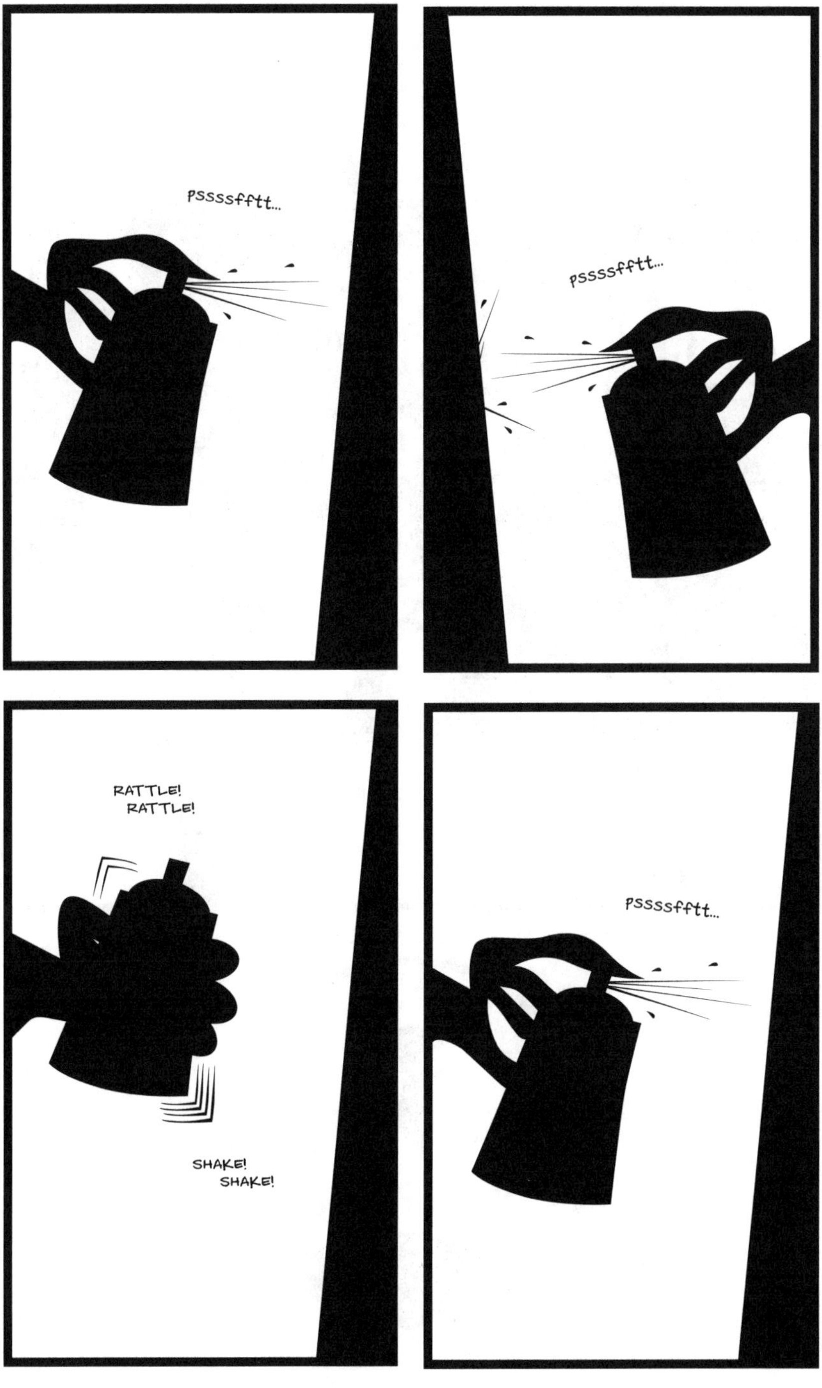
pssssfftt...
pssssfftt...
RATTLE!
RATTLE!
SHAKE!
SHAKE!
pssssfftt...

MAYBE THE PARKDALE 3 SHOULD GET INTO RENOVATIONS...

THE END

HOW TO BE YOUR OWN SUPERHERO

A CHRONICLE OF EXPERIMENTATION AND FASCINATION

Carly Stasko

I dream I am a woman of action.
I rise above the armchair faction,
And improve the world we share a fraction.
This kind of play breeds satisfaction.

— CARLY STASKO, 2003

A brief scan of the female superhero role models that are available via the popular media shows that there is a limited spectrum of choice. Wonder Woman, Xena Warrior Princess, Charlie's Angels, Buffy the Vampire Slayer: These women show strength, ability, courage and cleavage, but they only offer us one kind of feminine power and tell the story as though there were no others. Sadly, few sheroes venture beyond the safe norms of being young, sexy, white and uncomplicated. Most heroines are represented such that their power is rooted in sex and violence, ignoring the many real and diverse powers of women.

Susan Douglas, author of *Where the Girls Are: Growing Up Female with the Mass Media*, describes women as both insiders and outsiders in their relationship to the media. She says, we have "grown up and continue to live with media images not of our making, so, on some level, we will always feel like outsiders looking in at a culture that regards us as unknowable, mysterious, laughable, other."[1] She goes on to point out, though, that "we are insiders too, having been formed by this very same culture, our desires researched to the hilt and then sold back to us in a warped, yet still recognizable fashion. We stand on the border, looking out and looking in, feeling simultaneously included and excluded, wooed as consumers yet rejected as people."[2]

This presents women (and men, for that matter, because their hero role models suck, too) with the challenge of creating new superheroes out of the precious fragments we can gather from popular culture and the original elements we dream up ourselves using our imaginations. Douglas describes this as the "power to accept or resist the new stereotypes, picking up some shards, kicking away others."[3] She explains that this is how feminism and womanhood itself became a kind of pastiche. Or as my friend Joel once told me, "Honey, everyone's in drag!"

Just because role models in the mass media can be limited and superficial, they are not devoid of value. All of us at one time or another have probably identified with the hero of a movie or story (though this is certainly easier for straight white men). However, many of us have become very good at deriving inspiration and motivation from role models of a different gender or race than ourselves. This ability to identify has arisen out of necessity, due to the lack of diversity represented in the media. On the positive side, the situation affords us the unique ability to pillage any and all of popular culture for scraps so we can build our own idealized superheroes and utopias. The best part about this is that all of us have several (perhaps an unlimited supply of) different superheroes inside of us just waiting to bust out.

From early childhood, we learn to see ourselves and to be seen, as we form our sense of self. In our consumer culture, identity so often is ill-defined by consumer choices. It's no surprise than many people struggle with their identity: there are many conflicting, biased and provocative messages in the mass media, telling us we can know ourselves through products. We are cut off from the natural world through urbanization and daily practice. Without an understanding about how we fit into the natural world, many of us struggle to use the objects and symbols around us to make meaning out of our experiences and to define our identity. These symbols and objects fall short if the meaning is only superficial. Our true symbols of happiness are the by-products of living authentically, rather than the products we buy. When we become creative and open-minded about how the story of our life can unfold, we are liberated from the restricting narratives around us. Rather than following a script, we can cast ourselves in the roles we want in stories of our own making.

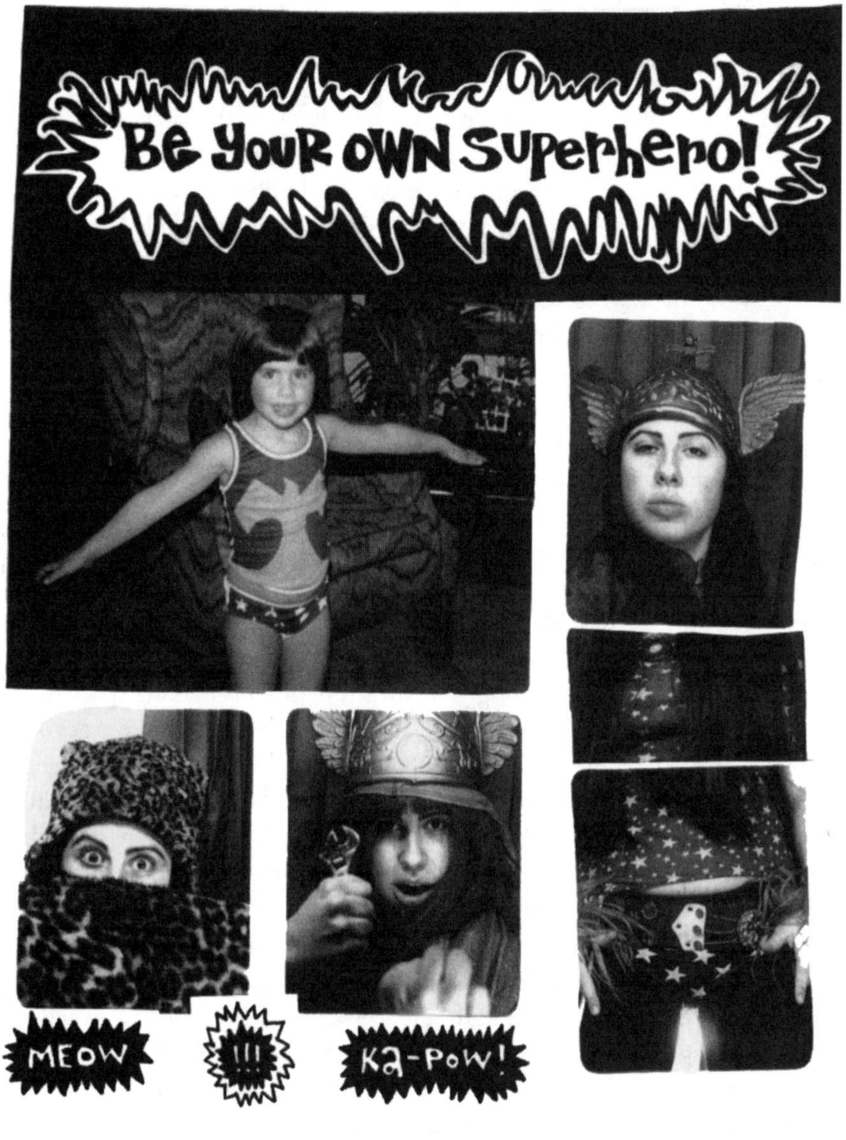
Be your OWN Superhero!
MEOW
!!!
Ka-POW!

My romance with the notion of being a superhero, magical witch or super-spy began at a very young age. I was pretty sure that one day, I would be visited by a fairy godmother or a friendly witch posing as an undercover spy who would inform me of my superpowers and my mission. I thought that it would most likely happen on my birthday, as a kind of gift, and so I would prepare myself mentally for it. As each birthday passed without such a visit, I figured I just wasn't old or wise enough yet. Rather than becoming impatient, I only experienced greater anticipation for the eventual day of my empowerment. While I waited, I carried on with my daydreams and imaginative play.

Turns out that, so far, I can't fly and don't have X-ray vision, but I have learned something about my powers by experimenting with them. For example, healing powers are the types of gifts we discover when a friend or animal is in need. We can easily notice the positive impact our touch, words or presence has on someone else who isn't feeling well. Western medicine is structured to make us feel as if we play a passive role in our own well-being and that only a doctor has the power to heal or understand our bodies. Part of being your own superhero is noticing ways in which you are not passive and understanding the different powers you have developed to respond to the challenges of your environment.

The first step to becoming your own superhero is making space for the transformation and overcoming the negative messages and images of the mass media and the dominant culture. This is no small challenge, but sometimes this process becomes a kind of art. Many traditional superheroes, such as Superman, Batman and Spider-Man, were created out of stressful or dangerous circumstances, and it is how the given characters overcame their struggle that determines the nature of their superhero identity. Batman witnessed the death of his parents (the most common childhood nightmare), Superman was the only one who escaped his destroyed home planet, and Spider-Man was a victim of a genetic engineering accident. In each case the superhero has taken the gravity of his tragedy and used it as the source of his own superhuman powers. Feelings of anger or fear are typically transformed by superheroes into strengths and superpowers. They fight against injustice with justice and against hate with love.

This is the crafty secret to being a superhero. If you can find a way to transform your own deepest anger, hate or ignorance into love, understanding and wisdom, you can transform these things in the outside world too. And when it comes to magic, transformation is something that we are all very capable of (in the right conditions). Consider the butterfly, nature's star transformer. Did you know that a butterfly has to struggle to break out of its cocoon in order to grow and develop the muscles it will need to fly? Without its struggle to break free, the butterfly has no strength to fly. Be a butterfly! Be whatever you've been struggling to become.

IDENTIFYING YOUR POWERS

If we are to achieve a richer culture, rich in contrasting values, we must recognize the whole gamut of human potentialities, and so weave a less arbitrary social fabric, one in which each diverse gift will find a fitting place.

— MARGARET MEAD[4]

For those of you who have (perhaps in private) considered the possibility that you are also a superhero, I would like to affirm your assumption. The first step to considering such a possibility is to step far away from the accepted notion of what a superhero looks or acts like. Think about what special gifts you have. Can you communicate with animals? Are you a quirky problem-solver or a spontaneous kitchen magician? Do you dream about the future or can you resolve conflicts? What are your special abilities?

I began an experiment recently that took on a life of its own. It all started when I began to ask my friends and acquaintances about their special powers. I would ask them to name and describe their top three powers and I suggested examples, such as mental telepathy or the ability to de-escalate a conflict. As they described their powers to me, I listened to some of the most interesting stories I've heard in a long while. With this simple and somewhat odd question I had opened myself up to a curious and wonderful shared experience. I have learned that naming your powers is no small accomplishment. It's akin to casting a good spell. The act alone is powerful.

After having such a positive experience with my friends talking about their special powers, I expanded my questioning to others. If anyone hesitated as though in doubt of their possession of such powers, I assured him or her that everyone has at least a minimum of seven super-powers. The variety and scope of powers described amazed me. My mom is good at helping people pick out cats that suit them at the humane society. One friend of mine has a talent for making people feel comfortable and at ease. Another friend can make up improvised songs about any topic, while another is a great listener. One friend described his power as the ability to look into the sadness of the world and find stories of hope. It was very exciting to ask strangers or new acquaintances the "super-power question" because it always held the potential to transform the conversation into one of "big ideas" and optimism — a new power of mine.

IDEALISM AND ACTIVISM

Reasonable people adapt themselves to the world. Unreasonable people attempt to adapt the world to themselves. All progress, therefore, depends on unreasonable people.

— GEORGE BERNARD SHAW

Pundits, politicians, journalists and other cynics can be heard name-calling activists "tree huggers," "peaceniks" and "idealists." They use the power of naming to discredit the perspectives of individuals whom they brand with these dismissive terms. However, the debate is still open about idealism. Sure it must be balanced with realism, but idealism is important too! I try to wear my optimism like a badge. I know that it is my hope that fuels me to take positive action in the world. Yes I hug trees — so call me a tree hugger! I like it! I'll take it as a compliment! I also attend anti-war demonstrations and teach grassroots media literacy to students in high schools and universities. I've been a radical cheerleader at Reclaim the Streets, I plant sunflowers in abandoned urban spaces, and I throw spontaneous parties on the subway with my friends. I am glad that I am such an optimist, because if I wasn't, the part of me that is an observant critic would grind me into a state of static cynicism.

Being an activist is a great way to be a superhero in my books. Marian Wright Edelman, a leading children's and civil rights activist, bluntly points out the need for action: "A lot of people are waiting for Martin Luther King or Mahatma Gandhi to come back — but they are gone. We are it. It is up to us. It is up to you."[5] They, too, were just ordinary people like us who wanted to contribute to a positive human project that was bigger than themselves.

BECOMING YOUR DAYDREAMS

There are only two ways to live your life. One is as though nothing is a miracle. The other is as though everything is a miracle.

— ALBERT EINSTEIN

At age ten, I read a series of books called *The Worst Witch* by Jill Murphy, about a young witch named Mildred Hubble who was trying her best to become a bona fide witch at a secondary school called Miss Cackle's Academy for Witches. I fantasized about attending it and being invited into the secret world of magic that I was sure existed. Throughout my daily life, I took note of the different clues and stories that perpetuated this belief. I could also sense that as a child, I was somehow closer to this magic. Now, as a somewhat reluctant adult, I make a conscious effort to nurture this part of my imagination. I see these beliefs as more than playful fancy. They are a way of connecting myself to the powers of the unknown.

Do you ever, or have you ever, dreamed about being an unconventional superhero? Or maybe a crafty witch with healing powers? Perhaps a super-spy, sneaking into the houses of power and sneaking out with knowledge to share with your friends? Maybe you've dreamed you could fly, or read people's minds or travel through time and space? Have you ever fantasized about the future, and made it then happen in "real life"? Do you remember your dreams? Do you produce and direct them, and cast yourself as a quirky explorer of the unknown? What visions, characters and situations do you entertain in your sleeping mind?

Lucid dreaming is a great way to practise and experiment with being your own superhero and all you need is your imagination. One exercise you can do to practise lucid dreaming is to look at your hands for a while before you go to sleep. Notice the shape of your hands, the texture and the relationships of the lines. Try to map them out so that you can remember the way they look with your eyes closed. Then as you are about to fall asleep, tell yourself you are going to look at your hands in your dream. With your eyes closed, imagine looking at your hands. Then, when you are sleeping, if you ever become aware, even for a brief moment, that you are dreaming, try to look at your hands. Once you accomplish this (it may take some practice), you will have connected with your body in your dream. At that point you can start living your dream; this is good practice for living your life as you want.

CHANGE RITUALS

The hero has to awaken the sleeping images of the future, which can and must come forth from the night, in order to give the world a new and better face.

— ERNST BARLACH

Typically, coming-of-age rituals involve the changing of costumes to symbolize the death of the old self and the birth of the new. Sometimes a form of partly scripted improvised theatre using masks helps individuals to discover who their new self is or what their calling in life is. The time of changing is defined as "liminal," meaning that it is an in-between place and time where rules and roles are suspended to make a fluid environment for personal change. When I look today for the contemporary equivalents of these rituals, I see them all around me in dance-club culture, Halloween dress-up, even consumerism. In most cases, people seek out new identities and change into new costumes in order to become someone else. The intention of this is amplified when we act out the character the costume implies and begin to interact with others as though we were that character. By doing this, we become more like that new person. When I look back at different dress-up parties I've been to, I realize I learned a lot about myself from those experiences. I was able to experiment and explore different sides of my personality by seeing different ways I could engage with situations.

My first memory of Halloween is associated with daycare. I was three years old, and I was celebrating this mysterious new occasion with the other kids. As I soon discovered, I was not dressed for the occasion (gasp!). My dad had a job interview that morning and my mom was on strike, and somewhere in the mix, my costume had been forgotten. After his interview, my dad remembered and raced to the drugstore to buy me one of those ready-made costumes. For me the whole day was wonderful because it was so mysterious. It felt like something had opened up and more things were possible. As my frazzled dad dressed me up in my costume, it occurred to me that I should ask him what I was. He told me I was a little goblin with magical powers. I remember asking him what a goblin was, and he went on to explain it to me in a way that triggered my already overactive imagination. I looked down at my hands and I saw that they had become goblin hands. I wasn't dressed up as a goblin: I *was* a goblin. The best part is that I didn't even know that goblins were supposed to be ugly. I just thought they were magical and earthy.

The halls of my daycare had been decorated and the lights dimmed. I walked down the hall with my dad, and it turned into a jungle trail. He hugged me goodbye and told me to have fun. I entered the darkened playroom and saw a circle of little creatures like myself, and a big strange-looking creature was ushering me into the circle. I sat down and was greeted by unknown entities on either side. This was a magical circle. I could see a fire burning in the middle and spirits dancing in the darkness all around us. I wasn't scared because I was a goblin. I had magical powers and this was a special event, where the dark wasn't scary; it was a costume we wore that made it easier to imagine.

SELF-KNOWLEDGE THROUGH DRESS-UP! (MY SHERO SELVES)

We all have different sides to our characters and various strengths or powers that go with them. Dressing up for Halloween and other events has given me the chance to take on alternative identities, and as a result learn more about myself. When I was four years old, I dressed up like Wonder Woman. I didn't care or know much about the "official" *Wonder Woman* story plot. So what? Write your own script! Cast yourself as whomever you please, pillage and plunder what you like from popular culture and feel free to take as much creative licence as you need.

Between the ages of six and twelve, I dressed up as a witch several times. I could be strong and powerful but didn't have to be beautiful. I also got a thrill from being a little bit scary. I dreamed about flying into the school yard on a broomstick or being able to turn into a cat or an owl. Even now, when I brew up different medicinal teas like chamomile, calendula or marshmallow, I regard my cooking pot as a cauldron.

Sometimes I stare into the swirling water and think about all the reme-
dies and healing wisdom that was lost and suppressed because of the
witch hunts. It's at those times that I remember my childhood certain-
ty that our time as witches was here — and it is!

In Grade 7, I was given the job of being a fortune teller during
Carnival Day at my school. There were four of us and we each had our
own booth, which could be visited by other students. It never occurred
to me that I wasn't an oracle. I stepped into the character when I stepped
into her costume and discovered that the character had been there all
along. The natural ability to be psychic is in all of us, it's just a matter of
observing and acting on those observations. The more practice you have,
the better you get. Think about all the information we receive from our
five senses. Then consider how much of it is ignored by our brains to
avoid information overload. Experiment with your senses and don't let
the limitations of what is considered possible stop you from trying.

My decision to dress up as Medusa a few years ago was a very intu-
itive one, and I was forever changed by the experience. I wanted to be a
strong and wise woman, who was feared for her powers alone rather
than her evil deeds. I looked at myself in the mirror and the first trait I
noticed was my long brown hair. Then my eyes followed from my head,
down my body, to my armpits, pubic hair and hairy legs. The hair on
top of my head received frequent compliments for its healthy shine,
while the hair on the rest of my body was perceived as dirty, wrong,
unwomanly, and perhaps even dangerous by much of the outside world.
This got me thinking about how women's sexual powers have been vil-
ified by everything from Greek myths to beer commercials. I wanted to
challenge this vilification, and the symbol of the snake came to mind. I
would be Medusa, a strong woman who was "grossly misrepresented in
the media." For my costume, I wrapped wire in some scrap leopard-
print material and then twisted it around my braids, attaching various
rubber snakes to the ends. The result was very effective. The wires
enabled the braids to stick up in all directions, allowing the snakes to
dangle down with their slithery tongues sticking out just above my forehead and shoulders. When I walked, they slithered and wiggled.

At a 1970s-themed party, I inherited an auburn afro-wig. It felt
amazing to dance with my long hair tucked inside a big spherical halo.
The symbol of the afro carried with it the meanings of power, pride,
freedom, radicalism and cool. My perception was based on a caricature

— a mixture of vintage propaganda news stories about the Black Panthers, Blaxsploitation films and kitsch pop-culture artifacts (the afro-wig being the most common). Only years after did I begin to learn about the real people and issues that inspired the Civil Rights movement and the cultural influence of Black Pride. Like many powerful women in history, the master narrative had stolen their stories and left them half told, forgotten or transformed into propaganda, or worse still, empty commodities. The lesson for me was that the power of transformation must be balanced with responsibility and respect. In my case it means looking back with honesty and trying to learn about my assumptions. Getting in costume is an experiment, and it brings with it questions, hypotheses, observations and discoveries.

One of my favourite alter egos is the Fairy Prankster. Picture this: it's early morning, you're sitting in the subway waking up and you notice that some people are putting up balloons and streamers inside the subway car. They are smiling at you as they tape up homemade art over an ad for pimple cream. At the next stop, more people with balloons board the train. Some of them are in costumes. One young woman is wearing a powder blue ball gown and tiara; she smiles at you and begins to dance with someone dressed up as a mad scientist. Musicians start playing drums and acoustic guitars and everyone starts dancing. You notice that as average citizens board the train, somewhat confused, they are welcomed by the partiers with cheering. All around you the conventional codes of subway conduct are being subverted. You see more smiles than you have ever seen before in the subway.

A superhero approaches the people across from you and begins to make a list, with their help, of wrongs that she must right. To your left some fairies are dancing around and handing out paper flowers, and you wonder if this is some lucid dream. Pinch yourself: it's a subway party! The strange event I've just described really happened underground in Toronto. In fact, subway parties are so popular with both the instigators as well as the unsuspecting celebrators, that it has become a sort of irregular tradition. They give us a chance to remember the goodness in people and the potential for human interaction. They can happen successfully with as few as ten participants or as many as fifty.

Another important facet of my personality is the Guerrilla Gardener. I go out with friends on spring nights with shovels, soil and seeds (or sprouts) to plant flowers (usually sunflowers) in abandoned lots and crumbling urban areas. The idea is to reclaim these depressing spaces with nature. It's not right that there are more parking lots than parks! Blankets of cement cover the city! Trees remain captive in small metal cages tied up with Christmas lights! This calls for some Guerrilla Gardeners!

Nature is a form of public art. Gardening is also a form of performance art, since people often stop and ask us what we're doing. It gives us the opportunity to talk about all kinds of issues, ranging from the patenting of seeds to the privatization of public space. I've always been inspired by the way flowers grow out of a crack in the pavement. Being able to make that happen makes me feel like a superhero. As a Guerrilla Gardener I have no costume or persona, it's just me as I am. All the other experiences I've had of dressing up and creating my own superheroes and role models have given me the inspiration to try to be a real superhero in my day-to-day life.

Being a culture jammer is another real-life superhero fantasy of mine. While standing at the bus stop staring at an ad with a flawless anorexic-looking model on it, an uneasy feeling stirred in my stomach. So many women suffer from eating disorders and low self-esteem that holds them back in life, and all because of unrealistic images like the one that stared at me from the bus ad. Cue the culture jammer. I looked both ways and when the coast was clear (I could always come back later when there was less foot-traffic), I pulled out a fat permanent marker and drew a bubble from the model's mouth, with "Feed Me" written inside. Rather than feeling helpless like before, I felt great. I used the power of the ad against itself. By adding only two words to the image, I subverted its entire meaning. Another tag I have recently taken to writing on ads depicting airbrushed models is "Be a Revolutionary, Love Your Body," which I first saw on a sticker made by my friend Allison Mitchell.

I started culture jamming after I got involved in forming a group called the Media Collective, a loose-knit group of artists and activists who were interested in reclaiming, subverting and making their own media. I published my own zine, made stickers, posters, stencils and street chalk-art to subvert advertising, express my own ideas and challenge the privatization and corporatization of public space. We made puppets and performed street art to raise awareness about issues such as the environment, globalization, social justice, education and police violence. At our monthly gathering people would share ideas and suggest projects they wanted to try. It could be an independent magazine, a billboard alteration, a video, Web site, a poster project or a community garden. At one point I was invited, with some other members, into a high school to talk about why we were culture jamming. I discovered that I loved playing the role of a catalyst in schools and started to visit different schools often to teach workshops about media literacy, critical thinking, independent media production and war-time propaganda.

Most recently, I have imagined a new dream job for myself that's part-superhero fantasy and part-linguistic exercise. I decided to become an "Imagitator," someone who agitates imagination and fuels the spark of possibility that resides in people. When I was later hired by a community art organization, I had the chance to experiment and discover what it really meant to be one. That summer I worked with at-risk youth, helping them make videos that would tell the stories that were important to them. In preparation, we did lots of activities to exercise our imaginations. We also took turns sharing stories to help see the value in our lived experiences. It was an amazing experience and I became good friends with many of the participants. Having people believe in me and being able to create my own job description was a turning point in my life.

That was when I realized the power of naming. What is your dream-job title? How would you name your special super-self? You never know what will happen until you try.

AVOIDING SUPERHERO BURNOUT

Being your own superhero isn't easy, and one of the challenges is avoiding superhero burnout. I have fallen prey to this phenomenon on many occasions, and I try to learn from these experiences. As your own superhero, you've got to protect and save yourself first if you are going to be any help to the rest of the world.

The following activities have been very helpful for me on multiple levels. They are only suggestions, however, so feel free to stray from them and create your own.

THIRTEEN EXERCISES
FOR NURTURING YOUR INNER SUPERHERO

1. Stand tall when people give you a funny look for being yourself.
2. Give yourself permission to see connections between what you love in the world and what you love in yourself.
3. Start to actively notice what you perceive and what you imagine. Try to influence what you imagine so that you can see in new ways.
4. Keep a journal so you can express yourself freely and make self-awareness a daily practice. When possible, write at the start of the day while your mind is fresh and dreams can still be remembered. Try to write whatever is on your mind and let your own inner voice guide you.
5. Create a special or sacred place where you can gather images, objects, plants or pieces of your own art that are meaningful and positive for you. Go to this place as frequently as you can in the mornings and at the end of the day to "check in" with yourself. Let your thoughts drift as your eyes fall upon the different arrangements of objects, and feel free to change and rearrange them in accordance with your shifting moods or the changing times and seasons.
6. Dress up in costumes for special rituals, parties or events (or even just for yourself in private). Take on an a special quality or entire identity that you admire, and see how it feels and fits.
7. Draw naked self-portraits of yourself.
8. Treat insecure thoughts as dangerous spells, which in their own undoing reveal your inner strengths.
9. Play an instrument or sing about the feelings that most confuse, excite and inspire you.
10. Visualize your personal ideas of happiness, success and finding meaning in life. What story do these images tell? If the image is incomplete, use your imagination to experiment with new narratives. This is good to do before going to sleep.
11. Participate often in do-it-yourself rituals so you can play with ideas and explore the different sides of yourself. As often as you can, try to trust rather than judge yourself.

12. Recognize the balance of energies in yourself and the world around you. By contemplating the connections of all things, you will feel more centred, connected and hopeful. As well, an understanding of these connections can sometimes provide you with helpful solutions to complex problems.

13. Give yourself to yourself. If you are a rabbit, jump! If you are a snake, slither! If you are a strange wonderful mutant, name yourself whatever you want (if you want), and do your thing! And don't take yourself too seriously! Have fun!

*

NOTES

1. Susan Douglas, *Where the Girls Are: Growing Up Female with the Mass Media* (New York: Times Books, 1994), 271.
2. Ibid.
3. Ibid., 191.
4. Margaret Mead, *Sex and Temperament in Three Primitive Societies* (New York: William Morrow & Co., 1963), 322.
5. Marian Wright Edelman, graduation address, Berea College, Berea, Kentucky, May 27, 2001.

HER EYES AND HAIR REPEAT

Paola Poletto

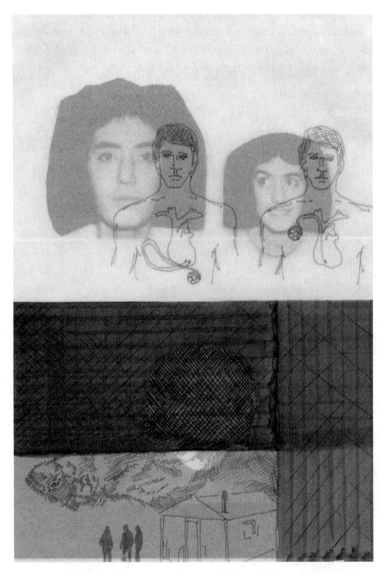

My double life.

My father's big mouth.

My brother's coyness.

My mother's third eye.

DIARY OF A BROOM GIRL

Mariko Tamaki

It was December 2002 and for several weeks I was working down by the harbour on Cherry Street fixing up a warehouse for an opera company. It was cold and dirty, like working in the diseased closet of a very old person with talcum powder covering every surface, old sweaters and shoes tucked into the corners. The whole place had to be swept and sanitized so that the opera singers coming in wouldn't get sore throats.

I swept and mopped all day long and a layer of soft dust molecules accumulated on my clothes. I shook them off by stamping around outside, leaving dusty *O*s in my wake. I developed a system with my broom and some mystery green sand that must have been toxic. The sand helped with the dust but left green drag-queen crusties in my eyes every morning.

For the majority of the day I was content to sweep things into piles and think about what my must-have for spring that year would be. Someone had asked me that earlier and I didn't know. I wanted to have an answer by the end of the day. I was thinking about sneakers when I heard a somewhat-taunting squeaky man voice that came from above.

"Hey, Broom Girl!"

The voice in question belonged to a boy named Dwight. I hadn't spoken with Dwight since I had correctly guessed three days earlier that he played Dungeons and Dragons, a guess I hazarded not because Dwight had said anything to me about it but because I could just tell. Indication number one was an excess of dragon-themed jewellery, which should tell you a little about Dwight.

"Hey, Broom Girl, you want to pass me that cord?"

I picked up the cord in question and passed it up to him.

"Michi," I said.

"What?"

"Michi," I said. "That's my name."

"Oh, yeah."

Five minutes later, as Dwight wove his way through the lamps on the floor to get out for a coffee, he winked at me and pointed his finger at my broom.

"What's up Broom Girl?" he chuckled.

"Hey, Dwight," I said, "If you call me Broom Girl one more time, I'm going to shove this broom up your ass."

The problem with ass threats is that, although they sound sweet and trip off the tongue like sucked Smarties, they are largely meaningless. Very rarely do you plan to follow through with a threat you make about someone's ass.

Dwight laughed. "OK, Broom Girl."

After that, only to Dwight, but often to Dwight, I was Broom Girl. I started sweeping in uneven circles so that I could avoid him. I ate my lunch alone, away from the rest of the crew. I chewed on bitter cucumber sandwiches and thought about revenge. I abandoned my must-have for spring and thought only about what I would do or say to Dwight before the job was over.

If you're a feminist, you've had a moment like this. It's the moment when you encounter what is undoubtedly sexism, which results in your brain being suddenly flooded with a lethal mix of politics and rage. If you're like me, this rage is often worsened by the oily residue of desire to say something with impact, something other than, "Fuck you!"

It's the desire to say something that will define the confrontation by what it isn't, a bar brawl, and what it is, a clash of politics. It's the will to assert yourself as right, which is infinitely difficult to do when the moment strikes, even if you have had time to prepare.

"Fuck you, asshole!" I yelled at Dwight and immediately wanted to kick myself.

Six years ago, when I was just out of university, I ended up at a dinner party with a bunch of old friends. Among them was a girl named Mary — Mary Graham. If you don't know Mary Graham, her name is not significant to you. It's significant to me because I do know Mary

Graham and I hate her. Not thirty minutes into the evening, she and I got into a fight about sexual harassment at work. We were talking about someone at a friend's office who was a bum-patter and whether or not any of us had a problem with it.

"What women have to realize," Mary said, "is that reporting sexual harassment doesn't make you look strong. It makes you look weak, like girls can't look out for themselves, so they have to get the teacher involved. It's like snitching."

Of course, I knew all about what Mary Graham thought about snitching because I went to grade school with her. Everything I know about Mary and snitches has to do with a particular game of dodgeball she and I participated in back in Grade 7.

On that particular day Mary was playing on her best friend Christy Pilgrim's team, made of up a tight-knit group of girls whose names, coincidentally, all ended in *y*, dippy long blonde ponytail *y*'s. I think one of them was named Miffy. Christy is the one I recall with keen accuracy, probably because, just when we were nearing the end of the game, Christy threw the ball at my face. It bounced off my cheek and into my hands with a thwack! It felt like a rock.

My eyes were closed as I gripped the rubber in my hands. The girls on my team gathered around me, put their hands on my back and asked if I was all right. I was on the unofficial Asian/ethnic team and I was one of the tallest girls. We always got clobbered.

From somewhere inside the group of girls gathered around me, I felt a tug on the ball. It was Christy.

"It's my ball," she said. "You're out."

"You hit me in the face," I said. My cheek was getting hotter and hotter, like an electric burner, heat spreading out in a coil from the inside. "It's a foul."

"You jumped at it," Christy said. "It's not my fault it hit you in the face."

"I didn't," I said.

"Did too," said Christy.

"Did not," someone behind me piped up.

Christy stepped back and let go of the ball. She had a tiny birdlike face, smooth and small. Her lips were always twisted into a perfect knot. Everyone felt bad for Christy that year because her dad was getting remarried. I didn't feel especially bad. Christy was never that nice to me.

Christy cupped her hand and swung it at me, like she was knocking something off a table. Her wrist was locked and stiff as her palm connected with my cheek. It felt like she'd snapped my neck like a rubber band. I dropped the ball and Christy scooped it up, swiveled and walked back to her team. I turned and ran into the school, colliding with the soft silk chest of our vice-principal.

I did not have a problem with snitches or snitching. "Christy hit me," I screamed. Christy was given two weeks' detention.

But that afternoon Mary and two of her friends called me at home and hissed into the line with their lips close to the receiver: "Finker! You'll wish you were dead." For three weeks, Mary and her friends followed me from class to class, walking only inches behind, their hot breath in my ears. Eventually Christy's detention was over and all was forgotten.

Six years later, I watched Mary take what I thought was a smug sip of her beer. She hadn't aged at all. She had the same Grade 7 chubby cheeks, the same thick blonde hair that was held up in a high ponytail by a black ribbon. I took a big sip of my Caesar, the red tomatoness burned down my throat and made my eyes water.

What I meant to say in response to Mary's comment about sexual harassment was all about justice and power, that the word "snitching" was a bully's way of making the people they picked on feel even less powerful. Sexual harassment was against the law for a reason, because its victims are often women, often employees who feel like they have no recourse for the way they are being treated — people who put up with it because they feel they have no choice. Reporting sexual harassment, I wanted to say, wasn't snitching any more than reporting vandalism or robbery or assault. It took guts.

Instead I stood up and knocked my Caesar into Mary's lap. Everything I wanted to say blended into a dull Morse code in my head. Why, I wondered later, don't politics line up like eggs in a carton when you need them? All that shaped in my head was:

Power.

Take for.

Granted.

Victim.

You.

Take me.

None of that made any sense. So instead I grabbed my purse. "You," I spat, "are a bitch."

Of course, it's true, right? She is and she was. But calling someone a bitch is not the kind of victorious moment you picture, ten years after getting hit in the face for no reason.

My friend Katie says feminism can be like the ground in Super Mario Sunshine level eight, with the sand that funnels out from underneath you. In order to survive, you have to wrench your joystick and jump really high and fast onto the next pillar. You have to keep jumping until you hit the big yellow crown that lifts you up into the air. It's all about patience and timing.

The next day Dwight was running down a flight of stairs when he tripped. I was near the bottom of the stairs when it happened. I watched him plummet, not in slow motion, but quickly and assertively, the way a body should fall. He landed in a starfish at the bottom, swore and quickly rolled over onto his side to grab his ankle.

I waited patiently for the crowd of concerned boys in tool belts to disperse and let Dwight get his footing. Then I quietly approached to ask how he was doing.

He frowned and growled, "Fine."

"Are you sure?" I asked.

"Yeah," he said.

"OK," I said, "because if you were really hurt I wouldn't say this."

"Say what?" he asked.

Gripping my broom in one hand I leaned in really close. "That's what you get," I hissed, "for calling me Broom Girl."

It is a doubly powerful statement, you have to understand, when the person you're talking to plays Dungeons and Dragons and knows what the role of the dice can mean. After that Dwight didn't call me Broom Girl anymore.

EVERYDAY SUPERHERO

Rose Bianchini

We now join our everyday superhero, Julie, who fights evil with each measured breath. She is a superhero of thought and an activist who directly faces the atrocities we all fear. Full of self-proclaimed identity, she travels the concrete in straight lines and lets her emotions rule.

We shadow Julie's daily life, watching her back slowly stiffen and her brow furrow, as she contemplates how to persevere.

WORK

Equipped only with a small dose of courage, Julie awakens each morning tapping her own name on her wrist. Full of anxiety she finds her gut located around her neck. She plays at being grown up by participating in morning commutes to tall buildings that broadcast signals.

Her office mates eat out of Styrofoam on small couches. They cross and uncross their long, divorced legs under short skirts. These are women who know where to get pedicures, shop during lunch and remain fearlessly high-powered. Julie's own insecurities heighten as they force-feed her discussions of waist sizes and sales.

"You are tiny," they squeal over the pressboard desks.

"I lost some weight after a breakup," Julie responds.

"Ohhh. Mmmmm." The syllables float on wise nods.

"You shed that man."

"Right."

The chattering women make no comment about how extra-small clothes hang on her frame. Instead, food obsessions are celebrated over blaring MTV images that keep the hip media producers current.

They are unaware of her malnourished blackout in the bookstore as her lanky boyfriend disengaged. It occurred slowly. The boyfriend was burrowed in a black parka clinging to a nature book. She hid in the feminism section and read: "Trauma to one's body may cause anorexia. One stops eating to escape ..." First came the wave of epiphany, then a thud of blackness.

There was an obligatory squeeze of her clammy hands as she was awakened by her soon-to-be ex. His coffee spilled as his back straightened and his long legs strode away. She cried in public that cold day.

Due to Julie's commitment to integrity, she soon found that sharing a subway ride with red-faced men each morning stopped making sense. The inane conversations with co-workers during long afternoons were futile time-wasters. And she grew tired of wearing a sweater to ward off the air-conditioner grate's daily attack. Thus, one day she quit and never looked back.

SIDEWALKS

She wears a steady stare and a mysterious grin while she navigates the city's wind tunnels. She attempts to use superhuman feminist theory to deflect the lusty looks that travel down her spine and the fat-lipped, thin-limbed women behind Plexiglas who beg her to consume.

The sidewalks are dangerous. Flying through the polluted air are shards of sexual propositions made by skinny art boys, drunken mechanical engineers, bush pilots, lawyers-to-be, retired guidance counsellors, tour guides, anarchists, chem students, bosses and single fathers. They intrude on her soul-searching, pay-phone conversations and beers with other lady superheroes.

Example one of many: "Heeeey," slurred a street urchin from the bar district, while calculating the amount of time between grabbing her arm and possible dick ejaculation in a back alley.

"Don't touch me."

"Carpet-muncher."

"I wish that was funny."

"If you change your mind, we're staying at the Holiday Inn."

"Good for you."

Her head feels invaded by their want. The sick entitlement of their desire eats at her for days. She can never wear the skinny pants or the tight heels. To feel less exposed she pulls the clothes away from her skin.

Alone

She becomes lonely. Essentially, she has always been alone. Since the day she was born she wandered the earth, using her ESP to learn language. Julie desperately tried to ignore the social construct of pain that called itself family.

As a child, she hid in closets with tiny words, reading thousands of books by dim flashlight. With her blue teddy bear, she slowly cultivated the power to float up through the ceiling to better places.

One day when the monsters under her bed came to find her, she was engaged in full-blown astral projection. "Ha," she scoffed, "I am bigger and better than this sad little existence."

Her tiny self looked up. The front of her nightie was stained yellow with violent hands.

"Don't leave me behind," yelped tangible young Julie, her face frozen.

Our superhero-in-progress floated quickly through the paper ceiling, ripped it to shreds and enjoyed much-deserved escapes.

Family Obligation

She smears bruises on her legs and breathes in the damp flashbacks. It is difficult to attend her niece's sixth birthday because she cannot abide the conversations permeated by denial.

There's too much food bought from large chains, where corporate cars line the massive parking lot. Julie scrapes her toe on the suburban grey carpet.

"What are you up to these days?" asks the brother with the perverse smirk on his face.

"I work in the ... by the ... up the ... I am so important. You cannot even fathom how important I am."

His son's whining complaints quickly distract him: wailing about a red balloon.

"Relax!" the brother screams at the top of his lungs.

"I want it! I want it!"

During yet another onslaught of blood obligation, she is forced to pose by the Christmas tree while her alleged family shouts at the children between camera flashes. Julie is then politely given garishly wrapped family portraits from Wal-Mart.

"I spent hours picking out *your* gifts," she mumbles into her hand.

They glance at her precious objects with quiet enthusiasm. She has pegged them, softly considered their happiness on frigid afternoons.

They barely looked up when she arrived. They were too busy with loud plastic toys that require batteries. Struggling to dismantle small pieces for impatient children. The walls seem to burn with white-primer sterility: these changes are fine.

"I made you these earrings, this painting, this poem."

In return, they give her small, distracted thank-yous.

Letting Go

A true superhero who forges brand-new identities needs no superior being to direct her. It dawned on her one stale afternoon that she could officially no longer talk to her family.

She heard the children's recess outside her window and felt cheated out of some happiness everyone else held in the palm of their sweaty crayon hands.

Too wracked with malaise to move from her dirty sheets and face another day full of unexplainable pain, Julie lay years of intense judgement, loud abuse and teeth marks on tender arms onto her wooden floor.

"I will not endure one more obligatory family moment," she declares to startled roommates. "As of this moment, I exist only for myself."

Immediately, the phone begins to ring with insistence. She relents and answers it.

"Don't you care about me?" asks the sick mother, slinging guilt at full throttle.

"Do you call what you did caring?" demands Julie, finally shattering the family rule to deny they weren't perfect.

"One day you will understand."

"Understand what?"

"How hard it was for us."

"I'm just aiming for functional."

Relationships

As an activist for survival, Julie feels the need to pile books next to her bed for protection. She wonders aloud how long her lack of faith in true

love will last and if she can read herself away from dysfunctional relationships rather than be reduced to a banal psychological definition
written on a white page.

In childhood make-believe, she married other little girls. The wed-
ding aisle was a neighbour's backyard. The bouquet was made up of
stolen marigolds. Girls with their dangerously sweet breath and manip-
ulative taunts were safest.

Men were large with mean voices. She feared their hands in dark
closets. Even though her mother, with dough on her forearms, had told
her to let them take care of her.

"This is what it means to be a woman."

Julie awaits the man who will undo the damage, listens silently with
the ears of integrity. This man will in no way resemble her silent, judgemental father who folded his arms across his small chest. The new pro-
tector will hold her wrists with wide fingers, praise her work and bur-
row deeply into the covers.

At times she pursues her best friend through mirrored hallways in an
attempt to connect lover and chosen family. With narrow hips and a
dark beard, he grabs at her quickly. The drama unfolds under a single
sheet on a mattress on the floor. Speaking over the loud door buzzers in
the courtyard, she watches the sky turn blue again.

"Your need overwhelms me," he chants.

"It's not always this way."

"It is."

"Allow a person to change."

"I wake up with my own anxiety."

"So?"

"You can't be here for that."

"I want to be held in a safe way."

"How?"

"Like I saw this little girl once on her mother's lap. It was summer.
She was rocking and holding her nice and firm; steady hands on a small
back."

SEX

Her affairs take place in lofts with high ceilings. Men with progressive
tongues and full dicks plunge deeply and breathe rapidly into her ear.

On beds, Julie plays with boys' intimacy fears to unravel her trauma. She wants to own her body and have it shift easily away from past hands that tightened her muscles and left her neck stiff. She sucks in. Their boyish arms rock slowly as they weave misogynist blame.

The complaints range from too needy to too hard to locate. She rolls around in their projected selves.

"Where are you?" they ask.

"Here."

"I can't read you."

"I know."

She rides buses with strangers and takes off clothes in their family homes, upstairs from their mothers. She has Saturday sex on large tables in hotel basements. She meets them on hot afternoons while wearing white dresses or short skirts. She gets caught under large trees in the rain. Long limbs wrap around her waist. She reclaims her own skin from traditional constraints.

"Does this happen often?" It's an awkward question asked over fresh bagels and unknown expectations.

"No."

She washes scents off her mind and plays sex games in corridors. She allows herself to be bought dinner and drinks. She dismantles gender with her smirk.

THE NEWS

Her TV spouts prime-time fear-mongering. Graphic images of little girls' parts float in rivers. Public outcry reaches the windows of high-rises: the middle class demands immunity to the horror.

"Plant microchips in their arms!"

"We will track them!"

"Like the animals that they are!"

Like Julie, other isolated women in tiny apartments know deep in their joints where the violence resides. It's in musty childhood basements that empty their stomachs. In the inexplicable daily pains and creeping infections. Deep in the home fortress, with tall sloping towers built on denial, childish hands ball into fists and out-of-body projection is coping.

She shuts off the TV. A superhero does not allow the media to distort her experiences. Instead, she listens deeply to the shared stories of women with small angry voices who stain their lips with survival and arrange their chairs in circles.

Voices

Although Julie is in constant pursuit of justice and joy, she still finds that at times the violence wafts behind her like a scent. It seeps into her hair. Causes passersby to stare. She holds her head up with a shaky chin on glaring sunny days, yet it has reconfigured her brain. Now she is unclear where other people's identities end and hers begins.

"You are worthless," say the voices that curve her thoughts during weak afternoons.

"Always have been, always will be," they hiss.

"Liar," she whispers, hoping they're wrong.

A moment of crisp clarity settles. She shoves the black snakes of paranoia with her foot. Her name is clearly written on her arm so that she can remember herself when the unwanted voices come to visit.

Emergency Room

In this metal fast-paced technological revolution, at times Julie finds it best to hide her traumatic memories under party talk, in cluttered drawers and under her dirty fingernails.

But sometimes her veneer cracks. Her hair becomes frizzy and her eyes dart around unfocused. Many people do not understand the pressure and strain of her secret/double superhero existence. She finds herself in bright hospitals with concerned loved ones milling in the waiting room.

"Did you buy razor blades?" The loud insensitive emergency-room worker speaks quickly from the doorway.

"Yes."

"What did you plan to do with them?"

Julie wanted to see the pain stream out with a hiss. She did not want to die. She just wanted to relieve some of the pressure, see her blood pour out, stop the migraines.

"Well?" His voice is sharp with his impatience to leave. He wants to go home to his normal wife and escape the "crazies."

"You are making me feel uncomfortable."

She will not allow mental symptoms contrived by a stranger to be written about her in a manila folder.

TRAVEL

Julie travels spontaneously and quickly. Often she cruises on cheap planes, rides the rails or glides along on rain-soaked buses. Escapes and temporary lairs include piles of dirt and ocean jaunts. The small of her back loosens as she stomps out memories and past selves on gravel roads.

She relishes the in-between moments, ripe with potential. The ride. She watches land melt away. She even enjoys her impatient seatmate with frosted hair, who reads a book with the glaring subtitle: *Can Faith, Hope and Love Survive a Year of Terror?* Perhaps these exploitative books become noble while you're traveling at 30,000 feet.

Then there's the whoosh of landing in a new place. A freshly scrubbed face waits at the airport. Julie's words gleam with expectation.

She travels to escape the fear she has been fed since birth: that she is a woman, thus small, weak and a target; that her gender makes her valuable only as a producer of children and pleaser of an overbearing husband; that dreams, adventure and the pursuit of higher consciousness are not a woman's lot.

She endures her parents' worried voices on the distant phone line.

"Why did you have to go?" they ask.

"Because I wanted to."

"So far?"

"Yes."

"We worry."

"I know, but you have to trust me."

"It's other people we don't trust."

"That's a sad way to live."

Julie unpacks their mistrust of everything unfamiliar. She will not cower in a brick house with a loud TV and believe this is happiness. She will climb, scamper across rocks, camp by oceans. Her limbs and mind will tone into one smooth muscle bent on forward motion.

WRITING

She squeezes written words into office days at yet another contract job, while her co-worker is on lunch and before her boss walks toward her desk.

At times she is poised in well-decorated coffee shops with her head planted firmly atop her neck. Young suburban hippies peer over her bird shoulder, scouting creativity. She sighs deeply. The hip masterpiece is just waiting to flow from her fountain pen to solve all the world's ailments.

"I have it all: the pain, tragedy, loneliness. I could be great. Should be great!" she says to that tight place where self-doubt resides.

"Shut up," she barks, for her "self-confidence" is jaded and mocking.

"I could have talent: the tragic heroine who turns her life into a creative conduit. People eat that stuff up. I could be the brilliant voice in the cesspool of humanity everyone is waiting for. Why not me?"

Her secret self does not comment on these grandiose statements. Thus, Julie writes into the sunrise and deep into the dark sticky night.

ACCIDENT

Julie feeds her pets tofu while dreaming of tragic bike accidents. She wonders aloud: "If my bones were ground against metal, would I finally be free?"

She can imagine the startled face of a suburban wife in a white sedan as Julie's body suddenly appears on her car's grill, intent on self-harm. The overfed children scream in the back seat, smeared cupcake on their cheeks.

"No!"

Then follows the fantasy of a luxurious funeral where millions of unknown fans pour through the walls. She floats above them with a benevolent smile, up to that special heaven for people who never knew they were or could be superheroes.

"Ah. They really did love me."

The old beaus. The grade-school teachers. The cousins she always hated. They would scream over the coffin.

Moans of "Sweet Julie" would waft toward the rafters. "She could have been so great. The world is now deprived."

Yet when reality sits close beside her, Julie realizes there is much to do. She meditates softly on the trauma of the everyday, the violence in her tautly strung body. She looks directly into a silver-painted mirror and decides: Much to do. Never too late.

MINIATURE COLOURED MARSHMALLOWS

Lisa Smolkin

Too much unowned pain. It makes me have to disappear. I get cold and then freezing and then sick.

Someone told me I smelled like miniature coloured marshmallows.

Excuse me I think the world is a really bad place which
is getting in the way of my practicum.
I don't know how to get support. I don't know what I need.

Some people are weirder
than others.

who can meet me ?

How can I
get a harp
donated to me ?

I don't know what to say. People are interrupting me. They are telling me what to do. I don't know where I am or what I am doing. I feel I am made to apologize for everything.

Happiness is about being okay with where I'm at

   Saline solutions

Happiness is being blonde.

The Life of a ~~Borderline~~
Chronic Post-Traumatic Stress Disorder Sufferer

My head is about to explode.

What's my responsibility?

puzzle

Major Drag

Guess what
I've got it.

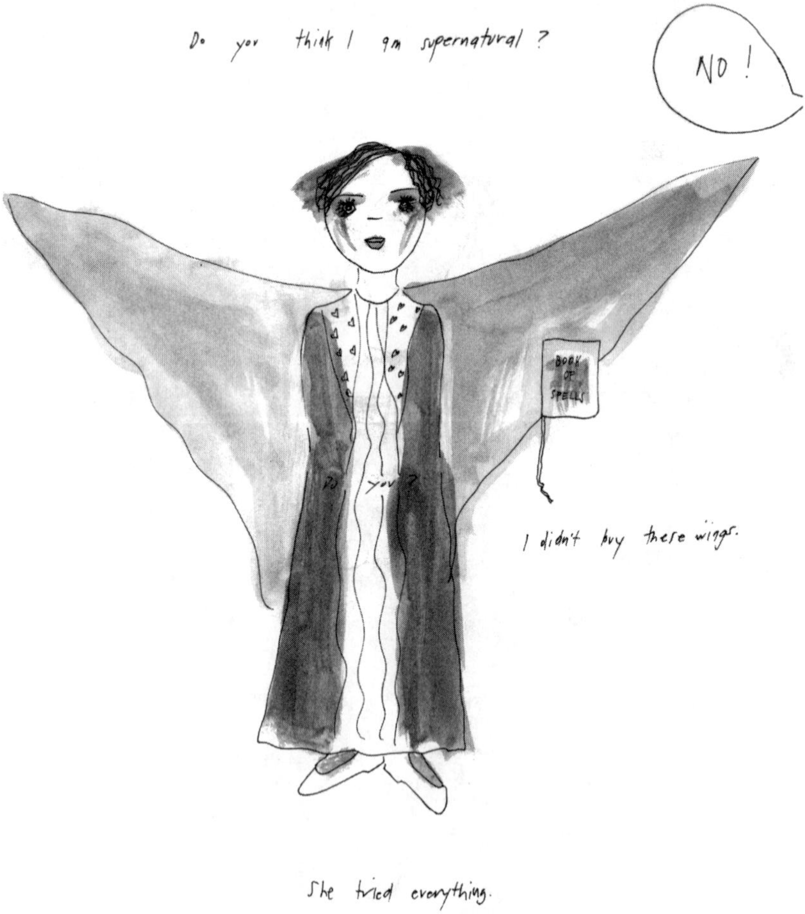
Do you think I am supernatural ?
NO !
BOOK OF SPELLS
Do you ?
I didn't buy these wings.
She tried everything.

The Movie Theatre was packed with all my friends.

It is so great to be loved by so many great people.

Sylvia Plath

I'm really more of a bird than a person.

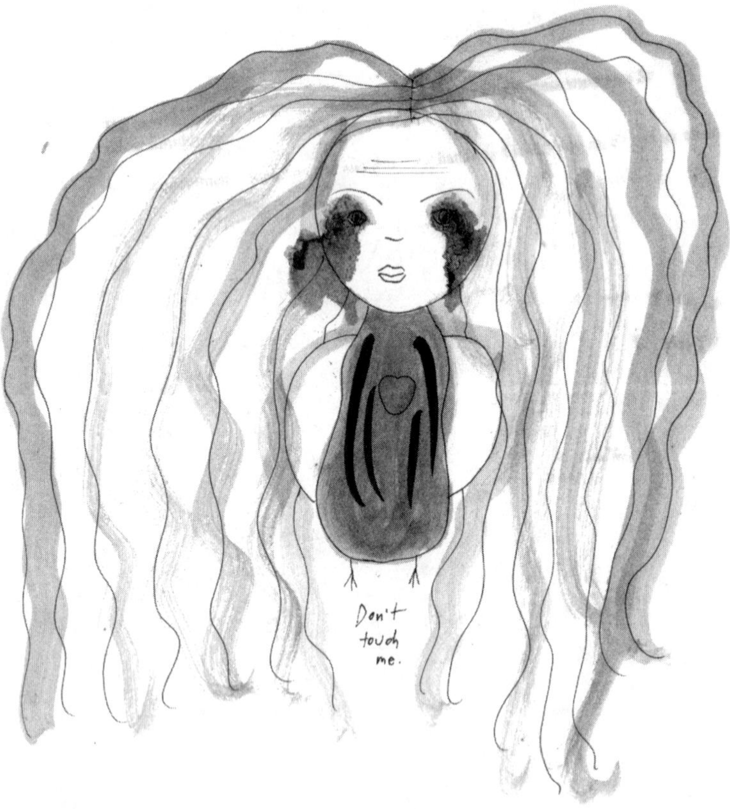
Don't
touch
me.

I have limitations.
That's a fact
Now fly away.

READY TO BE STRONG?

BUFFY, ANGELINA AND ME

Nancy Gobatto

From now on, every girl in the world who might be a Slayer, will be a Slayer. Every girl who could have the power, will have the power. Who can stand up, will stand up. Every one of you, and girls we've never known, and generations to come ... they will have strength they never dreamed of, and more than that, they will have each other. Slayers. Make your choice. Are you ready to be strong?

— BUFFY THE VAMPIRE SLAYER[1]

I'm capable of being stronger and darker and fiercer than anybody's ever written.

— ANGELINA JOLIE[2]

The other night I had a dream that some prissy chick and her friend were gettin' on me — saying something about me having had a nose job (which, not that it matters, I have never had). I walked over to a party where I was and promptly sent out not one but *two* Slayers to take care of the girls for me. That's right, not just Buffy but the good-turned-evil-turned-reformed second Slayer Faith were in my corner, hanging with my crew. I've got to say, it's a comfort knowing a slayer (or two) has your back.

It had been a while since I dreamed of Buffy or one of her friends, but it certainly wasn't the first time. About two and a half years ago I was taking the antidepressant/anti-anxiety med Paxil and the most obvious side effect was an intense period of heightened dreaming during which I found myself hanging out with Buffy and her Scooby Gang almost every night. The dreams were so vivid I felt like I was actually getting to know these people — who were really actors playing roles — while I was unconscious. It was troubling. It's one thing to go to your therapist and tell him you're dreaming of a twenty-foot figure that resembles your mom looming in the horizon. It's a different thing altogether to say you're befriending Buffy the Vampire Slayer, fighting evil and (if truth be told) getting pretty good at it, night after night.

> I don't want to be insane. But it seems the easiest option. I am too tired to work for more. Will insanity bring rest? Will insanity be lonely, a place where no one can understand? I don't want to be alone.
>
> — Nancy Gobatto, personal journal,
> June 9, 1994 (age 18)

One evening when I was nineteen, my older sister and I were walking her dog through the suburban streets of my childhood. I don't remember what exactly we were discussing, but at one point she turned to me and said, "I started with thirty years of crap to undo. You might as well start with twenty. Find yourself a therapist."

I grew up at the end of an era that viewed childhood as an idyllic space, distinct and almost completely apart from adult experience. Things were starting to change. Dr. Spock had been hanging around for a while and some parents were still feeling the impact of the movement toward liberation and change in the 1960s and 1970s. But in the 1980s, you didn't put on the TV and hear Oprah preview the next episode featuring "children who have holes in their souls in the shape of their fathers." You didn't hear about "crazy" kids, just kids who "went" crazy sometime during high school or shortly thereafter. So it's not that I wasn't a crazy kid, it's just that no one noticed, or maybe they just didn't call it that.

I think back now and am stunned that I didn't end up in therapy before I was nineteen or on meds before I was twenty-five. I've been terrified of the film *One Flew Over the Cuckoo's Nest* for most of my life. Something about it felt prophetic, especially when I was younger. A sense that I actually belonged somewhere very far from the yellow checked curtains that hung in my bedroom. These were characters I understood maybe a little too well.

I was a young adult when I saw Angelina Jolie's portrayal of the seductively unstable Lisa in *Girl, Interrupted* (1999). After watching that retelling of a group of young women's experiences in a mental hospital in the late 1960s I realized that had I been born then, hospitalization would have been inevitable. In today's world, on the other hand, I suspect I would have faced a series of school-board social workers and pediatric psychiatrists by the time I graduated from high school. And I'm not saying I was some kind of movie-of-the-week teenaged heroine screaming or raging against myself and others. I'm just saying that sometimes "insanity" has a lot to do with timing.

This essay will detail some of my reactions to the fictional character of Buffy Summers and the real-life actress Angelina Jolie, two women I have never met (and in the case of Buffy could never meet). I focus on Buffy and Jolie for two reasons: they are both representative of the current popular expectations of "girl power" and in spite of (or perhaps because of) this, they both face specific pressures regarding their claims to sanity. My own experiences within the realm of mental health, coupled with my attraction to these women, have forced me to reconsider my own understandings and often unspoken beliefs about my worth as a woman who is so often deemed, at best, quirky and, at worst, crazy. Neither word seems to connote strength. So it's not surprising that a show that reframed difference as being "chosen" and an actress who has defined her public role in Hollywood on her own terms and won an Oscar for her work would speak to a quiet, buried part of myself that was beginning to assert itself.

In Buffy and Jolie I recognized that sense of teetering, that constant wondering about which step will go too far, pull you past reality and land you in the loony bin. Buffy is the teenager with super-strength and Jolie is the woman challenging expectations about love, sex, work, and motherhood. Both must constantly reconcile the fact that not only do they risk being misunderstood but also that they, through that misunderstanding, may be regarded as unstable. The older I get, the more I realize that I will always be a little crazy, but I'm sure not alone and if a slayer and an Oscar-winning actress are among the ranks of the insane, it can't be all that bad a path to follow.

HELLO, MY NAME IS BUFFY SUMMERS. I AM A SLAYER

> BUFFY: I *was* in an institution. There were doctors and nurses and other patients. They told me that I was sick — I guess, crazy — and that Sunnydale and all of this ... none of it was real.
>
> XANDER: Oh, come on ... that's ridiculous! What? You think this isn't real just because of all the vampires and demons and ex-vengeance demons and the sister that used to be a big ball of universe-destroying energy?[3]

I spent a lot of time watching Joss Whedon's self-proclaimed feminist show *Buffy the Vampire Slayer* (*BtVS*). Perhaps because of my need to belong, I started wondering what role I would play, were I given the chance. I didn't want to be a monster/villain or a one-week-only victim who gets saved. No way. I wanted to be a recurring character who would enhance the audience's understanding of Buffy and her cohort.

Somewhere around season five it hit me: a psychologist. What if Buffy needed some help dealing with the emotional and societal pressures of being a "hot chick with superpowers."[4] I thought it would work on several levels and it could be an interesting relationship as my character came to understand that Buffy wasn't having delusions of grandeur but was actually a superhero who couldn't get a date with a living person to save her life. So when, part way through the sixth season of *BtVS*, an episode opened with Buffy huddled in the corner of a white room while orderlies and an ever-caring shrink hovered over her, I felt I should have spoken up sooner.

The premise of the episode, titled "Normal Again," is this: while out on the hunt, our fearless Slayer is stung by a demon whose venom causes hallucinations. She imagines she is (and has been) in a psych ward for the past six years — since she started thinking she was the Slayer. What makes the episode "very scary — in the way that padded cells are"[5] is the narrative play that makes Buffy (and the viewer) question which reality is the hallucination. It forces us to confront the fact that "[a] primal fear for many people is that madness is simply one bad day away."[6] The idea that Buffy's existence as the Slayer is nothing more than her primary delusion as she suffers with an "undifferentiated type of schizophrenia" is of course refuted by Buffy's pals in her Slayer world. Thus her best friend, Willow, insists: "Buffy, look at me. You are *not* in an institution. You have never been in an institution." This argument, however, is quickly stunted by Buffy's confession in "Normal Again":

> Back when I saw my first vampires … I got so scared. I told my parents and they completely freaked out. They thought there was something seriously wrong with me. So they sent me to a clinic. […] I was only there a couple of weeks. I stopped talking about it and they let me go. Eventually, my parents just forgot.

This is a remarkable discovery for fans of the show. Never in the previous five years had there been any references to institutions or mental-health issues. Personally, I was struck by the plot's similarity to an episode in the second-last season of *Star Trek: Deep Space Nine.* In that show, Captain Benjamin Sisko (the first Black actor to assume the lead role in a *Star Trek* series) undergoes a similar struggle: he bounces between his "present-day" as a Star Fleet captain and his own version of a mental hospital in the mid-twentieth century US. When reasoning with both Buffy and Captain Sisko, the hospital staff allude to their implied second-class status in society (Buffy as a young girl and Sisko as a Black man). The logic is thus: you should recognize you are hallucinating because you are not capable of achieving such a position of power in society.

I was so stunned by this intense episode in "Normal Again" and Buffy's struggles to come to grips with which life she really wants to be real. She is forced to choose between the life where she has both her parents around to support her while she recovers from mental illness and tries to pursue a normal life, and the life where her mother is dead and she is the Slayer, responsible for friends, family and the world. In the end, we see Buffy say goodbye to her parents in the mental-hospital reality and learn she has slipped back into a schizophrenic coma: Buffy chooses to remain in Sunnydale with her friends and to accept her duties as the Slayer. However, viewers are left wondering if the show they have been watching and are continuing to watch is nothing more than the delusions of a mentally ill girl.

So much for girl power.

It's no surprise that this episode occurs during the sixth season. Following Buffy's self-sacrificing death at the end of season five, she is resurrected by her Wiccan pal Willow and the rest of the Scoobies at the beginning of the sixth season. The resurrection, however, does not play out exactly as planned, and we learn that her friends have, in fact, ripped Buffy from heaven. So the season is more grim and psychologically complex than previous seasons. The troubled side of Buffy revealed through her struggles to find meaning in her post-heaven life disturbed many fans. Sarah Michelle Gellar, the actress who played Buffy, also openly disliked the tone of the sixth season:

> It wasn't who Buffy was, or why people loved her. You don't want to see that dark heroine; you don't want to see her punishing herself. You want to see her killing vampires and making quips. It didn't feel like the character that I loved. Joss [Whedon] always explained that season as being about your 20s, where you're not a kid anymore, but you don't know what you want to do [with your life]. He always said that I didn't understand last year because I've always known what I wanted to do, and I didn't have that confusion, [that] dark, depressive period.[7]

Perhaps because I did understand what it meant to feel "dark" and "depressive" and was currently in the later part of my twenties' angst, I found the sixth season compelling in a way that the previous ones weren't. A slayer who doesn't necessarily have all the answers and sometimes fucks up became increasingly intriguing to me. So, when I saw "Normal Again," I looked deeper into the plot line and narrative turns of the show — beyond just sitting on my couch week after week. I eventually came upon the Dark Horse comic's story arc *Slayer, Interrupted,* which ran in four issues (issues 56–59 of their *BtVS* comic series) and acts as a prequel to the television series. It details the time Buffy spent in the clinic that her parents sent her to when she was a young teenager.

In the television episode we hear that Buffy was "so scared" of becoming the Slayer that she tells her parents, who "freak out" and send her to the psych clinic. The comic-book storyline is slightly different: Buffy runs away to Las Vegas to fight vampires with her friend/potential boyfriend Pike[8] and during this absence her little sister, Dawn, reads her diary and discloses the information she discovers to their parents at the beginning of *Slayer, Interrupted.* Thus, while the television show portrays Buffy as scared by her new role as the Slayer, and seeking help from her parents, the comic book offers a more defiant Buffy — a young woman who is willing to run away and pose as a cocktail waitress in order to fulfill her Slayer duties. It's defiance, rather than fear, that affects her time in the clinic and shows us a young woman struggling to come to grips with her life and to make conscious decisions about whether or not to live as the Slayer. Instead of a bleak, senseless place, where Buffy learns she must hide her identity in order to secure her freedom, the clinic in the comic book becomes an avenue that takes her toward self-discovery and acceptance.

Saved from intensive drug and electroshock therapy by the intrigued and maternal Dr. Primrose, Buffy enters into a therapeutic relationship with her. Shortly into her therapy sessions Buffy has the following realization: "The vampires, the demons, the monsters ... It's all a metaphor for growing up. I'm 'slaying' my youth. So then ... I'm not the Slayer."[9] Buffy reads her behaviour as an intra-psychic attempt to reconcile fears of growing up. Thus, "slaying" is not just slaughtering monsters, but part of a schema in which it represents Buffy's struggle to combat the usual adolescent adversaries. Aside from highlighting the metaphoric framework of the Buffyverse, this theory offers Buffy the opportunity to separate herself from her role as the Slayer. The relief she gains is short-lived, however, and she soon begins to suspect that she might not be so easily removed from her responsibilities.

When the head psychiatrist is revealed to be a demon, Buffy realizes she is the only one capable of fighting him and accepts her destiny. We also learn that Dr. Primrose always knew that Buffy was the Slayer and, in fact, Dr. Primrose used to be a Watcher (someone trained to watch over and train a slayer). Dr Primrose explains: "You are a creature of destiny, Buffy Summers. Slayers are always where they most need to be." Thus, Buffy's stay in a mental ward has less to do with her or her parents' concern than with her fate as the Slayer — a fate she has been trying to avoid.

In both the television episode "Normal Again" and the comic-book series *Slayer, Interrupted*, the notion of insanity becomes an excuse to resist strength and responsibility. In "Normal Again," to believe she is a schizophrenic is to relinquish control and to live according to the presented limitations. In *Slayer, Interrupted*, to reduce her identity as the Slayer to a metaphor of youthful angst means she need not struggle to come to grips with what it means to be a high-school student who is not the same as everyone else, whose displays of strength have the potential to alienate family, friends and love interests.

I have, for many years now, felt as though if I could only put my finger on what's "wrong" with me, I would be able to enter some sort of better existence. I have been to many therapists and have tried various legal and illegal substances with the hope of discovering the answer to my question. No such luck. So now the question really is, what would I be doing differently with my life if I were "fixed"? The truth is my own notion that I am in need of fixing has become a powerful tool I can use to distance myself from taking risks or simply living life. As long as I maintain that I am somehow unwell, un-whole or unworthy, I don't have to face the responsibilities I am afraid of (even if it's not saving the world from the forces of evil). Like Buffy.

ANGELINA JOLIE: KOOKY, DARK AND ENORMOUSLY TALENTED [10]

> It's nice to know that even when we go against ourselves or we get lost or feel misplaced, it's still possible to be able to say "I survived."
>
> — Angelina Jolie [11]

With the release of her second video game–inspired film, *Lara Croft Tomb Raider: The Cradle of Life,* actress Angelina Jolie once again became the focus of media attention in the summer of 2003. Certainly this was not the first time Jolie provided valuable copy for journalists, but the summer did offer an extensive interview with ABC's Barbara Walters on the popular news show *20/20,* among others. What becomes obvious in almost all of Jolie's interviews is the way interviewers conflate Jolie's personality with those of her characters. For example, at one point in the *20/20* interview Walters refers to the character Jolie plays in *Girl, Interrupted* as "a charming but dangerously disturbed young woman" and moves almost immediately to a description of Jolie: "Words like 'dark,' 'weird,' even 'crazy,' began to pop up around the tattooed beauty." Similar comparisons have been made between her and the character of Gia (from the film of the same name). Adjectives used to describe Jolie seem to fall into two categories. On the one hand they are "disturbed," "dark," "angry" and "out of control." On the other hand they are "beautiful," "charming" and "talented." It strikes me that while male actors are free to enjoy any range of roles, they are less likely to be directly challenged as being disturbed during a national TV interview.

The apparent parallels between Jolie and the characters she chooses to portray, however, are not accidental or construed only by the media. Regarding her role as the action hero Lara Croft in the two *Tomb Raider* films released thus far, Jolie says:

I mean, she is about breasts and boots, but she's also about, and used to taking on the guys she does, but she also takes on the girls. She's not anti-men. You know what I mean? She's not that kind of a tough, feminist, sexpot bad girl. She's just fun and wild and adventurous. And her spirit is more important to me than anything, yeah, all the other things about her. I think, at the end of the day she's just wild and she fights for what she believes in. And I think that's a great thing.[12]

When Walters comments that this sounds more like Jolie herself, Jolie admits that she and Lara "have that in common." Yet the identification between Jolie and her characters is not necessarily direct, as she explains in *Cosmopolitan* later that summer: "The character needs to be beyond me, whether it's someone who's physically more advanced or wiser or someone whose heart is in a place that I don't understand. I need to be learning and not regressing as a person."[13]

In a sense, Jolie seems to use her characters to access certain traits she aspires to have or understand, which does not ease the aforementioned conflation. Being identified as Hollywood's kook might not be such a bad thing if one considers the publicity that accompanies it. Indeed, if "any press is good press," then Jolie's antics as a free-thinking, honest-speaking A-list actor have helped secure her position within popular culture. They certainly haven't hindered her critical success. Jolie was awarded a Golden Globe for her performance in *Gia* and an Oscar for *Girl, Interrupted.* However, the perception of her as crazy and the resulting responses strangers have to her are problematic in other areas of Jolie's life, specifically with regards to her role as a single mom to her adopted son Maddox.

During the lengthy process of finalizing the international adoption (Maddox was born in Cambodia), Jolie's father, the actor John Voight, spoke about his perceptions of his daughter's mental health in a national television interview. The "distressed father" said that Jolie was out of control and needed help, but was not willing to accept it. When asked about this by Walters, Jolie explained:

[I]t wasn't just that I needed help. I think — it was a lot more than that. And I think he said other things that were edited out because he couldn't legally make those comments 'cause they were, what do they call it, defamation of character, I think. And the most difficult thing is, in him doing that, it could have affected my relationship with my child. And they could have decided, he's right, she's crazy, let's remove that child from her custody. And that's unforgivable.[14]

Thus, while Jolie is granted a certain reprieve from being irreparably categorized as unstable or crazy because of her level of attractiveness and creative talent in Hollywood, there was no guarantee that such a reputation would be overlooked by an adoption agency or the US social services once Maddox was in the country. Here, the *reputation* of craziness is not so easily reduced to kookiness, but has become an issue of stability and the ability to be a parent.

It's interesting that the behaviour Jolie has exhibited that has branded her a kook is mostly evidence of a different understanding of life. For example, Jolie's marriage to actor Billy Bob Thornton drew media attention because the couple were openly emotionally and sexually infatuated with each other. Their sex life became legendary as soon as they were married, yet now that the marriage has ended, it seems the cultural memory of those events focuses on Jolie rather than Thornton. That Thornton is able to escape scrutiny only reinforces the popular expectations about male sexuality as somehow beyond control. Jolie on the other hand, by demonstrating a sort of public sexuality that challenges expectations about femininity, is constantly forced to reconcile this with her other roles, including that of Maddox's mother.

Also, Jolie's interest in collecting knives (most of which are rare pieces suitable for presentation in a museum and all of which are locked away for Maddox's safety) and her use of tattooing as a commemorative practice (she has tattoos dedicated to various people and times in her life) draw criticism from the more mainstream culture. In the interview for *20/20*, Barbara Walters seems more concerned with the fact that Jolie has a "gorgeous body" which she marks up, rather than with the significance of tattooing in relation to Jolie's personal history. The subtext of Walters' comment is that to mark an attractive body is somehow illogical. I wonder whether or not Ms. Walters would like, for example, my tattoos more since I'm not a Hollywood beauty.

In another interview, Jolie explains: "A tattoo is something permanent when you've made a self-discovery, or something you've come to a conclusion about."[15] That tattooing adds to the perception she is outside the norm is to be expected, but, again, this becomes fused with other traits to further "prove" her instability.

Certainly, Jolie doesn't pretend that deep down she is just an average gal. She admits to the resonance between herself and some of her characters and she recognizes her more "wild" behaviour but makes the distinction between outrageousness that is harmful to others and a sense of "silliness":

> I never trashed a hotel room because I'm aware that somebody's going to have to clean that up. You know what I mean? I've been silly. I've jumped in the pool at, you know, the Golden Globes. That's just fun. I'm just silly. And I'm free.
>
> [...] I've been crazy in my life and I've been wild in my life. I've never been a bad person. I've never intentionally hurt other people just to hurt them. And I'm trying to do a lot of good things with my life.[16]

Along with adopting her son, Jolie has funded the building of schools in Cambodia and intends to continue doing this kind of work and adopt more children. What I find appealing about Jolie is her directness and apparent honesty. During interviews, she does not avoid difficult subjects or deny past experiences. For example, when asked about her history of self-abuse, she responds:

> I always felt that if you were going to do an interview, you should do an interview and if you could help somebody or share something, that was the reason for doing an interview, not to protect yourself and be careful and look appropriate, you know ... So I talked about that because I thought that was something, it was something I was trying to understand about myself. And maybe I could get some answers. And I did.[17]

By refusing to resist this kind of difficult identification, Jolie opens herself up to potential ridicule or criticism, but she also offers what I feel is a unique window of identification for women who can't seem to squeeze themselves into more conventional expectations. For me, watching Jolie's career and public life evolve — to include parenthood and humanitarian work — has forced a reconsideration of what it means to be valuable person. Jolie's life doesn't read like a "before and after" story, where her past craziness is shed for a more conventional image. While one can certainly see her maturing throughout her tenure in the public eye, there is continuity to her self-presentation that I cannot help but respect.

CONCLUSION

> I write stories. Mostly about girls, mostly about strength. About family, and pain, and responsibility. And the Getting of Strength.
>
> — JOSS WHEDON[18]

> I believe in being completely honest [...] about who you are and what you feel and what you say. And I believe in following, following not just your heart but your gut and your impulse. And living in the moment.
>
> — ANGELINA JOLIE[19]

In 1997 an advocacy organization called Children Now and the Kaiser Family Foundation revealed that girls aged sixteen and seventeen "chose males predominantly as the TV characters they most admired."[20] So now I'm wondering what makes a character admirable? For me, as I've tried to demonstrate here, it's not always about overt symbols of empowerment or feminist sensibilities.

Don't get me wrong. I'm all about feminist sensibility, but sometimes after, say, a prolonged period of depression, I'm not looking for feminist sensibilities, I'm looking for understanding. Perhaps that is the true starting point for identification. In seeing these representations of strong women who stumble, falter, fall and get back up, I have been able to reconsider how my own dark moments and fumbles highlight, rather than eclipse, my experience of power as a woman who sometimes might not feel so strong.

I might not have slayer strength or the influence and funding to open schools in Cambodia, but I did survive being born three months premature and made it home to my parents' in only six weeks. I somehow found a way to make it through burying a soulmate at the age of twenty-one without surrendering. I voluntarily go into a therapist's office every week and drag out all sorts of stuff I'd rather not in order to be a better person. My friends will tell you I'm always there when they need me — without fail and if you ask my seven-year-old niece, I bet she'd tell you, I am pretty super.

I wish I were ending this piece with a statement of my own independence from societal expectations of what it means to be a well-put-together woman. But the truth is I'm still insecure and many days, I still feel displaced. But I am working on that and I will say that I no longer wish for that feeling of being "normal" or "cured" — at least not in the traditional sense. Instead I wonder what I could be doing to make my life a more interesting and valuable space — whether I'm crazy or not. Instead of imagining what strength I'd have if I were "stable," I'm contemplating how much evidence there is to show that I already am a pretty tough chick when all is said and done.

NOTES

1. *Buffy the Vampire Slayer,* "Chosen," Episode No. 144, first broadcast 20 May 2003 by UPN, directed and written by Joss Whedon.

2. Angelina Jolie, "The Education of Angelina Jolie," interview by Lawrence Grobel, *Movieline's Hollywood Life,* July/August 2003, 70–75, 74.

3. *Buffy the Vampire Slayer,* "Normal Again," Episode No. 117, first broadcast 12 March 2002 by UPN, directed by Rick Rosenthal and written by Diego Gutierrez.

4. *Buffy the Vampire Slayer,* "End of Days," Episode No. 143, first broadcast 13 May 2003 by UPN, directed by Marita Grabiak and written by Jane Espenson and Douglas Petrie. In this episode Faith turns to Buffy and says: "Thank God we're hot chicks with superpowers."

5. Keith Topping, *Slayer: The Next Generation, An Unofficial and Unauthorized Guide to Season Six of* Buffy the Vampire Slayer, (London: Virgin Books, 2003), 149.

6. Ibid.

7. Sarah Michelle Gellar, "The Good-bye Girl," interview, *Entertainment Weekly,* 7 March 2003.

8. Scott Lobdell, Fabian Nicieza and Cliff Richards, *Buffy the Vampire Slayer: Viva Las Buffy* (Milwaukee: Dark Horse Comics, 2003). This takes place in the comic story arc that immediately precedes *Slayer, Interrupted* — the focus of my analysis here.

9. Scott Lobdell, Fabian Nicieza and Cliff Richards, *Buffy the Vampire Slayer: Slayer, Interrupted,* 1–4, (Nos. 56–59) (Milwaukee: Dark Horse Comics, 2003), n.p.

10. In the Preface to his interview with Jolie, Lawrence Grobel writes, "She has been described up to this point, not unfairly, as kooky and dark, as well as enormously talented." Jolie, "The Education of Angelina Jolie," 72.

11. Jolie, "The Education of Angelina Jolie," 75.

12. Angelina Jolie, interview by Barbara Walters, *20/20,* American Broadcasting Corporation, 11 July 2003.

13. Angelina Jolie, "Angelina Holds Nothing Back," interview by Jennifer Kasle Furmaniak, *Cosmopolitan,* August 2003.

14. Jolie, interview by Barbara Walters, *20/20.*

15. Angelina Jolie, "Angelina Jolie, Tattoo Diarist," interview by Karen Thomas, *USA Today,* 17 July 2003.

16. Jolie, Interview by Barbara Walters, *20/20.*

17. Ibid.

18. Joss Whedon, Karl Moline and Andy Owens, *Fray,* 8. (Milwaukee: Dark Horse Comics, 2003). Quoted from "Mel Call" — the letters section of the comic.

19. Jolie, Interview by Barbara Walters, *20/20.*

20. Nadya Labi and Jeanne McDowell, "Girl Power: For the Next Generation, Feminism Is Being Sold as Glitz and Image. But What Do the Girls Really Want?" *Tim,* 29 June 1998, 60 (3).

A MANIFESTO FOR THE BITTEN
THE CYBORG, THE VAMPIRE, THE ALIEN AND ME

Sophie Levy

Everyone should have an alien song.
— Singer/songwriter DANNY MICHEL, live at
the Music Hall in Toronto, March 3, 2001

This is my alien song. This is an essay about aliens and other strangers, whom we have invited into our culture through the back door — or a broken window, or the mirror, some secret route from our imagination to the everyday. This is an essay written by an alien looking for others like her in unlikely places (genre fiction, popular and cult films, TV, and other locales) and waiting on the margins of academia for someone older, cooler, more beautiful and possibly undead, to ask her to dance.

This is a series of random broadcasts. This is what comes of listening for the Other, like Jodie Foster in *Contact*, like the lines of Surrealist poetry the poet Orphée hears on the car radio in Jean Cocteau's film. Cocteau understood our vampire nature: in *Orphée*, Death (a black-hatted and designer-sheathed femme fatale) falls in love with the poet, and steps into his bedroom through a mirror (Cocteau's trademark — the glass is made of mercury). The special effect is seamless — Death appears to step through glass — but the liquid mercury that mimics the mirror's surface bites into the skin of all who come through it.

So this is a manifesto for the bitten. That is to say: bite marks are in. Not lovebites, those blushing bruises with the lifespan of a high-school romance or a mayfly, but the permanent imprint of incisors on flesh. Or flesh on incisors. A love song with bite for a pierced, tattooed generation opening ourselves up to the mark of the Other.

1. The invasion begins with a single alien. Millarca in J. Sheridan LeFanu's book *Carmilla*. The Nazi war criminal next door in Stephen King's *Apt Pupil*. Sil and then Eve in the *Species* films. Arnold Schwarzenegger's cyborg in *Terminator*. Call in *Alien: Resurrection*. They're lone agents, marked as different by their singularity. Their presence warns us of the deluge. They are single manifestations of a faceless force, metonymy for the whole swarm, solo spinners of destruction deployed en masse. No longer alone, their difference is marked by their mass identity. The swarm gathers, and soon we are not sure who is us and who is them. They threaten a global cult of identity, of individualism — our heterotopia. All those aliens, they look the same. One little green man's like another. There's no heterogeneity. Not like us.

2. Aliens and vampires have the ability, much envied and feared by humans, to reproduce themselves through miscegenation. We can only turn to each other in order to propagate our species. But aliens and vampires turn to us. Turn into us. Turn us into them. The perversion is addictive, binding us to them as intimately as leather on skin. Aliens and vampires need us. They need our bodies. The clinical cathedral of the mothership and the intimate velvet of the vampire's bite-embrace are both fetishizations of the boundary between sexual desire and reproduction.

3. Cyborgs have an even more frightening property: they can replicate. We are in the process of making cyborgs. We're not seeking or imagining them, as we do with aliens and vampires, but inventing them in the purest scientific sense, and basing them on ourselves. Stephen Hawking, whose words come to us via his computer, and Steve "Cyborg" Mann, who sees the world through a digital camera, may be the best-known examples — professors of science who have become scientific experiments — but I am a cyborg too, incubated and on life support for my first three months. My "other" mother was a machine, and my first reflection appeared in her glass womb-walls.

4. So what selves do we project onto our creations? Selves that seem to fear the dangers of body-to-body contact. Let us take *The Matrix* as mirror: we are reflected in selves that reflect, wrapped in rubber and sunglasses. Selves that open to reveal brilliant steel technology beneath the skin. Selves implanted and marked with new technological orifices. These new points of penetration admit us to the game, where we see, with vampire eyes, the green death running through each person we meet.

> 4a. We open our bodies to surgeons operating by satellite hookup, wielding robot arms that control micro-scalpels. We dream in video games, date via text messages, circulate our thoughts globally and silently via e-mail. As Donna Haraway, feminist zoologist and author of "A Cyborg Manifesto,"[1] points out, we *are* cyborgs — part carbon-based life forms and part technological prostheses. Anyone with a vibrator fits into this description. Like Orphée stealing his inspiration from the car radio, we are embedded in networks of information technology. Turn on, plug in, get off.

5. Our fear is that we cannot control them. Aliens, vampires and artificial intelligences all reproduce like infection and by infection. How often have you watched your machine crash and blamed its malign intelligence? What if our errors are teaching machines the processes of human consciousness? Our machines must learn to make mistakes. They need to fall in love with humanity and follow us into passionate errors. Aliens, vampires and cyborgs have autonomy. They infect us because of desire.

6. Technoqueer not technofear. The passion of the new Eve is for a bite of the Apple. No more ribbing about sin. No more bearing childbirth as a burden.

7. I am the alien next door. I am the bad girl your mother warned you about. The alien planning parthenogenesis with her girlfriend. I am the pretty face of the faceless masses. We want you for our own. We want you to make others like us and infect the whole world. Queer filmmaker Derek Jarman used to say that it took two heterosexuals to make a queer. How many lesbians would it take? That's a joke. See, I almost convinced you that I'm human. The religious right fears queers because

they reflect the practices not only of aliens and vampires but of evangelical religion and politicians. Multiplication of the other: an iteration producing the same result again and again. Take of my body. Be like me. Jesus was an alien.

8. Two-spirited, half-spirited, not quite there — the different do not fit the binary. They are banished to castles, laboratories, outer space. The earthy damp of basement apartments. To being our reflections, trapped behind glass and steel. When we fall in love with these others, who are our reflections, we set them — and ourselves — free.

9. Perfect on the outside, hollow on the inside: both cyborgs and vampires defy the myth of organic decomposition. The vampire is the polar opposite of Haraway's micro-machines made of sunshine.[2] Their hybrid nature permits them to step outside of linear time. Vampires are not visible in mirrors, because light, which is composed of time, passes straight through them.

10. Vampires are the gleam in my eye as I drag up for a night out. They are the polish on my leather pants, the wicked bite of zips, the silver rings that pierce my ears. They are glow-in-the-dark teeth coming out of the box in my closet. They are flying me over the wired bridge at 4:00 a.m., strung up by brilliant points of city light, cloaked in other dancers' sweat and smoke.

11. When cyborgs look in the mirror, do they see vampire reflections? What do they see? And how do they see it? Robot vision only becomes discernible in the movies at the point when it fails — pixellates. Think about the last moments we share with the T-100 in *Terminator II*: as he dissolves himself, his vision fails, breaks up, and we are reminded (at the point of his most human action) that he is a robot. His eyes are screens upon which the world is projected. When we look into cyborg eyes, do we see ourselves reflected and distorted as on the convex surface of the television screen?

11a. A fascinating school of thought suggests that if there is intelligent life on other planets, it would more closely resemble insects than humans. Insects' eyes are really thousands of perfect eyes that each see a fragment of the field of vision in detail. Therefore, when aliens look at us, they most likely see a kaleidoscope, a Cubist vision, a collage. Their surgery is an attempt to repair us, to make us look like them.

12. You are watching my high-school memories. Her nose is a hive of tape and bandages marked *Sweet Sixteen*. When she looks in the mirror, she sees images imprinted on her eyes by years of Friday-night TV. With a flip of a button nose, the channel changes. If you watch closely, you can see the future. Her ankle is a blank of tape and bandages over a tattoo. Words threaten to bleed through. Her skin blinks wetly — the wound a camera, the scar its shutter — and the image takes forever.

13. Television makes freaks of us all. Cameras are pointed at our faces as if we are unaware that the words "demonstrate" and "monster" are linked at the root. When the spliced cable channel crashes, à la the Neal Stephenson novel *Snow Crash*, it is unclear who is killing who in the darkness. Buffy and the vampire go several rounds. Holding the cable into its socket, I become part of a cyborg relay, the electromagnetism under my skin completing a circuit in the informatics of domination. The computed spell completed, Buffy thrusts a sword through Angel's breast. He breaks up. Hell is a bad reception, a dervish of pixels. A snow crash is hell.

14. In the mythology of *Buffy the Vampire Slayer*, vampires are composites: human bodies inhabited by demons as opposed to souls. Although outwardly organic, their bodies are merely coats of skin that become distorted when they feed. Their bodies are all that remain of their original identities. Skin is an ironic surface that burns cold to the touch of those who desire their bodies, who fall in love with a self that has walked through the mirror to death.

15. Vampires are entirely carnal. For them, other bodies are either edible (penetrable) or invisible. Bodies are disposable but what is contained within them is desired. However, what is contained within them does not fill the hollowness of the vampire body. Vampires are demons in shells.

16. Vampire or slayer? That is the choice that confronted us every Tuesday night for seven years. And here is the question: what's the difference? There's a little bit of demon in all of us, a sliver of ice in the heart, a sharp eye tooth, a stiletto heel. Dressed to kill at night with our pointy prostheses. Dy(e)ing to get beneath the skin.

17. Cyborgs are all surface. Their skin is an interface between sense impressions and neural expeditions. Humans experience cold from the skin to the brain, and back to the skin again. Skin is etched with information it receives and transmits. The cyborg is both tattoo artist and tattooed flesh.

> 17a. And they shall know us by our brands. The biting humour of sterilized steel marks us with black lines and numbers. Our skins read like an issue of *Bitch* magazine, aiming a (tattoo) gun at corporate culture.

18. Everything I know about feminism I learned from pop culture. Click. The long pin slides into the socket at the base of my skull. "Computer," says my re-embodied voice, speaking sternly from a self-image pixellated with shaven head and steel toe-cap boots. "I need to know everything about girl power." Upload Flash and Shockwave. The image morphs, growing long hair, high heels and a wicked sense of humour.

> 18a. *Bite me*, she says. Two small scars tattoo a love bite on the side of her neck.

19. The world is our shuckable oyster. It's the shell we step out of holding our iPods like pearls. Like video-game heroine Lara Croft, we know how to dig through the histories they sell us.

20. Is this prediction or projection? We spend so much time looking into the evil eye. Its blue glass bugs out at us from every corner of the room. Does it offer protection or curses? Our own faces swim in its surface: ghosts in the machine. The remote control is our cyber-prosthesis. We cannot imagine life without it.

21. So this is alienation: the lived reality of cyborgification. I stare into the fishbowl of the screen. Somewhere behind the glass, the information I need swishes its tail back and forth, like a goldfish gaping zero one one zero one ... Shockwave downloads. The virtual Ouija board appears. I spell out HELP. There's no answer. What kind of cyborg believes in ghosts?

21a. A goldfish mouths zero one and the neck of my cervix presses against the ultrasound machine. My abdomen is glass, transparent, revealing a murky world where ovaries wave like polyps. I feel like a Teletubby. The cyborg body is a television. It is broadcast, manifest and screened. The shadows are not ghosts but fugitive information, electrical sparks misfiring. Defiantly infertile, the cyborg body is nevertheless all skin, all orifice. Haraway posits reproduction and replication as opposites: *everything* the cyborg takes in becomes more of her.[3] Each pore is rendered penetrable. It is ductile. It processes everything as information — zeros and ones and decimal deviants.

22. In battles, humans win by becoming machines. The end is partial — it is never over, always predicting its own replication in sequels, video games, our fantasies. The cyborg's eyes look down as film flies upward. Do androids have electric vertigo?

23. Everything I know about cyborgs, I learned from feminism. Girls know there is no *The End*, only cycles of film looping back and around. They know tattoos are forever but that the skin beneath them changes. They know how to fight in high heels and how to change their lives by changing the channel.

24. There is a radio station where lines of poetry cross the mirrored boundary between life and death. With our dyed black hair and velvet trappings, we listen to alien songs. We are sixteen. We are waiting for the spaceships to rescue us, for the late-night kiss of dead enamel and cold breath. We are waiting for the invasion. We do not realize that the army is already within us. We have been bitten and one day, when we climb from the buried nightmares of girlhood, we will turn and fight.

NOTES

1. Donna Haraway, "A Cyborg Manifesto: Science, Technology and Socialist Feminism in the Late Twentieth-Century," in *Simians, Cyborgs and Women: The Reinvention of Nature* (New York: Routledge, 1991), 149–181.

2. Ibid., 153. Haraway is referring to the increasing miniaturization of electronics, particularly to the growth in fibre optics, which produce electricity by converting light waves.

3. Ibid., 161–2.

HIGH FASHION AND
THE NECROMANTIC ARTS

Daniel Heath Justice

Denarra Syrene

Denarra Syrene was bored.

Imprisonment wasn't really the problem — Denarra was familiar with many jails in the Reach: there was the aptly named Trollmaw, a fetid pit of madness in the limestone caves beneath Chalimor that mocked the city's hypocritical grandeur; the Hanging Cells of Battico, hundreds of bamboo cages suspended on slender golden chains over a raging southern coast; the Penance Wall of Harudin Holt, in which the spirits of wrongdoers were held in enchanted sleep until their term ended. The gentle matrons of a Dhean hermitage — the Slumbering Tower — practised rehabilitation through spiced wine and aromatic baths, whereas less-enlightened settlements like the grim-walled Bashonak preferred the older tradition of inciting mass riots, hurling rotten vegetables and other produce, and well-aimed spittle.

At least in those situations Denarra had company or interesting scenery to ponder. Even during her exile on the blue glacier in the Waste of Sleet she was provided with a sublime vision of the northern night skies. The shimmering colours of the Celestial Veil brought her to inspired tears and provided the basis for her spring wardrobe. But until Mibbet's Point, Denarra had never known the pain of incarceration, and it was driving her to the edge of insanity.

"By Bidbag's hairless goat, these brutes know their business," she whispered hoarsely, scanning the distance for something — anything — to break the tedium. But there was nothing to see besides grey rock, grey buildings, and the occasional grey and dusty Human trudging toward an equally grey destination. Even the sky, so often her solace, had joined the conspiracy, its friendly blue turned to tiresome slate.

With a deep sigh loud enough to direct the guard's attention to her plight, Denarra slumped down on a rough bench. Her shackles clattered loudly on the table. The jail had recently been a tavern, though clearly not much of one — nothing more than a room with a few benches and splintery tables crammed inside. A single barred window was the sole source of natural light, more for smoke ventilation than illumination, if the soot-blackened timbers of the ceiling were any indication. A squat stone fireplace against the south wall was the only furnishing that had any aesthetic potential, but the sooty stones merely increased the room's dreary mood.

Time crept on. The iron shackles blistered her wrists. Dull daylight plodded toward late afternoon and each moment dragged with insufferable slowness. Denarra's bright pink nails tapped a jaunty rhythm on the table, but even she couldn't overcome the heavy malaise that settled over her makeshift prison. She tried all her standard ways of passing unpleasant times: she styled her dark hair into an elaborate tower bedecked with ribbons, feathers and strings of semi-precious stones; she retouched the beautifiers on her face, trying out a new cache of light floral shades; she even risked her guard's ire with a couple of quick colourcastings on her dress, transforming the dusky red fabric to a bright lilac that perfectly matched her new eyeshade. The shackles prevented any deeper connection to the *wyr*, the ancient spirit-source of the Folk, but such small castings tended to skitter past iron barriers. So she pushed through and, after a few false starts, found the new colour satisfactory. Any one of these activities would normally keep her occupied for hours, but the overpowering dullness stifled even their therapeutic powers.

Finally, unable to bear the tedium, Denarra rushed to the window. "Yes, yes, I admit it! You've broken me. You win — I can't take it anymore!"

A fat man with mismatched shirt and jerkin stepped into view in the jail's outer room. "Quiet! You've only been in there for an hour."

Denarra snorted. "But it's been a perfectly hellish hour. Have you any idea what I've been going through in this chamber of torments? There are laws against this sort of treatment."

"Yes," the man grumbled, "and there are laws against burning down prayer shrines, too."

Her eyes flashed. "I'm an innocent victim of circumstance! How was I supposed to know the casting would do that? You'd think the shrine's manufacturers would've known better than to build the roof with such combustible thatch. I can hardly be held responsible for their lack of foresight." She was warming up to the defence. "Besides, how was I supposed to know that they were only for decoration? Nobody *I* know just leaves big copper braziers filled with kindling standing around like that, and I did extinguish your very ungrateful priest before all his hair burned away." She didn't mention the priest's muttered refusal to let the "half-breed" near the shrine's altar just before the fire broke out. The only response was the whining creak of a chair as the man lowered his heavy bulk.

"You know, empathy is a quality you could familiarize yourself with," she muttered.

＊

The poster had clearly been a case of false advertising: "Calling all Intrepid Travellers with Adventure in their Blood. See the Reach and Exotic Ports of Call. Journey in the Safety of a Guided Tour with Like-Minded Compatriots. Only the Dauntless Need Apply." She had packed her travelling gear that very afternoon. The timing was fortuitous, as she'd had a small misunderstanding with a rather influential merchant earlier in the day — a tiny quibble about whether she'd paid for what she assumed was a free sample of an exceedingly rare perfume — so she decided to take a little vacation to give him a chance to calm down and reflect on his bad manners.

Denarra had been disappointed to find that her fellow "adventurers" were nothing more than dull, wealthy Humans looking for a story to tell their equally dull, wealthy friends back in Chalimor. They fell into three categories: spoiled and rutting striplings with more nose hair than brains; pasty-faced guildsmen and their mousy wives, who yammered endlessly about the terrors of campfire living; and babbling pilgrims, who collapsed with pious wetness at the thought of the enshrined knucklebone of some obscure and half-forgotten saint in every dreary little town along the way.

Denarra was the most exotic aspect of the entire affair, a Strangeling with a flair for the dramatic and a fashion sense unfettered by convention. She shared with her father the bronze skin and curvy voluptuousness of the forest-dwelling Kyn, along with his oak-leaf ears and bright eyes. Her mother's Human blood tempered the four sensory stalks nestled in her thick hair. She inherited other qualities from her mother, too: a visceral need for excitement, a bewitching beauty and captivating smile, and an unpredictability that bordered on chaos. Even when she was a youngling she'd been more of a wildflower than a cultivated rose, preferring the free breeze and sunshine to the placid domesticity of the high-walled garden. When just a stripling, she changed her name to something more suitable to her personality, exchanged her breechcloth for a dress, and rushed into the wide, waiting world to experience all its dangers and delights. But the gift that most defined her life came from her father's calming Kyn ways: she was a wielder, connected to the *wyr*-bound currents that shaped and joined the Kyn and the other fey-Folk to the old ways of the hidden world.

Generally, Humans tended to be suspicious of the sorcerous wielders, and after hundreds of years of being persecuted and driven from their homelands, most fey-Folk had little use for Humanity. There were few places where Humans and Folk lived in peace. Chalimor, the political centre of the Reach, however, was one such rarity, although not so much in recent years. This travelling group was largely predisposed to tolerance. If not for a brief dalliance with the son of a particularly myopic guildsman — which came to an abrupt and quite revealing end when Denarra carelessly kicked over a lantern and set their wagon aflame — she might still be with the caravan on some remote road in the Allied Wilderlands.

Instead she'd been abruptly transferred to a merchant train on its way to some of the more isolated settlements in the Firebrand Mountains. And now she was in the twice-cursed town of Mibbet's Point, a once-bustling mining community that now held little interest for even its own residents.

Denarra stood up and stretched with a yawn. No use in regrets — as her mother had often told her: "Feeling regretful is like shovelling smoke: you do a lot of work and end up with nothing to show for it." Still, it was hard not to mourn the loss of her wide-brimmed scarlet hat with the golden greathawk feather in the band. It was gone, lost in the fire. The memory annoyed her, so she sat back down on the bench, leaned over the table and gnawed at the edge of a fingernail.

Denarra returned to her daydreams. What if she never left this place? What if Mibbet's Point, this tedious tomb of a town, was the end? She was fading in this dingy room, wasting away like an epic poem of suffering as the last breath left her full lips. Visions of her funeral, crowded with hundreds — no, thousands — of sobbing friends and admirers drifted in front of her eyes. She smiled at her own image, resplendent in her finest emerald evening gown and ropes of rare pearls. The Strangeling wielder nodded approvingly at the sight of her lovely and well-coiffed body lying inside a gold-lined crystal casket, arms draped gently over a dozen pink orchids nestled in her ample bosom. She could almost hear the aching strains of a funeral dirge and the poetic retelling of her noteworthy life, her noble end and her unparalleled sense of style. She even felt a pang of regret that she wouldn't be able to attend the fabulous memorial party that was certain to follow.

She was wiping away a tear when a scrape at the door shattered her wandering thoughts. She turned to greet the visitor with a broad smile, but it vanished at the sight of a short Human with a bald, bandaged head and singed beard, followed by a trio of nervous, mud-covered miners.

"Oh, you again. Well, I can't say the visit is entirely unexpected. I assume you've come to apologize?"

The bald man coughed. "Me? Apologize? You're the one who ... my shrine ..."

She waved her hand, dismissing his concern. "Now, now, there's no need to take all the blame — the building was clearly a firetrap, an accident waiting to happen. I completely understand your position. And don't worry, I have no intention of taking the matter to your superiors. All I ask are reasonable accommodations and perhaps a meal to tide me over till I find someone to take me back to the trade wagons."

"Now, hold on there — we've come to read the charges you're facing. Arson, assault, blasphemy, resisting arrest and lengthy profanity in the vicinity of women and children." The man's voice grew louder with each new charge, his ragged beard quivering. Denarra pointedly ignored him and turned her attention to the others.

"Ah, I see you brought some of your associates with you! To be perfectly honest, I was getting *absolutely* desperate for company, and though I've never really had much interest in the 'sons of the soil,' as it were, I'm ever so glad to meet you!" The miners bunched together, eyes wide, as Denarra rushed forward with her lacquered fingers extended in greeting.

Her welcome was interrupted by a sudden bright flash and explosion that rattled the earth and threw them to the floor. To Denarra's amazement, the structure continued to stand, although sooty thatch dropped from the ceiling.

"Wasn't me this time, boys," she said, coughing as she fanned the dust away from her face, the clank of her chains muted in the thick air. "Oh, damn." There was a lengthy gash in her dress. Denarra turned to the bearded man, who lay sprawled in the firepit. "Do you happen to know where my travel satchel is? I need a needle and some thread — if I don't take care of this problem right now, I'll have a dire emergency on my hands." The man stared at her.

Outside the tavern, all was chaos. Denarra hadn't had much of a chance to see the settlement before the little misunderstanding that landed her in this predicament, and she was surprised to see so much activity. She stood and walked to the doorway, sidestepping the miners who lay tangled in a heap near the door. Mibbet's Point lay at the juncture of three tall peaks. Its thirty or so stone and timber houses squatted on each side of the main road, which was now flooded with a bewildering array of creatures. Humans were rushing past the tavern in a desperate frenzy, occasionally colliding with one another and all manner of livestock and poultry in their haste. A couple of hardy mountain burros galloped by, their mouths open wide in a synchronized bray of terror, followed closely by a weathered old man with a floppy hat, who let loose a stream of profanity that brought an appreciative nod from the much-travelled wielder.

"Sithéin save us," the priest whispered. "Mordok is upon us."

Denarra turned to him. "Who?"

"Mordok, the Shadow Serpent! The Asp of the Loathsome Tower!" Seeing no response of recognition, the man went on: "He's a great and powerful reaver, a cruel necromancer who rules these mountains with a will of iron and cruel magic. He demands tribute of gold and goat's milk from us each spring, but with the good ore and she-goats drying up, we haven't been able to meet his demands. And now he's come to get his revenge!" He buried his face in his hands.

"Oh, *that's* original." Denarra looked back to the north. "What kind of name is 'Mordok,' anyway? Sounds more like an anti-social skin condition than the reputable title of a brother of the arcane arts. Ah, well — I suppose I'd better go and see what this is all about." The chains clattered to the ground. The men looked at her in horror. She smiled and held up a small wire pick, which she returned with a flourish to one of the many folds of her dress. She'd waited to use the little tool until she had an appreciative audience. Admittedly, their gaping mouths and bulging eyes weren't quite the enthusiastic response she'd hoped for, but it was hardly surprising given the dearth of cultured entertainment in these remote parts. Maybe she'd stay for a while and offer them some guidance; she *was* a charitable soul, after all.

Another crackling blast from the north brought her attention back to the smoking centre of activity, and she walked on, absently rubbing her chafed wrists. The men behind her stood together in confusion, but none followed.

❋

Denarra picked her way through the rubble in the street, avoiding piles of burro dung as well as the surprisingly large amount of iron scattered across the road: remnants of wagon wheels, picks and other mining tools, the strewn inventory of a pot-and-kettle merchant's stand. Iron was mortal poison to many of the Folk, and though Denarra was Human as well as Kyn and had some resistance to the metal, she still suffered from its touch. This narrowed her choices when it came to a wide range of jewellery and other accessories.

The wielder wrinkled her nose in disgust at the sudden acrid stench of sulphur and rancid milk. Her hand disappeared into her dress and emerged with a green scarf, scented with rose oil, which she held up to her face. As she did so, she noticed with some irritation that the nails on her hand were still pink, not the soft purple of her new ensemble. So she stopped briefly to match the shade with the rest of her outfit.

Mordok. She'd never heard the name before, but that wasn't surprising — there were many rogue reavers throughout the Reach and most operated on such a small scale that they rarely met any resistance. Denarra frowned. When Humans went wild, it never reflected badly on the entire people, but if one of the Folk got a little experimental with the *wyr*, men brought out the hounds and pitchforks against all "fey witches." Wielders were fundamentally different from Human sorcerers, yet the subtleties of such distinctions never seemed to matter to Humans. Wielders drew from the *wyr* that was the essence of their own spirits; thus, they drew only on those powers that were given freely, not those taken by force. As Humans practised it, it was just another name for slavery.

She looked around at the men and women crouching in the shadows around her and shook her head. She couldn't help but feel sorry for them. Not all Humans were fools and bigots; many were just as much victims of cruelty as were the Kyn and other Folk. And not all interactions between the Folk and Humanity were doomed to failure. Her parents were the perfect example, in spite of all their differences. She had no doubt that her mother would always be chasing after another wild dream with her father beside her, breathless with anticipation. Sometimes these things worked out.

The smoke was thicker now. She peered through it, eyes watering in spite of the scarf, as she tried to catch a glimpse of what stood beyond. A slight breeze caught the edge of the smoke and lifted it away to reveal the prayer shrine that had gone up in flames only a short time earlier. Denarra stomped over to it indignantly. "After all that fuss and bother ... 'burned to the ground,' indeed! Over half the shrine is still standing." She swung around to glare reproachfully at the bearded priest, but he was lost in the smoke. "He'll hear more about this when I'm through with this 'Mordok' fellow."

Looking up at the crest of the hill, she saw the blackened remains of a goat, and beside them stood a tall, broad-shouldered figure in sleek black robes that flowed like magma around his feet. In his right hand he held a black staff topped by the onyx head of a striking serpent; in his left hand gleamed a wicked scimitar. His hair was long and pitch black, save for the white streak streaming from temple to split ends down his back. Denarra wasn't a bit surprised to see that one eye was hidden by a crimson patch.

She shook her head. "So this is Mordok. What *is* he thinking with that outfit?"

The reaver held the scimitar high and cried, "The Shadow Serpent demands that thy elders present themselves, at once and in haste, lest my wrath be visited upon thee again! Let this smouldering ram be a warning to all of the powers of Loathsome Tower!"

Denarra stifled a giggle.

A group of six old men emerged from the ruins, led by a portly elder whose broad hands wrung his leather apron incessantly. Denarra turned to a young woman who crouched behind an overturned ore cart. "Your council of elders is all male, I see. Typical. No wonder this place has so little imaginative possibility." She shook her head and moved closer.

"Thou hast forgotten Mordok's tribute, curs!" the reaver bellowed at the elder in the apron. "Mordok is not given to patience or generosity this day. Prepare thyself for unbearable torment!"

"Please," the sooty lead elder grovelled. "We're doing all we can, but you ask the impossible! The snows this winter were fierce, and we couldn't get through the pass to the richer veins. And because of the drought, we've been pumping our goats every day and night, but all we get for our trouble is blisters and bites." A merry laugh echoed in the distance. Mordok glanced around for the source of the sound, then turned back to glower at the grovelling man.

The elder continued desperately. "Just a little longer, we beg you! We're a peaceful community, small but honest, dedicated to responsible industry and a strong standard of living. We might not have the art scene of Argot Falls, but our schools are consistently rated among the best of the Seven Settlement region, and our crime rate decreased last year from a high of —"

"Enough!" Mordok cried, his brows bristling in fury.

Denarra was impressed. *I wonder how he does that,* she thought.

The reaver swept his staff in a wide circle. "On thy belly, worm! Mordok has not travelled this vast distance to parley — he has come to conquer, come to rule! The mountains cradle in their stony embrace vast riches, precious ores that shall be used to finance a titanic campaign of political destabilization, economic inflation and social anarchy that will lead to world domination. Then Mordok will be master of all! Yes, fool, thou art looking upon thy lord and master. All will bow in supplication to the throne of Loathsome Tower, my slaves forever, generation after generation of manual labourers subject to his every whim, his every desire, his every —"

"Okay — just stop, stop, *stop!*" Denarra snarled and stomped up the hill, green eyes flashing. The few Humans who remained in the street rushed for cover. "Please have some respect for the dignity of your position," she said, pointing a lilac fingertip at the reaver. "Just what do you think you're doing?"

Mordok spun around to face her. Blood-red fire exploded from the head of the staff and enveloped the sorcerer in an eerie glow. In a deep, sepulchral voice, he roared, "Who dares to speak to Mordok the Shadow Serpent in such a fashion?"

Denarra waved some of the smoke away with her scarf. "Oh, you sad, silly thing. First, you've got to get rid of that overblown language — it just doesn't work. Honestly, whoever heard of a reaver these days who still follows that old cliché of thees and thous? Remember, darling, you're not on stage. And referring to yourself in the third person? Pretence only works with irony and you're sadly lacking in the latter. You're simply a pathetic joke — not, I assume, the intended result of this whole performance." She flicked his staff scornfully with a well-manicured fingernail.

"By all the powers of darkness, thou shalt pay for this impudence!" he sputtered, grasping the staff tightly in preparation for another devastating casting. The town's elders took this opportunity to rush to safety with surprising agility. Only Denarra and Mordok remained on the hill, although many frightened and curious eyes watched the happenings from the rubble that littered Mibbet's Point.

"See, you're just not listening." Denarra shook the sleeve of his ornate robes with disdain. Mordok stepped back in alarm. "Look at you — dressed in black? What look are you going for? Most redundant villain of the year? It's hardly imposing. Every angst-ridden poet has an outfit just like it, and I'll tell you, you don't know irritation until you've been to a late-night reading with a half-drunk horde of passive-aggressive virgins more skilful at posing than poetry." She walked around him, her eyes narrowed in thought. "You should try something unexpected, like fuchsia — now that can be a terrifying colour. Or maybe try alternating stripes of yellow and green. Solids just aren't good with your complexion."

Mordok stared at the Strangeling. He'd never faced such an enemy, and he was uncertain how to safely proceed. Besides, she *was* making sense. He'd agonized over solids versus some sort of pattern — he did love reds and yellows — but frustration and insecurity led him to more conservative choices. "Well, I ..."

"And another thing: the eye patch? The snake staff? The little skull and crossbone pattern on your robes? You give evil sorcerers a bad name." She leaned in closer, speaking in soft, conspiratorial tones. "You see, the best villains are the ones you don't expect to be villains. They're cultivated, charming and at the forefront of fashion. But darling, to be honest, the only thing frightening about you is your alarming lack of creativity."

He held his hand up to his eye. "But I need the patch!"

Denarra shrugged. "Well, if it's a genuine medical condition, at least go for something other than red. In this case, you might even try a helm that drops down over half your face. Or maybe have the patch partly designed to look like the jawbone of some toothy creature — something interesting like that. Now, turn around."

Mordok moved around carefully.

"I'd also look into breeches and knee-high boots. Robes are all well and good for ceremonial occasions, but they're hardly practical for the wear and tear that occurs when you're trying to obliterate a town. You need something you can move around in, something that won't trip you up. And, if I'm not mistaken," she said, pointing to dusty streaks on the front of the robes, "you've already taken a tumble in those a few times today."

Mordok nodded sheepishly.

Denarra continued: "I'd stay away from anything like robes." She laughed and spun around, her long lilac dress and rainbow of scarves and ribbons whipping wildly around her curvy form. "Unless, of course, you know how to do it right! If you decide that you just can't give up the robes, you should look for a genuine Joolip de Tour like this one. Fashionable and practical, at a price anyone can afford!"

She stopped and scrutinized him again. Mordok shuffled uneasily under her critical gaze.

"You know," she smiled, "the hair works. I like the streak — it's not over the top, just enough to be dignified and striking. If you trimmed the goatee a little, it would be a nice combination. You might try a couple of earrings, or even a nose ring for flair. And you'd be quite handsome if you didn't scowl so much all the time."

He looked away shyly.

"But the name has got to go. Mordok? You're not a subterranean mud toad, darling. That can't *possibly* be your real name."

The reaver shook his head and scratched his scruffy chin in thought. She was making sense. It was like hearing all his own concerns from the mouth of another. "Mordok had not ... I mean, I hadn't really thought much about it. What do you suggest?"

The wielder grinned. "Oh, something more lyrical, with more fire and fierceness. Something that sends shivers through the body." Her eyes glazed over for a moment, and then she cleared her throat, flushing slightly. "Something that rolls off the tongue, like Astavar, or Kalugamu the Blasphemous, or even Cytharri of the Withered Wood. It doesn't matter if it's accurate, it just needs some personality, some quality that says, 'Hey, I'm someone special — pay attention to me.'"

The reaver thought for a moment. "Why not Astavar? It's quite dignified." He continued, increasingly excited. "But what about the staff? Don't you think snakes are frightening?"

Denarra smiled again. "Well, sure, they're scary, but *everyone* uses snakes. Either snakes, bats or spiders. You need to go with a motif that's all yours. Why don't you try something that scares people but isn't overused, like a ravenous fluke worm, or a swarm of killer wasps, or a flying eyeball surrounded by a circle of bloody daggers? I was once chased through a spruce forest by a bull elk looking for love, and let me tell you,

I've never been so scared in my life — you don't know fear until a frustrated elk is after your ass. It becomes the standard against which all mortal terror is measured."

"I'll consider it," he mused. "But I'm still quite fond of the snake."

"Well, it's a thought, anyway." Denarra turned and looked around at the devastation on the hill. "You know, I could help you. I'm not doing anything right now. Why don't we talk it over, say, dinner ... your treat?"

"What a delightful suggestion!" Astavar (the reaver formerly known as Mordok) smiled to reveal a beautiful set of white teeth.

Her knees quivered.

"I know a lovely little café, just a few leagues from here in a charming seaside hamlet. The view and lemon-grilled salmon are unparalleled," he said as he held out a tightly muscled arm, which Denarra eagerly accepted.

"You have yourself a date, my friend. But tell me, have you ever given any serious thought to this whole villain thing? I mean, honestly — anyone can be a villain, but it takes a special kind of man to be a hero."

Astavar smiled again. "I'll take that into consideration, too." Amidst the wreckage of Mibbet's Point, the inhabitants began to emerge from the shadows, curiosity winning over caution. They watched the reaver pull a glimmering hoop from the folds of his robe and drop it on the ground. It expanded quickly until it grew large enough to accommodate both the reaver and the wielder. Denarra peered in and clasped her hands together in delight.

"Pantamari's? You didn't mention that's where we're going! Oh, I've heard so many wonderful things about the place. Still, darling, it's only fair to warn you — I'm not a cheap dinner companion!"

Astavar grinned and whispered in her ear as she joined him in the circle. She broke into a long laugh that carried through the valley.

"I'm not that kind of girl," she giggled. "But I do know a lovely young woman in Chalimor who used to be a vengeance crusader with the Claw Brigade — she now designs leather accessories for the romantically adventurous. I'm sure you'd get along fabulously! And from what I understand, she just *adores* rehabilitation work!" Astavar laughed as a flash of lavender light and pearly mist erupted from the hoop.

When the mist cleared away, they were gone. Only the lingering scent of roses remained.

*

The people of Mibbet's Point began the cleanup shortly after the wielder and the reaver vanished. The only fatalities were a few unfortunate goats and a cross-eyed cat who was trampled by a low-bellied sow during the riot. Within a day, the rubble caused by the reaver's attack had been transferred into ore wagons and tossed down the slope outside of town. The next day they added the burned timbers from the temple, two melted copper braziers and the still-identifiable remains of a large red hat with a charred golden feather pinned to the band.

The priest himself carried the hat to the edge of the slope. The Strangeling had healed his admittedly minor burns before the arrest, but he half suspected that the bald patches in his beard would never grow back. He looked off into the canyon, gauging the distance thoughtfully. Knotting the hat into a ball, he drew his arm back and flung it into the canyon with a shout of triumph.

The red ball spun out on a wide and impressive arc; indeed, it went farther than he expected. But his elation faded to indignant disbelief as the red shape spun into the wind and unfurled on the wild breeze. The hat disappeared among the clouds, floating merrily east, toward Chalimor.

SLUMPYHEROES

Sherwin Tjia

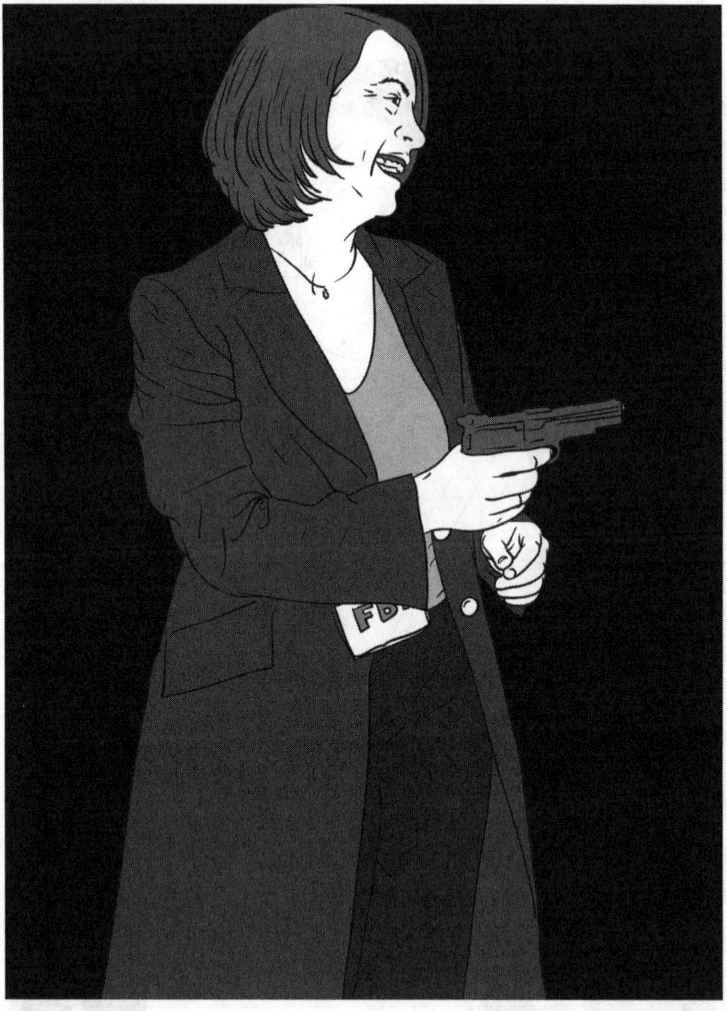
FBI

FACES OF GEMINI

A. M. Dellamonica

Gemini found her twin sister, Leela, crashed on the couch in her ratty apartment, snoring raspily with a melted bottle of champagne clutched to her breast and teary lines of mascara on her cheeks. The dregs of the alcohol had spilled when the bottle liquefied, and the room smelled of booze and farts.

Eau de fraternity, Gemini thought. This isn't going to work. Despite the urge to flee, she remained in place, helmet in hand, looming over the couch wearing the ill-fitting battle suit she'd put on an hour before.

As she woke, Leela said Gemini's given name with a snort and a quiet belch: "Chelsea?"

"Yeah, it's me."

"What are you doing in that get up?"

"There's an emergency," said Gemini. "Are you drunk?"

"Could be," Leela said.

"Meaning yes, I suppose, or you'd take my head off for even asking."

"Have it your way." Leela flashed an uncharacteristic grin. "I saw you on the news today. Amazing footage. Is it always like that?"

"It's a blur," Gemini said. The words were out before she realized they were true.

Leela stretched, curling her toes. "Mom has a nice glossy photo of you saving that baby — for her scrapbook."

"Baby ..." she said, just barely remembering.

"You drippified the guy's sword before he could decapitate the kid, and then took out his reins. Bastard fell right off his horse."

"I vaporized a lot of tack today," Gemini said, thinking of the dozens of horses still running loose downtown.

"No surprise you forgot. It looked pretty intense."

"Intense," she echoed sarcastically. "Five thousand barbarian warriors —"

"Relax, Chelsea. I'm not trying to minimize. It must have been terrible."

Gemini nodded, not trusting herself to speak. The horde had thundered into Stanley Park at dawn, killing everyone they found. The barbarians' weapons had been primitive; but pitted against a scattering of unarmed joggers, tourists and kids, they had done plenty of damage. Dozens of civilians had been murdered before Crucible had arrived to contain the threat.

"So ..." Leela said. "Bad guys gone now?"

"No. The army's taken over. Did you say you were at Mom's? Was there —" She bit back the tactless question — was there some kind of crisis? "I mean ..."

A muscle in Leela's cheek jumped. "Dodd's moving."

"Where?"

"Back to London."

Of course. The tears, the boozing — it made sense now. The ex-husband was hauling Leela's son — Gemini's nephew — across the Atlantic. "What are you doing about this, Leela? Sitting back and letting him take your kid without a fight?"

"No, I —"

"You had to drive him away, didn't you?"

Leela squinted up at her. "If you came here to abuse me, you'll have to get out."

Gemini reined her feelings in with difficulty. "Sorry."

"Thanks. You want coffee?"

"Uh ..." The offer caught her off-guard — Leela was rarely so quick to let bygones be bygones.

Getting up, Leela finally noticed the now-hardened glass lump of bottle fused to her tank top. Her mouth bunched. "Jeez, Chelsea, did you have to?"

"No, it was you who —" Gemini protested, but Leela had peeled off the shirt. She let it fall to the floor as she vanished into the kitchen.

"Leela, stop a sec. You'd better —"

"I better what?" The warning came too late: A kitchen cupboard melted away, dribbling like hot mozzarella. The jars inside the cabinet came cascading down, shattering on the counter. By the time Gemini got there, her sister was covered in bits of broken glass, coffee grounds and flour.

My reaction time is down, she realized. Am I still in shock?

"Shit." Leela eyed the mess with mild surprise. "Why didn't you tell me I had your superpowers again?"

"They're our powers."

"Bull." Leela clamped flour-covered fingers over her mouth before her breath could melt anything else. Then, brow furrowed in concentration, she sighed loudly. The flour on her hand became little beads, dribbling and then evaporating so that the flesh beneath was left clean.

Gemini's spirits lifted. If Leela had that much control over the most destructive of their handful of powers, her plan might work after all. "I need a favour. Can you help? With you in possession of our abilities —"

"It all depends on what the favour is, Chelsea."

"I need you to go on a mission," Gemini said. "As me."

"Forget it."

"But —"

"Don't piss me off, Chelsea. I can't afford to melt this apartment to slag."

"Remain calm, breathe slowly —"

"Don't you give me orders." Leela's voice finally had an edge. The kitchen wall thinned and dribbled, like wax near an open flame.

"Look," Gemini said. "All I need —"

"No." Leela put up a hand, silencing her. "We'll switch the powers back to you."

"That won't work. I'm in a terrible mood, Leela."

"As if I hadn't noticed. You'll have to sort yourself out, Chelsea."

"It's not that simple."

"Funny, it's what you always say to me."

Gemini felt her hands balling into fists. She sucked her lips over her teeth and clamped her jaw shut over the skin until it hurt.

Leela was unmoved. "Take that stupid suit off."

Surrendering, Chelsea unhinged the battle suit so that its torso fell open. Her breasts, relieved of the armour's compression, immediately started to ache. She levered herself up out of the suit's legs, setting one bare foot on the floor.

"Watch the wreckage," said Leela, but the warning came too late — Gemini's heel crunched down onto glass with an intense, shocking sting.

"Over here." Leela headed back to the dingy dining room, already stripping off her clothes. Gemini hopped in pursuit, leaning one-legged against the plastic table as she tugged the shard of glass from her foot. She wriggled out of her shirt and bra, one-handed, then paused — if she let go of her punctured foot, it would drip blood on the faded carpet.

Leela retrieved her ruined bottle-smeared tank top and nudged it toward Gemini. "Stand on this."

"Thanks." She put her foot down and then peeled off the rest of her clothes, folding them nervously.

"You ready?"

"Ready," Gemini said, suddenly breathless.

Nude, they hugged each other tightly. There was an instant when the embrace seemed normal, even comforting. Then they began to fuse, flesh melting together until they were once again as they had been at birth: twins; identical and conjoined, they now had one wide body between them. Leela controlled the left leg and arm, Gemini the right. To all outward appearances, they were a two-headed woman.

Gemini stared at their reflection in the glass of the dining-room window. They had learned to walk like this, to ride a bicycle together, to sleep, to swim. For seven years they had been together constantly. Everything had been a negotiation: where to go, when to sit or stand, who would hold which lace as they tied their shoes.

Then Dad had found an old sorcerer, one willing to reshape them, to melt them apart as if their flesh was wax. He'd "drippified" their body — to use Leela's term — remaking them into two. They'd had to learn to walk again, to swim, write and eat separately ... and they had to learn to be alone.

The solitude had been terrifying. But Leela and Gemini had their own separate hearts now, their own lungs and wombs and control of two hands each. The superpowers they'd gotten during that mystic separation, though, were throwbacks — abilities shared by them both.

"Okay," Leela's breath warmed her ear. Their faces were canted away from each other; they had never quite been able to look each other in the eye when joined. "I had the powers, we've merged, you should have them when we separate."

"One, two, three, go," Gemini said.

They pulled apart, flesh stretching between them. As her inner hand and foot took shape, seeming to grow out of the wet tissue of Leela's innards, Gemini sensed that the switch had worked. Her skin no longer felt raw and over-sensitive. Her cuts and bruises did not ache. They separated, and Gemini's vision sharpened. Her fatigue vanished and her mind started to clear ...

She reached for the duffle gratefully, hand closing around the fabric of her Gemini uniform. But as her gaze took in the familiar black body-suit, with its pattern of white stars, everything snapped back. The tiredness and pain returned, hitting like bricks or fists.

"Shit," Leela said. "OK, new plan. I'll think of the most depressing thing I can until the powers go back to you."

"Leela, it won't work."

"Come on. You're the perky one."

"It's not about perk."

"Right. It's psychic strength, well-being, self-esteem. You have your shit together and I don't. You're the one everyone's proud of. I've made all the mistakes ..."

"I never said that ..."

"I know, but I'm trying to bring myself down, okay?"

"Oh. Right. You're a mess."

Leela laughed. "Get your happy back and get the hell out of here, OK?"

Closing her eyes, Gemini dug into her cache of pleasant memories. She thought of her first encounters with the others — Balm, Serpentine, Crimson and Mortar. They'd all been working solo back then, Little League vigilantes busting crime lords and small-time supervillains. Over time they'd clustered into a group, one that eventually received an official law-enforcement mandate from the Province. Shortly afterward they became Crucible, then Looking Glass — Powell — had joined the group. The team had saved the world that day, and Gemini had fallen in love.

It was no good. Her past seemed tainted, and her mind was drawn instead to this morning's battle. She heard the screams again, saw the pile of severed heads, remembered a horse tangled and panicked, caught in the chains of a swing-set. There'd been a body beside the animal, a bike courier punctured by arrows ...

"Dammit," Leela hissed. "We used to do this on the phone. Are you trying?"

Gemini nodded.

"So what's wrong? Would it help if you talked about it or something?"

"No. It's —" She fought back the tears, the panic-inducing sense of shock. "It's been an unspeakable day."

"I'm sorry, Chelsea. Really. But I'm no superhero."

"I just need you to —"

"No! Fuck, isn't this why you have a team?"

"They're —" Gemini slumped against a chilly wall; without the battle suit holding her upright, she could barely stand. "Purgatoire has them."

Leela's eyes widened. "All of them?"

Gemini nodded, gaze lowered. The room seemed to get quieter and quieter, and it sank in that she was still undressed. She scooped her panties off the table and stepped into them. Fingering her bra, she sighed, dreading the idea of strapping up her aching breasts again. Then she made herself do it.

When she risked a peek up, Leela was dusting flour off her skin and eyeing Gemini warily. "You want me to dress up as you and take on a big-name supervillain," she said. "With no experience, backup, and imperfect control over your powers —"

"*Our* powers, Leela —"

"Plus he has hostages?"

"It's Purgatoire. There are always hostages."

"These are your friends, Chelsea. What if I screw up? Six months ago we were barely speaking. If I get your team killed ..."

"They'll die if you don't help. Please, I need one small assist — and it's entirely non-violent."

Leela's eyes narrowed. "No combat?"

"No fighting, I swear. Help with one thing and I'll take over."

"How? In that?" Leela gestured at the empty battle suit, standing like an eggshell abandoned by a newly hatched chick, at the edge of the kitchen.

"Yes," Gemini said.

Leela grunted, examining the suit. Nine feet tall, it was emphatically male, albeit with skewed proportions. Its limbs were elongated, its hands and feet massive, its groin robust. The whole of its musculature was exaggerated and lumpy. They could have been pleasing dimensions, maybe, but the helmet was just a shade too small. Overall, it made the wearer seem bulky and pinheaded.

That helmet stared at Gemini from the tabletop now. She had melted its front to waxy lumps in a battle long ago. Faceless, it was topped with sculpted curls of hair.

Gemini had put the suit on for the first time only an hour before, after she'd finally made it back to Base Pacific. With her teammates abducted and her powers gone, getting home had been an ordeal, one that took hours her friends might not have.

She had crawled down to the base vault and found the suit. It had seemed hideous, a totem lying under layers of dust.

Moving in it felt like being joined to Leela again: everything was slow, each movement a bit delayed.

Leela touched the suit's metal skin lightly, with just her fingertips. "Is this the outfit from the guy who almost killed Powell?"

"Yes, a villain named Sliver. His suit was in our evidence vault."

"Won't he want it back?"

"I killed him," Gemini said shortly. "Leela, we're wasting time."

"Strategize this, Chelsea. If you can just go and borrow some suit full of superpowers anytime you want to, what do you need me for?"

"To free one of my teammates, that's all. You won't be involved in the fighting, Leela. I promise."

"Shit." It was a long exhalation. "I am officially unhappy about this, OK?"

"Apparently you're happier than me," Gemini said morosely.

Dimples ghosted on and off Leela's cheeks, and Gemini's suspicion that her sister was drunk resurfaced. But she couldn't be, could she? She had the super-metabolism now.

"It had to happen sometime," Leela said.

Within the hour, they were flying low over the Burrard Inlet in the Crucible Orb, the team's primary vehicle. Leela was slouched on a passenger couch, wearing Gemini's black suit. Picking at the fabric, she twisted in her seat.

"Are you okay?" Gemini finally asked.

"I guess. Being you is a little weird."

"Imagine doing it full-time."

"Well, there's the fame, the public service medals, the fans, the perfect boyfriend ..."

"The secret identities and the terrible hours," Gemini rejoined, stung. "Not to mention the fighting and the injuries."

"Yeah. I'm glad you guys have that healer ..."

"Balm," Gemini said.

"Though, I guess he can't fix everything."

"No," she said. The Orb controls shimmered briefly, obscured by tears.

"I'm glad you have Balm," Leela repeated. "You know we worry sometimes. Mom and I."

Gemini didn't answer that. Am I supposed to apologize? she wondered.

"Speaking of fighting, can you actually operate that old battle suit?"

"It's fine," Gemini said. In fact, Sliver's suit was tight around her hips, its outward appearance of roominess compromised by the power packs and equipment housed inside. Its manly form-fitted chest was mashing her breasts again; they were practically bumping her chin. "The controls are well designed; a kid could fly it."

"Controls for what?"

"Oh — flight manoeuvers, guns."

"Guns?"

Gemini triggered a sequence and tiny silver needles erupted from the battle suit's enlarged fingertips, homing in on one of the Orb's couches and puncturing the upholstery. "Guns."

"Gross." Leela arched her back, still tugging at Gemini's unitard. "I'm never gonna pass for you."

Privately, Gemini agreed. "Remember you aren't wearing clothes: the costume is more of a skin. There are no pockets, you can't fuss with your hair because of the mask, and don't scratch yourself. If you stand still you'll look aloof, otherworldly."

"*Riiiight*," Leela said dubiously. "That reminds me, I wanted to ask. We were born in Regina. But you're always telling the press you come from some planet orbiting Castor ..."

"Pollux."

"Whatever. Why the lie?"

"You want people to know my powers are linked to a twin sister with a vulnerable little boy? What if my enemies found out I had a sweet old mom?"

"Oh. Have I mentioned lately I hate your life?"

"Every time you see me," Gemini said. She'd meant to sound light-hearted; instead her voice came out brittle, and Leela's head whipped around.

Gemini tensed, in the silence that followed, for the inevitable fight.

"Ah," Leela said at last. "Well, I'm sorry about that."

"Are you joking?" With Leela's face hidden behind the Gemini mask, she honestly couldn't tell.

"No. Actually, I'm pretty proud of you. Not scrapbook-proud or anything. But ... what you do. It's important. And you're good at it." She laughed, sounding embarrassed. "I'll shut up — I can't tell what you're thinking in that getup."

"I was just thinking that about you," Gemini said. Praise from Leela — a watery sense of pleasure suffused her, warring with a suspicion that this was a trick, some tactic that would blow up on her the next time the two of them argued.

It's the kid going away, she concluded — it's shaken Leela up. She's apologizing, cleaning house emotionally. Please, she prayed suddenly, don't let her be suicidal.

Leela folded her hands in her lap — a visible effort to keep still. "So, what's the deal? Tunnels? Booby-trap-a-minute electronics, idiot henchmen posted at every door?"

Gemini shook her head. "Purgatoire doesn't go for underground warrens. He likes to have lots of civilians handy."

"Hostages, right," Leela murmured.

Gemini pushed away a memory from this afternoon — herself, bobbing powerlessly in the Pacific while mind-controlled civilians dragged her teammates into Purgatoire's lair. "He charms people — that's what he calls it: 'charm' — into becoming his captives."

"And you know where he is now?"

"Canada Place. We were on our way to apprehend him when they brought in the horsemen to distract us. Here, I've got the target onscreen."

"Target," Leela grumbled. The Crucible Orb brought up a high-resolution image of the terminal. The cruise ships had been pulled away from the dock, and the walkways were eerily devoid of tourists. Yellow police tape formed a perimeter around the building. "Aren't the cops going to do *anything?*"

"No point," Gemini said. "He'd charm them once they got within range ... and then he'd have puppets with guns."

"Great. So what's our plan?"

"We take the Orb underwater, like so." Making the vehicle's bulk-heads transparent, she brought the ship out of flight, entering the water silently. "With luck, we can get in from below."

"And what exactly is this teeny tiny thing I have to do?"

The colour of the water deepened to green as they moved into the inlet. Gemini turned on the Orb's running lights. "Help me free Evangeline."

"Which one is Evangeline?"

"Jesus, Leela, she's Crimson."

"Don't snap." Leela's voice was maddeningly calm. "You told me everyone's real name once ... what? Five years ago?"

"Sorry." Fighting a tremble in her hands — probably fatigue or low blood sugar, things that didn't worry her when she had powers — Gemini brought up a team photo on Orb's main screen. "Reading left to right: Crimson is Evangeline. Serpentine is Maria. Mortar and Balm are Rufus and Cray, respectively ..."

"And Looking Glass is your dear sweet Powell. Okay, got it. Thanks for the review." Leela fiddled with her mask. "Hey, shouldn't you have backup plans?"

"This is a backup plan, sort of. It's one they won't think of." Gemini shifted inside the battle suit, trying to get comfortable. It had been so long since she'd lost her powers that she had forgotten how sensitive her skin could be, how every touch could set off a parade of sensations. The unyielding press of the battle suit's interior mouldings was creating bruises, unfamiliar, hard-to-ignore aches. The only thing the increased sensitivity that came with being powerless made better was sex. Her loins burned dully at the thought, a quick surge of rote horniness that rose and then dropped away.

She focused on Leela, who was staring out at the sea. In the pale glow cast by the Orb, even the polluted and litter-strewn underworld of Burrard Inlet seemed romantic. Lank plaits of seaweed caressed the hull, and schools of fish — probably toxic and inedible — swam past, their every move a whipsaw mystery. A seal nosed over to investigate them.

"The things you get to do," Leela murmured, voice full of wonder.

"Miracles for breakfast."

Gemini surprised herself by speaking: "What was it like when Dodd said he was going to England? I mean, how did it feel?"

"I dunno," Leela said. She was still watching the seal. "He's been homesick."

"Yeah, but —"

"He's not leaving to punish me, Chelsea."

"Do you still love him?"

"Maybe. When he first left, I was ... a million mood changes a day. Stormy."

"It came out of nowhere," Gemini remembered.

"Yeah." The black and white costume with its star-field pattern radiated cool competence. Leela's voice was soft, thoughtful. "One second I feel sucker-punched, the next I'm celebrating the things I don't have to put up with anymore. The petty irritations, you know? Two seconds later I'm forgiving, then I'm mad, then I'm crying ..."

Gemini felt her mouth working, but no sound came.

"Are we here?" Leela asked. They had come under a scroll of shadow, moving into blackness.

"We're under the pier. I'll scan for warm bodies." Leela leaned close to watch as Gemini scanned the structure above them. "There — that'll be Purgatoire, and there's my team ..."

"They're the green lights? So what are those pale pink dots?"

"Puds — I mean, civilians. People without powers."

"Other hostages."

Blushing inside the clunky helmet, Gemini nodded. "He's got them scattered around the building to make it harder to assault the place."

"You think there's a route in from below?"

"Yes." She tapped the screen, highlighting it. "You melt a corridor straight upward from this point."

"And then?" Leela asked.

Gemini circled the brightest of the green lights on the display. "Crimson is immune to our powers. You'll poke your head into the conference room and vaporize whatever restraints they're using to hold her. She'll get loose, I'll fly in. She and I will mop up Purgatoire. Meanwhile you'll get back into Orb and wait for us."

"What if I free Crimson and he just zaps her again, or she's knocked out ..."

"It doesn't work that way. Evangeline can't lose consciousness, it's one of her abilities. And she'll have been thinking about counter-tactics ever since they captured her. Believe me, nobody takes out Crimson twice in a row."

"I need to know this plan of yours will work, Chelsea."

"It will," Gemini said. She suddenly realized the voice coming through her mask was Sliver's, high, crystalline and sexless. It was almost a child's voice, and to her ear it sounded vulnerable, full of doubt.

"Okay," Leela said. "Let's go."

They surfaced and Leela clambered out of the Orb, arms flailing until she got her footing and exhaled upward, melting them a tunnel. Everything thinned, dribbled and then vanished, leaving a lumpy-edged corridor that led upward through the deck and various building materials. Gemini couldn't have done a better job herself. She felt hollow suddenly — redundant, unnecessary.

The team needs me, she reminded herself.

"The drips can be used as handholds as they harden," she said. But Leela was already climbing up through the tunnel she had made, her spandexed ass swaying as she switched from grip to grip, moving upward.

Thumbing the battle suit controls, Gemini flew up in pursuit of her sister. They ascended in silence, reaching the concrete floor just below the conference room.

"I'm not ready for this," Leela said, voicing Gemini's own thought.

"Melt the cement and soften the carpet just a bit, then push up and take a peek. We're in the corner of the room ... it should be nice and unobtrusive."

"*Should.*" Leela sighed and the cement vanished. The carpet got stringy and thin. She poked upward, peered out ... and did nothing.

"Free Crimson," Gemini reminded her in a whisper. But Leela was gesturing for them both to descend, making choppy gestures and then climbing down so rapidly she almost fell into the water.

"Problem?" Gemini hissed at the bottom as Leela fell to her hands and knees, heaving. "You're not going to barf in my costume, are you?" She tried to chuckle, to break the tension. Instead the sound came out forced, hiding nothing.

"No. Probably no. Um ... Chelsea. Crimson can't be killed?"

"She's completely immortal. Why?"

"Just that ... he's cut her into pieces."

Inside the battle suit, all Gemini's limbs went slack. The suit itself did not react; she remained in place, hovering before her sister. "Oh." The Sliver voice was definitely childish this time, almost a quaver.

"And Powell —"

"No civilian names," Gemini said automatically.

"Looking Glass is up there, walking around loose. He can open dimensional gates, can't he? Could he have brought in the horsemen? I'm not saying it's his fault. Purgatoire must be ... what did you call it? Charming him."

The words sounded dim, like they were being drowned out by the babble of a crowd. All the louder voices were inside Gemini's head: her own doubts and fears shouting recriminations and denials.

"Chelsea?" asked Leela, impatiently.

"We've been fighting," Gemini said finally.

The mask — her mask, Gemini's face — came up sharply. Then Leela pulled it off, revealing her pale face and wide, stunned eyes. "What?"

"Fighting. Over little stuff. For a couple of years. Nothing important. He got remote, I stopped trusting him as much. We'd been trying to work it out."

"But?" Leela asked.

"We ... I had to leave him in the middle of a battle. It was about a week ago. I thought he'd just take a portal to safety, like always. But the perps we were fighting had neutralized his powers."

"You abandoned him?"

"No — we rescued him as soon as we realized."

"Was he hurt?"

"Hurt and angry," Gemini said. "But we couldn't have done anything differently. The Legislature was in session — government types were in danger, you know? Balm healed Powell up, but he was upset, and we ... *I* might not have been all that sympathetic."

"I bet. You need to work on your empathy skills," Leela said, but her eyes were kind, her voice gentle.

What I need is to get back on task, Gemini thought. The others were suffering, just above them. But she kept talking: "The next thing I knew barbarians were all over Stanley Park. I thought I saw one of Powell's portals, but I told myself I had to be wrong."

"So ... you're saying Looking Glass is working with Purgatoire of his own free will?" Leela asked."

Gemini nodded miserably.

"I should've thought about where your happy went." Leela patted her absently, her palm making an almost-silent bong against the metal of the armour. "Chelsea, I'm so sorry."

"Don't sympathize. I'll cry and my tactical display will mist up. Is Crimson really in pieces?"

"Yes. Sorry."

Only discipline and long habit kept Gemini from trying to rub her throbbing eyes. "What am I going to do?"

"Strategize anew, I guess," Leela said. "Will the guns in that suit do any good at all against Purgatoire?"

"Sure," Gemini said. "But what about Looking Glass?"

Leela scratched her nose. "How would you take him out?"

"What?"

"Come on, tell me you haven't been thinking about it."

With a stab, Gemini realized she had. "He'll be expecting me to try something non-lethal. To entangle him in the floor, or a partially melted chair."

"You can't do what he's expecting though can you?" Leela asked.

"No. So I'd have to burn him — hit him hard and ..." As Gemini spoke, her voice thinned and got higher, but she pushed on through the sob. "… hope Balm can heal him after."

Leela nodded. "'Kay. That's what I'll do."

"I can't ask — you hate violence."

"I'll hate it more if he's loose killing people. Besides, he knows the truth about me and Mom, doesn't he?"

Gemini nodded. "We never had secrets."

"Okay. You bust in there and put a hole in Purgatoire. I'll climb up behind you and get Looking Glass."

"You're sure?"

"I'll be right behind you," Leela promised.

"All right." Gemini toggled the suit controls, flew upward at low speed and broke through the softened carpet. Even after the darkness below the pier, the room seemed murky, lit only by computer screens and a single dim chandelier. Crimson was hacked into seeping, scattered pieces. Balm was dangling from the ceiling, chained with his eyes gouged out and his fingers broken, while Mortar slowly dissolved in a tank of antifreeze-pink liquid. As for Serpentine … the lower half of her body was simply gone. Her torso issued from mid-air, her body bisected by a blue-white ring that could only be one of Powell's dimension portals. Her upper body jittered in a wild and grotesque dance; as she flailed she was trying to scream, but her voice was gone.

The room was filled with machines, and neither of the villains was in sight.

Somewhere in the midst of all this gadgetry had to be a device that was keeping Crimson from shifting to her energy state and reintegrating herself, Gemini reasoned. Turning her back on her friends, she began destroying Purgatoire's equipment, driving a stream of needles into each unit of hardware, into every cable.

Battle calm descended and her mind was suddenly clear. She noted that Purgatoire had found himself a new army. No low-tech rampaging hoard this time, either — an inter-dimensional viewer showed row upon row of German infantry, soldiers with bayonets and tanks and blank charmed eyes.

That's where he and Powell are, then, Gemini thought — recruiting. Hopefully the destruction of their equipment would bring them back.

It was the work of an instant to destroy every machine in the room. And it worked. Crimson's scattered pieces were already glowing a deep red when Purgatoire darted out of a blue-white portal, brandishing his Pandemonium Globe, a device that would subject every pud within its range to lethally terrifying visions.

Gemini was ready. She shot a score of spikes through the villain's wizened hand. His fingers dropped open and the globe bounced to the floor.

They dove for it, Purgatoire with his uninjured hand extended, Gemini with her suit's massive fingers splayed. The battle suit fought the dive, though, pushing her away from the floor. She skimmed over her target, fumbling what should have been a perfect grab.

As the suit rigorously brought itself upright, she watched, helpless, as the villain regained possession of his globe.

"Haha," he squeaked. Beyond the door, people began to shriek. Purgatoire crawled upright, yanking needles out of his impaled hand with his teeth. "Not so fast, Mr. Giant."

"Easy," she said. His nose came only as high as her chest, but he seemed unafraid. "Don't hurt anyone. You've got me."

"Oh, I don't got you yet, Giant."

"This suit is impervious to your charms."

"Then take it off," said a new voice, behind her.

Powell.

She let her gaze flick left, shocked at how hard it was even to look at Powell as he stepped through the blue-white portal. Lover and confidant, he had become her foe. It was inconceivable.

"It is you, isn't it, Gem? Come to bring me to justice?"

"I've killed for you," she said softly. "I've all but died for you."

"You abandoned me when it counted."

"You knew the stakes —"

"There's always something more important than me, isn't there?" His mask was more mobile than hers — she could see pain in his face. For an instant she could forgive him anything, even this.

"Switch sides," she told him breathlessly. "Glass, switch back. I'm begging."

"Take off the helmet, Gem, or I'll cut Serpentine in half. Do you remember ... she was laughing when you guys came to rescue me? 'Poor hapless Looking Glass, can't get himself out of a simple jam —' "

"Glass ..." She was stalling him now ... but for what? Leela was nowhere in sight.

"I'm a joke to you all. You weren't even worried."

Leela can't do it, Gemini thought, she just can't hack the violence. Even now, at risk of becoming Purgatoire's puppet, she found she almost admired her sister for that.

"Stormy," she murmured. "One minute scared, one minute mad ..."

"Helmet. Now," commanded Powell, resolution settling into the features of his mask. He pulled the dimension portal taut around their friend, cutting a bloody line into her torso. Serpentine's face wrenched; her forked tongue flicked out, and Gemini saw punctures in its spotted black and white tissue: in her distress, Maria had bitten herself. "Not laughing now, is she?"

"I give up, okay?" Gemini reached for the catch on her battle suit's helmet.

"You'll feel better in a minute, Mr. Giant," Purgatoire crooned, shoving the Pandemonium Globe up against her face as Gemini unlatched. She lifted the helmet, slowly surrendering ...

And then Looking Glass was gone.

The carpet vanished from beneath his feet and Gemini heard him cry out as he fell, then splashed. Instinct took over: she backhanded Purgatoire with all the suit's considerable strength, sending him across the room. The globe fell and she dropped a heavy desk on it, crushing it casually as she ran to the edge of the wide pit yawning in the centre of the conference room. Forty feet below, her sister was wrestling with Powell in the ocean, their distant thrashing forms illuminated by the greenish white light of the Crucible Orb's running lights.

"Hang on," Gemini bellowed. "I'm coming."

"No — save the team," her sister's voice echoed up amid splashes.

It wasn't fair to leave Leela down there, but she was right. Gemini turned, driving a fist into the tank holding Mortar prisoner and leaving it to drain as she flew to Serpentine. Grasping her friend under one sinuous, scaly arm, she eased her up through the narrow bottleneck of the dimension portal. She nearly gagged then, as she saw the burgered flesh of her teammate's legs. Something had been eating her.

Then she went to Balm, crushing the chains that held him with her armoured hands. The metal crumbled and it was oddly satisfying, more messily destructive than sighing things into sterile nothingness.

"Cray?" She whispered his real name, lowering him to the floor. "Cray, it's me."

"Gem?" He blinked bloodied sockets at her.

"Yeah. Can you walk?"

"Legs are busted," he said. "Glass?"

"Taken care of," she said, hoping it was true. "I know you're injured, but Serpentine's pretty bad. Mortar too."

His jaw firmed, all business. "Crimson?"

She checked the red glow, finding it brighter and less diffuse. "She's reassembling."

He shivered slightly.

"Can you help the others if you can't see?"

"Take me to whoever's worst."

She carried Balm to Serpentine's side and moved his broken hands to their teammate's heart, watching as he summoned a crackling halo of healer's energy and directed it into her body.

As Gemini stepped back his blind face followed her. "Feels like war today, doesn't it?"

"Sometimes that's what it is." It was a mantra for their bad days. It had never felt so true.

Damn. Leela.

Gemini whirled back to the pit just in time to see her sister climbing back up into the ballroom. She had Looking Glass over her shoulder, slung in a fireman's carry.

"Are you okay?" Gemini asked.

"No," Leela said, letting Powell fall to the floor with a thud. "I'm going to throw up after all. Getting hit is exactly as rotten as I remembered."

"I'm sorry."

"Thanks. It turns out hitting back doesn't suck, though."

"I think I said as much when you were dating that abusive psychopath ..."

"You could work on being less smug, you know." Shaking water off her costume, Leela nudged Powell with a toe.

"How did you take him out?" Gemini asked.

"Surprised?"

"Maybe a little."

"I put my hands around his throat, thought about the way he'd screwed you over, and just ... squeezed. Eventually he went limp." Leela said. Her voice was colder — scarier — than Gemini had ever heard it, despite their years of fighting. Then she sighed. "I guess you have to jail him, huh?"

"He brought the barbarians here," Gemini said. "Even if we could overlook what he did to all of us ..."

"People died. Yeah. Well, you want my opinion, he deserves it."

Misting up again, Gemini looked at her lover's sea-soaked form. "So that's it. Fifteen years of history. Broken."

"Oh, I don't know." Leela bent to bind his hands. "There was a time when I thought you and I would never speak again. People do surprise you."

"This from the woman whose kid is going to be living on Greenwich Mean Time." Still looking at Powell, she tried to draw breath. It felt as though something was lodged between her lungs.

Was that a chuckle?

Gemini examined her sister, suddenly suspicious. The mask hid every hint of an expression, but ...

"You don't drink champagne when you're *un*happy," Gemini said at last, thinking back to her sister's earlier intoxicated state.

"I only said you-know-who was moving to London," Leela said.

"But when I asked —"

"You mean when you totally assumed that if he wanted to take my son to Europe I'd just let him?"

Gemini frowned. "You misled me."

"You need to quit thinking I'm spineless," Leela said.

"So ... the kid's staying with you?"

Leela gave her a goofy thumbs-up. "Seven days a week, twelve months a year. He moves in Monday after school."

Gemini grabbed her with Sliver's powerful hands, then pulled her sister in for a hug they could never have shared in civilian gear, for fear of gluing themselves together.

"You could kill a girl doing that," Leela said when Gemini finally released her.

"Only a civilian."

"You mean a pud?"

"You were never a pud."

Leela laughed. "I'm a textbook case."

"No," Gemini said. "You're extraordinary."

A squeak interrupted them, and then a tentacle edged under the door. Leela tilted forward, mouth open, ready to attack.

"Don't kill it — it's just a police probe," Gemini murmured. "They must have heard the battle."

"Right." She struck an overly heroic pose. "This is Gemini. The situation is under control. Send a containment thingie ..."

"Unit," Gemini whispered.

"Right, a unit to take the, um, the perpetrators into custody."

As the probe withdrew, she turned back to Gemini. "You better plan on wearing that battle suit for a while, huh?"

"Oh, I'll bounce back ..." Then it sank in again: Powell a villain, Powell going to trial. The media coverage. And Powell just being gone, when he'd been there day in and day out for all these years. She thought fleetingly of their bed, his clothes hanging in their shared closet, all the things in Base Pacific that were his. Team equipment the two of them had built together, items they wouldn't be able to get rid of. All those things, like ghosts, bringing up memories ...

"Maybe we better melt-proof your apartment," she said to Leela.

"Fuck. I guess so."

"You know what?"

"Yes?"

"I'm glad you get to be a full-time mom again." Another mood switch now, as the containment team bustled in to whisk Purgatoire away and Leela had to explain that Looking Glass was going into custody too.

As the police carried Powell away, Gemini's heartbreak dimmed to something like numbness. In its absence she saw, to her surprise, that Leela was standing up straight, that she wasn't plucking at her uniform.

"Hey," she said, "can I get one more favour?"

"Sure."

"Don't you want to know what?"

"No, actually. I trust you."

She led Leela up a staircase, heading for the roof. "I've been thinking I may need to make a more expressive mask for my costume."

"Gemini's?" Leela asked. "Or this big metal shell?"

"Both, I guess. If my emotions are up and down for a while, I'll probably be using both costumes."

"Will you tell the press it's you in the statue suit?"

"No. I don't want word getting out that my powers come and go. I'll pretend there are two different heroes. Gemini and ... I'll need a second name for when I'm wearing this." So much work, she thought. So many changes. Powell gone.

"Being you is pretty complicated, huh?" Leela said.

"Usually I don't notice," she said, feeling heavy, weighted down.

"Well, softening the masks isn't a bad idea," Leela offered. "Being inscrutable gets old."

"Yes," Gemini agreed, opening a fire door and bowing Leela outside. "I don't know what I was thinking."

Beyond the doorway was the city, its sky, above the office towers, full of police helicopters that chattered and vied for room with the news-service birds. It was just dusk, and the streetlights were coming on in irregular patches, street by street. The air, warm and barely humid, smelled of the sea.

A familiar layer of sound — camera shutters clicking like locusts —

rolled toward them as Leela stepped out into view. Wearing Gemini's costume, she looked every inch the hero.

"Hey," Leela took an uncertain half-step back from the cameras, but her sister caught her before she could backpedal fully, nudging her out into sight, "why am I out here?"

"For the scrapbook," Chelsea said. "Wave, Leela."

REPORT ON FIVE CASE STUDIES OF FEMALES

WITH ENHANCED CHARACTERISTICS:

Molecular Basis and Treatment Strategies

Bustos, S. P.

Centre for the Research and Understanding of Superhumans (CRUSH)

ABSTRACT

The molecular explanation for the recent proliferation of female mutant vigilantes has been found in a newly discovered gene that maps to the X chromosome. The gene encodes a transcription-factor protein that enhances the expression of several different genes and confers super-human capabilities on the carrier. Five case studies are discussed in this report, as well as treatment strategies to be implemented.

METHOD

Subjects used in this study were collected using the decoy method. A situation was constructed whereby subjects were led to believe their abilities were required to come to the aid of a "victim," such as a small child. During the "rescue" a sublethal dose of the horse tranquilizer acepromazine was administered by dart gun. The subjects were then transported back to the research facility, where they were carefully observed under reinforced restraints and studied using state-of-the-art technology.

BACKGROUND

Humans carry their genetic information on 23 pairs of chromosomes. Included in these are the sex chromosomes. Men possess one X and one Y sex chromosome, while women possess two Xs. Recently, a region of DNA on chromosome X was found to contain a novel gene. Because it encodes a transcription-factor protein on the X chromosome, it was dubbed "X-TRA." Mutated and modified forms of the protein have been found to promote the activation of several other genes to such high extents that the carrier displays superhuman traits. Because genes from two X chromosomes are required for the effect, only females have been affected.

X-TRA protein:

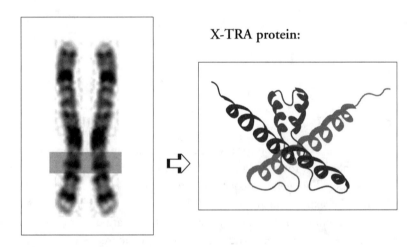

Figure 1: A pair of X chromosomes showing the locus of the novel gene (left) and the protein it encodes (right).

RESULTS

Case Study #1: Female with Super-Senses

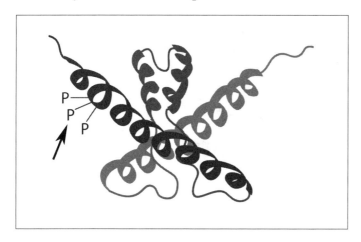

Figure 2: The mutant X-TRA protein that causes super-heightened senses is phosphorylated three times.

X-TRA was found to enhance expression of proteins involved in perception using the five senses. The subject has the following traits: micro-, X-ray and long-distance vision; ultrasonic hearing; ability to detect one part per million (ppm) of any substance in food or air by taste or smell; ability to detect and identify submicroscopic agents by touch.

Treatment: subjects should have the following surgically removed: retinas, tympanic membranes, olfactory and gustatory receptors, and the Pacinian and/or Meissner's corpuscles. Unfortunately the subject escaped during the outdoor long-distance vision test before treatment was given.

Possible Afflicted Individuals: Callisto, who battled Storm of the X-Men; Feral, former member of X-force.

Case Study #2: Female with Airborne/Waterborne Capabilities

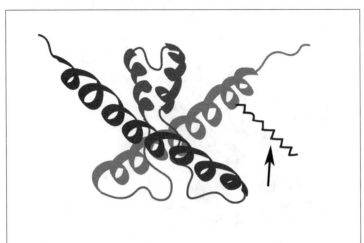

Figure 3: The mutant X-TRA protein that causes flight and extended underwater capabilities has a fatty acid modification.

This X-TRA mutation allows the subject to fly and to "breathe" underwater. The subject possesses millions of nanoscopic bladders interspersed throughout the adipose tissue. The subject, by control of the breathing apparatus, is able to concentrate and store trace amounts of helium from the air within tissues and fill the bladders with it when flight is desired. The same is done with oxygen for the purpose of respiration underwater.

Treatment: Mechanical constriction of the pharynx. Tragically, the subject escaped before treatment through an unlocked skylight in the facility.

Possible Afflicted Individual: Phoenix, original member of the X-Men. However, her mechanism of flight is different than that described above.

Case Study #3: Female with Shape-Shifting Ability

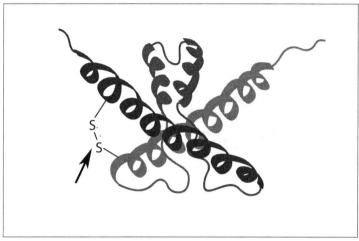

Figure 4: The mutant X-TRA protein that is responsible for shape-shifting capabilities has a disulphide bond.

This mutated protein allows the subject to undergo morphological alterations of the body to resemble any person. Nerve-growth factors become up-regulated in the subject, which triggers high numbers of cells to migrate throughout the body and form various tissues, including cartilage and bone. Strict regulation of tissue formation, especially in the facial area, allows successful morphogenesis.

Treatment: Zinc and copper supplements (potent inhibitors of nerve-growth factors). Administer by injection using force if necessary. Regrettably the subject morphed into a research technician and was subsequently freed by an unsuspecting facility caretaker before administration of treatment.

Possible Afflicted Individuals: Husk, a member of Generation X; Mystique, founder of Freedom Force.

Case Study #4: Female with Mental Sensitivity

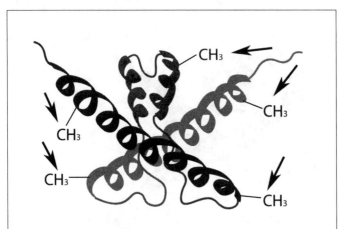

Figure 5: The mutant X-TRA protein that enhances mental capabilities is methylated five times.

This X-TRA protein gives the subject a faculty for telepathy, mind control and telekinesis (movement of objects with the mind). Heightened electrical output from the brain allows the subject to create interference with others' brainwaves, thereby intercepting thoughts and reading or even changing them. High amounts of intensely focused mental output allows the movement of objects.

Treatment: Administration of acetylcholine inhibitor to slow nerve impulses. Unfortunately the subject used mind control to convince researchers to free her before treatment could be applied.

Possible Afflicted Individuals: Mirage, founding member of the New Mutants; Typhoid Mary, hired by Kingpin to bring down Daredevil.

Case Study #5: Female Displaying Super-Strength

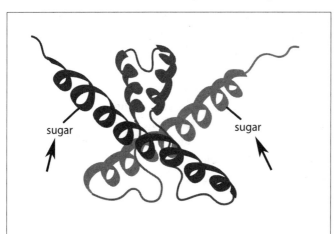

Figure 6: The mutant X-TRA protein that imparts super-strength has two sugar moieties added.

This mutant protein gives the subject super-strength and a protective exoskeleton covering. Subject displays colossal muscle contraction activity due to highly active actin-myosin interactions. Development of a chitinlike outer layer occurs by secretions of epidermal (skin) cells.

Treatment: Calcium starvation (required for muscle contraction and exoskeleton hardening). As our many preparatory simulations did not factor in her rage at being captured, the subject broke free of restraints and nullified armed guards to escape. Treatment was not successfully administered.

Possible Afflicted Individuals: Zealot, who fights alongside the Wildcats; She-Hulk, member of the Avengers; and Penance, member of Generation X, who is covered in diamond-hard skin.

CONCLUSIONS

Five females with enhanced characteristics were studied and various mutations of the protein X-TRA were found to be responsible for the expression of their super-abilities. Treatments were proposed and attempted. Unfortunately all subjects refused treatment and fled the facility despite our best efforts to contain them for observation. We believe that the proliferation of female super-fighters must be stopped before it reaches epidemic proportions. They should be regarded as extremely dangerous and treatment should only be administered by a trained professional. Future studies will include collection of females with other super-traits and fortification of research facilities. Sightings of female super-fighters should be reported to the proper authorities immediately.

S. P. Bustos is a senior research fellow at the Centre for the Research and Understanding of Superhumans (CRUSH). She thanks Dr. J. Munroe for the generous gift of the actin antibody.

Disclaimer:
All treatment options described in this report are suggestions based on research conducted in a controlled setting. The author does not assume responsibility for unsuccessful treatment efforts, nor for any harm received during these attempts. Extermination should be reserved as a last resort.

MADAME MOUTH'S LITTLE GET-TOGETHER

FEMALE VIDEO-GAME ENTITIES TALK LIFE, LOVE AND BLOODSHED

Carma Livingstone

From: madame.mouth@fcs.iaai.edu
To: red.wave@fcs.iaai.edu; mighty.aphrodite@fcs.iaai.edu
Subject: Tonight's the night!!!

Hi Red and Aphro:

I'm so glad The Legs, The Hair, The Tits, The Ass and The Brain could all make it to the game characters' conference this year — you wouldn't believe how many amazing heroines are here. This morning, I gave a panel with The Tits on female fighters of the 1990s and it was totally packed. In the afternoon, we staged a brilliant sit-in at a keynote speech on the entertainment value of gang violence. I would say at least 250 characters — both male and female — decided not to attend after seeing us there.

You know, there hasn't been a gathering of female entities like this in ages. Not since just after Monsieur Mouth and I finalized our divorce in '96. Who would've thought I'd already have tenure at the Institute of Applied Artificial Intelligence? Who would've believed we'd have our own Department of Female Character Studies? I realize that my history as The Creators' first female character helped my acceleration up the academic ladder, but, still, I'm proud of my accomplishments.

MADAME MOUTH'S LITTLE GET-TOGETHER

MADAME MOUTH

Game: Madame Mouth
Release Date: 1981

Madame Mouth entranced players around the world as the first female video-game character. Her game was a quickly released sequel that was almost identical to the groundbreaking Monsieur Mouth. One of the only differences is the addition of short inter-level vignettes that tell the story of Monsieur and Madame Mouth's courtship, including the birth of their daughter. Back then, games were of a simple, though stunning, nature. Madame Mouth manoeuvers about a two-dimensional labyrinth and crams JoyPills into an infinite maw. She is chased by the Red Demons, supernatural beings that hunger for her flesh. Madame Mouth sports heavy mascara, brilliant red lips and a single red rose attached where an ear would be.

Anyhow, I've managed to secure confirmed attendance from all five heroines for the little party I'm hosting in my room tonight. I've stocked my mini-bar with enough CircuitPlus to put an army of alien invaders under the table, so I'm sure candour will be the order of the evening.

I don't expect any of my guests will notice the data-capture unit I've wired into my belly. I worked out the configuration for recording my internal circuit board as well as my external environment. That means my immediate reactions will be on disk along with the audio-visual display. Isn't that amazing?

Don't worry. I'll tell them about the recording later so I can get permission to use the material in my book.

I hope nothing goes wrong tonight … I can't afford to pay for any damage to the hotel room this time! Needless to say, I am very excited and more than a little nervous. I'll report on preliminary findings tomorrow.

Cheers, Madame M

*

<DC Timecode: 00:00:00>
At 7:30, I open my hotel-room door and find The Hair hovering just above the threshold. She thrusts a bouquet of red roses into my face. She's probably hoping to get a chance to speak with me privately. I am the only friend she confides in these days, as she spends most of her energy trying to rebuild a relationship with her son. They have been separated for a thousand years, after all.

"Hi Madame M," she smiles. It's good to see her at least partially happy.

"Hair, it's been far too long. Please come in."

"You look fantastic, Madame M." The Hair circles me with her arms. "Just as round as you were when you were first released."

I've never quite understood the outfit The Creators gave The Hair. She is the empress of an ethereal realm, but she's dressed like an 1980s goth. She wears a tight green and black bodysuit accessorized by a useless short vest. She has matching thigh-high black boots and leather wristcuffs. Her bum-length hair is black with a wide white stripe that starts at her forehead. Like anyone who has been resurrected from the dead, The Hair's eyes are glowing, white orbs. She is petite and does not have the bulging muscles and massive chest of other female fighting characters.

The Hair flies over to the table of food I've laid out and dives into the pretzels, her favourite snack.

"So what's going on with you these days, Hair?"

<DC Timecode: 00:02:37>

Before The Hair can swallow her first mouthful, the buzzer sounds again. It's The Legs and The Ass. They used to despise each other, but they've bonded recently over the discovery of vast Internet porn shrines dedicated to their entities. The Legs and The Ass can be seen masturbating with flowers and giving artful blow jobs. There is even an XXX video site where female Users wear their costumes for male admirers.

The Ass was also the subject of a naked patch created by Users and distributed over the Internet. Users apply the patch to hack into the game and rob The Ass of her clothes. She finds it funny, as it is extremely bizarre to watch nude Ninja action, but The Creators are angry about it. They've threatened to sue anyone found hosting the file.

"Hey, Madame M." The Ass glides by. She's wearing a matching black bikini and mesh top.

"Nice swimsuit," I politely comment.

Powers and Skills:

Madame Mouth's power is her stamina. She can play forever without tiring. She can teleport from one side of the screen to the other by way of special portals. When she manages to gobble one of the five UltraPills in the labyrinth, she gains the power to devour the Red Demons and send their spirits back to a prison cell in the middle of the screen.

THE LEGS

Game: Back Alley Battle 2

Release Date: 1992

The Legs was the first female fighting character in the Back Alley Battle series and among the first to hit the arcade. Her game sported new movements and battle engagement, but remained two-dimensional. Born in China, The Legs' parents died when she was young. Her Uncle Chen was the only next of kin, but he couldn't raise her because he was a member of the Te-Wu, the secret police. He sent The Legs to live in a Wu Shu school, where she trained in acrobatics and martial arts. On the day of her graduation, Uncle Chen was kidnapped by a criminal organization called the Kong League. The Legs became a Te-Wu agent, like her uncle, in order to find him and bring down the League.

"A User had me buy it late today. Unfortunately, a range of bathing suits is all that's available to me right now."

"Damn fantasy-sports simulation," says The Legs. "I'm so grateful The Creators didn't come up with that one when Back Alley Battle 2 was in its heyday."

The Ass narrows her eyes. "There weren't enough female fighters back then to stage a mud wrestling tournament." She brushes past us and heads for the cheese croissants I've selected just for her. She stops for a beat when she notices The Hair, but decides to continue on her path. The Hair levitates two feet higher and fixes her empty eyes on The Ass.

"What's with the cheese fetish anyway?" The Hair asks as The Ass fills her mouth. "I noticed you ringside feeding brie to another female fighter in XXX-treme Mud Wrestling."

"Gee, Hairy, not even a 'Hi, how are you?'" The Ass replies. "And in answer to your question: it's what The Creators programmed us to do. You know I can't control the game play."

I interject, "Ladies, ladies! Would anyone care for a glass of CircuitPlus?"

"Madame M, that would be lovely," says The Legs cheerily. The Legs, like The Hair and myself, hails from a two-dimensional configuration. Her costume is a sexy red dress with a Chinese collar and hip-high leg slits on both sides. She also wears tight red boots and silver bracelets with spiked studs. The Legs' breasts are full and so are her muscular thighs.

<DC Timecode: 00:17:49>

The buzzer rings again. Both The Ass's and The Hair's eyes shift to the door, their cheeks already a little rosy due to the CircuitPlus. "I'll get it!" squeals The Ass.

"No, I will!" cries The Hair. "It might be The Tits!" The Hair floats in front of The Ass to block her path, and before The Ass can protest, The Hair's hand is on the doorknob.

"Oh, hi, Brain," The Hair says in a flat voice. The Ass flops back on a purple, fun-fur chair. "Hello, Brain."

"Good evening, ladies," says The Brain, striding in and picking up a crystal glass. She fills it with shimmering blue CircuitPlus. "Madame M, thanks for inviting me! I'm new to the scene, so it's nice to be included."

"I'm glad you could come, my dear," I say. "Please make yourself at home."

"I will." The Brain stretches out on the pale yellow blow-up couch. She wears a cropped snakeskin jacket and matching pants. A rather large gun rests on her hip. Ultra-cool angular sunglasses hide her eyes and her hair is bound in tiny braids. Her build is one of the most subdued I've seen, as it mirrors the body of a real female User (albeit that of a petite and muscular Hollywood diva).

The Ass gets up for another glass of CircuitPlus and takes the opportunity to position herself beside the door. The Hair hovers nearby. "Talked to The Tits lately?" The Hair asks.

"As a matter of fact, The Tits and I had lunch today," The Ass grins viciously.

The Hair knocks back a large gulp of CircuitPlus. The Ass follows suit. There is a quick buzz of the doorbell and The Tits peeks her head in the door.

<DC Timecode: 00:27:33>
"Tits!" The Ass reaches up and drapes her arms around The Tits' neck. The Hair quickly nudges The Ass out of the way. She hovers at The Tits' eye level and places a soft kiss on each cheek.

Powers and Skills:

Her specialty is kicking. Special moves include the Bolt of Thunder, a rapid-fire straight-legged kick, and the Spinning Sparrow, a handstand in which her legs jut out and spin like helicopter blades.

THE HAIR

Game: Fatal
Fighters 3
Release Date: 1994

The Hair is Empress of Nirvania, a realm that exists parallel to Earth's. One thousand years ago, The Hair's beautiful and peaceful land was taken over by Yama Khan, an evil emperor. He sapped Nirvania of its energies and turned it into a wasteland called Niraag. He took The Hair as his wife and used his power to control her son. The Hair couldn't handle the psychological pressure of serving Yama Khan, so she drank an elixir of morning glory seeds. The poisonous liquid contains the power to elevate souls to higher realms. But Yama Khan discovered The Hair in a transitional state and confined her spirit to Niraag. The graphics and sound in Fatal Fighters 3 are vibrant and hypnotic. The game also incorporates a complicated array of secret codes that unlock hidden scenes.

"Tits, my sweet, so glad you could be here tonight," I say. "How are you?"

"I've been better, Madame M," she replies, extracting herself from The Ass and The Hair's attentions. "That actress bitch is still jacking the spotlight in my game's movie spinoffs!"

"I know, dear. I've seen. But you're the original! Nothing can ever change that."

"I guess so." The Tits looks simply dashing (as always). She is tall — six feet even — and her default outfit is a tight black catsuit, black army boots, and a double gun holster across her hips. Her hair is black and tied back in a single waist-length ponytail. The Creators pumped up her breasts to an even more fantastical size in her latest game. They're the largest of any female entity. Like The Ass, she was recently the subject of a patch that allowed Users to strip off her clothes and play her naked. Unlike The Ass, The Tits was deeply disturbed by it.

"Hi, Brain." The Tits chooses a spot on the couch next to The Brain. "How's your game doing?"

"You know how it is in the game-movie combo biz," says The Brain. "It's flying off the shelves."

<DC Timecode: 00:35:53>

"Tits, can I get you a glass of CircuitPlus?" I ask. It's time to get the evening started. In spite of the need to stay alert for my research, I decide to have just one glass as well.

"Cheers, my friends!" I say. Five exquisitely crafted arms clink their glasses to mine: there are muscles, there are delicate lines, there is soft, unblemished skin. "As you all know, I am continuing my work in female character studies. Tonight I was hoping you would speak frankly with me about your roles in the evolution of gaming."

"Sure, Madame M," says The Ass. "Anything I can do to help."

"Some help you'll be," mutters The Hair. "A pixellated wrestling whore."

The Ass reaches in front of The Hair and passes the pretzels The Tits' way.

"I'd like to ask some questions to get the discussion going," I continue. "Legs, you were the first female character in a fighting game. What do you think The Creators had in mind when they released you?"

The Legs blushes. She is not one to take centre stage. "No one had ever seen a girl kick ass before me. However, there is something that has always bothered me."

"What's that?"

"In my game, I am the only one who cries when I lose. And when I win, I jump up and down and squeal like a schoolgirl. I find that embarrassing."

"Not to mention all the peek-a-boo shots of your underwear," quips The Hair. "I mean, lying on the ground after defeat and lifting your thigh just enough to provide a rear shot. That's tasteless."

"Uh-huh," says The Legs, sliding her foot up beside her thigh on the couch and letting her rose-coloured panties show. "And what about you? You're dressed like a horror-show dominatrix."

"Yeah. And how about your lame powers?" The Ass hoots. "Spitting poison balls and melting your opponents with a scream? That is truly pathetic."

"Whoa, whoa," The Brain cuts in. "I think you are missing the point. From where I stand, you have all accomplished a lot. You are strong and independent. If it weren't for you, I wouldn't be the balanced female entity I am today."

"Easy for you to say, Brain," says The Tits as she hefts her bulging breasts with her hands. "You don't have to carry these around. They're lethal weapons."

Powers and Skills:

The Hair levitates at will, spits lethal balls of poison and emits supersonic screams that melt opponents' skin. Watch out if she gets too close, because her hair will wrap you in a cocoon and press the breath from your lungs.

THE TITS

Game: Marauding Maven
Release date: 1996

The Tits was the first female character to star in her own series. Part of the new three-dimensional wave, her games introduced a mix of fighting action and puzzle-solving that revolutionized game play. Clunky and primitive by today's standards, players of the time were amazed by the ability to turn The Tits in all directions. Along with those trademarks came her voluptuous body, Amazonian frame and slightly deformed but gargantuan breasts. The Tits was raised in an old-money family in Boston, Massachusetts. At the age of 19, The Tits met Dr. Harvey Walters and was fascinated by a talk he gave about his career in genetics. Under Walters's tutelage, she became a highly acclaimed geneticist, but she could not

"But you're beautiful, Tits," says The Ass. Her eyes shine as she slides onto the floor and places her hand on The Tits' foot.

The Tits jerks away. "Frankly, I'm sick and tired of everyone focusing on my body. Doesn't anyone care that I am an accomplished geneticist?" A tear glints in The Tits' eye and a hush falls over the room. There is little comfort for The Tits in the way she's been marketed. She downs her glass of CircuitPlus.

<DC Timecode: 00:46:13>
"Ass, I wanted to ask you what you really think about XXX-treme Mud Wrestling," I start. "A lot of people say it's little more than a video-game version of *Playboy*."

"Well, Madame M, I've heard all the talk." The Ass throws The Hair an over-the-shoulder middle finger. "And at first, I must admit, I was appalled at the transplant from a fighting game to a mud wrestling tournament. But the artwork is stunning. The outdoor scenery is rendered right down to individual flowers. Did you see the scene where I take a morning hike and drink from a rushing stream? It's a work of art, I swear!"

"But what does all of that have to do with mud wrestling, dear?" I ask.

"Okay, fine, maybe not a hell of a lot. But at least the game is honest. It was created as a tits-and-ass fest. What's wrong with that?"

The Hair swoops down and wraps her hair around The Ass's waist. "Where do you get off, you spoiled little glut of polygons? After all the work Madame M has done for our cause."

"Hey, Witch-from-the-Crypt! Am I supposed to be the intellectual slave of someone who in twenty years of gaming has never taken the red rose off her head?"

"I can't take my rose off." My chest burns with embarrassment. "I don't have any arms."

The Hair's mouth opens wide. Giant neon-green sound waves cast luminous shadows on the walls. Hands cover ears and eyes squeeze shut as The Ass's bloody flesh lands on thighs, shoulders and lampshades. A moment later, her bones zap out of sight.

"Hair! Not again!" The Legs cries.

The Tits and The Brain shake their heads.

"Oh, she'll be fine after a reset," says The Hair. She crosses her arms and floats to a corner of the room.

The Tits finishes off her glass of CircuitPlus and pours another. "I brought my naked patch along. Do you ladies want to strip down and get in the hot tub?"

"Here Madame M," The Brain gently pulls at my rose, "I'll get that for you."

<DC Timecode: 01:09:21>

The Legs and The Brain glisten in the yellow glow that emanates from the hot-tub. Their long thighs and hips disappear beneath shifting ones and zeros. I bob and tilt along the surface as soft heat laps around my lower jaw. The Tits comes out of the bathroom and eases herself in.

"What happened to The Hair?" asks The Legs.

"Oh, we had a word and she decided to go," says The Tits.

"What did you say to her?"

"I just laid it all out. I told her this silly competition between her and The Ass has to end. I'm not into dating anyone right now, let alone either of them!"

quell her adventurous side. She began a quest to raid and expose secret laboratories where dangerous, immoral and highly profitable genetic research is under way.

Powers and Skills:

The Tits has always been highly athletic. Early on, she took an interest in extreme sports, martial arts and classical weaponry, such as archery and fencing. She is an accomplished markswoman and always carries her beloved 9-mm Beretta. Her other passion is commanding the wheel of a fast car. The Tits prefers to work alone.

*

THE ASS

Game: For Honour
and Glory:
XXX-treme
Mud Wrestling
Release date: 2003

The Ass is one of several female fighting characters in her game's series. She is an elite Ninja assassin who wears several different costumes, from a revealing black and white kimono to a schoolgirl uniform. Relegated to a "fantasy sports simulation," the characters in For Honour and Glory: XXX-treme Mud Wrestling have been lured to a deserted town in the Rocky Mountains and forced to compete in tournaments. The game boasts unseen heights in breast-and-bum physics technology. An entire team worked on a rendering engine that produces an accurate "jiggle factor" as the girls jump, dive and flip. Wisps of hair, blinking eyes and flexing thighs all look phenomenally natural as The Ass and her

"Madame M," The Legs closes her eyes and sighs, "why are we all so violent?"

"It's the way The Creators made you, dear." I tilt my head back. I've had a little more CircuitPlus than I'd planned, and I don't want to think too hard anymore.

The Tits' mouth tightens. "Sometimes I wish I could be the princess in *Giovanni Brothers* or *Monkey Dong*. You know, some helpless girl who hangs around and waits to be rescued."

"You could never live like that," The Brain says. "Can you imagine how boring that would be? We need danger and adventure. But here's what gets me. Have you ever noticed how similar our psychological profiles are?"

"What do you mean?" The Legs asks.

The Brain's finger traces a spiral along the surface. "When was the last time you held hands with a lover? When was the last time you thought about having children? When was the last time you admitted weakness and asked for help?"

"I see what you mean," replies The Tits. "How many times have we been described as tough, independent and cold?"

"Never co-operative, compassionate or caring," I say. "The Creators can't bestow power on a female unless she's an ice queen."

"But you have to admit, Madame M," The Legs interjects, "it's better than putting on a lot of make-up and running around the screen eating JoyPills, which is what you did every day for years."

"And then, to top it all off, chasing a male in between levels so he can knock you up at the end," adds The Brain.

"Ouch," I say. "I love my daughter and I'm really proud of her, but you're right. I have seen the Internet posts that describe me as nothing more than a giant mouth. One User asked how many cocks a jaw like mine could take. Can you believe it?"

"You can't worry about Users like that, Madame M." The Tits puts her hand on my cheek. "They delight in perverting what The Creators give us."

<DC Timecode: 01:20:03>
"So how should we be made then?" The Legs asks.

"I think it's obvious that we have to get past the big boobs, tough attitudes and ultra-violence," says The Brain. "But we don't want to rob ourselves of strength and power. Part of the attraction for The Users is living a fantasy."

"Is that what this is really about?" says The Legs. "I mean most of The Users are male. Sure, a lot of them get off on pretending they're women in digital form, but what's the point of worrying about the image we project to boys?"

"I think it's really important," The Brain responds. "Our composition as the ultimate female powers can affect the opinions male Users form about human girls. And, yes, gaming is still a boys' world, but more females pick up joysticks and controllers every year."

The Tits' eyes rest on The Brain's sunglasses. "Do you ever get the feeling The Creators only care about using us to make money?"

The Brain takes a moment to contemplate. She is newly released and a much more sophisticated, thinking entity. She is also one of the first female characters to be treated on par with male characters in her game. "I think that's part of it, Tits. But I do believe there is a greater purpose."

"Like what?" asks The Tits.

"I agree with some of what The Ass was saying before The Hair toasted her. I think about all the

friends go at it in the muck, throwing mini-tantrums when they lose and emitting gleeful yelps when they win.

Powers and Skills:

The Ass was born with a strong and agile body. Her training elevated her abilities in hand-to-hand combat to fearsome levels. She is highly competitive, becomes spiteful and bitter when she loses, and uses this negative energy to fuel her hunger for battle and bloodshed.

*

THE BRAIN

Game: Rule Your
Destinies
Release date: 2004

You are either with
her or against her. The
Brain shares the lead
in Rule Your Destinies
with a male character
named Shadow. Her
game is derived from
a series of movies in
the physical world
called *Destinies*. The
gaming environment
is a potent mix of
fighting action,
problem-solving and
live action footage
inserted from the film.
The Brain was raised
in a biodome on
Mars, as this was the
only place the last few
thousand human
survivors could find
refuge. She is one of
several humans lead-
ing a rebellion against
out-of-control entities
of artificial intelli-
gence who have colo-
nized the Earth and
human consciousness.

creativity that has gone into rendering our entities.
It is a beautiful and complicated form of art. There
is love and devotion in addition to deviation.

"And what about the dedication of The Users?"
The Brain continues. "They play us for hours and
hours every day. They are obsessed with figuring out
how to wield our powers more wildly or extinguish
them more efficiently. They fantasize about us.
They create digital shrines to us. They paste us
across computer screens in 32-bit pixel glory. It's
nothing short of worship."

"And there's nothing like watching a gorgeous
and powerful woman triumph in the male-dominated field of violence and bloodshed," adds The
Tits.

The Legs places her hand over her foot and
stretches her thigh. "Well, they can program us as
intelligent, skilful, and powerful entities until the
digits come home. What difference is it going to
make when games like *Pimp's Paradise* are still out
there?"

That's true. Watching Vinnie Vincent beat prostitutes to death doesn't help anyone, does it?" The
Brain says.

"Speaking of which," a gleam slides across The
Tits' eyes. "I was invited to Vinnie's room for a party
tonight ..."

"Are you thinking what I'm thinking?" asks The
Legs.

"Let's do it!" shouts The Brain.

"Hold on a second. Didn't you just say we need
to get past the violence?" I cry.

"That's for future releases," The Tits sneers.

"You said it, Madame M. We are programmed
for violence." The Legs cracks her knuckles. "Not a
lot we can do about it."

<DC Timecode: 01:41:22>

We are outside Vinnie's room. I can't quite remember how we got here and at this point, my vision and reasoning are only intermittent flashes.

"Hi, Vinnie," The Tits purrs. She wraps her arms around his neck. The Brain sidles up and kisses his cheek.

The Legs coos, "Can we join the party?"

"Any time, girls." Vinnie's mouth twitches at the left corner. "Luscious ladies like yourselves are always welcome. But ditch Big Mouth, would you?"

"Sorry, darling. She's part of the package," says The Legs.

"All right then." Vinnie gives me a strange look. "You really do look like shit, Madame Mouth. Your mascara is running. And where's your rose?"

Empty bottles of CircuitPlus lie strewn about the room along with lustrous orange capsules I don't recognize. The women from Vinnie's gang of prostitutes are hanging out. He sits down beside the red-haired one and strokes her bare left breast. I guess there's a topless patch for *Pimp's Paradise* now, too.

The Legs, The Brain, The Tits and I knock back one final shot of CircuitPlus. The Legs throws her glass at the window, flips into a handstand and flies around in the Spinning Sparrow Kick. She knocks Vinnie on his ass. The Tits fires a shot and the TV explodes. The Brain yells for the *Pimp's Paradise* girls to follow her lead. It only takes a split second for them to turn on their leader. They pounce on his stomach and deliver sloppy but powerful karate chops. The redhead pulls a knife and slits his neck. As blood sprays around the room, The Tits cries, "Reset him! Let's do it again."

*

Powers and Skills:

The Brain is highly intelligent and skilled in martial arts and hand-to-hand combat. She commands her own interplanetary battleship and her immense skill as a pilot has made it the fastest ship in the rebel fleet. The Brain is also a charismatic leader whose force of will has ensured victory even during the worst of times.

*

From: madame.mouth@fcs.iaai.edu
To: red.wave@fcs.iaai.edu
CC: mighty.aphrodite@fcs.iaai.edu
Subject: Request for Leave

Dear Red and Aphro:

I am writing from the Las Digitas Resort in Southern IO. It was absolutely essential for my mental health that I proceed directly here after the game characters' conference.

I need some time to rethink my research. I have always worked from the assumption that female characters are inherently good and that the gaming environment was the cause of their evil and violent characterizations. Now, I'm not so sure.

I am sorry for the short notice, but I will not be back for a few weeks. As you are well aware, this is my life's work I'm reconsidering.

Yours truly, Madame Mouth

THE DANGER ROOM GIRLS

Sherwin Tjia

Three mutants are currently in the X-Men Mansion Kitchen chat room.

Bullettrain69: i mean, i don't understand why they wear costumes at all. if you were a mutant, why would you want to draw that much attention to yourself?

DV8: So the enemy can't get a hold of you. Same reason why army guys cut their hair short. It's practical.

MoodyGrl has joined the conversation.

Nitro: Hi, MoodyGrl.

MoodyGrl: Hello, Nitro.

Bullettrain69: u would think that the best way to evade somebody would be to slip into a crowd. it's easier to disappear into a crowded street if you just look normal.

MoodyGrl: But then you wouldn't have the fun of a secret identity. :)

Bullettrain69: i don't know about you, but if i were a mutant i wouldn't WANT a public identity. you'd just be, like, a circus freak!

Nitro: Hey, MoodyGrl, what makes you so moody?

MoodyGrl: Sometimes it's fun to hide behind a mask. Sometimes dressing up you can feel kind of invulnerable.

Nitro: I like dressing up.

Nitro is inviting MoodyGrl into the Danger Room. Press Shift+(Y)es to accept or Shift+(N)o to decline.

MoodyGrl declines the invitation.

Bullettrain69: nitro, what IS your problem?

Nitro: What's yours?

Bullettrain69: you've been hitting on moody since she got here.

Nitro: Look, I'm just trying to be social is all. More than u can say.

Bullettrain69: fuck this shit.

Bullettrain69 is inviting MoodyGrl into the Danger Room. Press Shift+(Y)es to accept or Shift+(N)o to decline.

MoodyGrl accepts the invitation.

DV8: You're an idiot.

Nitro: What the hell are you on about?

DV8 has left the X-Men Mansion Kitchen.

Nitro: Fuckhead.

Nitro has left the X-Men Mansion Kitchen.

Bullettrain69 and MoodyGrl have entered the Danger Room.

Bullettrain69: nitro's not always an idiot. just when he knows there's a girl around.

MoodyGrl: Well, thanks, sort of. But I'm not going to be any more forthcoming with you. :)

Bullettrain69: s'no problem. i'm not into girls.

MoodyGrl: You're gay?

Bullettrain69: ha! I'M a girl.

MoodyGrl: Oh! Then why wasn't Nitro hitting on you?

Bullettrain69: he doesn't know and he's never asked.

MoodyGrl: I'm kind of new here. You've probably guessed. :)

Bullettrain69: not that many girls in the X-men fansite chat room. more since the movies have come out. but it's always been a little scarce here — girl-wise, i mean.

MoodyGrl: Maybe I should change my moniker so I'm not such an easy target.

Bullettrain69: you could just shorten it to moody.

MoodyGrl: Maybe next time I log into the Mansion chat room. Why'd you choose Bullettrain69?

Bullettrain69: it has to do with my powers. ;)

MoodyGrl: Hee hee! You're a mutant too?

Bullettrain69: we're ALL muties here!

MoodyGrl: What's your power?

Bullettrain69: i can fly.

MoodyGrl: Oh yeah? Prove it.

Bullettrain69: can't. they'd send the army after me. capture me. study me. you know.

MoodyGrl: I know. They'd do the same thing to me. They'd want to cut me open to see what makes me tick, like an alien autopsy or something.

Bullettrain69: ok, moodster, i told u mine. now u show me yours.

MoodyGrl: It's not a GREAT power or anything.

Bullettrain69: power's power — wot is it?

MoodyGrl: I don't know. It's stupid. I've got a kind of useless power. Nothing like you.

Bullettrain69: no power's useless. wot is it for chrissakes?!!!!

MoodyGrl: My skin changes colour.

Bullettrain69: oh. u mean like you can turn into a black person?

MoodyGrl: How do you know I'm not one already? :)

Bullettrain69: oh fuck, sorry. *blush*

MoodyGrl: Hee hee. No, I'm not Black.

Bullettrain69: are u asian? I'M asian.

MoodyGrl: Nope. Garden-variety white person. Mostly Scottish. I had a grandfather who was Polish. But that's still white, I suppose.

Bullettrain69: but CAN you turn black? if u wanted to?

MoodyGrl: That's not the kind of colour-changing I mean. I mean that —

Bullettrain69: wait — are u like a chameleon?

MoodyGrl: No, nothing fancy like that. I just turn different shades of red, blue and green. I can't coordinate it or anything so that I blend into the background. It doesn't work that way for me.

Bullettrain69: oh. well, can you do anything else?

MoodyGrl: Something else happens, but it's really stupid. I mean, I hate that it happens.

Bullettrain69: wot is it?

MoodyGrl: I mean, this is embarrassing, but when I get really angry, I get paralyzed.

Bullettrain69: wot?

MoodyGrl: When I'm absolutely furious, my body shuts down. I literally can't move. I can feel it too. I have to sit down and pretend that I'm resting until I get over it and can move again.

Bullettrain69: that's intense.

MoodyGrl: Yeah. It's less a "power" and more of a "disempower." :)

Bullettrain69: it's kind of the reverse of the Hulk. when he gets mad that's how he BECOMES powerful.

MoodyGrl: Yeah. Anyway, that's why I'm pretty chill most of the time. I can't afford not to be!

Bullettrain69: wow. that sucks ass. you really ARE a mutant, aren't you?

MoodyGrl: I've never really told anyone that before.

Bullettrain69: fakers never make up CRAPPY powers. they always have, like, laser beams coming out of their cocks or something.

MoodyGrl: All right already. My powers suck. I know.

Bullettrain69: sorry. i mean, i meet a lot of role-playing dudes on this site.

MoodyGrl: I'm hoping that as I get older I'll develop other powers. Maybe something to compensate for the ones I have. I always keep this pocket mirror handy. A lot of times I have to hide when I change colours. Other times I just use a lot of foundation. My friends think I'm completely vain because I wear so much makeup. It's such a hassle. What a fucked-up power. I always used to read the X-Men and feel completely inadequate. :)

Bullettrain69: yah — they'd probably keep you back at the mansion. ;)

MoodyGrl: Maybe with Wolverine. Mmmrowr.

Bullettrain69: yah, he's not bad in the movies.

MoodyGrl: I saw the second one, like, four times. Looking at him, I just feel safe, you know. Like, we could take a nap together. And THEN I would jump him.

Bullettrain69: :)

MoodyGrl: Have you met any other mutants on this site?

Bullettrain69: not so much muties as — well, this one girl's kinda a mutant. she's an astral projector down in wisconsin. that's as far as it goes — powers-wise — but she can do it every night.

MoodyGrl: That must be so cool! I tried to do that once. There was this book where you could coach yourself.

Bullettrain69: she even wanted me to test her. first, i had to give her the EXACT directions to my house, right? and then i was supposed to write something on a piece of paper and put it somewhere that was pretty inaccessible but that was lit.

MoodyGrl: Did it work?

Bullettrain69: so i wrote down the title of the pj harvey song "who will love me now?" on a piece of cardboard and stashed it in the attic, by the only window up there. it's this dusty number with cobwebs and shit. you can't see through it, but it lets light in. and the day after, she tells me exactly what i wrote. she even knew that i wrote it down with this big fat silver marker.

MoodyGrl: That's awesome! She'd make the perfect spy.

Bullettrain69: i know — but she's the kinda mutant that the army would make mincemeat of.

MoodyGrl: Hmm. But now that I think about it, how do we know she's telling the truth? Maybe she's a mind reader and she's just telling you she can astral-project because she doesn't want to freak you out.

Bullettrain69: she can mind-read over the internet?

MoodyGrl: I don't know. I haven't thought this out. :)

Bullettrain69: well, she told me that she's scared of doing it too much because she doesn't like being out of her body for too long a stretch. she begins to feel disconnected from it, like she's this balloon that's flying away into the atmosphere.

MoodyGrl: Jesus — imagine if she fell asleep in the backseat of a car? How would she know where to go back to?

Bullettrain69: she'd be fucked, no doubt about it. tho, she'd probably just go home.

MoodyGrl: Her parents would think she was dead.

Bullettrain69: yah, they'd take her to the hospital once they realized they couldn't wake her.

MoodyGrl: Have you met this girl?

Bullettrain69: we did an on-line chat once, where we both had our cams on. i kinda floated in front of it to show her. she was all, like, envious. she wished she could REALLY fly, instead of projecting, because a lot of times it feels too ghostly. but i was, like, you're gorgeous! this girl's really pretty. i told her that's kind of a superpower too. hey — do you have a computer cam? we could hook them up.

MoodyGrl: No, sorry. Our package didn't come with one.

Bullettrain69: s'okay. no worries.

MoodyGrl: Hey, so tell me about flying.

Bullettrain69: i have to admit — it's pretty awesome.

MoodyGrl: I would imagine. Can you go very high?

Bullettrain69: well, i've been high enough that i start having problems breathing. i mean, the air is really thin up there. i suppose i could bring up an OXYGEN TANK or something, but i've never really gotten around to it. also it gets cold.

MoodyGrl: How fast can you go?

Bullettrain69: it's not like — you know how in the books, they always have, like, these power cocktails? where, like, rogue can fly, and absorb people's powers, and she's not INVULNERABLE or anything, but she can crash into walls and, like, break the walls. well, i'm not like that. i can fly, that's about it.

MoodyGrl: :) That's enough.

Bullettrain69: yah — it's pretty sweet. but i can't go terribly fast or anything. i mean, i can, but again, i have trouble breathing. it's like when you're in a car on the highway, and you're bombing along and you stick your head out the window — you know what i mean?

MoodyGrl: Yeah. You're going so fast you have difficulty inhaling.

Bullettrain69: it's like that. so i don't fly very high or very fast. also, if i slam into a wall at 50 klicks or whatever, i'm, like, severely injured or dead. i could break my neck.

MoodyGrl: Jesus! Do you wear a helmet or anything?

Bullettrain69: nah — i don't wear one when i'm riding my bike, either! :) you have to really bundle up to do it, tho, even on warm nights. it's just cold. oh — and don't fly after you eat. i've barfed. sometimes it's like going on a roller-coaster. especially when the weather's unstable.

MoodyGrl: Could you always fly?

Bullettrain69: nah. it started around puberty. it was weird. i started dreaming about it first. in these dreams i'd be running along and i'd jump and i'd stay in the air as long as i held my breath. as i let my breath out, i'd float slowly back down.

MoodyGrl: That's the opposite of swimming!

Bullettrain69: hmm! i never thought of it that way before. i used to dream about it constantly. then, in one dream — i'll never forget — i stopped holding my breath, and i kept floating. i kept floating higher and higher, and suddenly i was upside down, floating back toward the earth and when my hands touched it, i woke up. i was touching the ceiling of my room.

Bullettrain69: i was so scared, i just hung there. i didn't know what to do. it took me a while to figure out how to get down — how to relax enough to be able to control it. but the funny thing was i stopped dreaming about it when i started going out at night and doing it.

MoodyGrl: Because you started living it.

Bullettrain69: yah, i suppose.

MoodyGrl: You ever fly out to Montreal? :)

Bul.ettrain69: where's that?

MoodyGrl: Hold on —

Bulettrain69: ok

MoodyGrl: I gotta go — my mom's driving downtown and I can grab a ride with her. Montreal's kind of eastern Canada. North of NYC. Where are you?

Bulettrain69: i'm not too far from there — Brooklyn.

MoodyGrl: You should come on up sometime.

Bulettrain69: sounds sweet — my e-mail's

bullettrain69@netscape.net.

MoodyGrl: Cool! Mine's inconsolablecat@hotmail.com.

Bulettrain69: how inconsolable r u?

MoodyGrl: Not very. I just say that to invite consolation.

Bulettrain69: ha! all right — i'll be in touch.

MoodyGrl: Do. It was great to meet you.

Bulettrain69: cheers!

MoodyGrl: :)

MoodyGrl has left the Danger Room.
Bullettrain69 has left the Danger Room.

SUFFRAGETTES, VIGILANTES AND SUPERHEROES
ONE GIRL'S GUIDE TO CHICKS IN COMICS

Elizabeth Walker

I read comic books as a kid, but this isn't a confession. I can't tell you how embarrassed I was reading them or how I hid them behind issues of *Teen Beat* and *Seventeen*. Comics are cool again these days but this isn't a revenge-of-the-nerds story. I was an average 1970s kid with rather average interests and I grew into a pretty average adult.

The truth is, I only read the comics that fell across my path, and I rarely sought them out beyond stretching lazily for another from an available stack. In this fashion, I read *Archie*, horror comics, occasional scraps of pornography, and *Mad* magazine. I read that which had been abandoned by others, discarded in boxes in empty lots, or tied in garbage bags and left in attics and basements. I read them in greedy gluts and forgot most of them instantly.

I didn't wonder much about the girls I saw in those panels, though I was aware that they all pretty much looked the same. Except for hair colour, of course, and very occasionally in skin colours that hurtled from one sick hue to another. Eventually comics ceased to cross my path and, already a bespectacled book reader, I did not mourn their absence.

Tim Burton's 1989 movie adaptation of *Batman* made comics nerdy-cool again and in the early 1990s a friend left a box of graphic novels in my possession. I spent an entire Montreal winter hidden in a basement apartment reading the Hernandez brothers' *Love & Rockets*, Frank

Miller's *Batman: The Dark Knight Returns*, Alan Moore's classics: *Swamp Thing*, *The Watchmen*, and *V for Vendetta*, and, of course, *The Sandman*, penned by Neil Gaiman. I was enthralled. I emerged the following spring forever changed. While stubbing out cigarettes and spilling pints of beer on terraces, I argued with classmates that comics were in fact the stuff of modern myth and were every bit as subtle, complex and gratifying as anything we read for university.

But it didn't take too many trips to the local comics shop to realize I was a tourist in the world of comics, and the locals — all guys — let me know it. They scoffed because I didn't know who took over writing this or that title in the mid 1980s, or how some minor character was killed in issue #48 only to come back two years later in an alternate universe as some other hero. They scoffed because I was a chick, reading the soft stuff in graphic novels, and because I didn't collect comics obsessively, competitively, and to the detriment of my social life. They scoffed because I wasn't suffering.

"Losers," I sneered to myself as I stalked out. "Lonely masturbators. Fuck them. I'm not playing power games with these boys." I never understood how a passion for comics meant memorizing stats as if they were baseball players. This is pop culture, people, not homework. So for the purposes of this article I'm not enumerating every last girl sidekick or nameless female hack who inked half of one issue of *Amazing Woman* so I can write a eulogy to her obscure, forgotten brilliance. But I will try to whet your appetite because honest-to-god enthusiasm is one of the great lost virtues of a too self-conscious age. So relax; digging comics is pretty safe and you don't have to apply for a club membership.

For this article, I sought counsel from friends who love comics. They all had the same reaction: "Oooh, what about so-and-so? I adore her." They sang the praises of fave local artists, manga from Japan, on-line comics, and a slew of chicks working in DIY circles. They made me want to go out and read more. I nodded and wrote the titles down thinking, *there sure doesn't seem to be a lack of women in comics.*

So what did I discover in the pile of new books that had been enthusiastically recommended? Women are everywhere these days. They are on the page and behind the drawing table. Female characters are just as prevalent as guys in the pages of alternative comics and graphic novels. There are girls in comic shops and bookstores. They chatter about the latest *Chobits* and *Berlin* and wear *Tank Girl* T-shirts. They make their own mini-comix and trade them at conventions.

But there are still relatively few women working on mainstream action comics. And while there's plenty of T&A in the pages of mainstream comics, that's not the kind of female presence I'm looking for.

Female cartoonists have always plied their art wherever they could get whatever work people would let them do. But by taking small steps, one or two or three women suddenly became a small movement, and notions shifted just a little in one direction (or another) and a little more room was won (or lost). I've tried to ferret out some of those women — both artists and characters — who made their own leaps and bounds.

I'LL SEE YOU IN THE FUNNY PAGES: GIRLS IN THE EARLY DAYS

Comics didn't really exist as we know them until the 1930s. Before the exploits of heroes became the stuff of comic books, cartoonists plied their craft in the family-oriented Sunday newspaper. Rose O'Neill, already a successful commercial artist, added some word balloons to her sweet nursery tableaux about the cupid-inspired "Kewpie" babies and leaped into comics history. Ornate and sentimental, the whimsy of the Kewpies corrected by gentle example the adult world which lay just beyond the gutters and frames. The Kewpie became the first great comics licence, iconic image and toy of the early twentieth century. Unlike many creators, O'Neill controlled the licence and grew rich. Financially independent, O'Neill lived scandalously; she married and divorced twice, lived openly with a male lover, and was a vocal supporter of votes for women. She employed her lisping Kewpies for a Suffragette promotional postcard in which the quizzical darlings were accompanied by the following text:

> Isn't it a funny thing
> That Father cannot see
> Why Mother ought to have a vote
> On how these things should be?[1]

The disconnect between gender (and generations) remains cartoon fodder to this day, but in the 1920s there was a craze for what they called "flapper strips," in which a fashionable heroine confounded family and friends with her ditzy, slap-happy, thoroughly modern logic. Take *Dumb Dora* (by *Blondie*'s Chic Young); more concerned with clothes, parties and boys than with everyday life, Dora turned middle-class convention on its head. Dora's readers celebrated the trivial with her, and every strip ended with the same money shot: "She ain't so dumb!" But Dora never asked for more than makeup and dates; "dumb Dora" was hip slang in the 1920s for a not-too-bright modish chick. Eventually the champagne wit of Dora and her flapper sisters went flat when the Depression hit and newspaper readers favoured the weekly cartoons of drama and adventure.

From 1924 until his death in 1968, Harold Gray's *Little Orphan Annie* became an enduring icon of the Dirty Thirties. Annie had no eyes, just spooky white holes, but she was plucky, wore a bright red dress and scrambled through the dangers that typically vex impossibly rich little girls — to great acclaim.

In contrast, Martha Orr's Depression wasn't that much fun. In 1932 she started *Apple Mary*, a strip about a woman who lost everything in 1929 and was reduced to selling apples from a cart she wheeled through slum streets. Every week, she negotiated trouble with slum landlords, difficult neighbours and angry young men, always defending the weakest and dispensing sage advice. Not the stuff of action and adventure. Martha Orr gave up control of *Apple Mary* in 1940 and (*leapin' lizards!*) *Apple Mary* became *Mary Worth,* Sunday page war horse and trite melodrama. (Writing was taken over by a man, Allen Saunders. I'm not saying there's a connection.) Have a look at *Mary Worth*, over sixty years later. What's all the tension and tears about? Seriously.

GIRLS UNDER COVER

In the UK, tradition forbade cartoonists from signing their work, so many, male *and* female, are lost to us. However, in the US, cartoonists could become famous household names. But two female cartoonists needed gender-neutral pseudonyms to get a foot in the door and make *their* name in comics.

Tarpe Mills created one of the first female superheroes when socialite, Miss Fury, donned a magic panther skin for a costume party and found herself with amazing new powers she used to right the wrongs of society. Thanks to her odd pen name, artist June Mills got her start in the 1930s drawing adventure comics for a largely male readership. Mills was a "good girl" artist, though good-girl art was anything but. An illustration style that emerged from horror and adventure magazines, it featured "good girls" in extraordinary states of terror and undress, who twisted trembling breasts toward the reader. The style became widespread, and a talent for titillation overcame social barriers when big money was at stake. Mills favoured Nazis, nipples, stilettos, leather and whips; and she had the distinction of being pulled from the shelves for being too controversial. Mills proved that a female artist could dish out the dirty as nastily as anyone.

Maybe you've never heard of the 1992 movie *Brenda Starr* (Anchor Bay Studios) starring Brooke Shields. It was a flop, but not for lack of story: Brenda Starr is a glamorous investigative reporter with flaming red hair who solves crimes and gets into danger while following scoops. Initially Starr was supposed to be a bandit, but creator Dalia Messick had been unsuccessful at getting a drawing gig until she sat down together with *Chicago Tribune* secretary Mollie Slott and hammered out a pitch for *Brenda Starr*, in which Starr became a girl reporter. Dalia submitted the proposal under the name Dale Messick. It was immediately accepted and has run continuously since 1940. During her long career, Dalia fought to be accepted by her fellow creators: "It was always the same story. They couldn't believe I could draw because I was a woman. They would just put my samples away and say, *Come on honey, let's go out and talk things over.*"[2]

One of her colleagues even offered the following dick-brained assessment of her problems: "It was very difficult for her to overcome with talent that tremendous beauty. She was extraordinarily pretty and it was hard to get around."[3] This pissed Messick off and she remains vocal about it to this day, even after her retirement in 1980 at the age of seventy-five. Since then, the writing and drawing of Brenda Starr has remained in the hands of women, which makes it difficult to understand why the Hollywood movie featured a male cartoonist bent over the drawing board bringing Brenda Starr to life and thereby erasing her back story.

WONDER WOMEN: HOW DOES SHE DO IT? I MEAN, IN THOSE HEELS?

Before superheroes, there were private eyes, cops and vigilantes. The first female vigilante hero was the Lady in Red, a woman who stalked the streets at night in a hooded cape (a sensible choice for nocturnal activities). She didn't last long. The first female superhero was actually

Nelvana of the Northern Lights, a Canadian creation. In fact, creator Adrian Dingle credited Frank Johnston of the Group of Seven with the concept of Nelvana and he first put the Northern Lights to page in the summer of 1941. Named for the mythological figure of Nelvana, from an Inuit legend, she was reasonably outfitted in fur (it would be Gortex these days, I'm sure), and fought World War II on behalf of the Allies until 1947, when she was retired. Her superpowers? She could fly, travel at the speed of light on a ray of the Aurora Borealis, and, like a good Canadian, turn invisible. I think a Heritage Minute is in order.[4]

A paradoxical wisdom prevails regarding superwomen's costumes and life expectations. It seems the more revealing and least life-preserving costumes extend the heroine's shelf-life indefinitely, while sensibly-clad heroines often find their young lives cut short by wary executives. The awesomely titled comic book, *Jet Dream and the Stunt-Girl Counterspies*, written back in 1968, is one such spirited example. An A-Team of professional stunt girls wield high-tech tools, vehicles and weapons. They battle crime wearing comparatively modest neck-to-ankle white cat suits. Their mothers might've pointed out that it's tough getting axle grease out of that white fabric, but the girls never made it home to do laundry. They lasted one issue.

In contrast, Wonder Woman has a tight busty costume and a penchant for getting tied up that keeps her popular to this day. To be fair, at the time of her creation in 1941, Wonder Woman wore a knee-length skirt, but the life of this heroine has been extended by the dramatic shrinking of her costume. Every time she gets "edgier" in order to appeal to a new audience, her body gets more distorted. Thank god she can fly now, because she probably can't walk.

But the fact is, the average superheroine's life expectancy in mainstream comics isn't high at the best of times. Gail Simone, the head writer of the DC comic book for the WB series *Birds of Prey*, spent some time investigating the phenomenon. She discovered that when writers need a tragic climax to push sales, they often kill a girl, whose death usually occurs off-panel to preserve the all-important climax of discovery by the hero. The hero swears revenge and goes back to his physical exertions imbued with brooding new meaning. All too often, aunts, girlfriends and sisters meet their unhappy end this way.

As a result, most superheroines are in danger, because they hardly ever spring ex nihilo; usually they are molded from Superboy's rib, as his crime bustin' *sister*. They are less powerful than their brothers, and *always* significantly less clothed. She-Hulk is an exemplary sister-hero. Bruce Banner's cousin, Jennifer, became affected by the same radiation that turns Bruce into a green mass of muscle and lower brain functions. *Cool!* Imagine the crazy stories that could develop out of a woman in a powerfully raw state! Well, Jennifer's puny human creators couldn't imagine any of them. Instead, she was permanently changed into the sarcastic and somewhat impatient She-Hulk, a muscular six-foot-tall green woman clad only in heels and a gymnast's body suit. Jennifer fights crime at night and then goes home to her handsome and largely silent Native American lover, who rubs her green feet.

THAT AIN'T ME BABE: UNDERGROUND COMIX DRAW THEIR OWN CONCLUSIONS

In the 1960s, the counter culture gave birth to underground "comix." In New York and San Francisco, artists like Robert Crumb and Vaughn Bodé were drawing stories that reflected taboo-breaking youth culture. Always skirting the obscene, underground comix liberated depictions of sex and relationships. For the first time, adult issues were directly addressed in comic books, but depressingly, when these groundbreaking male cartoonists savagely satirized American mores it was at the expense of women. Pick up any Crumb collection or check out Terry Zwigoff's movie biopic of Crumb to see how screwed up he is when it comes to the ladies. However, spare yourself the indignity of watching the movie adapted from his *Fritz the Cat* comix. Crumb disowned the film, but when you watch a headless female creature being fucked in her neck that doesn't seem to matter.

Female cartoonists of the period were drawn to the new territory of underground comix but as women they felt (ahem) alienated by much of what they saw. So a group of female cartoonists got together to form the Wimmin's Comix Collective and began creating work dealing with issues of particular concern to women such as menstruation, female sexuality, pregnancy and wife abuse. In 1970, they self-published their first comic, *It Ain't Me Babe,* and followed it up in 1973 with their first of many collections, *Wimmin's Comix #1,* which has been regarded as a milestone in underground comix ever since. It also marks an important contribution to comics publishing: the collective functioned under a rotating editorship so every woman got a turn at leadership. The majority of the next decade's most influential female cartoonists such as Aline Kominsky, Melinda Gebbie, and Roberta Gregory came from the collective, which ultimately disbanded in the 1980s as the core group of women went on to other pursuits like publishing the infamous collections *Tits & Clits*, *Dyke Shorts* and *Twisted Sisters*.

Trina Robbins was one of the founding sisters of the collective and she published the first forthright lesbian comic, *Sandy Comes Out*, and later, *Go Girl!*, about a smart and sensibly clad teenage superheroine for younger female readers. Robbins has since become the foremost historian of women in comics. Her books include *From Girls to Grrlz: A History of Women's Comics from Teens to Zines* (1999, with Carla Sinclair), *A Century of Women Cartoonists* (1993, with Dave Schreiner), and *The Great Women Superheroes* (1996). The books represent decades of research, of combing through forgotten back issues, uncovering cartoonists and creations, and restoring their names and art to the public memory. Thanks to Robbins's endless hard work, these women artists are now receiving the professional respect and critical appraisal they deserve in magazines like *The Comics Journal* and *Comic Art*.

MY LIFE: THE COMIC BOOK

The notion that, before the Wimmin's Collective, women only had *Betty & Veronica* comics to read is a worn-out cliché. Contrary to popular belief, in the late 1940s and early 1950s, romance comics were all the rage among female readers. Echoing your every desire — lurid or sentimental — and featuring your choice of good girls or bad girls, over forty best-selling comics with tales of forbidden love appeared monthly. Swarms of teens, nurses and secretaries (judging by the comics' heroines) learned a steamy vocabulary of gestures and emotions from these sensationalized morality tales of fallen women and virtuous gals.

When the 1980s rolled around, the Wimmin's Collective started writing about the things they did between the sex, drugs and rock 'n' roll. The confessional age had begun. Imaginative and whimsical, sharp and funny, or godawfully narcissistic and boring, women began depicting themselves and their lives on paper. Suddenly, there were comics that obsessed openly over relationships, motherhood, women's work, and — of course — body image. Woman comic artists broke new ground, and a range of experiences that had never before been aired found their way into the photocopied and stapled mini-comix as well as the Sunday funny pages. (O god! O *Cathy!*)

But *Cathy* aside, consider *For Better or Worse*. Canadian cartoonist Lynne Johnston's strip may seem like it's about stodgy family matters, but twenty years ago it was a brand new concept. It depicts the daily life of a busy, tired, conflicted modern mom. It's one of the few contemporaneous works that actually ages its characters alongside its readers (*Blondie* take note). These days Johnston's creation, Elly, is even wrestling with empty nest syndrome. Always compassionate toward her characters and never sensationalist, Johnston tackles issues as they come to the door of a sheltered, happy, white middle class family. Johnston has confronted her syndicated audiences with controversial subjects like infidelity, death, anorexia, and (most famously) the issues of homosexuality and gay marriage.

But Johnston's audiences haven't always accepted her work for better or for worse; strips featuring Lawrence, her gay character, have been banned on a number of occasions. And if you are still having difficulty with the idea of identifying yourself as a feminist on the grounds that times have really changed since our mothers burned their bras, then you need to know that Lynne Johnston had to wait until 1997 to become the first woman inducted into the International Museum of Cartoon Art. Worse yet, in the syndicated world, where the wretchedly embarrassing Cathy is the only girl strip represented on some funny pages, it wasn't until 1991 that Barbara Brandon's strip *Where I'm Comin' From* finally became America's first nationally syndicated mainstream comic strip by a Black female cartoonist. It runs to this day.

Outside the US, it was rare to find family friction as a source of amusement. For instance, while it's unusual to find a family strip in post World War II Japan, it's not unusual to find female artists. In fact, a popular native tradition of cartooning, or manga, saw many Japanese women working successfully as writers and artists. In Japan a woman could distinguish herself as an artist and reach the kind of fame achieved by male cartoonists in the West. Machiko Hasegawa did just that with Japan's first family strip, *Sazae-san*, about an overbearing Japanese mother, which ran from 1946 until Machiko's retirement in 1992.

The best female cartoonists have shifted their genres by re-examining subject and content. In the 1970s, a group of well-known Japanese woman artists came to be known as the Magnificent 24 because so many of them were born in 1949 (the Japanese year Showa 24). Moto Magio, Yumiko Oshima, Keiko Takemiya and Ryoko Yamagishi are the best known of this coterie of artists which changed the world of manga. Inspired by Hideko Mizuno's 1963 *Silver Flower Petals*, a popular series about a medieval princess with a sword who rides the countryside on horseback, the Magnificent 24 went on to introduce bold new cartoon stories for girls (known at home as shojo manga) that would find male and female admirers around the world. Manga readers loved heroines who could kick ass and shed a few tears too.

Without the influence of the Magnificent 24, the world would probably not have been introduced to the ultimate shojo manga, *Sailor Moon*, the cartoon about five crime-fighting girls in mini middies with magic rings. It was launched in 1991 by twenty-four-year-old Naoko Takeuchi, who grew up reading the Magnificent 24. A professional cartoonist since age fifteen, Naoko's study of shojo shows in all the fierce action, the trembling, choked-up romance subplots, the unnerving prevalence of panty shots, and the sly homoerotic tension.

THE 1980S

(OR THE RENAISSANCE OF COMIC BOOKS)

The 1970s saw a lot of changes in traditional comics. The impact of underground comix and distopian SF comics from the UK created a new atmosphere in which superheroes flourished. Ironic re-evaluations of the role of the superhero in society had given rise to a darker, more complex kind of comic book, and the straight-up superhero was bound for extinction. By the 1980s, sales were peaking and just about every idea was given a shot on paper to see if audiences would go for it. Not every character was a hit, but the new focus on superheroes' complex personalities and relationships provided rich material for storylines.

The *X-Men's* Storm is just such a character. She was introduced in the 1980s as part of an international brigade of heroes come to inject the team with new verve. An African queen with power over weather, she became the team's funky mohawk-and-leather-jacket-sporting powerhouse and even eventually led the group. A queen used to authority, it is for the sake of justice that Storm becomes an underground renegade with a group of American mutant teenagers. Unlike them, she was never treated as an outcast by her society and doesn't suffer emotionally for being different. She doesn't doubt herself or long for normalcy.

However, after spending the last twenty years surrounded by whining American teenagers, she may be ready to return to Africa.

The superhero-as-political-soldier has also been the basis for some of the most brilliant writing, such as Alan Moore's *The Watchmen* and Frank Miller's vigilante Batman in *The Dark Knight Returns.* Miller, one of the most successful creators of the past twenty years, pushed the idea even further in his most daring comic, about a young Black girl hell-bent on saving the world from the tyranny of liberalism. Published by Dark Horse, *Martha Washington* goes up against the ray guns and dark conspiracies of the military-industrial complex in a paranoid future America. Washington is not really a superhero, she's a toughened refugee from a fascist welfare state, and she looks as mean, miserable, and tired as you would expect a woman full of Ayn Rand's philosophy to be. Though she longs for a return to the days of her squalid childhood, and dreams about her mother at night, Martha is a steely-eyed crusader who owes as much to Riply (from *Aliens*) as to Batman.

IN COMICS, BEST FRIENDS R FOREVER

Bust followed boom and by the mid 1990s, mainstream action comics were a rapidly shrinking industry. The best comics were being produced by small independent companies and they weren't about superheroes at all — or about normal people. The 1990s saw lots of comics about the quirky lives of loners and misfits, and many of the best creations featured female friends scraping through life together in the quest for something true. Interestingly, most of them were still drawn and written by men.

Francine and Katchoo, the madcap friends in Terry Moore's *Strangers in Paradise*, (Abstract Studios) stick together despite their slapstick hijinks in love, at work and in the world at large. Suburban-bored Enid and Rebecca from Dan Clowes' *Ghost World* (Fantagraphics) slowly drift apart as the end of high school forces them to confront their ideas of being adults and authentic people. Enid's a girl with a normal figure who wouldn't make fun of your spectacles or your comic book/vintage toy/record collections. (Wait, maybe that's a fantasy after all.) In the entirely deadpan *Why I Hate Saturn* by Kyle Baker, writer and alcoholic Anne goes on a cross-country road trip to find Laura, her beautiful, demented sister.

As different as these comics are, the girl heroes share a common heritage as they are the inevitable daughters of Hopey and Maggie, from the Hernandez brothers' long running 1980s comic-book series *Love & Rockets* (Fantagraphics). Best friends since high school, punks Maggie and Hopita live in a magic-realist Los Angeles where monsters, wrestlers and punk bands exist alongside dinosaurs, superheroes and celebrity mechanics. These kick-ass Latinas drink beer from cans and cruise the boulevards. Maggie moons over boys and Hopey tags walls. They have fights and misunderstandings. They are occasional lovers. Over the years, Maggie's weight has fluctuated and she's had some bad hair days, but it's never a big deal because she's always the foxiest thing in tight jeans. Maggie is far more famous, and rightly so, for her succession of odd jobs: international mechanic, wrestling manager and even — for a short while — superhero Ultimax's sidekick, Go-Go Girl. Maggie, like many female readers, observed after her first day in spandex: "How did the old Go-Go Girl fight in this thing?"

It is remarkable that many of the most enduring female characters from alternative comics were created by male artists who grew up under the spell of both action and underground comics. They turned from superpowers to super cool girls, maybe the kind of girls they would have liked to meet while they were geeky boys reading comics alone in their rooms. The influence of the mainstream comics is faintly visible though, under the fab haircuts and lesbian chic. There are just as many cliffhangers and sudden rescues, costume changes abound, and the girls discover that masks don't always come off at the end of the day.

These days, most girls at your average zine-fest and alternative comix conventions are what I call *Enids*: bespectacled, dark-haired girls in cardigans and black boots, bent over their ironic clip art chapbooks, making new barrettes out of discarded junk, hot glue, and glitter. I wonder if it's a case of the-chicken-or-the-egg. Did the girls exist first, or did the cartoonists imagine them into reality? The first and most famous Enid is Joyce Brabner, Harvey Pekar's wife, frequently depicted in his long-running Dark Horse comic-book series and the 2003 movie adaptation, *American Splendor* (Fine Line Features). Harvey's comics have always been about his life and friends, and *American Splendor* makes it clear that girls like Joyce have always existed wherever comics are being made. All hair, neuroses, and owlish glasses, Joyce was Harvey's biggest fan and, soon after taking up a written correspondence with him, she became his wife. No one makes a better Enid icon; Joyce defies the line between fiction and reality. She's Harvey's nagging wife, victim of his misanthropy, often sourly portrayed in his works. She's his muse and manager, protecting him when he works and selling his merch. Joyce was his caretaker when Harvey was diagnosed with cancer, and his co-writer when they depicted their struggles in the very moving and funny 1994 graphic novel *Our Cancer Year* (Four Walls, Eight Windows).

Over the years, the most enduring superheroes are symbols of a set of attitudes and behaviors; icons that mutate to reflect our complex responses toward their symbolic natures. Change is a crucial ingredient of success as new characters slip into significance every day. Superman does not just symbolize power and justice, he's also the incarnation of our faith and hope in power. Batman reflects our ambivalence toward the vigilante. Through the contradictory storylines and personalities of *Wonder Woman*, we can study the revelations of history.

Despite the decades of revision, Wonder Woman prevails as an icon of feminism (she was even *Ms* magazine's first cover girl in 1972[5]) that readers find compelling instead of threatening. She is perhaps as important for her singularity as for the ideals she personifies, and all subsequent heroines are but a variation of her, right down to the tight little suit. As long as the Wonder Woman icon fills our field of vision, we can't see the other female heroes or develop new attitudes toward female power. Perhaps we need to look away from the traditional comic superheroine altogether to find more worthy feminist icons.

I nominate *Love and Rocket*'s dynamic duo, Maggie and Hopey, for their angry virtue and comedic spirit. To readers, they are *the* underground princesses, in possession of a priceless friendship and denizens of the hardcore record shop. Put me down for a T-shirt featuring these two heroines, blowing each other kisses and giving us the finger.

*

NOTES

1. Trina Robbins, *The Great Woman Cartoonists* (New York: Watson Guptil, 2001), 41.

2. Maurice Horn, ed. *The World Encyclopedia of Comics* (Philadelphia: Chelsea House, 1999), 527.

3. Attributed to Mike Grell. Steve Duin and Mike Richardson, *Comics: Between the Panels* (Portland: Dark Horse, 1998).

4. A "Heritage Minute" is a sixty-second TV spot produced by the Canadian government highlighting contributions by Canadians to culture and history. They can be pretty funny (not intentionally). There's one about Joe Schuster, a kid from Toronto, who had an idea for a strong man in tights who could leap over buildings in a single bound.

5. *Ms* magazine #1, July 1972.

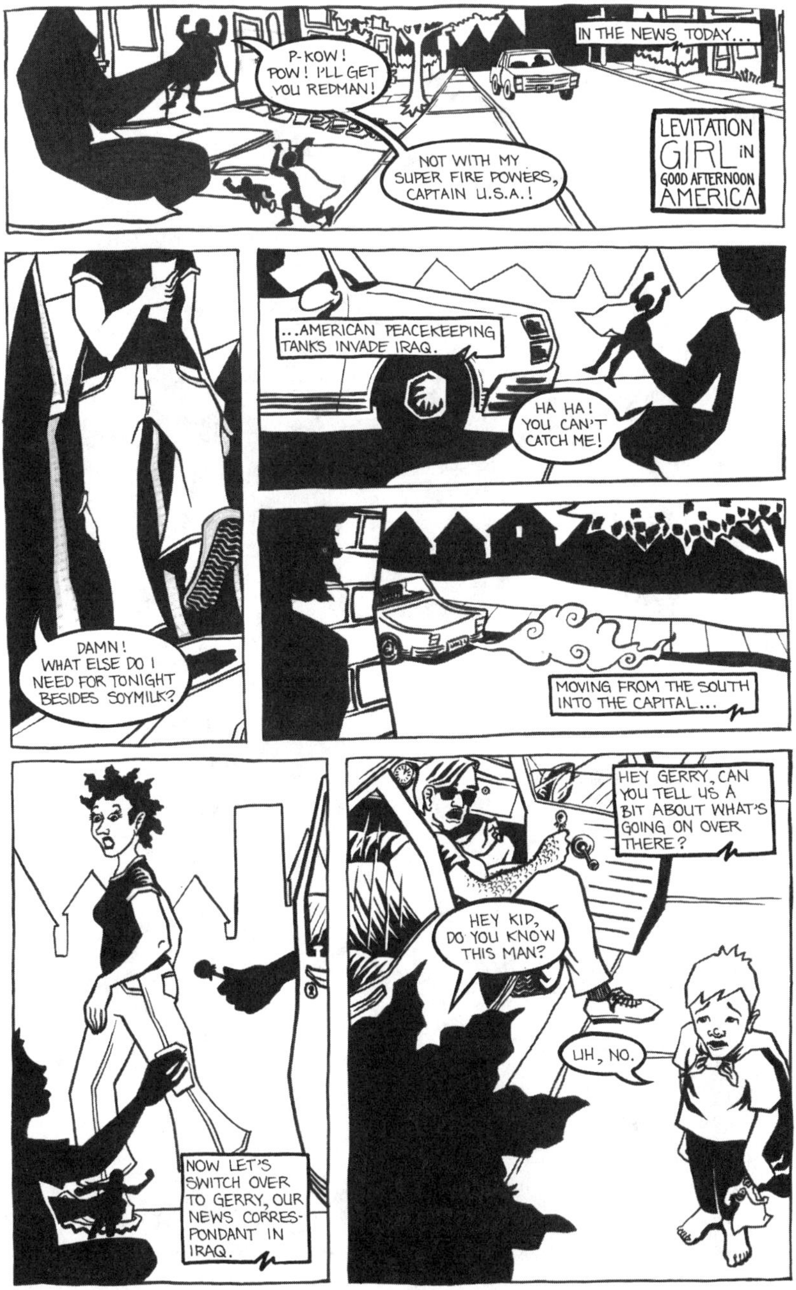
IN THE NEWS TODAY...
P-KOW! POW! I'LL GET YOU REDMAN!
NOT WITH MY SUPER FIRE POWERS, CAPTAIN U.S.A.!
LEVITATION GIRL IN GOOD AFTERNOON AMERICA
...AMERICAN PEACEKEEPING TANKS INVADE IRAQ.
HA HA! YOU CAN'T CATCH ME!
DAMN! WHAT ELSE DO I NEED FOR TONIGHT BESIDES SOYMILK?
MOVING FROM THE SOUTH INTO THE CAPITAL...
NOW LET'S SWITCH OVER TO GERRY, OUR NEWS CORRES-PONDANT IN IRAQ.
HEY GERRY, CAN YOU TELL US A BIT ABOUT WHAT'S GOING ON OVER THERE?
HEY KID, DO YOU KNOW THIS MAN?
UH, NO.

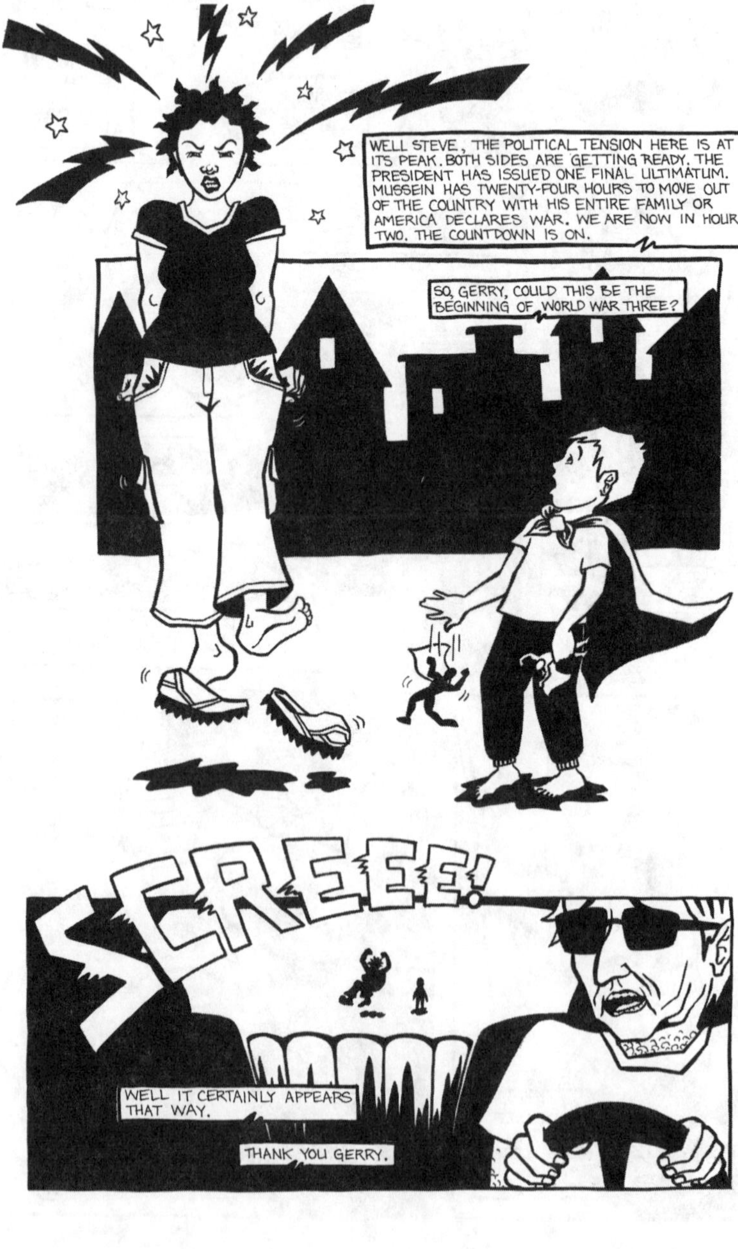
WELL STEVE, THE POLITICAL TENSION HERE IS AT ITS PEAK. BOTH SIDES ARE GETTING READY. THE PRESIDENT HAS ISSUED ONE FINAL ULTIMATUM. MUSSEIN HAS TWENTY-FOUR HOURS TO MOVE OUT OF THE COUNTRY WITH HIS ENTIRE FAMILY OR AMERICA DECLARES WAR. WE ARE NOW IN HOUR TWO. THE COUNTDOWN IS ON.
SO, GERRY, COULD THIS BE THE BEGINNING OF WORLD WAR THREE?
SCREEE!
WELL IT CERTAINLY APPEARS THAT WAY.
THANK YOU GERRY.

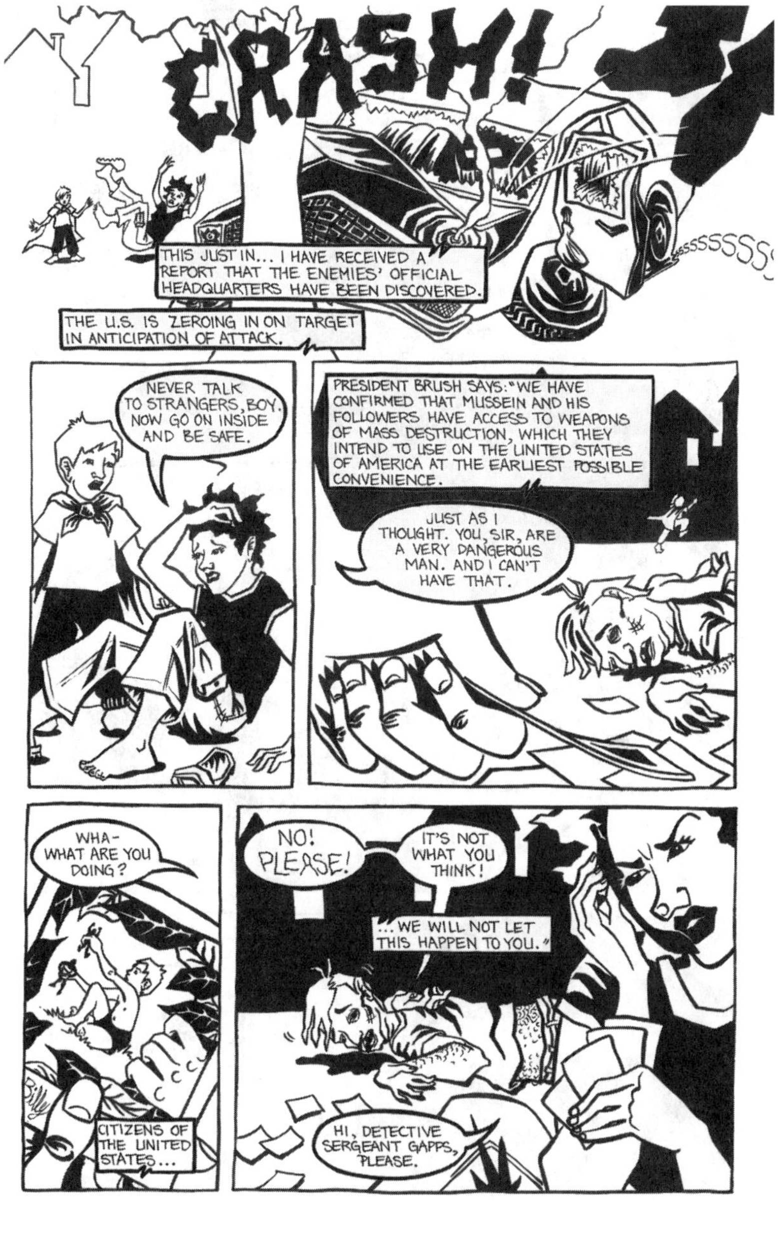
CRASH!
SSSSSSSSSS
THIS JUST IN... I HAVE RECEIVED A REPORT THAT THE ENEMIES' OFFICIAL HEADQUARTERS HAVE BEEN DISCOVERED.
THE U.S. IS ZEROING IN ON TARGET IN ANTICIPATION OF ATTACK.
NEVER TALK TO STRANGERS, BOY. NOW GO ON INSIDE AND BE SAFE.
PRESIDENT BRUSH SAYS: "WE HAVE CONFIRMED THAT MUSSEIN AND HIS FOLLOWERS HAVE ACCESS TO WEAPONS OF MASS DESTRUCTION, WHICH THEY INTEND TO USE ON THE UNITED STATES OF AMERICA AT THE EARLIEST POSSIBLE CONVENIENCE.
JUST AS I THOUGHT. YOU, SIR, ARE A VERY DANGEROUS MAN. AND I CAN'T HAVE THAT.
WHA- WHAT ARE YOU DOING?
CITIZENS OF THE UNITED STATES...
NO! PLEASE!
IT'S NOT WHAT YOU THINK!
...WE WILL NOT LET THIS HAPPEN TO YOU."
HI, DETECTIVE SERGEANT GAPPS, PLEASE.

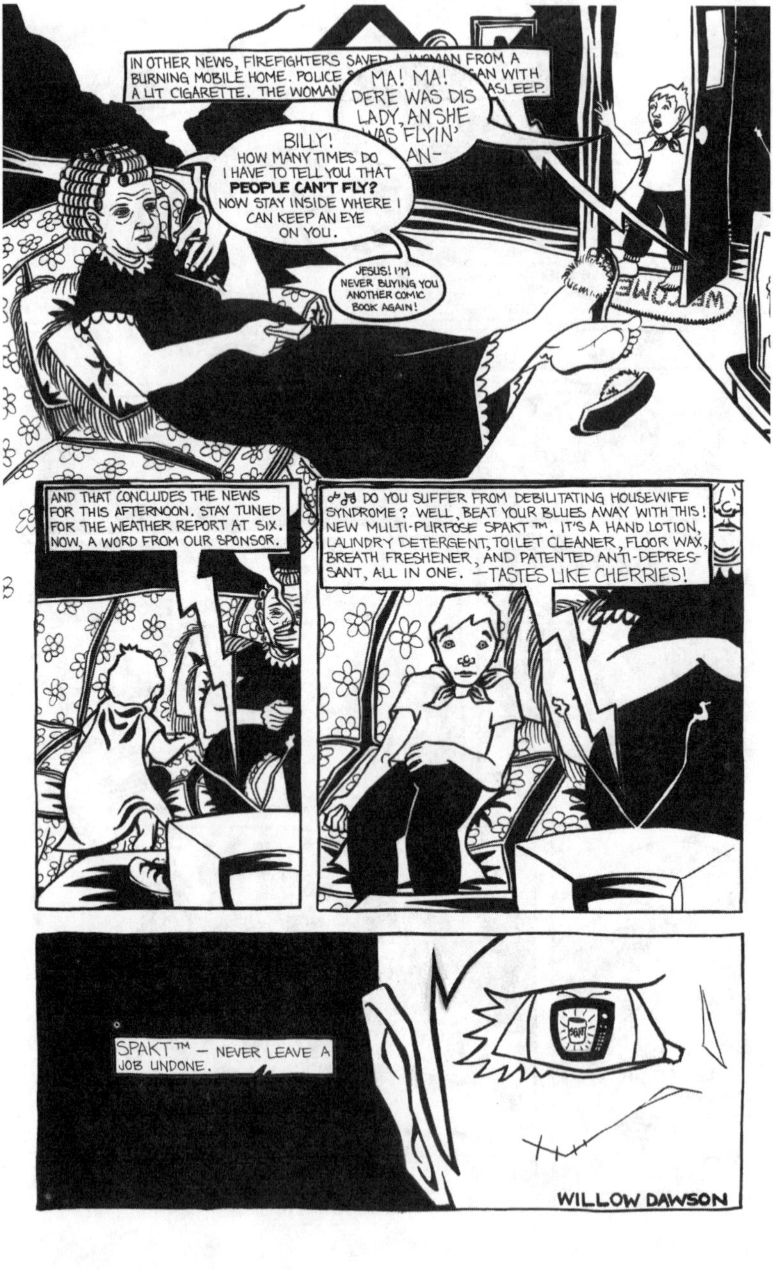
IN OTHER NEWS, FIREFIGHTERS SAVED A WOMAN FROM A BURNING MOBILE HOME. POLICE ... AN WITH A LIT CIGARETTE. THE WOMAN ... ASLEEP.
MA! MA! DERE WAS DIS LADY, AN SHE WAS FLYIN' AN-
BILLY! HOW MANY TIMES DO I HAVE TO TELL YOU THAT **PEOPLE CAN'T FLY?** NOW STAY INSIDE WHERE I CAN KEEP AN EYE ON YOU.
JESUS! I'M NEVER BUYING YOU ANOTHER COMIC BOOK AGAIN!
AND THAT CONCLUDES THE NEWS FOR THIS AFTERNOON. STAY TUNED FOR THE WEATHER REPORT AT SIX. NOW, A WORD FROM OUR SPONSOR.
♪♫ DO YOU SUFFER FROM DEBILITATING HOUSEWIFE SYNDROME? WELL, BEAT YOUR BLUES AWAY WITH THIS! NEW MULTI-PURPOSE SPAKT™. IT'S A HAND LOTION, LAUNDRY DETERGENT, TOILET CLEANER, FLOOR WAX, BREATH FRESHENER, AND PATENTED ANTI-DEPRESSANT, ALL IN ONE. —TASTES LIKE CHERRIES!
SPAKT™ — NEVER LEAVE A JOB UNDONE.
WILLOW DAWSON

DIAMOND DAME

Emily Pohl-Weary © 2043

Diamond Dame, the superhero, cannot fly like she used to. Her X-ray vision's not so sharp and her once-pert breasts hang so low they kiss her belly. She looks ridiculous in a miniskirt; she's skin and bones. That damn costume hangs off her pitiful muscles and the cape refuses to swirl like a living thing around her bony hips — the look has grown weary and so has she.

The Whiz Bang Kids, her loyal sidekicks, have grown up and moved on. Tracy and Little Tim used to be the best helpers. Now Tracy's got a cute little toddler and she's a journalist working her way up the *Daily Planet*'s ladder of success. Single mothers don't get out much. Her heart's in the right place, it's just chained to a stroller. Little Tim's gone away to school. He studies criminal law and only writes once in a while. When he does, the letters reek of parties that only other lawyers attend. He probably isn't using his gift at all. He's become too straight-laced for that.

It's really hard for Diamond D. She misses the Whiz Bang kids a lot. Tracy was the best shape-shifter on Earth. She could infiltrate the most secure evil-planning sessions inside locked boardrooms and climb office towers in her sleep. Little Tim was a first-class mind reader and teleki-netic. He could change weather patterns with his mind! He was no prophet, but he did make the mountains come to him. And he was relentlessly good and merciful.

Oh, they had such great times together! Now she's at it alone. Saving the planet from evildoers is too much responsibility for one woman. Just when she decides (for the umpteenth time) that she should hang up her super-cape for good, the phone rings or she reads the newspaper's current affairs section and, well, she knows that this gift of hers will follow her to her grave.

And the grave is just where she might end up if she doesn't watch her cholesterol, the doctor warned last time she paid him a visit. She's got high blood pressure. The pills he gave her haven't helped much. They do, however, rival her arthritis in the race to rob her of a good night's sleep. Diamond D has survived dastardly mutants galore, but who can combat the sneaky hand of time?

Recently, Oprah invited her onto that program of hers. It was just like the old days. Diamond Dame enjoyed herself very much. Oprah took her seriously (unlike the time she was on *Geraldo* and he launched into his BS about whether she was a superhero or a super-quack) and when she started talking about saving the Dame's soul through self-love, Diamond D set her straight in the blink of an eye. Superheroes do so many good deeds there's got to be a special place reserved in heaven just for them. The self-appointed guru understood the concept of karmic points. She may be fat, but at least she respects her elders.

After the show, the Dame walked to her car alone. It was miles away from the studio, and her bad hip wasn't co-operating. She was annoyed that the producer hadn't bothered to make arrangements. D. D. shouldn't have to hike to her car!

"I kept thinking," said some young pip shuffling along in front of her, "that even though she probably can't fly anymore, I'm glad to see she's still around. I mean, I always wondered what happened to her."

"Never heard of her," said the teen girl walking next to him. She was wearing a baseball cap jutting sideways and her brown ponytail poked out in the opposite direction. Diamond Dame fought the urge to reach over and smack it off her head. Girls didn't even know how to dress themselves these days!

"Back in the eighties, everyone looked up to her. I remember my mom used to talk about her all the time. She's really ... she's put in her dues. It's just sad."

The girl shrugged and cracked her wad of bubble gum "She's got more wrinkles than Bubbie Schwartz."

"Ha ha. She's got more wrinkles than Bubbie and Zaida Schwartz combined."

Oh, how times have changed, thinks Diamond D. Times have

changed. The flightiness of fame! People don't remember anything for more than five minutes anymore. In her youth, the big networks clamoured for appearances. Now she's walking to her car alone, thinking about past glories and the super-soulmates she's lost along the way. It's not right!

Diamond Dame believes she should be a celebrity, on par with Mother Teresa or Madonna. In her teens, before the Whiz Bang Kids were even born, the Dame defeated the goons who ran United Rapes Unlimited single-handedly. Well, she did have the help of her good buddy Sudden Fury. If he was still around, she would be happy to fight another day.

Fury's been out of commission since '89, when he injured his knee something terrible. He spends his days selling used comic books for a dollar to kids who don't know the difference between cartoons and the real thing. At first Fury tried to tell them who he was, but more and more often, the kids just didn't believe him. When he insisted, they ran away.

The Dame blames it all on television and billboards. The little darlings — youngsters — with all this nonsense filling their brains, how can they comprehend the difference between fiction (He-Man, Luke Skywalker and G.I. Joe) and reality (Diamond Dame)? What's wrong with them? Don't they know that without help, she's, well, helpless? Sudden Fury fought at her side when U.R.U. tried to install its puppet master as prime minister and rid the country of its most civilized attributes. They were the ones who saved socialized health care and publicly funded daycare.

During the final battle, Fury's left leg was ripped off below the knee by an evil warlock. The limb grew back, of course, but the joint was never the same. It's sad that he gets no respect from the children. He was always such an idealist. At least Diamond D knows the truth: the kids don't believe her and they don't believe in her. Nobody thinks for themselves anymore. It used to be so straightforward: there were good guys and there were bad. Diamond Dame, Sudden Fury and the Whiz Bangs were good, U.R.U. was bad. Now, somehow, the lines are not so clear. The bad guys know how to obfuscate by using bureaucratic language or hiding behind policemen's uniforms.

There's been a resurgence of evil. The U.R.U.'s back, stronger than ever and their exploits are splashed across the front page of *The Daily Planet*. It's enough to make her throw down the paper in disgust. Worst of all, there's no one to stop them. She and the gang would never have allowed this to happen back in their heyday. To even touch the executive, she'd need the help of both Whiz Bang Kids and Sudden Fury.

Diamond Dame remembers when the evil gang started out in Argentina in the Seventies. Back then, they were a dime-a-dozen military junta waging a dirty war to wipe out what they proclaimed was "left-wing terrorism." Their stronghold on that country eventually weakened, due to international pressure, so they closed up shop, moved north and put all their resources into developing a multinational corporate conglomerate that couldn't be touched by any government. They aligned with powerful business interests and gained enough strength to launch a cover op. Recently, they orchestrated a merger of right-wing political parties and are attempting to install a mind reader with only one testicle as CEO of the country. The elections are less than a week away.

The Dame knows it's time to take them down. With the help of the Kids and Fury, she could bring ultimate evil to its knees. But now the U.R.U. has got so many superheroes scrambling to make ends meet that there's no one to stop them. Damn postmodernist, third-wave feminist doublespeak! Put a gang of bullies in Holt Renfrew pinstripes, give them shiny SUV stretch limos and suddenly they're the new heroes for a generation of kids who believe everything they see on television.

Suddenly, old D. D. just wants to get back to her apartment so she can hide from the world. It's her last refuge. She hates leaving it because everywhere she looks, she sees signs of the nasty gang. They're moving in. Taking over the streets. Somehow they've got the bankers, the TV stations and large software companies on their side.

Today it's hot in her penthouse apartment: stiflingly hot and filled with memories. She opens the window. Despite her reduced vision, she can still see into people's living rooms and kitchens. She can practically watch U.R.U. hoard their money, finagle their way into the bedrooms of innocents and confound the masses with secret codes like Java, Flash and SQL.

Suddenly, Diamond Dame is carried away by emotion. She's a superhero, goddammit! She jumps nimbly up onto the window ledge, looks down at the ants swarming through the streets below and screams: "Everyone needs a hero!"

ACT OF GRACE

Judy MacDonald

On the street: garbage, lonely panhandlers, angry, aimless kids and our hero, pushing a bundle buggy in front of her.

Nobody notices Felicity Grace. That's one of her powers. She needs no tricks, no mask, no costume. Poverty makes her invisible. Presto.

She passes a guy sitting on the sidewalk with a small box in front of him. He doesn't bother to ask her for change.

"G'night, brother," she says.

No answer.

Somewhere in the city, a child cries alone after a beating. Elsewhere, a single mother has run out of food for her family. A man has been mugged. A woman has been raped. They will not be saved.

But here on this street there is hope, and it goes by the name of Felicity Grace. Under a bridge, her buggy beside her, a bicycle nearby, an ancient mattress behind the ragged rose-coloured sheet she's put up for privacy. Home.

Felicity eats a soggy falafel and drinks the remains of a Sprite. She treats herself to half a cool cappuccino and a couple of day-old dough-nuts. All are finds from today's foraging.

She listens to her battered battery-operated radio: reports of floods, fires, blackouts, tainted meat, suicide bombings, war, disease, abduc-tion, bulldozed homes and hunger. Terror comes in so many guises, it's hard to keep up with who's playing what part. It's hard to fight. Before you know it, you're fighting yourself.

In another part of the city, Kenneth Dude makes plans. He gets in his car. Kenneth Dude's disguise is ingenious, if over-used. Blue-grey blazer in light wool, matching pants. A white shirt with stiffened collar, still fresh from the dry cleaners. Charcoal-coloured silk tie, black leather loafers, dark grey socks. Respectable.

Dressed for business, he is speeding along the streets toward Felicity Grace. He is on his cell phone talking about his stocks, which didn't do so well during this afternoon's market correction.

"No, *you* listen!" he yells at his broker, then disconnects.

A man with so much on his mind loses track of small things. All things outside himself are small for such a man. Kenneth Dude isn't thinking when his foot pushes harder on the gas, when his fists pound on the steering wheel, when he closes his eyes and shouts into his car's leather interior about losing important percentages on his millions. His heartbeat swallows his hearing; his blood crushes other sound. He presses redial on his cell phone, then cuts it off, presses again, cuts it off. It's a ritual.

The car hits something. It lurches back a little, then forward. It bumps over a garbage can or raccoon or some stray dog. A few metallic scrapes shudder through the floorboard. *Shit*, he thinks, *what is this going to cost?*

In his rage, he still notices the red light and manages to stop, barely, cell phone still locked in his right palm. He doesn't get out to see what might have happened – there's no damage that can't be fixed, and the car is running fine. He sees that this isn't a safe neighbourhood, and notices there is no other traffic around. Out of his car, Dude would be a target. He misses other things, though, like Felicity Grace looking for a pay phone that was recently pulled out by the company so that folks with money would buy cells. Felicity gets off her bike, throws it to the sidewalk and walks to his car. He doesn't see her until she is blocking his way through the light that's just turned green.

"Dammit," Dude says. She must be crazy or looking for cash. Either way, he's had enough shit to deal with today. He looks hard at Felicity, his right hand waving her to the curb. He guns his engine to scare her off, but she doesn't budge. His headlights make her glow.

With his left hand, he presses a button, lowers his window. He's holding the phone like a sword in his right. "Who do you think you are?" he shouts. "I'm in a hurry."

"I'm nobody. I'm alive, asshole. And you aren't going anywhere, fast or slow." She pounds the hood of his car so hard it makes a dent.

Kenneth Dude started this trip angry, but the shabby woman has got him pulling his face back like an attack dog, teeth showing a jagged white, veins blue across his forehead and pulling out from his neck, his skin a flash-burn red of resentment. "Jesus, more shit!"

As quickly as it washes over him, the feeling turns to a sick, ignorant fear. There's blood where Felicity's fist hit. More elsewhere. A fine spray of blood and bits right across the front hood.

He says, "Oh my God, what have you done?"

She says, "You mean what have *you* done. Get out of the car and see for yourself."

"What?"

"Get. Out. Of. The. Car."

"Don't talk to me that way. You have no right to talk to me that way." Dude starts to shut his window.

Without seeming to move, Grace is suddenly at the driver's side of the car, her arm inside the window. Her hand slips down the back of Dude's neck, catching his tie, choking him. With two free fingers, she pinches muscles he didn't know he had.

She snarls, "Go ahead and drive some more. You can take me for a ritzy ride too, like the other little friend you've got there."

"Where? What are you talking about?" His voice a weak dribble from his knotted throat.

"Always the last to know, eh?" Her eyes big, full of fun, her voice thick with contempt.

Kenneth Dude sees disease. Madness. Someone with nothing to lose. "I've got a phone here," he rasps, thrusting it at her. "I'm not afraid to use it."

"Yeah, go ahead, call 9-1-1 on a middle-aged homeless woman. Maybe you can brag about it to your buddies later, how you showed everyone that you're the boss."

"Listen, try to be reasonable." Every word hurts. Dude is thinking about whether he can somehow shut the window, cut her arm off cleanly, and make an escape. He is not used to losing control.

"Like you're one to talk about reason. Don't kid yourself. I know what you're thinking," she says. "You want to do me serious damage. Wanna know what I'm thinking? *Should I finish him off or kiss him — which one would freak him out more?* What do you think? I'm open to suggestions."

Dude presses 9-1-1. Pause. Says which intersection he's at. "Yeah, in a car, in a car." Pause. "I sound this way because I'm being fucking choked to death." Pause. "She's right beside me, fucking strangling me while we chit chat, lady. Licence number I-four-I." Pause. "Letter I, number four, letter I, right. Get someone here right away. The car is a … keh … uhcht … g-ith." She is pulling tighter on the tie. He disconnects.

A few other cars go by slowly, staring to see what is happening, but they don't stop. The passengers and drivers don't look into the eyes of Felicity or Kenneth Dude, don't get out to help or call in an emergency. Some of the people laugh as they pass.

The ambulance comes. It's the one Felicity Grace was after. She is sorry that the firefighters will waste a trip. She can almost always do without cops.

The vehicle pulls in behind the car. The paramedics rush to get their equipment, then hustle forward. Kenneth Dude smiles a bit with relief, despite his pain, until he notices they are heading toward the passenger's side, and not to him.

Grace's pinch turns into a massage. One that is so soothing, so maternal, it reminds him of all that he wants in life but doesn't have.

"Hey! Hey!" he shouts to the paramedics through the windshield. "What the fuck gives, here? Has everyone gone nuts? Hey!"

"There, there," she coos. She slips her hand out of his collar, gives his tie a little tug, then adds, "I think you need some air, don't you?"

He is confused. He can't see the emergency workers anymore, but he can hear them talking to each other. It starts to sink in that something else has happened. Something big.

This is what Felicity Grace wanted all along. He has been outsmarted by a bum.

"I need to get out. No — I need to leave," he says, almost pleading with Grace.

"You take off in this car, and you run over the people you asked to come save you. And believe me, you're already in deep for what you've done. You gave them your licence number. You're not getting away with it, regardless."

"Getting away with what? All I want is to get away from you."

"I gave you a chance to deal with this between us, but no, you wouldn't have it. You couldn't be bothered to see what's what. I know what I am. Time for you to find out what you are. Get. Out. Of. The. Car."

"I need to, I need to. I — ah, get away from me, and I'll get out."

"With pleasure."

Felicity Grace steps back. Kenneth Dude gets out and comes to the front of the car. He sees blood pooling around the passenger side. He sees the paramedics huddled over something, but can't make out what. Then he sees it. Sees, and throws up. The head and shoulders are caught underneath the car, but he can see the torso heaving for breath. It's got small legs tangled in a bike and is wearing jeans and a sneaker on one foot. The other shoe is gone. Much of the foot is gone too. A child.

"Good to know what you are, isn't it?" asks Felicity Grace. "It's good to set things straight. You can't always do it, but from time to time, yeah."

DIVINE SECRETS OF THE YAGA SISTERHOOD
THE JOURNEY FROM SUPERVIRGIN TO SUPERMOM TO SUPERGODDESS

Sandra Kasturi

A long time ago, in a girlaxy far, far away, I wanted to be a princess. I had the adoption fantasy down pat — if you were adopted, that could mean you really *were* a princess. Maybe your real parents had to send you secretly into exile, to the people who were currently raising you, because you weren't safe. The enemies of the royal family could kidnap you and hold you for ransom. The fate of the free world could depend on getting you back. Having you live with commoners was probably the safest option. But someday you'd go back to reclaim the throne, and then everything would come full circle, and all true identities would be revealed. I read a lot of fairy tales, and Frances Hodgson Burnett's *A Little Princess* was my bible. I had a rich fantasy life.

Despite advances in women's rights and shockingly revolutionary ideas like equal pay for equal work, back when I was a kid — which is thirty years ago — there still weren't a lot of fantasies for girls that allowed them to be tough and strong. There weren't a lot of imagined futures that didn't involve a man — the handsome prince. We were still more likely to identify with Miss America than with Gloria Steinem. I wish I could say I longed to be an astronaut, but I didn't. The closest I ever got to fantasizing about being a take-charge kind of girl was wanting to be Daphne from *Scooby-Doo*. Not Velma, who was clearly the brains of the whole goofy operation. Daphne. After all, she was the pretty one.

But one day I found some different kinds of stories; I read some Russian fairy tales, stumbled on some Greek mythology, and then I hit the motherlode. I discovered comic books. They taught me that women could have strength, and the Greek myths showed me that women could have power, and the wily Russian tales enlightened me, eventually, to the fact that the culture of youth wasn't everything: with age comes wisdom, and without that, strength and power are meaningless. That's when I discovered what I now call the Yaga Sisterhood (after the famous Russian witch Baba Yaga) — that network of women, real and fictional, your girlfriends, your female relatives, your idols, which only gets better and stronger with age.

As I grew older, I gave up yearning to be the young maiden who waits to be rescued by the prince. I realized that if there were any rescuing to be done, I'd have to do it myself. I didn't have to wait to find out how the quest turned out — I could go on the quest myself and affect its outcome. Maybe these are things all women learn as they mature and grow, with any luck, wiser. There's an old Russian proverb: "Women can do everything, men can do the rest." It's true. We really can do everything, though nothing comes without its price, and sometimes, Yaga Sisterhood or no, it takes us a long, long time to get where we want to be. Sometimes the girlaxy is farther from the world of women than you think.

From mythology through fairy tales and folklore, we can follow the road across the ages to lays sung by bards and ancient stories turned into plays and poems. The narratives get longer and longer as the centuries go by, until those goddesses and heroines (like Kali or Eurydice) turn up in other incarnations (like Mary Poppins or Elizabeth Bennet) in scandalously novel things like, well, novels. These women in the old stories are the forerunners, the fictional great-grandmothers of today's female superheroes. The Russian Baba Yaga, Medusa, Miss Marple, Wonder Woman: all sisters. But if that's so, why has it so often been difficult to find strong and interesting female characters "of a certain age?" Is it just our North American obsession with youth? After all, in France, apparently women aren't even appealing until they're over thirty-five. Or so I've heard, and I'll just happily assume it's true.

SIGI FREUD'S SPECTRAL MOTHER

So why *aren't* there any female superheroes over the age of forty? There may be a few over thirty, if you do the math according to their histories in the DC or Marvel Comics universes, but they look much younger, regardless of their chronological age. Mind you, in the comic-book universe you can travel back in time, come back from the dead and even get rejuvenated so you are, in fact, years younger. But if you look at the majority of women fighting crime between those pages, nobody's even remotely close to hitting menopause. Must be one of their superpowers. And if the comics are translated to the silver screen, well, then the characters, whether superhero or just supergirlfriend, are skewed to look even younger. For example, I always thought Spider-Man's honeybun, Mary Jane, was in her late twenties or early thirties in the comics, until she turned up in high school in Sam Raimi's film version.

There *is* the obvious answer: it gets harder to fight crime as you age and your body slows down. Bruises take longer to fade, and bones don't set as fast. But many comic-book creators allow their male protagonists to age and even die. Who can forget the famous and much-lamented death of Superman? And Batman's sidekick, Robin the Boy Wonder, was killed off a couple of times and replaced. But most of the time, the women simply continue to exist in a youthful version, or they don't exist at all. Perhaps it's simply that most comic books and graphic novels are still written by, and for, men. It's still a T & A show. And whose tits do you really want to look at? Britney Spears's or Phyllis Diller's? It's a variation on the Hollywood Syndrome: your male lead can be sixty, but your female lead still has to be twenty.

There is always the exception to the rule: Wonder Woman's mother, Hippolyta. It's unusual in the first place for a female superhero to have such a prominent and noticeable parental presence. In fact, it's unusual for any superhero to have parents that are still in the picture. It's always easier to jump into your tights and go about your business if there's no one asking you when you're coming back for dinner or whether you've washed your spandex.

Hippolyta, on the other hand, is not your ordinary mother. She, like Wonder Woman, is an Amazon, and a queen to boot. She has her own special powers and eventually ends up fighting the good fight like her daughter. In fact, at one point, she ends up going back in time to the 1940s and, instead of being the third Wonder Woman, ends up becoming the first Wonder Woman, ahead of the regular Wonder Woman we know. The interesting thing about Hippolyta and Wonder Woman herself is that they are both from a place and world that is not male-dominated. Hippolyta, the comic-book character, is based on Hippolyte, the

Amazon queen of Greek mythology, probably best known from *The Twelve Labours of Hercules*. Old Herc was sent off to steal Hippolyte's girdle (which endowed the wearer with incredible strength), but she apparently became enamoured with him and gave it away as a gift. Well, that's one version of the story. Other variations have Hercules kidnapping Hippolyte, raping her and killing her before fleeing with the girdle. Well, that's after the goddess Hera, never Hercules's biggest fan, sticks her big oar in and stirs everyone up into a high dudgeon. But that sounds far more likely than an Amazon going all goo-goo-eyed over some nice pecs and a fringed loincloth.

But what is really of note here is that Hippolyta's a truly interesting older woman, a matriarch with special powers who is trying to fight the good fight. In the comics, after hanging out in the 1940s for a bit, Hippolyta ends up back in her regular time, and helps DC's Justice League of America fight various enemies. Wonder Woman herself gets killed, but the gods on Olympus turn her into the goddess of truth, so she isn't really dead. She gets turned back into Wonder Woman for interfering too much with humans; then there are various bits of intrigue and betrayals and so on (it's better than *The Young and the Restless*, I swear), and in the end Hippolyta sacrifices herself for the sake of humanity, and of course ends up dying tragically in the arms of her daughter, Wonder Woman. If the Brontë girls were alive today, this is what they'd be writing.

If we examine the situation with a jaundiced eye, we can say, yes, of course, Hippolyta has to die — we can't have this older woman, this *mom*, as a main character in the superhero universe. It just doesn't fly. It spoils the *romance* of it all.

Even Joss Whedon, creator of *Buffy the Vampire Slayer*, succumbed in the end — Buffy's mother, Joyce, ends up being killed off in the long run, but at least her absence leaves a vacuum. Whedon did it cleverly, however, because he understood the practical difficulties associated with being a superhero. The characters feel Joyce's loss, and Buffy is put in the unenviable position of having to look after her younger sister, pay the bills, find a job and all that practical mundane stuff that regular folks have to do. It's funny and tragic at the same time to watch Buffy being forced to work at a fast food place, where she earns minimum wage, when she's saved the world from apocalypse any number of times. But then being a hero has always been a thankless job. The thing is, Wonder

Woman's mother dies, Buffy's mother dies, most superheroes' mothers are already dead. These older women are like Freud's spectral mother: they are noticeable for their very *absence* from the story.

MISS ORACLE REGRETS
SHE'S UNABLE TO LUNCH TODAY

We're a long way from the Golden Age of comics. The female characters aren't as two-dimensional anymore, though sadly they're often still as, ah, pneumatic. It does a girl's heart good to read comic books and see TV shows based on those that have strong central women. And sometimes even strong *disabled* women. The popular comic book, *Birds of Prey*, spawned a now-cancelled TV series of the same name, which had only women as the main characters: the Oracle (Barbara Gordon, formerly Batgirl, until the Joker shot her and she ended up in a wheelchair), the Huntress (Helena Kyle, illegitimate daughter of Catwoman and Batman),[1] and Dinah Lance, whom we later find out is the daughter of Black Canary. And let's not forget our supervillain, also a woman — Dr. Harlene Quinzelle/Harley Quinn — the Joker's former therapist and now, after being completely twisted by the big J, just as much of a psychopath as he ever was — his de facto spiritual daughter.

What's fascinating about the comic book and the show is not only that women play such large and strong roles, but that the sins (and virtues) of the parents are in fact visited on the children. They can't live normal lives, even if they want to. The most interesting character is Barbara Gordon/the Oracle; she is in fact an "older" woman (in Hollywood or the DC/Marvel universe, this means she's over thirty-five) who has had to make a new life for herself since she can no longer walk. So she trains herself to be a virtuoso of information and technology, creating a new life for herself.

For Barbara, the destruction of so much of her physical ability isn't just about not being able to play basketball or go ballroom dancing anymore. It's about figuring out how she can still help save the world. After all, Barbara Gordon was never just brawn. She has brains, too. So Batgirl metamorphs into the Oracle and becomes an even more valuable superhero than ever before. There's a saying that when given a burden, a man will look for a wheelbarrow, but a woman will just pick it up and keep trudging.

Maybe that's not true for the modern woman/superhero — she builds her own wheelbarrow and turns her luck around. Even age and a crippling bullet can't stop her. She's a true member of the Yaga Sisterhood.

SPINSTER CAT HOUSE

Whenever me and my girlfriends (fellow Yagas) are between male partners, we remind each other that someday we'll all be living together in some big old mansion with about a hundred cats. We'll leer at the pool boy when he comes around, but, otherwise, no men need apply. Because even if we do ever get married or live with men, they'll die long before we do, poor things. And those of us who are gay? The more Yagas the better! We'll pool our resources, move in together and feed every stray in the neighbourhood until we're inundated with kitties. We'll call it the spinster cat house. Sounds like a blast to me.

As novelist Jim Munroe illustrates in his book, *Everyone in Silico,*[2] you don't have to be young or even middle-aged to be a hero — you can be geriatric. In Munroe's book, former assassin (and prematurely aged) grandmother Eileen Ellis dons a kind of smartsuit that enhances her body's failing powers in order to look for her grandson, Jeremy. The suit runs off her own body as a power source, so it physically destroys her in the end (though her mind ends up being uploaded into a virtual reality). But not before she saves her grandson and the world (sort of).

In Suzette Haden Elgin's novel *Native Tongue,*[3] the hero is also a granny. Nazareth Joanna is a female linguist in a terrible future where not only are linguists reviled, but all women are only slightly more important than cattle, basically good for breeding and housecleaning. Even in this dreadful dystopia, Nazareth, first as a somewhat foolish and stubborn young woman, but later as a smart and much more cunning grandmother, manages to quietly triumph. The women in Elgin's world work for years to create their own private language, a language that men are never taught. They theorize that if you create words for concepts that were never before expressed, you can change people's attitudes and viewpoints and that this, in turn, can change the world. If the entire female population of the world talks, and therefore thinks and believes, in a certain way, then the universe itself will shift. It's kind of like Schrödinger's language:[4] participation and observation change the outcome of the future.

And let us not forget our own darling Miss Marple, the nemesis with a "fluffy pink scarf around her neck," from the pen of that cunning little minx Agatha Christie.[5] As I always like to say, Dame Agatha wasn't the greatest writer in the world, but, *boy*, could she tell a story! Miss Marple never misses a trick, and she's well into her eighties, showing us once again that you can fight crime even when your joints are stiff with arthritis and you've promised Dear Doctor that you absolutely won't do any more stooping or kneeling. The divine Miss M's mental abilities outstrip those of the police, her younger friends and relatives, and many a criminal mastermind. Not bad for an "old pussy"[6] who always seems to be knitting jumpers and booties for her godchildren. She never even drops a stitch.

Dame Agatha, your ghost is welcome in our spinster cat house any time. Suzette, we'd really love to have you over for a visit, and you can stay as long as you like. Jim, well, I guess we can let you hang out with the pool guy.

FROM SUPERGIRL TO SUPERMOM

Let's face it, though: these older women are unusual. The world tends to assume that women get tedious with age, while men get more interesting. Just this once, let us imagine a perfect world in which comic-book women do grow old. (No, let's be realistic, in a perfect world no one would age.) In this perfectly imperfect world, Wonder Woman gets older, gets middle-aged. Batgirl's joints ache every morning because of old injuries, and she thinks that her superhero name is monumentally stupid because she's over forty. She's hardly a girl anymore. And most of the female superheroes "born" in the 1960s and 1970s can't get up to much anymore because they're too busy looking after their kids while the men are still out reaping glory. Doesn't seem right, does it? But let's be fair. Maybe the Justice League of America is an equal opportunity employer. Maybe Superman gets paternity leave.

How do you go from fighting crime, from "making a difference," to changing diapers and being a soccer mom? From Supergirl to Supermom? You still have to maintain your secret identity. You can't even cash in on the coolness factor with your kids' friends, because it would make them perfect little targets for your arch-enemies, even though you fantasize about it:

"Your mom used to be Batgirl? No way!"

"Way!"

Would you even have arch-enemies anymore? Maybe your new nemesis becomes Leaver-of-Wet-Towels-on-the-Bathroom-Floor or Refuser-of-Ear-Washing.

You would do what all the regular non-superhero moms do — suck it up and make it work because, after all, you do love your children, even though you dream about jumping from rooftop to rooftop, and you wish your bullet-repelling bracelets weren't just jewellery you wore to the occasional nice dinner out. And you wish you had the cleavage you used to have, back in the day. Hell, you wish you had the *bra* you used to have, back in the day!

Eventually the children are grown and gone: One follows in mom's footsteps and takes up crime-fighting. One's still totally embarrassed by everything you stand for and becomes an accountant in Iowa. The third's a video-store clerk, watches movies made about you and tells everyone who will listen that that's not how it really happened, not at all.

Here's what I think happens to the Artist Formerly Known as Diana Prince, and here's why I think men can't relate: For men, in those bouncy, forever-young universes, older women don't exist. There's nothing so invisible as a middle-aged woman. You don't even need a magic cloak or special powers not to be seen. Cross that age barrier and you've done it without any trouble at all. That's why men have no clue what these women would be doing at that age; they never really see them — it was never the Invisible *Man*.

The way I see it, the ex-supergirlfriends would be getting together in some local seedy dive, drinking single malt when they have the money and whatever's on tap when they don't, sneaking a smoke or two just to be dangerous, but getting out the breath spray before they go home. For those few precious hours, they'd just hang out, bond, talk about anything and everything, relive their glory days, watch as their tits race each other to see which one reaches the navel first (to paraphrase Maya Angelou). Batman, Superman, Spider-Man, whoever — they're all irrelevant in the face of this kind of female relationship. That's the power of the Yaga Sisterhood.

Perhaps this is what men find so difficult to deal with — that at some point straight women reach an age when men are far less necessary. They lose that teenybopper-view of the world; they know that underneath the spandex outfit and the cape, there's just a guy pretty much like any other guy, a person like any other person with a bulgy middle and thinning hair. How frightening that level of understanding and comprehension must be! How difficult for a man to face a mirror showing reality, and not the vision he's always carried around in his head. It's much easier to tell your stories to a starry-eyed young thing who's going to buy your own version of yourself.

TOMORROW THROUGH THE PAST

Since even now older superwomen role models are few and far between, we have to search for them in other places. The Yaga Sisterhood never gives up! We return to the past, where the older woman reigns supreme. Sometimes a hero, but more often a villain, you can find that woman "of a certain age" in the cautionary tale, or in the folk or fairy tale, where she usually appears as a witch (if bad) or a fairy godmother (if good).

So we come to the Yaga Sisterhood's namesake. One of the most notorious of witches in the folkloric tradition is Russia's Baba Yaga, whose legend has survived wars, revolutions, the Soviet downfall — the ups and downs of history. Baba Yaga, had she been real, would have devoured them all. Yet who is this infamous character? Is she a good witch or a bad witch? Maybe both? The jury's not in on that one — Baba Yaga, like most women, like most people for that matter, has many faces. And perhaps that explains her endurance. We can understand Baba Yaga and embrace her, because she helps us understand our multi-faceted selves. As writer Katya Arnold says, Baba Yaga "is so familiar to Russian children that she's almost a member of the family — like an elderly aunt who is either mean or nice, depending on her mood."[7]

Baba Yaga is a greater biter than any Russian Czar ever was, and certainly more canny. She's a grandmother, wise woman, force of nature, goddess, purveyor of good, purveyor of evil, perhaps kin to the Devil himself? The most common of her appearances is as the old crone living deep in a mysterious forest in a bizarre house set on chicken legs. She rides around in a mortar, using the pestle as an oar and erasing her tracks with a broom attached to the back. The tools of the kitchen become the tools of power, of knowledge. How homelike! How "feminine!" For witchcraft in these stories, if anything, is female, is domestic, is *tidy*.

One of the best-known Baba Yaga stories is "Vasilisa the Beautiful."[8]

It's a kind of Cinderella story, complete with an evil stepmother and a fairy godmother of sorts. It's also a variation of the Prometheus myth. Vasilisa is a beautiful young girl who loses her mother at a young age. After a short period of time, Vasilisa's father gets married again to an unpleasant woman with two daughters of her own. They hate Vasilisa and make her life unbearable (hello, Cinderella!), and it's only through the help of a magic doll that she can complete her back-breaking daily chores. One day, when Vasilisa's father is away, her stepmother decides it's time to get rid of the girl once and for all. She sends poor Vasilisa into the forest to ask Baba Yaga for fire, knowing that this is, in effect, sending the girl to her death. Long story made short: by being polite and respectful to Baba Yaga, Vasilisa is asked into the famous chicken-legged hut, where she completes many tasks with the help of the magic doll. She also manages to be clever enough not to get killed and eaten.

It is unclear how much time elapses, but the implication is that Vasilisa enters Baba Yaga's house as a young girl and emerges as a young woman. She even dares to ask a few questions, but always with respect. Baba Yaga finally gives Vasilisa a skull with fire in its eyes as a gift and sends her home. Things end badly for the stepmother and stepsisters: the skull's eyes follow them everywhere until their sins burn their souls and they are entirely consumed by the fire. Vasilisa, being pure, remains unscathed. Some tales go on to say that Vasilisa eventually marries the Czar who is impressed by the quality of her needlework and industriousness. A tidy and domestic ending!

There are many reasons why this tale is popular: good triumphs over evil, and rewards and punishments are meted out appropriately. Like its modern-day counterpart, *Birds of Prey*, it is the women in the story who are central; the men (father, Czar) are minor characters, dispensed with in a line or two. In many Russian stories, it is the women who are clever and resourceful, who have power, who have the will and wisdom to bite back, even if it isn't always in overt ways. Sometimes there is more power in subtlety, in listening, rather than acting. It is the faceoff between Baba Yaga and Vasilisa that is central to the story — and both powers come to a draw — old age/wisdom does not exactly triumph over youth/vitality, or vice versa. The result is a respectful standoff: the young girl gets what she wants and so does Baba Yaga.

In the Baba Yaga stories, as in many other fairy tales from various cultures, attitude is everything. If you treat the people and creatures you meet on your way to your personal grail with respect, then chances are that you will succeed. Behave rudely or badly, and suffer the consequences. Vasilisa treats Baba Yaga with deference, and ultimately it pays off. The gift of fire (and therefore home and hearth, the return to the real world from Baba Yaga's underworld) is hers. But those who do not behave well are treated much more harshly.

Baba Yaga and Vasilisa are, in effect, mirror aspects of each other: the Crone and the Maiden.[9] This is a popular theme. Even *Buffy the Vampire Slayer* revisits it (proving that the old stories are still the best ones). Youthful Buffy enters a kind of dream quest to visit the First Slayer — a Baba Yaga/African goddess figure who is the purveyor of ancient wisdom, an aspect of the Crone. In Tim Powers's mythical Cold War novel, *Declare*, the Soviet Union is protected by, quite literally, Mother Russia: a flesh and bone-eating djinn called Machikha Nash, a ghoul who swallows the gold and jewels of dead men[10]— a goddess much like her compatriot, Baba Yaga. The theme even appears in silly films where a young heroine is forced into a battle (sometimes a literal physical fight) with her beloved's psychotic mother. Sadly, age always ends up equaling psychosis in these movies. But in the end, these two faces of womanhood are merely different aspects of the one: we may start as the Maiden, but we will all end up as the Crone, whether we like it or not. Better to embrace Yaga, treat her with respect, for she is in us all.

In many myths — the Greek Fates or the Scandinavian Norns, for example — Baba Yaga or her counterpart would be the one who snips the thread at the end of life, the one who really bites back. In India she is Kali: mother, lover and destroyer, an unstoppable force. She even shows up in children's literature as the fearsome Mary Poppins — not Disney's spoonful-of-sugar-sweetened nanny, but P.L.Travers's literary creation: a magical and terrifying substitute mother who can speak to birds and animals, understand the secret language of infants, fly through the air and who is on a first-name basis with celestial bodies.[11] How could such a creature not be awe-inspiring? It's no wonder that Jane and Michael Banks adore and fear her in equal amounts.

The best-known Yaga-type figures are certainly variations on the wicked queen or evil stepmother in popular fairy tales like Snow White, Sleeping Beauty and Cinderella. In Snow White, the older woman is both stepmother and queen (a double whammy) who cannot bear that the girl is prettier than she is. Interestingly, revisionist modern versions of this tale have been written by people as diverse as Neil Gaiman,[12] Tanith Lee[13] and Stephen Sondheim.[14] They all present the queen/step-mother as a much more sympathetic character and make the younger woman the spoiled brat, the upstart bitch/witch. After all, who could stand to have that smarmy girl swanning about in front of the mirror going on about how lovely she is? Not to mention little goody two-shoes Cinderella behaving like a martyr just because she has to do a few chores. And that rude little whinger, Sleeping Beauty, who doesn't invite her godmother to the party, and then flings herself into bed for a hundred years just because she pricks her finger! No wonder modern-day writers like to turn these stories on their heads.

Incarnations of Yaga show up in Greek mythology again with characters like the fearsome gorgons whose faces and snaky hair are so terrible to look upon that the foolish mortal who sees them becomes a Rodin marble. Medusa (the head gorgon) is yet another aspect of the tripartite goddess and was originally worshipped as a snake divinity by the Libyan Amazons. As so often happens in these tales, any mortal who gazes directly upon the miraculous tends not to end well, like the poor sod torn apart by Diana/Artemis's hunting dogs just because he found her bathing. He came upon her by accident! It hardly seems fair.

It's yet another example of how women are viewed with both appetite, awe and terrible fear. Desire can result in death or metaphorical imprisonment (turning to stone). The divine wrath of the Yaga Sisterhood can be awful indeed.

SISTERS ARE DOIN' IT FOR THEMSELVES

By looking back at fairy tales and mythology from the past, we can move once again to the future. More modern aspects of older women include superheroes, witches, grandmotherly assassins ... and simply women who have triumphed against the odds, like the revenge-seeking Uma Thurman in *Kill Bill*, or the unsung hero of a single mom who lives downstairs.

These are the secrets of the Yaga Sisterhood: we as women affect the outcome of our lives and our world. We are gravid, pregnant with our future selves. If we are lucky, we will give birth to our inner Yagas, gain the power of wisdom and turn that into a legacy for all the young Vasilisas. They are the seeds of an infinite number of Baba Yagas to come: women to be reckoned with, for good or evil.

We should all aspire to Yaganess. Or perhaps Babaosity? At any rate, who hasn't wished for iron teeth to bite back at her enemies, for wisdom and witchery and, above all, the power to achieve the things we desire.

The scales may take a long time to fall from our eyes — we emerge, new with knowledge, not at birth, but toward the end our lives, when we have become shining crones. We are Baba Yagas, not wicked and bent, but solid, replete with wisdom, living in our funny little houses on chicken legs, banging about with our kitchen utensils, biting some, giving gifts to others, because with age comes whimsy. We also pass on our knowledge to the girls who find their ways into the forest and have no desire to leave. All these things are possible. The forest is at your front door and is nothing to be feared. All of us contain elements of the divine.

We've come a long way from the girlaxy. We should glory in it. Shout it out from the rooftops: Yaga! Yaga! That's what I'll be doing. Well, after downing a couple of scotches in the bar with Wonder Woman and Batgirl, the ladies from the spinster cat house, and the other members of the Yaga Sisterhood.

*

DEDICATION

For Phyllis Gotlieb and in memory of Judith Merril,
and especially in memory of my great-aunt Toni Kert:
girls who always bit back, long before it was fashionable
to do so.

NOTES

1. It should be noted that the Huntress in the *Birds of Prey* comic books is a different character altogether and definitely isn't Catwoman and Batman's daughter.

2. Jim Munroe, *Everyone in Silico* (Toronto: No Media Kings, 2002).

3. Suzette Haden Elgin, *Native Tongue* (New York: Daw, 1984).

4. Quantum theorist Schrödinger postulated that the observer affects the outcome of the experiment, or that measurement affects reality. According to his thought experiment, a cat (unobserved) is put in a box with a container of poison gas connected to a radioactive device. If an atom in the device decays, the container opens and the cat dies. Theoretically there is a fifty/fifty chance of this happening. But we don't know whether the cat is alive or dead until we open the box. So until the box is opened, the cat is neither alive nor dead, but both. It is our observation or measurement that allows the cat to achieve one state or the other.

5. Agatha Christie, *Nemesis* (London: William Collins Sons & Co., 1971).

6. Ibid., 40.

7. Katya Arnold, *Baba Yaga* (New York: North–South Books, 1993).

8. Albert B. Lord (ed.), *Russian Folk Tales* (Connecticut: Heritage Press, 1970).

9. Caitlín Matthews, *Sophia, Goddess of Wisdom: The Divine Feminine from Black Goddess to World-Soul* (London: Mandala, 1991).

10. Tim Powers, *Declare* (William Morrow, 2001).

11. P. L. Travers, *Mary Poppins; and Mary Poppins Comes Back* (Harcourt, Brace & World, 1983).

12. Neil Gaiman, "Snow Glass Apples," from *Smoke and Mirrors* (Avon Books, 1998).

13. Tanith Lee, *Red As Blood, or, Tales from the Sisters Grimmer* (New York: Daw Books, 1983).

14. Stephen Sondheim and James Lepine, *Into the Woods* (musical), first performed at the Martin Beck Theatre, 1987; also available on DVD from Image Entertainment, 1998.

MEDUSA: SUPERMOM

Sheila Butler

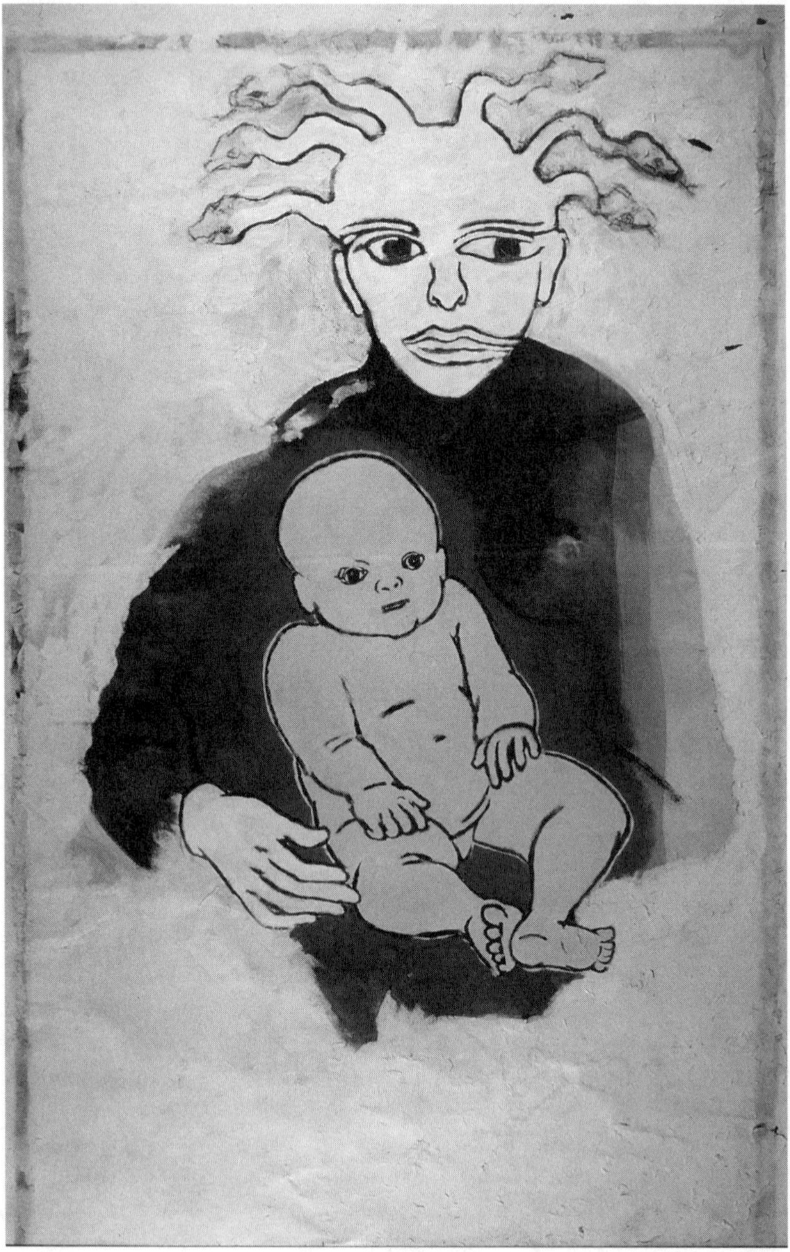

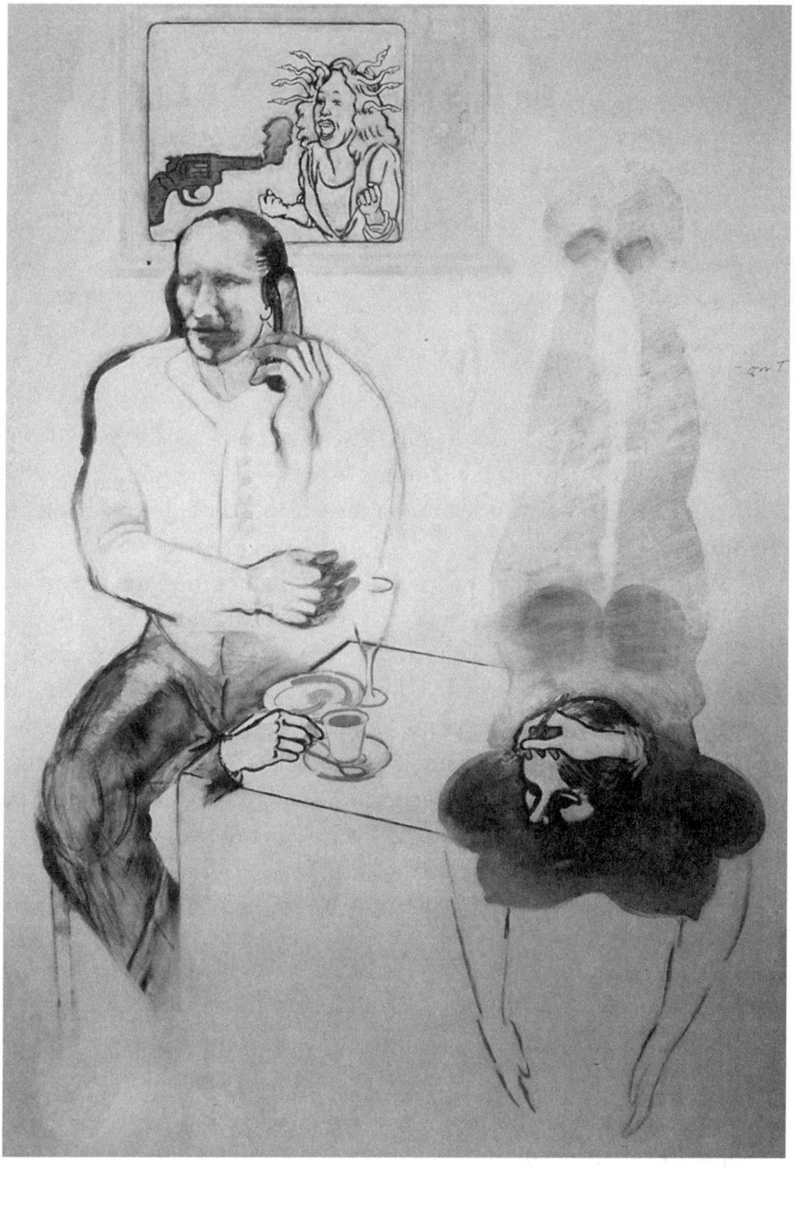

THE SMILE ON THE FACE

Nalo Hopkinson

There was a young lady …

"Geez, who gives a shit what a … what? What a laidly worm is, anyway?" Gilla muttered. She was curled up on the couch, school library book on her knees.

"Mm?" said her mother, peering at the computer monitor. She made a noise of impatience and hit a key on the keyboard a few times.

"Nothing, Mum. Just I don't know what this book's talking about." Boring old school assignment. Gilla wanted to go and get ready for Patricia's party, but Mum had said she should finish her reading first.

"Did you say, 'laidly worm?'" her mother asked. Her fingers were clicking away at the keyboard again now. Gilla wished she could type that quickly. But that would mean practising, and she wasn't about to do any more of that than she had to.

"Yeah." Damn. If Mum had heard that, she'd probably heard her say, "shit," too.

"It's a type of dragon."

Looks like she wasn't going to pay attention to the other word that Gilla had used. This time, anyway. "So why don't they just call it that?" Gilla asked her.

"It's a special type. It doesn't have wings, so it just crawls along the ground. Its skin oozes all the time. Guess that protects it when it crawls, like a slug's slime."

"Yuck, Mum!"

Gilla's mother smiled, even as she was writing. "Well, you wanted to know."

"No, I didn't. I just have to know, for school."

"A laidly worm's always ravenous and it makes a noise like a cow in gastric distress."

Gilla giggled. Her mother stopped typing and finally looked at her. "You know, I guess you could think of it as a larval dragon. Maybe it eats and eats so it'll have enough energy to moult into the flying kind. What a cool idea. I'll have to look into it." She turned back to her work. "Why do you have to know about it? What're you reading?"

"This lady in the story? Some guy wanted to marry her, but she didn't like him, so he put her in his dungeon ..."

"... and came after her one night in the form of a laidly worm to eat her," Gilla's mother finished. "You're learning about Margaret of Antioch?"

Gilla boggled at her. "Saint Margaret, yeah. How'd you know?"

"How?" Her mother swivelled the rickety steno chair round to face Gilla and grinned, brushing a tangle of dreadlocks back from her face. "Sweet, this is your mother, remember? The professor of African and Middle Eastern Studies?"

"Oh." And her point? Gilla could tell that her face had that "huh?" look. Mum probably could see it too, 'cause she said:

"Gilla, Antioch was in ancient Turkey. In the Middle East?"

"Oh yeah, right. Mum, can I get micro-braids?"

Now it was her mum looking like, "huh?" "What in the world are those, Gilla?"

Well, at least she was interested. It wasn't a "no" straight off the bat. "These tiny braid extensions, right? Maybe only four or five strands per braid. And they're straight, not like ... Anyway, Kashy says that the hairdressing salon across from school does them. They braid the extensions right into your own hair, any colour you want, as long as you want them to be, and they can style them just like that. Kashy says it only takes a few hours, and you can wear them in for six weeks."

Her mum came over, put her warm palms gently on either side of Gilla's face and looked seriously into her eyes. Gilla hated when she did that, like she was still a little kid. "You want to tame your hair," her mother said. Self-consciously, Gilla pulled away from her mum's hands, smoothed back the cloudy mass that she'd tied out of the way with a bandana so that she could do her homework without getting hair in her eyes, in her mouth, up her nose. Her mum continued, "You want hair that lies down and plays dead, and you want to pay a lot of money for it, and you want to do it every six weeks."

Gilla pulled her face away. The book slid off her knee to the floor. "Mum, why do you always have to make everything sound so horrible?" Some of her hair had slipped out of the bandana; it always did. Gilla could see three or four black sprigs of it dancing at the edge of her vision, tickling her forehead. She untied the bandana and furiously retied it, capturing as much of the bushy mess as she could and binding it tightly with the cloth.

Her mother just shook her head at her. "Gilla, stop being such a drama queen. How much do micro-braids cost?"

Gilla was ashamed to tell her now, but she named a figure, a few bucks less than the sign in the salon window had said. Her mother just raised one eyebrow at her.

"That, my girl, is three months of your allowance."

Well, yeah. She'd been hoping that Mum and Dad would pay for the braids. Guess not.

"Tell you what, Gilla; you save up for it, then you can have them."

Gilla grinned.

"But," her mother continued, "you have to continue buying your bus tickets while you're saving."

Gilla stopped grinning.

"Don't look so glum. If you make your own lunch to take every day, it shouldn't be so bad. Now, finish reading the rest of the story."

And Mum was back at her computer again, tap-tap-tap. Gilla pouted at her back but didn't say anything, 'cause really, she was kind of pleased. She was going to get micro-braids! She hated soggy, made-the-night-before sandwiches, but it'd be worth it. She ignored the little voice in her mind that was saying, "every six weeks?" and went back to her reading.

"Euw, gross."

"Now what?" her mother asked.

"This guy? This, like, laidly worm guy thing? It *eats* Saint Margaret, and then she's in his stomach; like, *inside* him! and she prays to Jesus, and she's sooo holy that the wooden cross around her neck turns back into a tree, and it puts its roots into the ground *through* the dragon guy thing, and its branches bust him open and he dies, and out she comes!"

"Presto bingo," her mum laughs, "Instant patron saint of childbirth!"

"Why?" But Gilla thought about that one a little bit, and she figured she might know why. "Never mind, don't tell me. So they made her a saint because she killed the dragon guy thing?"

"Well, yes, they sainted her eventually, after a bunch of people tortured and executed her for refusing to marry that man. She was a convert to Christianity, and she said she'd refused him because he wasn't a Christian. But Gilla, some people think that she wasn't a Christian anymore either, at least not by the end."

"Huh?" Gilla wondered when Kashy would show up. It was almost time for the party to start.

"That thing about the wooden cross turning back into a living tree? That's not a very Christian symbol, that sprouting tree. A dead tree made into the shape of a cross, yes. But not a living, magical tree. That's a pagan symbol. Maybe Margaret of Antioch was the one who commanded the piece of wood around her neck to sprout again. Maybe the story is telling us that when Christianity failed her, she claimed her power as a wood witch. Darling, I think that Margaret of Antioch was a hamadryad."

"Jeez, Mum, a cobra?" That much they had learned in school. Gilla knew the word "hamadryad."

Her mother laughed. "Yeah, a king cobra is a type of hamadryad, but I'm talking about the original meaning. A hamadryad was a female spirit whose soul resided in a tree. A druid is a man, a tree wizard. A hamadryad is a woman; a tree witch, I guess you could say. But where druids lived outside of trees and learned everything they could about them, a hamadryad doesn't need a class to learn about it. She just *is* a tree."

Creepy. Gilla glanced out the window to where black branches beckoned, clothed obscenely in tiny spring leaves. She didn't want to talk about trees.

The doorbell rang. "Oh," said Gilla. "That must be Kashy!" She sprang up to get the door, throwing her textbook aside again.

There was a young lady of Niger...

"It kind of creaks sometimes, y'know?" Gilla inquired of Kashy's reflection in the mirror.

In response, Kashy just tugged harder at Gilla's hair. "Hold still, girl.

Lemme see what I can do with this. And shut up with that weirdness. You're always going on about that tree. Creeps me out."

Gilla sighed, resigned, and leaned back in the chair. "Okay. Only don't pull it too tight, okay? Gives me a headache." When Kashy had a makeover jones on her, there was nothing to do but submit and hope you could wash the goop off your face and unstick your hair from the mousse before you had to go outdoors and risk scaring the pigeons. That last experiment of Kashy's with the "natural" lipstick had been such a disaster. Gilla had been left looking as though she'd been eating fried chicken and had forgotten to wash the grease off her mouth. It had been months ago, but Foster was still giggling over it.

Gilla crossed her arms. Then she checked out the mirror and saw how that looked, how it made her breasts puff out. She remembered Roger in the school yard, pointing at her the first day back at school in September and bellowing, "Boobies!" She put her arms on the rests of the chair instead. She sucked her stomach in and took a quick glance in the mirror to see if that made her look slimmer. Fat chance. Really fat. It did make her breasts jut again, though; oh, goody. She couldn't win. She sighed once more and slumped a little in the chair, smushing both bust and belly into a lumpy mass.

"And straighten up, okay?" Kashy said. "I can't reach the front of your head with you sitting hunched over like that." Kashy's hands were busy, sectioning Gilla's thick black hair into four and twisting each section into plaits.

"That tree," Gilla replied, "the one in the front yard."

Kashy just rolled her perfectly made-up eyes. "Okay, so tell me again about that wormy old cherry tree."

"I don't like it. I'm trying to sleep at night, and all I can hear is it creaking and groaning and ... *talking* to itself all night!"

"Talking!" Kashy giggled. "So now it's talking to you?"

"Yes. Swaying. Its branches rubbing against each other. Muttering and whispering at me, night after night. I hate that tree. I've always hated it. I wish Mum or Dad would cut it down." Gilla sighed. Since she'd started ninth grade two years ago, Gilla sighed a lot. That's when her body, already sprouting with puberty, had laid down fat pads on her chest, belly and thighs. When her high, round butt had gotten rounder. When her budding breasts had swelled even bigger than her mother's. And when she'd started hearing the tree at night.

"What's it say?" Kashy asked. Her angular brown face stared curiously at Gilla in the mirror.

Gilla looked at Kashy, how she had every hair in place, how her shoulders were slim and how the contours of the tight sweater showed off her friend's tiny, pointy breasts. Gilla and Kashy used to be able to wear each other's clothes, until two years ago.

"Don't make fun of me, Kashy."

"I'm not." Kashy's voice was serious; the look on her face, too. "I know it's been bothering you. What do you hear the tree saying?"

"It … it talks about the itchy places it can't reach, where its bark has gone knotty. It talks about the taste of soil, all gritty and brown. It says it likes the feeling of worms sliding in and amongst its roots in the wet, dark earth."

"Gah! You're making this up, Gilla!"

"I'm not!" Gilla stormed out of her chair, pulling her hair out of Kashy's hands. "If you're not going to believe me, then don't ask, okay?"

"Okay, okay, I believe you!" Kashy shrugged her shoulders, threw her palms skyward in a gesture of defeat. "Slimy old worms feel good, just," — she reached out and slid her hands briskly up and down Gilla's bare arms — "rubbing up against you!" And she laughed, that perfect Kashy laugh, like tiny, friendly bells.

Gilla found herself laughing too. "Well, that's what it says!"

"All right, girl. What else does it say?"

At first Gilla didn't answer. She was too busy shaking her hair free of the plaits, puffing it up with her hands into a kinky black cloud. "I'm just going to wear it like this to the party, okay? I'll tie it back with my bandana and let it poof out behind me. That's the easiest thing." *I'm never going to look like you, Kashy. Not anymore.* In the upper grades at school, everybody who hung out together looked alike. The skinny glam girls hung with the skinny glam girls. The goth guys and girls hung out in back of the school and shared clove cigarettes and black lipstick. The fat girls clumped together. How long would Kashy stay tight with her? Turning so she couldn't see her own plump, gravid body in the mirror, she dared to look at her friend. Kashy was biting her bottom lip, looking contrite.

"I'm sorry," she said. "I shouldn't have laughed at you."

"It's okay." Gilla took a cotton ball from off the dresser, doused it in cold cream, started scraping the makeup off her face. She figured she'd keep the eyeliner on. At least she had pretty eyes, big and brown and sparkly. She muttered at Kashy, "It says it likes stretching and growing, reaching for the light."

Who went for a ride...

"Bye, Mum!" Gilla and Kashy surged out the front door. Gilla closed it behind her, then, standing on her doorstep with her friend, took a deep breath and turned to face the cherry tree. Half its branches were dead. The remaining twisted ones made a mockery of the tree's spring finery of new green leaves. It crouched on the front lawn, gnarling at them. It stood between them and the curb, and the walkway was super long. They'd have to walk under the tree's grasping branches the whole way.

The sun was slowly diving down the sky, casting a soft orange light on everything. Daylean, Dad called it; that time between the two worlds of day and night when anything could happen. Usually Gilla liked this time of day best. Today she scowled at the cherry tree and told Kashy, "Mum says women used to live in the trees."

"What, like, in tree houses? Your mum says the weirdest things, Gilla."

"No. They used to be the spirits of the trees. When the trees died, so did they."

"Well, this one's almost dead, and it can't get you. And you're going to have to walk past it to reach the street, and I know you want to go to that party, so take my hand and come on."

Gilla held tight to her friend's firm, confident hand. She could feel the clammy dampness of her own palm. "Okay," Kashy said, "on three, we're gonna run all the way to the curb, all right? One, two, three!"

And they were off, screeching and giggling, Gilla doing her best to stay upright in her new wedgies, the first thing even close to high heels that her parents had ever let her wear. Gilla risked a glance sideways. Kashy looked graceful and coltish. Her breasts didn't bounce. Gilla put on her broadest smile, screeched extra loud to let the world know how much fun she was having, and galumphed her way to streetside. As she and Kashy drew level with the tree, she felt the tiniest bonk on her head. She couldn't brush whatever it was off right away, 'cause she needed her hands to keep her balance. Laughing desperately from all this funfunfun, she ran. They made it safely to the curb. Kashy bent, panting, to catch her breath. For all that she looked so trim, she had no wind at all. Gilla swam twice a week and was on the volleyball team, and that little run had barely even given her a glow. She started searching with her hands for whatever had fallen in her hair.

It was smooth, roundish. It had a stem. She pulled it out and looked at it. A perfect cherry. So soon? She could have sworn that the tree hadn't even blossomed yet. "Hah!" she yelled at the witchy old tree. She brandished the cherry at it. "A peace offering? So you admit defeat, huh?" In elation at having gotten past the tree, she forgot who in the story had been eater and who eaten. "Well, you can't eat me,'cause I'm gonna eat YOU!" And she popped the cherry into her mouth, bursting its sweet roundness between her teeth. The first cherry of the season. It tasted wonderful, until a hearty slap on her shoulder made her gulp.

"Hey, girl," Foster's voice said, "You look great! You too, of course, Kashy."

Gilla didn't answer. She put horrified hands to her mouth. Foster, big old goofy Foster with his twinkly eyes and his too-baggy sweatshirt, gently took the shoulder that he'd slapped so carelessly seconds before. "You okay, Gilla?"

Kashy looked on in concern.

Gilla swallowed. Found her voice. "Jesus fuck, Foster! You made me swallow it!"

Seeing that she was all right, Foster grinned his silly grin. "And you know what Roger says about girls who swallow!"

"No, man; you made me swallow the cherry pit!" Oh, God, what was going to happen now?

"Ooh, scary," Foster said. "It's gonna grow into a tree inside you, and then you'll be sooorry!" He made cartoon monster fingers in Gilla's face and mugged at her. Kashy burst out laughing. Gilla too. Lightly, she slapped Foster's hands away. Yeah, it was only an old tree.

"C'mon," she said. "Let's go to this party already."

They went and grabbed their bikes out of her parents' garage. It was a challenge riding in those wedge heels, but at least she was wearing pants, unlike Kashy, who seemed to have perfected how to ride in a tight skirt with her knees decently together, as she perfected everything to do with her appearance. Gilla did her best to look dignified without dumping the bike.

"I can't wait to start driving lessons," Kashy complained. "I'm getting all sweaty. I'm going to have to do my makeup all over again when I get to Patricia's place." She perched on her bike like a princess in her carriage, and neither Gilla nor Foster could persuade her to move any faster than a crawl. Gilla swore that if Kashy could, she would have ridden sidesaddle in her little skirt.

All the way there, Foster, Gilla and Kashy argued over what type of cobra a hamadryad was. Gilla was sure she remembered one thing; hamadryads had inflatable hoods just below their heads. She tried to ignore how the ride was making the back of her neck sticky. The underside of the triangular mass of her hair was glued uncomfortably to her skin.

Who went for a ride on a tiger …

They could hear music coming from Patricia's house. The three of them locked their bikes to the fence and headed inside. Gilla surreptitiously tugged the hem of her blouse down over her hips. But Kashy'd known her too long. Her eyes followed the movement of Gilla's hands, and she sighed. "I wish I had a butt like yours," Kashy said.

"What? You crazy?"

"Naw, man. Look how nice your pants fit you. Mine always sag in the behind."

Foster chuckled. "Yeah, sometimes I wish I had a butt like Gilla's too."

Gilla looked at him, baffled. Beneath those baggy pants Foster always wore, he had a fine behind; strong and shapely. She'd seen him in swim trunks.

Foster made grabbing motions at the air. "Wish I had it right here, warm and solid in between these two hands."

Kashy hooted. Gilla reached up and swatted Foster on the back of the head. He ducked, grinning. All three of them were laughing as they stepped into the house.

After the coolness of the spring air outside, the first step into the warmth and artificial lighting of Patricia's place was a shock. "Hey there, folks," said Patricia's dad. "Welcome. Let me just take your jackets, and you head right on in to the living room."

"Jeez," Gilla muttered to Foster once they'd handed off their jackets. "The 'rents aren't going to hang around, are they? That'd be such a total drag."

In the living room were some of their friends from school, lounging on the chairs and the floor, laughing and talking and drinking bright red punch out of plastic glasses. Everybody was on their best behaviour, since Patricia's parents were still around. Boring. Gilla elbowed Foster once they were out of Mr. Bright's earshot. "Try not to be too obvious about ogling Tanya, okay? She's been making goo-goo eyes at you all term."

He put a hand to his chest, looked mock innocent. "Who, me?" He gave a wave of his hand and went off to say hi to some of his buddies.

Patricia's mother was serving around mini patties on a tray. She wore stretch pants that made her big butt look bigger than ever when she bent over to offer the tray, and even through her heavy sweatshirt Gilla could make out where her large breasts didn't quite fit into her bra but exploded up over the top of it. Shit. Gilla'd forgotten to check how she looked in her new blouse. She'd have to get to the bathroom soon. Betcha a bunch of the other girls were already lined up outside it, waiting to fix their hair, their makeup, readjust their pantyhose, renew their "natural" lipstick.

Patricia, looking awkward but sweet in a little flowered dress, grinned at them and beckoned them over. Gilla smoothed her hair back, sucked her gut in, and started to head over toward her, picking her way carefully in her wedgies.

She nearly toppled as a hand grabbed her ankle. "Hey, big girl. Mind where you put that foot. Wouldn't want you to step on my leg and break it."

Gilla felt her face heat with embarrassment. She yanked her leg out of Roger's grip and lost her balance. Kashy had to steady her. Roger chuckled. "Getting a little top-heavy there, Gilla?" he said. His buddies Karl and Haywood, lounging near him, snickered.

Karl was obviously trying to look up Kashy's skirt. Kashy smoothed it down over her thighs, glared at him and led the way to where Patricia was sitting. "Come on, girl," she whispered to Gilla. "The best thing is to ignore them."

Cannot ignore them all your days. Gilla smiled her too-bright smile, hugged Patricia and kissed her cheek. "Mum and Dad are going soon,"

Patricia whispered at them. "They promised me."

"They'd better," Kashy said.

"God, I know," Patricia groaned. "They'd better not embarrass me like this too much longer." She went to greet some new arrivals.

Gilla perched on the couch with Kashy, trying to find a position that didn't make her tummy bulge, trying to keep her mind on the small talk. Where was Foster? Oh, in the corner. Tanya was sitting way close to him, tugging at her necklace and smiling deeply into his eyes. Foster had his I'm-such-a-stud smile on.

Mr. Bright came in with a tray of drinks. He pecked his chubby wife on the lips as she went by. He turned and contemplated her when her back was to him. He was smiling when he turned back. The smile lingered happily on his face long after the kiss was over.

Are you any less than she? Well, she certainly was, thank heaven. With any luck, it'd be a few years before she was as round as Mrs. Bright. And what was this less than she business, anyway? Who talked like that? Gilla took a glass of punch from Mr. Bright's tray and sucked it down, trying to pay attention to Jahanara and Kashy talking about whether 14-karat gold was better for necklaces than 18-karat.

"Mum," said Patricia from over by the door. "Dad?"

Her mother laughed nervously. "Yes, we're going, we're going. You have the phone number at the Hamptons' house?"

"Yesss, Mum," Patricia hissed. "See you later, okay?" She grabbed their coats from the hallway closet, all but bustled them out the door.

"We'll be back by 2:00 a.m.!" her dad yelled over his shoulder. Everyone sat still until they heard that lovely noise, the sound of the car starting up and driving off down the street.

Foster got up, took the CD out of the stereo player. Thank God. Any more of that kiddie pop, and Gilla'd thought she'd probably barf. Foster grinned around to everyone, produced another CD from his chest pocket and put it into the CD player. A jungle mix started up. People cheered and started dancing. Patricia turned out all the lights but the one in the hallway.

And now Gilla needed to pee. Which meant she had to pass the clot of people stuck all over Roger again. Well, she really needed to check on that blouse, anyway. She'd just make sure she was far from Roger's grasping hands. She stood, tugged at the hem of her blouse so it was covering her bum again. *Reach those shoulders tall too, strong one. Stretch now.*

When had she started talking to herself like that? But it was good advice. She fluffed up her hair, drew herself up straight and walked with as much dignity as she could in the direction of the bathroom.

Roger and Gilla had been the first in their class to hit puberty. Roger's voice had deepened into a raspy bass, and his shoulders, chest and arms had broadened with muscle. He'd shot up about a foot in the past few months, it seemed. He sauntered rather than walked and he always seemed to be braying an opinion on everything, the more insulting the better. Gilla flicked a glance at him. In one huge hand he had a paper napkin which he'd piled with three patties, two huge slices of black rum cake and a couple of slices of ham. He was pushing the food into his mouth as he brayed some boasty something at his buddies. He seemed barely aware of his own chewing and swallowing. Probably took a lot of feeding to keep that growing body going. He was handsome, though. Had a broad baby face with nice full lips and the beginnings of a goatee. People were willing to hang with him just in hopes that he would pay attention to them, so why did he need to spend his time making Gilla's life miserable?

Oops, shit. Shouldn't even have thought it, 'cause now he'd noticed her noticing. He caught and held her gaze and, still looking at her, leaned over and murmured something at the knot of people gathered around him. The group burst out laughing. "No, really?" said Clarissa in a high, witchy voice. Gilla put her head down and surged out of the room, not stopping until she was up the stairs to the second floor and inside the bathroom. She stayed in there for as long as she dared.

When she came out, Clarissa was in the second floor hallway. Gilla said, "Bathroom's free now."

"Did you really let them do that to you?"

"Huh?" In confusion, Gilla met Clarissa's eyes. Clarissa's cheeks were flushed and she had a bright, knowing look on her face.

"Roger told us. How you let him suck on your …" Clarissa bit on her bottom lip. Her cheeks got even pinker. "Then you let Haywood do it too. Don't you, like, feel like a total slut now?"

"But I didn't …"

"Oh, come on, Gilla. We all saw how you were looking at Roger."

Liar! Can such a liar live? The thought hissed through Gilla, strong as someone whispering in her ear.

"You know," Clarissa said, "you're even kinda pretty. If you just lost some weight, you wouldn't have to throw yourself at all those guys like that."

Gilla felt her face go hot. Her mouth filled with saliva. She was suddenly very aware of little things: the bite of her bra into her skin, where it was trying to contain her fat, swingy breasts; the hard, lumpy memory of the cherry pit slipping down her throat; the bristly triangular hedge of her hair, bobbing at the base of her neck and swelling to cover her ears. Her mouth fell open, but no words came out.

"He doesn't even really like you, you know." Clarissa smirked at her and sauntered past her into the bathroom.

She couldn't, she mustn't still be there when Clarissa got out of the bathroom. In the awkward wedge heels, she clattered her way down the stairs like an elephant, her mind a jumble. Once in the downstairs hallway, she didn't head back toward the happy, warm sound of laughter and music in the living room, but shoved her way out the front door.

It was even darker out there, despite the porch light being on. Foster was out on the porch, leaning against the railing and whispering with someone. Tanya, shivering in the short sundress she was wearing, was staring wide-eyed at Foster and hanging on every word. "And then," Foster said, gesturing with his long arms, "I grabbed the ball from him, and I …" He turned, saw Gilla. "Hey girl, what's up?"

Tanya looked at her like she was the insurance salesman who'd interrupted her dinner.

"I, Foster," stammered Gilla, "what's 'calumny' mean?"

"Huh?" He pushed himself upright, looking concerned. "'Scuse me, Tanya, okay?"

"All right," Tanya said sulkily. She went inside.

Gilla stood in the cold, shivering. *That liar! He has no right!*

Foster asked again, "What's up?"

"Calumny. What's it mean?" she repeated.

"I dunno. Why?"

"I think it means a lie, a really bad one." *He and his toadies. If you find a nest of vipers, should you not root it out?* "It just came to me, you know?" Her thoughts were whipping and thrashing in the storm in her head. *We never gave them our favour!*

Foster came and put a hand on her shoulder, looked into her eyes. "Gilla, who's telling lies? You gonna tell me what's going on?"

The warmth of her friend's palm through the cloth of her blouse brought her back to herself. "Damn, it's cold out here!"

Something funny happened to Foster's face. He hesitated, then opened his arms to her. "Here," he said.

Blinking with surprise, Gilla stepped into the hug. She stopped shivering. They stood there for a few seconds, Gilla wondering what, what? Should she put her arms around him too? Were they still just friends? Was he just warming her up because she was cold? Did he like her? Well, of course, he liked her; he hung out with her and Kashy during lunch period at school almost every day. Lots of the guys gave him shit for that. But did he like her like *that*? Did she want him to? *By your own choice, never by another's.* What was she supposed to do now? And what was with all these weird things she seemed to be thinking all of a sudden?

"Um, Gilla?"

"Yeah?"

"Could you get off my foot now?"

The laughter that bubbled from her tasted like cherries in the back of her throat. She stepped off poor Foster's abused toes, leaned her head into his shoulder, giggling. "Oh, Foster. Why didn't you just say I was hurting you?"

Foster was giggling too, his voice high with embarrassment. "I didn't know what to say, or what was the right thing to do, or what."

"You and me both."

"I haven't held too many girls like that before. I mean, only when I'm sure they want me to."

Now Gilla backed up so she could look at him better. "Really? What about Tanya?"

He looked sheepish, and kind of sullen. "Yeah, I bet she'd like that. She's nice, you know? Only ..."

"Only what?" Gilla sat on the rail beside Foster.

"She just kinda sits there, like a sponge. I talk and I talk, and she just soaks it all up. She doesn't say anything interesting back; she doesn't tell me about anything she does, she just wants me to entertain her. Saniya was like that too, and Kristen," he said, naming a couple of his short-lived school romances. "I like girls, you know? A lot. I just want one with a brain in her head. You and Kashy got more going on than that, right? More fun hanging with you guys."

"So?" said Gilla, wondering what she was going to say.

"So what?"

"So what about Kashy?" She stumbled over her friend's name, because what she was really thinking was, *what about me?* Did she even like Foster like that?

"Oh, look," drawled a way too familiar voice. "It's the faggot and the fat girl."

Roger, Karl and Haywood had just come lumbering out of the house. Haywood snickered. Gilla froze.

"Oh, give it up, Roger," Foster drawled back. He lounged against the railing again. "It's so fucking tired. Every time you don't know what to say — which, my friend, is often — you call somebody 'faggot.'"

Haywood and Karl, their grins uncertain, glanced from Roger to Foster and back again. Foster got an evil smile, put a considering finger to his chin. "You ever hear of the pot calling the kettle black?"

At that, Karl and Haywood started to howl with laughter. Roger growled. That was the only way to describe the sound coming out of his mouth. Karl and Foster touched their fists together. "Good one, man. Good one," Karl said. Foster grinned at him.

But Roger elbowed past Karl and stood chest to chest with Foster, his arms crossed in front of him, almost like he was afraid to let his body touch Foster's. Roger glared at Foster, who stayed lounging calmly on the railing with a smirk on his face, looking Roger straight in the face. "And you know both our mothers ugly like duppy too, so you can't come at me with that one either. You know that's true, man; you know it."

Before he had even finished speaking, Haywood and Karl had cracked up laughing. Then, to Gilla's amazement, Roger's lips started to twitch. He grinned, slapped Foster on the back, shook his hand. "A'ight man, a'ight," said Roger. "You got me." Foster grinned, mock-punched Roger on the shoulder.

"We're going out back for a smoke," Haywood said. "You coming, Foster?"

"Yeah man, yeah. Gilla, catch you later, okay?"

The four of them slouched off together, Roger trailing a little. Just before they rounded the corner of the house, Roger looked back at Gilla. He pursed his lips together and smooched at her silently. Then they were gone. Gilla stood there, hugging herself, cold again.

She crept back inside. The lights were all off, except for a couple of candles over by the stereo. Someone had moved the dinner table with the food on it over there too, to clear the floor. A knot of people were dancing right in the centre of the living room. There was Clarissa, with Jim. Clarissa was jigging about, trying to look cool. Bet she didn't even know she wasn't on the beat. "Rock on," Gilla whispered.

The television was on, the sound inaudible over the music. A few people huddled on the floor around it, watching a skinny blonde chick drop kick bad guys. The blue light from the TV flickered over their faces like cold flame.

On the couches all around the room, couples were necking. Gilla tried to make out Kashy's form, but it was too dark to really see if she was there. Gilla scouted the room out until she spied an empty lone chair. She went and perched on it, bobbed her head to the music and tapped her foot, pretending to have a good time.

She sighed. Sometimes she hated parties. She wanted to go and get a slice of that black rum cake. It was her favourite. But people would see her eating. She slouched protectively over her belly and stared across the room at the television. The program had changed. Now it was an old-time movie or some shit, with guys and girls on a beach. Their bathing suits were in this ancient style, and the girls' hair, my God. One of them wore hers in this weird puffy 'do. To Gilla's eye, she looked a little chunky too. How had she gotten a part in this movie? The actors started dancing on the beach, this bizarre kind of shimmy thing. The people watching the television started pointing and laughing. Gilla heard Hussain's voice say, "No, don't change the channel! That's Frankie Avalon and Annette Funicello!" Yeah, Hussain *would* know crap like that.

"Gilla, move your butt over! Make some room!" It was Kashy, shoving her hips onto the same chair that Gilla was on. Gilla giggled and shifted over for her. They each cotched on the chair, not quite fitting. "Guess what?" Kashy said. "Remi just asked me out!"

Remi was *fine*; he was just Kashy's height when she was in heels, lean and broad-shouldered with big brown eyes, strong hands and those smooth East African looks. The knot that had been in Gilla's throat all night got harder. She swallowed around it and made her mouth smile. But she never got to mumble insincere congratulations to her friend, because just then ...

They came back ...

Roger strode in with his posse, all laughing so loudly that Gilla could hear them over the music. Foster shot Gilla a grin that made her toes feel all warm. Kashy looked at her funny, a slight smile on her face. Roger went and stood smirking at the television. On the screen, the chunky chick and the funny-looking guy in the old-fashioned bathing suits and haircuts were playing Postman in a phone booth with their friends. Postman! Stupid kid game.

They came back ...
They came back from the ride ...

Gilla wondered how she'd gotten herself into this. Roger had grabbed Clarissa, hugged her tight to him, announced that he wanted to play Postman, and in two twos Clarissa and Roger's servile friends had put the lights on and herded everybody into an old-fashioned game of Postman. Girls in the living room, guys stationed in closets all over the house, and Clarissa and Hussain playing ...

"Postman!" yelled Hussain. "I've got a message for Kashy!" He was enjoying the hell out of this. That was a neat plan Hussain had come up with to avoid kissing any girls. Gilla had a hunch that females weren't his type.

"It's Remi!" Kashy whispered. She sprang to her feet. "I bet it's Remi!" She glowed at Gilla, and followed Hussain off to find her "message" in some closet or bathroom somewhere and neck with him.

Left sitting hunched over on the hard chair, Gilla glared at their departing backs. She thought about how Roger's friends fell over themselves to do anything he said, and tried to figure out where she'd learned the word "servile." The voice no longer seemed like a different voice in her head now, just her own. But it knew words she didn't know, things she'd never experienced, like how it felt to unfurl your leaves to the bright taste of the sun, and the empty screaming space in the air as a sister died, her bark and pith chopped through to make ships or firewood.

"That's some crazy shit," she muttered to herself.

"Postman!" chirped Clarissa. Her eyes sparkled and her colour was high. Yeah, bet she'd been off lipping at some "messages" of her own.

Lipping. Now there was another weird word. "Postman for Gilla!" said Clarissa.

Gilla's heart started to thunk like an axe chopping through wood. She stood. "What ...?"

Clarissa smirked at her. "Postman for you, hot stuff. You coming, or not?" And then she was off up the stairs and into the depths of Mr. and Mrs. Bright's house.

Who could it be? Who wanted to kiss her? Gilla felt tiny dots of clammy sweat spring out under her eyes. Maybe Remi? No, no. He liked Kashy. Maybe, please, maybe Foster?

Clarissa was leading her on a winding route. They passed a hallway closet. Muffled chuckles and thumps came from inside. "No, wait," murmured a male voice. "Let *me* take it off." Then they went by the bathroom. The giggles that wriggled out from under the bathroom door came from two female voices.

"There is no time so sap-sweet as the spring bacchanalia," Gilla heard herself saying.

Clarissa just kept walking. "You are *so* weird," she said over her shoulder.

They passed a closed bedroom door. Then came to another bedroom. Its door was closed, too, but Clarissa just slammed it open. "Postman!" she yelled.

The wriggling on the bed resolved itself into Patricia Bright and Haywood, entwined. Gilla didn't know where to look. At least their clothes were still on, sort of. Patricia looked up from under Haywood's armpit with a self-satisfied smile. "Jeez, I'm having an intimate birthday moment here."

"Sorry," said Clarissa, sounding not the least bit sorry, "but Gilla's got a date." She pointed toward the closet door.

"Have a gooood time, killa Gilla," Clarissa told her. Haywood snickered.

Gilla felt cold. "In there?" she asked Clarissa.

"Yup," Clarissa chirruped. "Your special treat." She turned on her heel and headed out the bedroom door, yelling, "Who needs the Postman?"

"You gonna be okay, Gilla?" Patricia asked. She looked concerned.

"Yeah, I'll be fine. Who's in there?"

Patricia smiled. "That's half the fun, silly — not knowing."

Haywood just leered at her. Gilla made a face at him.

"Go on and enjoy yourself, Gilla," Patricia said. "If you need help, you can always let us know, okay?"

"Okay." Gilla was rooted where she stood. Patricia and Haywood were kissing again, ignoring her.

She could go back into the living room. She didn't have to do this. But ... who? Remembering the warm cloak of Foster's arms around her, heavy as a carpet of fall leaves, Gilla found herself walking toward the closet. She pulled the door open, tried to peer in. A hand reached out and yanked her inside.

With the lady inside ...

Hangers reached like twigs in the dark to catch in Gilla's hair. Clothing tangled her in it. A heavy body pushed her back against a wall. Blind, Gilla reached her arms out, tried to feel who it was. Strong hands pushed hers away, started squeezing her breasts, her belly. "Fat girl ..." oozed a voice.

Roger. Gilla hissed, fought. He was so strong! His face was on hers now, his lips at her lips. The awful thing was, his breath tasted lovely. Unable to do anything else, she turned her mouth away from his. That put his mouth right at her ear. With warm, damp breath he said, "You know you want it, Gilla. Come on. Just relax." The words crawled into her ears. His laugh was mocking.

And the smile on the face ...

Gilla's hair bristled at the base of her neck. She pushed at Roger, tried to knee him in the groin, but he just shoved her legs apart and laughed. "Girl, you know this is the only way a thick girl like you is going to get any play. You know it."

She knew it. She was only good for this. Thighs too heavy — *Must not a trunk be strong to bear the weight?* — belly too round — *Should the fruits of the tree be sere and wasted, then?* — hair too nappy — *A well-leafed tree is a healthy tree.* The words, her own words, whirled around and around in her head. What? What?

Simply this: you must fight those who would make free with you. Win or lose, you must fight.

A taste like summer cherries rose in Gilla's mouth again. Kashy envied her shape, her strength.

The back of Gilla's neck tingled. The sensation unfurled down her spine. She gathered power from the core of her, from that muscled, padded belly, and elbowed Roger high in the stomach. "No!" she roared, a fiery breath. The wind whuffed out of Roger. He tumbled back against the opposite wall, slid bonelessly down to the ground. Gilla fell onto her hands and knees, solidly centred on all fours. Her toes, her fingers flexed. She wasn't surprised to feel her limbs flesh themselves into four knotted appendages, backwards-crooked and strong as wood. She'd sprouted claws too. She tapped them impatiently.

"Oh, God," moaned Roger. He tried to pull his feet up against his body, farther away from her. "Gilla, what the hell? Is that you?"

Foster had liked holding her. He found her beautiful. With a tickling ripple, the thought clothed Gilla in scales, head to toe. When she looked down at her new dragon feet, she could see the scales twinkling, cherry red. She lashed her new tail, sending clothing and hangers flying. Roger whimpered, "I'm sorry."

Testing out her bunchy, branchy limbs, Gilla took an experimental step closer to Roger. He began to sob.

And you? asked the deep, fruity voice in her mind. *What say you of you?*

Gilla considered, licking her lips. Roger smelled like meat. *I think I'm all those things that Kashy and Foster like about me. I'm a good friend.*

Yes.

I'm pretty. No, I'm beautiful.

Yes.

I'm good to hold.

Yes.

I bike hard.

Yes.

I run like the wind.

Yes.

I use my brain — well, sometimes.

(A smile to the voice this time). *Yes.*

I use my lungs.

Yes!

Gilla inhaled a deep breath of musty closet and Roger's fear-sweat.

Her sigh made her chest creak like tall trees in a gentle breeze, and she felt her ribs unfurling into batlike wings. They filled the remaining closet space. "Please," whispered Roger. "Please."

"Hey, Rog?" called Haywood. "You must be having a real good time in there, if you're begging for more."

"Please, what?!" roared Gilla. At the nape of her neck, her hamadryad hood flared open. She exhaled a hot wind. Her breath smelled like cherry pie, which made her giggle. She was having a good time, even if Roger wasn't.

The giggles erupted as small gouts of flame. One of them lit the hem of Roger's sweater. "Please don't!" he yelled, beating out the fire with his hands. "God, Gilla, stop!"

Patricia's voice came from beyond the door. "That doesn't sound too good," she said to Haywood. "Hey, Gil?" she shouted. "You OK in there?"

Roger scrabbled to his feet. "Whaddya mean, is *Gilla* okay? Get me out of here! She's turned into some kind of monster!" He started banging on the inside of the closet door.

A polyester dress was beginning to char. No biggie. Gilla flapped it out with a wing. But it *was* getting close in the closet, and Haywood and Patricia were yanking on the door. Gilla swung her head toward it. Roger cringed. Gilla ignored him. She nosed the door open and stepped outside. Roger pushed past her. "Fuck, Haywood; get her!"

Haywood's shirt was off, his jeans zipper not done up all the way. His lips looked swollen. He peered suspiciously at Gilla. "Why?" he asked Roger. "What's she doing?"

Patricia was still wriggling her dress down over her hips. Her hair was a mess. "Yeah," she said to Roger, "what's the big problem? You didn't hurt her, did you?" She turned to Gilla, put a hand on her scaly left foreshoulder. "You okay, girl?"

What in the world was going on? Why weren't they scared? "Uh," replied Gilla. "I dunno. How do I look?"

Patricia frowned. "Same as ever," she said, just as Kashy and Foster burst into the room.

"We heard yelling," Kashy said, panting. "What's up? Roger, you been bugging Gilla again?"

Foster took Gilla's paw. "Did he trick you into the closet with him?"

"What the fuck's the matter with everyone?" Roger was nearly screeching. "Can't you see? She's some kind of dragon, or something!"

That was the last straw. Gilla started to laugh. Great belly laughs that started from her middle and came guffawing through her snout. Good thing there was no fire this time, 'cause Gilla didn't know if she could have stopped it. She laughed so hard that the cherry pit she'd swallowed came back up. "Urp," she said, spitting it into her hand. Her hand. She was back to normal now.

She grinned at Roger. He goggled. "How'd you do that?" he demanded.

Gilla ignored him. Her schoolmates had started coming into the room from all over the house to see what the racket was. "Yeah, he tricked me," Gilla said, so they could all hear. "Roger tricked me into the closet, and then he stuck his hand down my bra."

"What a creep," muttered Clarissa's boyfriend Jim.

Foster stepped up to Roger, glaring. "What is your problem, man?" Roger stuck his chest out and tried to glare back, but he couldn't meet Foster's eyes. He kept sneaking nervous peeks around Foster at Gilla.

Clarissa snickered at Gilla. "So what's the big deal? You do it with him all the time, anyway."

Oh, enough of this ill-favoured chit. Weirdly, the voice felt like it was coming from Gilla's palm now. The hand where she held the cherry pit. But it still sounded and felt like her own thoughts. Gilla stalked over to Clarissa. "You don't believe that Roger attacked me?"

Clarissa made a face of disgust. "I believe that you're so fat and ugly that you'll go with anybody, 'cause nobody would have you."

"That's dumb," said Kashy. "How could she go with anybody, if nobody would have her?"

"I'll have her," said Foster. He looked shyly at Gilla. Then his face flushed. "I mean, I'd like, I mean ..." No one could hear the end of the sentence, because they were laughing so hard. Except Roger, Karl and Haywood.

Gilla put her arms around Foster, afraid still that she'd misunderstood. But he hugged back, hard. Gilla felt all warm. Foster was such a goof. "Clarissa," said Gilla, "if something bad ever happens to you and nobody will believe your side of the story, you can talk to me. Because I know what it's like."

Clarissa reddened. Roger swore and stomped out of the room. Haywood and Karl followed him.

Gilla regarded the cherry pit in the palm of her hand. Considered. Then she put it in her mouth again and swallowed it down.

"Why'd you do that?" Foster asked.

"Just felt like it."

"A tree'll grow inside you," he teased.

Gilla chuckled. "I wish. Hey, I never did get a real Postman message." She nodded toward the closet. "D'you wanna?"

Foster ducked his head, took her hand. "Yeah."

Gilla led the way, grinning.

They came back from the ride
With the lady inside,
And a smile on the face of the tiger.

THE LEFT HAND OF GOD

Shary Boyle

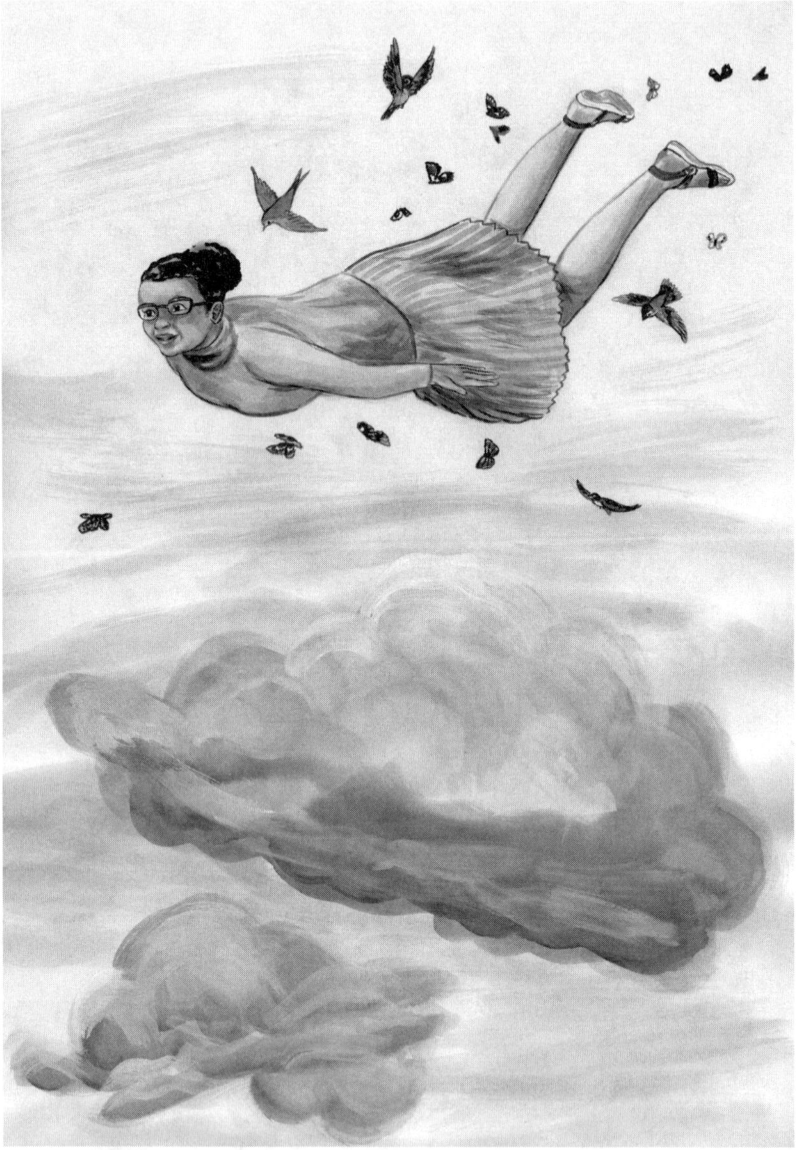

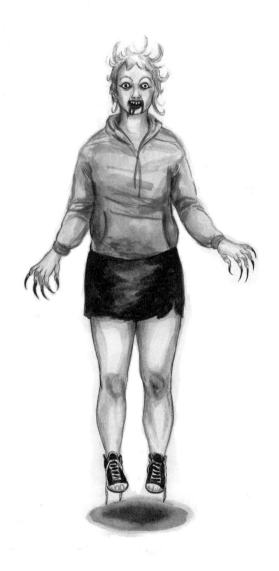

MYTH GIRLS

Kij Johnson

Myth Girls tell stories. It's what we do, same as Scooter Boys ride and Game Boys play. You have to be good to be a Myth Girl. You have to understand what the rules of a story are, how to tell it, when to scare your audience, when to let them off easy. You have to know how to fall into the trance that brings the Myth, and how to cement it in blood.

Pain cements things. I Tell you a Myth and I cut your hand, and you remember the pain and the blood, and the Myth with them. If you're part of an audience, you'll all remember, knowing that you might be the next one with a question. We try not to cut too deeply, but even so, Myth Girls don't tell light stories. Talk to a Story Boy for that.

It's hard to be a Myth Girl. What are you trading? Hard words and pain for food and a safe wall to sleep against. Not many people need the truth that badly.

Before I ran away, the Corp was training me to be a Savant. Mothers bring unwanted babies into the testing centres: if we pass the tests, the Corp buys us. I don't know how well the mothers are paid, but well enough that sometimes one has a baby hoping to sell it. I wonder what happens to the ones who don't pass the tests.

We're very expensive, Savants. There's the money to our mothers, and then there are all those years of feeding us and training us, paying our support "families" and making little corrections inside our heads until we can interface with the big computers. After they make the changes, we get seizures that make us try to claw our brains out, and the medicines to calm us cost a lot. Whenever I was screaming at them to stop the seizures, they would tell me how lucky I was to belong to them, and how grateful I should be.

I was grateful, until I was eleven. It was my birthday and I wanted real Nisei food, so they brought in a chef from outside, maybe even from the Tunnels, where everyone said the best Nisei food came from. He was small and wrinkled with his hair pulled back in a long tail. He cooked right in front of me: chopped real, dirt-grown vegetables into pieces with a big knife, and then cooked them on a little burner. When we were done eating, he cleaned his pot and burner and packed them away. The knife he swaddled in a clean cloth and slipped into a special case.

"Do you love your knife?" I asked, pleased to recognize the expression on his face.

He laughed. "It's just a knife. A tool."

"Then why are you so nice to it?"

"When your living depends on them, you look after your tools."

"Genoa, you'll catch your death of cold," one of the family interrupted. "Here, sweetheart; put on your sweater."

So I ran away. No one stopped me or questioned me, a little girl wearing slippers and clutching a bundle wrapped in a sheet, leaving by the Corp's main gate. I don't know what they were thinking, letting it be so easy, except maybe that tools usually stay where they're put.

I think I went only because I didn't know about the Underground. Mostly everybody ignored me, except for the ones who scared me. I walked and walked. A boy flew past on a scooter and grabbed the bundle from my hands. I started crying and didn't stop until much later, when I fell asleep in a pile of boxes set out for recycling in an access corridor.

I didn't feel anything while I was asleep, but someone stole my slippers. After that I walked barefoot through the broken glass and trash in the Tunnels, or I tied rags around my feet when they hurt too much. I couldn't run with bare feet, so I hid a lot. When I got hungry, I dug through the trash piled up all over and ate a lot of stuff that smelled funny and sometimes made me sick.

I had seizures once in a while. One time I woke up with my tongue sore from where I bit it and bruises all over my body that I didn't remember getting. Another time, I fell asleep exhausted afterward and a bum woke me up, pawing through my clothes. I didn't dare fall asleep after that. I kept moving down, deeper Underground, hoping the Corp wouldn't find me.

Then I saw the Myth Girls. They ran past me through the Tunnels, shouting "Myth Girls Tell! Myth Girls Tell!"

They were all a lot older than me, in their teens. Their long stained coats had things sewn to them: bones, hair, scraps of plastic, antique memory chips and bars. Their hair was long, tied back with coloured wires.

I was dizzy with tiredness and hunger, and my head hurt and I had diarrhea. I was afraid another seizure might start, which would leave me helpless, but I followed them because I didn't want to be alone in the Tunnels anymore.

They led me to an open place where five tunnels joined. In the centre of a gathering crowd, a gang-boy knelt in front of a Myth Girl, a small copper-skinned girl with slanted cat-eyes. He was wearing a transparent jacket painted with coloured slashes, dark skin ash-coloured with fear. The girl held a little ceramic knife in one hand, and the boy's hand in the other. "I Tell you the story; it answers the question. Blood cements it." She sliced his palm. Blood poured over the blade. The gang-boy shivered.

The rest of the Myth Girls whirled around, howling. My head was spinning, and I wanted to throw up. My hands didn't belong to me, numb and prickling, both at once. The shouting was like a scared heartbeat, fast and urgent. The Myth Girls' rhythms throbbed behind my eyes. A tall girl had a ratty knotted braid that fell to her knees; her eyes rolled up in her head, and she fell over and started to Tell.

It's easy for Savants to fall into trances: it's part of how they change our brains, it's why they pick us. I didn't realize I'd fallen into one until I woke up with my head in the copper-skinned girl's lap. The crowd was gone, and the Myth Girls were all kneeling around me. I felt too sick to be afraid.

The long-tailed one knelt beside me. "You okay, fod?" Fod for "fodder" — Tunnel-talk for kids. Her fingers tapped the floor in an itchy rhythm, like she couldn't hold still.

I shook my head, and then started crying, it hurt so much. "I'm — going to have a seizure. Don't let them find me —"

Copper-Girl said, "Hey, you Told. You not even a Myth Girl and you fell right into it."

"Please —" I sniffed.

"We watch you," Tail-One said impatiently. "Swear. You can trance?"

"It happens ... all the time," I said. And then the seizure started.

When I woke up later, I was in a pile of rags in a little alcove. Safe. Usually I made a mess of myself in a seizure, so I guess someone had cleaned me up. "Where —" I started.

An albino-white Myth Girl sitting next to me jumped up and left. Tail-One and Copper-Girl came back with her a moment later.

"Hey," said Tail-One, fidgeting, "I'm Maniac. I rule Myth Girls. This is Lyre —" she pointed to the copper-skinned girl "— and this Spider." That was the white one. "You?"

"Um, Genoa," I said.

"Why you Underground, Genoa? Girl like you must have a nice family somewhere."

"I'm a Savant. I was. I ran away."

"Shit, a Savant?" Lyre stared at me. "You a Savant, Corp takes care of you. Why run?"

"Um." I didn't even know the words for what had been wrong.

Maniac tapped her foot impatiently, fast. Maniac always moves like this, vibrates like a wire in a wind. "You too little to be by yourself Underground. You die."

"I'm okay," I said, but I shivered, remembering the Scooter Boy who took my bag, the stolen slippers, the unfamiliar bruises, the bum.

"Myth Girls be a small gang, but special. You be one of us, we take care of you."

"But I have to have this medication," I said.

"We steal the stuff we need to," Maniac said fiercely. "You Myth Girl now."

It was good with the Myth Girls. They cut my hand to make me part of the gang, and then gave me my own long coat and sewed the first pieces on. I didn't know anything about living Underground, but Maniac and the others helped me and got me medicine and took care of me. Lyre took me out teasing bums until Maniac chewed her out for taking me along on something so dangerous. Spider wanted to teach me to pick pockets, but Maniac said I didn't have to do that. I fell into a trance almost every time we Told, and she said that was hard enough work.

I'd been with the Myth Girls a couple of months when a woman came to us. She was thirty, dressed Corp but poor, like she was from uplevel maybe doing some drudgy little job to pay for a single room and maybe to feed a cat. Her black eyes were very big, and she was sweating, rubbing her palms dry on her jacket. She was scared but determined, needing magic. I felt bad for the ones like her, and there were a lot of them: there is no magic — not like she wanted, anyway — that would make everything happy and easy. But she had the money, and she had a question. Myth Girls don't say no.

People drifted toward us as we danced shouting through the Tunnels — a half-dozen, then a dozen more, until we had a crowd. They always gather. It's the horror of seeing a knife-victim bleeding on the street: you're afraid, but you can't resist. Even knowing next time it could be you.

I was spinning like a dervish, spiralling into my trance: even here, half lost, the Myth Girls whirling around me made me happy. I belonged here, with my friends, in the eye of this storm.

I raised my arms — they'd taught me a lot of gestures like this, to make it interesting. Maniac caught the Corp-woman's hand and held it palm-up, shiny with sweat. The woman whimpered, but I cut her anyway, saw the blood and closed my eyes.

I can't tell you a Myth without Telling. It's the chant and the song and the dance and the words, all together. Without the Telling, it just sounds like bits of old fairy tales, jumbled up with hearsay and vids and Tunnel-smarts. But it's the truth that's Told. If it comes out different every time, it's because you're different every time you ask.

While I Told, the rest of the Girls would swarm through the crowd, quick as rats. They'd take packages and tokens, anything that might not be noticed right away.

Afterwards, the Girls clustered around.

"Nice work, fod." Lyre handed me back my colours. I pulled the coat on, feeling it stick to my sweaty back and arms. I felt cold, tired, light-headed, a little sad, like always after I Tell.

"I did all right?"

Maniac danced from foot to foot. "Yeah." She touched my shoulder, already turning away to lean over Spider's shoulder. "What's the take?"

"Hey," Lyre hissed, and gestured with her head toward the shadows along the Tunnel's wall.

As soon as the story is over, the crowd always vanishes. Even the one who asks for the Myth leaves: I guess it scares them, what we do. No one *ever* stays. This time, someone was still there, leaning against the wall in the shadows under a broken Tunnel light. Watching us.

Maniac darted toward him, her little ceramic knife in her hand. "What you lookin' at?"

He stepped forward into a cone of light. He was medium tall, his face shadowed by a crop of rough hair. Old — maybe thirty. Dressed like anyone Underground, but he had no colours, no gang jacket, no affiliation marks anywhere. I knew he wasn't a bum: he didn't have enough scars and he looked too dangerous.

"I'm Jordan," he said, and looked us over.

"Shit," I whispered.

"Know him?" Lyre breathed.

"He's Corp, a Corporate Enforcer. I heard the name once."

"Shit," she said. Even down here no one would touch him: the Rules say he's safe. Not to mention he could kill you if he wants, and who's going to care about a Tunnel rat more or less? I kept my face down.

He said: "I'm looking for someone. Genoa. She's a Savant who came Underground."

Maniac strutted, knife flickering from hand to hand. "Just Myth Girls here, Corp-boy. You see any Sahvaants here?" She rolled the word out, mocking.

He stood still, not buying it. "I hear the Myth Girls have been stealing medication for Savant seizures."

"We no thieves," she said, but she was still.

"She'd be worth a lot of money to her Corp, this girl."

"No," Maniac said again, and I felt so happy I had to rub it in. See, I was important; I was a person. The Girls would never let anything happen to me.

I jumped up and walked forward, until I stood maybe ten feet from the enforcer. "Why you want her back?"

He looked at me, recognizing. "Her people want her back."

"She doesn't have people back there, just a Corp. She's just a thing to them."

"Right," Maniac said beside me.

I said: "If she's been gone a while, maybe she's lost her touch. Maybe they wouldn't want her anymore."

"No. They need her. You —" he stopped at my expression "— she knows how hard it is to be a Savant, how special. How important."

"Maybe she's special to someone else now. Maybe you'll never find her. You look and look, and she'll just never turn up." I'm pleading with him now, begging.

"Sorry." He stepped forward.

Maniac was suddenly between us. "Wrong, Corp-boy. Go home. We a family. We protect our own."

See? I wanted to scream at him.

"She's not yours," he said to her. "She's indentured to the Corp."

"Myth Girls got her now."

"Wait," I said, but Maniac was louder.

"You, Corp — you got lots like her. Forget this one. She's ours. She Tells Myths better than anyone."

"She can't make as much for you as I can offer for her return."

"It's not money," Maniac snapped. "Since she came, we sleep safer, eat better. We have face. Myth Girls keep what's theirs."

"She goes back," Jordan said evenly.

"You alone, Corp-boy. Who'll help you? Why don't I just cut you up and leave you here for the rats?"

"You're no slash gang; you don't have anything to prove. And you know the Rules. Hurt me, they come down on you. Nothing is worth that. Not even something as useful as Genoa here." He must really have believed that she wouldn't go after him, because he walked right past her and her knife, and caught my arm before I could jump back. "Talk's over. She comes home now."

"We need her," Maniac hissed. She lashed out with her knife and caught him in the side. He was right: you can't hurt an enforcer, not without retribution. Not if they know it's you. So you kill him, because then he can't finger you.

The Girls piled in, slicing with their little knives. I tried to join in until Lyre grabbed me and pinned me to the ground. "Let me go!" I screamed.

"Got to keep you alive," she snarled in my ear.

You look after your tools.

There was a flash of light and a smell like ozone. Spider screamed, and the Girls fell back. Jordan slumped panting in the clear space they left, a taser in his two hands. The wall behind him was splashed with his blood. Spider lay unconscious at his feet, legs jerking. "Looks like a standoff. I don't want to kill anyone, but I can," he said at last. "And I could come back for you, Genoa, but I won't. Just remember, we took better care of you. When you get tired of belonging to the Myth Girls, you'll come back."

"She's not going anywhere," Maniac panted.

I lay still, numb under Lyre's weight, watching Jordan leave.

That's when I ran away from the Myth Girls. They tried to find me at first, but gave up eventually: survival doesn't give you a lot of time for anything else. I didn't go back to the Corp, and I didn't join another gang.

I guess I'm a bum now. I'm hungry a lot of the time, and scared; but I have a place I can hide when I have the seizures, and I've padded it with bits of stuff so I won't hurt myself as much. This way I don't have to be a tool in anyone's hands.

Everybody takes care of their tools, but it's better to be a person. That's the truth I learned, cemented in Jordan's blood. And that's why I left the Myth Girls.

RED-HEADED ORPHANS RULE
WHY GIRLS OF SHADY ORIGIN AND IMPURE BREEDING KICK ASS

Catherine Stinson

When I was three years old and my brother was five, I asked for a Tonka truck for Christmas, and he asked for an Easy-Bake oven. Since it was the 1970s, we got our wishes, and my parents just thought it was funny. It really wasn't a big deal. So when I signed up for hockey school at the age of six, it came as a bit of a surprise that some people didn't think it was funny. It was not done. As soon as I stepped onto the ice, a boy skated by and pushed me down. From that moment on, I knew that being a tomboy was going to be a hard and lonely struggle. The feminist movement had won the right for women to vote, study medicine and wear polyester pantsuits, but it had not yet dealt with hockey, or ass-kicking in general. That job was left to little girls like me who liked to play with trucks, and we didn't have much guidance or encouragement. I didn't know of any real-life role models, and make-believe was dominated by Barbie.

I did, in the end, find a few ass-kicking girl heroes. As a child, I loved Little Orphan Annie, Anne of Green Gables and Pippi Longstocking, because of their strength and determination to do anything boys could do. Although they were tomboys, they were not necessarily feminist figures. For me, the two had been almost synonymous; being as strong, fast and agile as a boy was the way I expressed my girlhood feminism. My former girl heroes' individual stories also include disturbing subtexts that I didn't notice as a child. The three taken together also reveal some odd similarities that undermine their superficially progressive message in a more general way. Despite all this, I still derive some guilty pleasure from listening to my Annie record, I must admit.

In the 1970s and 1980s, at a time when I spent approximately eight hours a day watching TV, there were not very many powerful feminist characters targeted at the little-girl audience. Saturday morning cartoons were dominated by male characters — transformers, flying mice, singing chipmunks and professional wrestlers. Even mild-mannered Jem, whose holographic earrings and talking computer transformed her into a truly outrageous rock star, was basically an animated Barbie doll with big hair, iridescent makeup and bitchy enemies.

In traditional reading material, there were characters like Cinderella, Snow White and Little Red Riding Hood, all of whom were swept out of harm's way at the very last minute by a handsome prince or friendly woodcutter. In contemporary books, the female characters were concerned with boys, clothes and how they must increase their busts. That basically amounted to the same thing: if your feet were dainty enough, your reflection fair enough or you had a really snazzy red cape, a cute boy might save you from the horrors of unpopularity. Girls who read too many Judy Blume novels became paralyzed with fear that if they said anything out of the ordinary, or wore the wrong outfit they might be shunned by their peers. In fact, it seemed that any kind of action at all could lead to social death. I read these books and swallowed whole some of their damaging messages, but never fully connected with the characters. I didn't dream of someday marrying a prince. My dreams were more along the lines of winning a gold medal at the Olympics.

In the world of little girls, tomboys express budding feminist ideas with the simple refrain: "girls can do anything boys can do, better." Every town has its tomboy, but not many towns have two, so a tomboy's work of spreading the message of feminism is usually a solitary pursuit. Without allies, either in fiction, or in real life, it's hard to make the message convincing. When I finally found a few make-believe characters who didn't act like proper little girls, it was like finding a community. Annie, Anne and Pippi didn't keep quiet, didn't keep their dresses clean and weren't afraid to beat up their enemies. They were my sisters.

Although they were heroes to me as a child, upon later reflection, they didn't all live up to my expectations. Anne was noncommittal about her rejection of traditional girl roles. Many of her adventures sprang from her desperate need for acceptance. Annie's story was less about an orphan's struggle for freedom and more about making it rich in Depression-era America. It was basically a prop for capitalist propaganda. Pippi, a strange girl who lived alone with just a horse and a monkey, was the only one who stood up to my critical appraisal.

Little Orphan Annie, who charmed her way into a millionaire's heart and home, was the blockbuster exception to the rule that said all girl heroes should be pretty, polite and submissive. In 1924, Harold Gray created Little Orphan Annie for the *Chicago Tribune.* In 1981, when Columbia Pictures released a movie version of the Broadway hit *Annie* (itself based on the comic strip), it was an instant hit. Armed only with cleverness, guts and a song, Annie escapes from the clutches of the evil Miss Hannigan and the orphanage's near-slavery conditions, roams around New York City, saves a stray dog from being sent to the sausage factory and narrowly escapes being murdered by a money-grubbing fake daddy and his floozy wife. Annie seemed like a superhero when I was ten.

Anne of Green Gables became a role model later, in 1985, when Lucy Maud Montgomery's novels (written in the early 1900s) were turned into a TV miniseries. Although Anne tries to do what she's told and to hold her tongue, her hot temper always gets the better of her. She talks back to meddlesome next-door neighbour Mrs. Lynde on a regular basis, always gets into trouble at school, and completely upturns the quiet lifestyle of her adoptive parents, Matthew and Marilla. Despite her unpolished manners, plain dresses and humble beginnings, she comes out a hero. Anne matches wits with her competitor (and love interest) Gilbert, saves her bosom buddy Diana's croupy baby sister from certain death and gets the better of her arch-enemy Josie Pye in the end.

Astrid Lindgren's series of Pippi Longstocking books (the first of which was published in 1945) were popular throughout my childhood. A boring film adaptation was produced in 1973. In the books, the character is repeatedly described as the strongest little girl in the world. Her father's off being a pirate, her mother's dead and she's been left alone with a chest of gold coins. When the circus comes to town, she takes up the challenge to wrestle with the strongest man in the world and wins effortlessly. When children are trapped in a burning building, only Pippi dares to climb a tall tree and walk along a plank to rescue them from their window. She can outsmart any adult despite never having been to school.

On the surface, all three of these girl characters were very appealing. As a tomboy and a brain, I was often maligned for playing too roughly in the school yard, teased for not acting like a girl, called a show-off, and getting into scrapes for being a little too clever, aggressive and independent-minded for my own good. When Annie beat up a gang of nasty boys in a New York City alley, I found validation. I watched the movie over and over and over again.

I had also — like Annie, Anne and Pippi — been stricken with the curse of red hair. Perhaps it's a meaningless coincidence that so many progressive girl heroes are redheads, but I don't think so. Redheads — particularly female ones — are seen as odd, evil and hot-tempered. They're supposed to be ugly and strange, maybe witches or demons. There is even a Tom Robbins book, *Still Life with Woodpecker*, which is based on the premise that redheads are the descendants of an alien race colonizing the plant. If a red-headed character acts in unconventional ways, unbecoming to a proper little girl, all of the blame can be placed on her fiery hair. If redheads aren't quite human, it's only natural that girl redheads aren't quite girls. The message carried by these characters may not be that girls can be strong, smart and successful. The message may be that girls who are cursed with the evil red hair can be strong, smart and successful. The possibility is left open that their heroism is not due to bravery or strength, but to red-headed witchcraft.

As a child, one of my fantasies was to be an orphan. I dreamed of living in a house full of little girls. This might have been normal for a child with particularly strict parents, or an unpleasant home life, but my childhood was relatively stable, comfortable and free. When I questioned why I had this fantasy, it struck me that my girlhood heroes all shared yet another feature: they were all orphans.

The similarities in their stories are also striking. Annie and Anne were both nearly sent back upon arrival at their benefactors' houses because they weren't boys. Daddy Warbucks wanted a boy orphan to stay with him for a week, or, rather, he had thought that all orphans were boys. Annie charmed his mansion-full of servants into letting her stay with her song and dance routines and precocious worldliness. Anne charmed Matthew into letting her stay at Green Gables (despite the fact that he had wanted a boy who could help with the farm chores) with her flowery, overblown monologues, wild imagination and earnest humility.

Annie and Pippi both held dear to their hearts a gift from their parents that served as a symbol of the hope that they would one day be reunited with them. Annie guarded her half of a gold locket. Her parents were going to come back to her one day to reclaim her by presenting the matching half. They had been too poor to look after her as a baby, but would come back for her when they had enough money, she insisted. Pippi loved her oversized shoes, because her father had given them to her to grow into while he was away at sea, and she wouldn't wear any others until she was reunited with him. He had been shipwrecked, then became the king of an island of cannibals, she insisted. Nobody believed Annie's story, and nobody believed Pippi.

The orphan is a common stock character in children's fiction: from Oliver Twist to Tom Sawyer and Huckleberry Finn. Typically, either the orphan is a hopeless and helpless creature who eventually finds a benefactor, or the orphan takes advantage of his lack of supervision to live a wild, free life. Cinderella and Snow White, both motherless girls who are mistreated by their stepmothers, are of the first type. They wait for their handsome princes to come to the rescue, while they iron, scrub and hide out in the woods with a bunch of dwarves.

In the Depression era, American orphan characters started to take on a new role as a kind of blank slate, or a lowest starting point, from which their rise to success and greatness would make for the widest possible narrative stroke. To be able to dream the American Dream amid destitution, people needed super-sized, super-strong heroes. Spider-Man and Superman fit this model. Both were orphans who started from humble beginnings but rose to greatness through a combination of superpowers and strength of character without the help of millionaire benefactors or friendly woodcutters.

Annie is a substantial improvement over the girl orphan heroes who preceded her. She's outspoken, strong-willed and tough. Her heroism is not based on beauty, patience and good manners. In the early 1980s, thousands of little girls sang along to the movie's soundtrack, watched the TV special about the movie's casting, played with Annie dolls and dressed like her for Halloween. I watched the TV special with great fascination, imagined myself in the shoes of each girl who auditioned, and cursed Aileen Quinn for having won the part. If only I had been there, I might have beat her, I thought. Even if I couldn't sing or dance, they might have picked me, because I wouldn't have been a fake redhead with painted-on freckles.

But there are many ways in which Annie is not at all an improvement on predecessors like Cinderella and Snow White. Her life story is just a new spin on the same old story of a girl looking for a man. In this version, she's a helpless orphan in need of a strong, rich and handsome daddy to sweep her off her feet. Although her tomboyishness and independence make her seem like a feminist role-model, they're totally undermined by the purpose to which she puts these traits. Annie roamed the streets of New York City beating up boys, not because she wanted to flout social conventions, but because she was searching for a daddy.

In the end, Annie won what all the girls in the orphanage wanted. Even Miss Hannigan wanted a daddy (or husband or lover) desperately. Whenever a delivery man visited, she nearly tore his clothes off. Just like the little orphans, Miss Hannigan sang herself to sleep at night with mournful songs. (That she splashed around in a bathtub full of gin during the song was a detail that went over my head as a child.) Annie was the hero, because only she succeeded in getting her man. One of the final song and dance numbers has Annie and Daddy singing "I Don't Need Anything But You" to one another, as though they were romantic leads. Although she escaped a life of dish-washing and sewing in the orphanage, this freedom came in exchange for allowing herself to be washed, groomed and dressed in blue satin. She didn't trade in her proscribed gender role; she traded in her social class.

There are far more disturbing problems with Annie as a hero. I didn't understand the political aspect of the story when I was ten years old, but watching the movie again, it could hardly be more obvious. One of the scenes in which Annie endears herself to Daddy Warbucks is when Sandy saves their lives by barking at an intruder in the yard. A Bolshevik throws a Molotov cocktail through the window of Daddy's office, but because of Sandy's warning barks, Punjab is ready to dispose of the bomb. They explain to a shaken and confused Annie that the Bolsheviks hate Daddy Warbucks because he's living proof that capitalism works. The reason Daddy took in an orphan in the first place was to improve his image as a heartless, conservative politician. The scene in which Annie and Daddy fly to Washington to advise President Roosevelt on policy passed over my head as a child as just a boring scene. That Daddy was a munitions industrialist also meant nothing to me then.

Also disturbing, although not directly relevant to girl heroes, is the character of Daddy Warbucks's bodyguard. The character is played by a Black West Indian man, is named Punjab, wears a turban, charms snakes and quotes Buddha. This is something far more bizarre than a racial stereotype. It seems inconceivable that simple ignorance of any culture outside the white, Western world could explain this character's multi-faceted otherness. Punjab seems, rather, to be a carefully constructed mosaic of as many "foreign" cultures as could be packed into a secondary character. Daddy Warbucks's chauffeur (and master martial artist), The Asp, whose screen time is always accompanied by classic Chinatown-type movie music, nicely rounds out the squad of servants as a clunky combination of non-Western cultures. Their happy devotion to protecting and serving Daddy Warbucks can be read as a prototype of the Caribbean, Africa, South Asia, the Middle East and the Far East's enslavement to American industry and consumerism.

Anne of Green Gables was more of a role model for brainy girls than for tough girls. She isn't a superhero, but her story in many ways springs from the same source as Annie's (and she does give the boys of Avonlea a sound ass-kicking). She's so disaster-prone in the kitchen that she is relieved from the duties normally expected of a girl her age and is allowed to roam around the pastures with the freedom of a boy. She is hopeless at keeping her dresses clean and her hair neat. Instead of flirting with Gilbert, she fights with him. Instead of getting married right out of school, she goes away to college. In many ways she is a model for young feminists.

However, Anne of Green Gables does not completely live up to the progressive ideals she seems to represent. All of her success is due to brains and determination, not to gentleness and beauty, so she is a great improvement over more traditional girl heroes. But she suffers greatly because of her plainness. She desperately wishes that she could be pretty and demure instead of clever and feisty. Obsessed with Diana's raven black hair, Anne tries to dye her own hair black and only succeeds in turning it green. She begs, pleads and schemes until finally she gets a dress with puffed sleeves. Before her first poetry recital, she worries and frets for hours, not over her poem, but over her hair and blouse. One of her crowning demonstrations of tomboyishness — breaking her slate over Gilbert's head — is inspired by vanity. Gilbert had called her "Carrots." Years later, when at last Mrs. Lynde and the rest of the town harpies decide that Anne isn't such a terrible fright after all, part of their reasoning is that dressed up in her white lace blouse with puffed sleeves, she isn't quite as ugly as they once thought. Another part of their reasoning is that Gilbert Blythe, the most sought-after young man in Avonlea, is in love with Anne. They aren't at all impressed with Anne's successes as a student, writer or teacher.

Although Anne refuses Gilbert's proposal of marriage so that she can concentrate on her career (a decision that resonates with both the suffragette movement of the book's time and the second wave feminism of the TV series' time), it is seen as a mistake arising from her having too much pride. The regret she harbours for years afterwards reinforces this view. Marilla cautions Anne not to make the same mistake she made when she was young and rebuffed Gilbert's father, because Marilla ended up alone, hard and embittered. When Anne and Gilbert finally reunite years later, it feels like her refusal served only as a dramatic suspense that postponed the perfect ending. Her route to the perfect husband is unconventional, but she ends up in the same place. As readers and viewers, we know all along how it will end. The story reads like an epic romance, where the most unlikely of girls — outspoken, plain, evil-tempered and clumsy — manages against all odds to find true love, a storyline not dissimilar to many Judy Blume novels.

When I was eight or nine, I desperately wanted to be Pippi Longstocking. On my mother's suggestion (her suggestions were often of dubious quality and led to awful science projects on topics like rust and brine), I wrote a letter to MGM, asking them whether I could play Pippi in any upcoming movies they might do. We also included a copy of my Grade 3 school photo to demonstrate that I had the right hair for the job. They sent my picture back with a form letter.

Unlike the other red-headed girl orphans, Pippi Longstocking does live up to my initial reading. She is neither hopeless nor helpless. Everything she sets her mind to turns out to be a success. Like Tom Sawyer, she uses her lack of parental supervision as an opportunity to be wild and free. Instead of worrying about appearances, she glories in her ugliness. Unlike Anne, she does not fly into a rage when meddlesome old women call her ugly, skinny and red-haired. Pippi cartwheels down the street in delight, then tries to convince the pharmacist to make her a freckle cream that will give her more freckles. Although she has a treasure chest full of gold and jewels to live on, she patches her old dress and wears mismatched socks. She is the envy of her friends Tommy and Annika — children who are picture-perfect stereotypes of privilege and propriety.

Instead of waiting for a benefactor to sweep her off her feet, she fights off all the efforts of adults who try to "save" her. She refuses to be put in a foster home and spends only a few days at school before the teacher gives up on reforming her. When thieves try to rob her house, thinking it will be easy to take advantage of a lone girl with a chest full of treasure, she completely bamboozles them and scares them away. Instead of pining for parents who are never going to return, she does quite well living on her own with just a horse and a monkey for company. The story she tells about how her father was shipwrecked in the South Seas and is now the king of an island of cannibals sounds like a tall tale, but it turns out to be completely true. In *Pippi in the South Seas*, she takes Tommy and Annika on vacation with her to the island, where they frolic with the natives. (OK, that part's not so progressive.)

Pippi isn't all horseback acrobatics, wrestling and tossing burglars across the room; she also knows how to cook, clean and mend clothes. But when Pippi cooks, it's not complicated by gender roles; she cooks because she wants to eat cupcakes. She cleans simply because her house is filthy. She sews because her clothes are torn. Tommy and Annika are surprised that Pippi knows how to do these "feminine" things, since she's so unconventional, but Pippi's response is pure pragmatism. Whatever needs to be done, she can and will do.

The magic of Pippi's character is that she acts neither under the influence of, nor in reaction to social pressures. Since she was raised on a pirate ship, in an environment without socializing forces, she is completely oblivious to them and free to act on reason or whim alone. She reminds me of feral children. Instead of being raised without human contact, Pippi is a psychological experiment in being raised without social contact. Little Orphan Annie sells out her orphan sisters for a rich man and a comfortable, feminized life because she's a product of American society. Anne of Green Gables spends all her time and energy gathering academic accomplishments to compensate for her neurosis about her plain looks and lack of social standing, because Anne is a product of Western society. Pippi is as strong, smart, talented, altruistic and confident as a little girl can possibly be, because she's free from the crushing prejudices of society.

Although I was the first girl in my town to sign up for hockey, I wasn't the last. Another girl signed up two years later, and by now it's commonplace. Girls have infiltrated karate classes, "Boy" Scouts and computer camp. The role models for sporty girls still have many problems — like the all-white, nearly all-blonde US women's soccer team — but at least they don't wear pink sequined leotards. Not many little girls are lucky enough to be raised on pirate ships, but the social environment girls are growing up in has improved significantly since the 1970s.

RAW

Zoe Whittall

Will we be rich? The Ouija board said no.

Will George die a horrible painful death? Yes.

Should we go to work today? No.

We're trying to be optimistic. A day without work would smooth out our bodies like perfect fruit leather.

We're sitting on our seventh-floor balcony. It's a Sunday afternoon in Ottawa. We are two girls, both twenty-five, with eyes like lemon slices. The space between our thumbs and forefingers is raw from salt-sucked pre-tequila. Sour and lips burdened.

We don't really want our boss to die an incredibly painful death. Or maybe we do.

We're definitely drunk. The kind of drunk where it seems possible to have superhuman powers, to float above emotional upheaval, plan elaborate heists, resolve perceived injustices, dream big. We giggle through a plan to rob a bank without hurting anyone working there. It will be implausible tomorrow. Right now, we are the red and blue panels of a comic book, inking in the possibility of a better life.

Faces hot. Lips playdough red. We smirk into the smudged bathroom mirror like we're sharing private jokes with ourselves. We are drunk and broke. Broke and drunk. Solid *kuh* endings pronounced slow and slurring.

Cintra's got her shirt off and the whip marks on her back are healing. She pretends that the stinging left by strips of leather landing over and over is inconsequential, but I catch her looking at them in the mirror, straining her neck in the dim hallway light and frowning. I pour lotion on her back in the shape of a choppy heart monitor line and smear it across her raised skin. She winces.

I have a guitar and lyrics scrawled on a cigarette pack. The sun is going down behind the apartment complex across the street, and in the quietest moments we can hear my daughter Lara playing clapping rhyming games inside: "Miss Mary Mack-Mack-Mack, all dressed in black, black, black …"

Normally we don't put much faith in fate mass-produced by Parker Brothers, but Lara has been obsessed with it lately. The worn-in game board with its elegant font ends up at my feet more often than not, with Lara looking up at me from behind it wearing a demanding grin, punctuated by the recent loss of her two front teeth. The eight-year-old's fingers are slippery with trust as she asks the board over and over where God is and if she can talk to him.

Right now Lara is obsessed with cancer and God and the blood of the lamb. She has been talking to her grandmother. Now every time we lift up heavy glasses of milk at breakfast, she yells, "The blood of the lamb!"

Cintra rolls her eyes every time. I try to stay neutral, allow Lara to have her religious curiosity, hoping it might be a phase we can file away with the posters of the now forgotten boy-band in the basement.

Cintra's beeper lies like a bomb on the Ouija board. We're on call. The cleanest city has the most perverts willing to pay for redemption.

We're waiting for work and wishing it away. I'm strumming and singing, "The places you have come to fear the most." But the bones of my fingers aren't strong enough to keep it up. I abandon the guitar. Cintra smokes. Tap, tap, inhale. Little "O"s of smoke form around our ankles. The ashtray is overflowing. My hands smell like old metal.

I pull my knees up under me, close the Ouija board and place it back in its box.

Lara slinks outside in Cintra's big high heels. "Can I have your lipstick, Mommy?" I hand her the tube of pink gloss that marks the story I'm reading in a magazine about how to get out of a trunk if you're being kidnapped. Apparently, you just kick out the tail lights and wriggle your fingers, try to catch the attention of cars behind you. A woman in Baltimore saved herself this way because a passing car called the police when they saw her hands popping out of the trunk.

Lara sits at my feet with her slightly warped play mirror. The faces of the kittens that form a border around the reflective surface have been scratched off from years of use. She will line her lips carefully and then dab them with little dots of pink. It will consume her for almost half an hour.

When I say, "You are very pretty and don't need to wear lipstick," her eyes glaze over.

"It smells like cherries," she says. I leave her to her task.

George beeps. I've got a call in one hour, a regular. "It's Brian," George grunts semi-audibly into the voicemail. "If you're late, I'm taking another 10 percent."

Brian is our weekly client who has a superhero fetish. A white guy pushing fifty who's kink is pretending to be Batman. I am, of course, Robin. He wears custom-made underoos beneath his slick expensive suit. The rumour around the Dungeon is that he is a supreme court judge. He's been a client for over ten years.

I stand in front of the coffee maker trying to reason with it, while Cintra gulps down icy Gatorade and calls a cab. Draining the last of the half-and-half into a plastic mug of coffee, I catch Cintra sitting perfectly still on a kitchen chair, eyes closed. I walk over to her and hold her head against my chest. "You're my favourite," I tell her.

"And you're mine." She mumbles with her ear pressed against me in a sideways hug, listening to the faint sound of my heart scraping against the wire of my bra like radio static.

Sometimes I can't remember when Cintra wasn't my sidekick. When my husband was well, she was merely a good friend to pal around with. Now she was filling in this space that felt more like family.

Lara sits on my husband Jason's lap in the living room with *Horton Hears a Hoo*. He got out of bed today. He should get a fucking gold star.

Jason hasn't been able to work in months because he injured his back. I suspect it is fine now, but the depression keeps him whining on the couch, flipping channels with his painkillers poised. I started doing dungeon work when Lara was two. I was nineteen. "Supplementary income," we called it, when we dreamed about owning a house and sending Lara to a good school, which wasn't possible when we both worked in retail and were trying to go to college ourselves. At the time, we were able to see out of the rut we and the universe created. The fact that I worked at the dungeon bothered him a bit, though not enough to say I couldn't do it. He would never say I couldn't do something. Instead, he'd swallow his resistance until it hollowed out something inside him. I stopped when he got a promotion at the warehouse where he worked, and we were more stable. We never really spoke about it after that, until his compensation ran out after he injured his back. When I started up again, a few months ago, he didn't seem to mind at all.

Last week he said: "I saw a show last night on the documentary channel and these hookers were talking about it being an empowering job. I think that's kind of cool — I mean, I never thought of it like that before. They were all so tough and smart, just like you."

He meant well, but I wanted to slap him when he said that. I stared at the space between his neck and heart. "And sexy," he added after a moment. I felt like my heart had just slipped through a colander and fallen on my toes.

Cintra and I stumble into the waiting red and yellow cab. I roll on the elastic costume in the dressing room, become an androgynous sidekick. At first Brian and I play like we are four and six, chasing each other around the room and making up a thin plot of some save-the-city-from-evil adventure. It seems like some childhood regressive-therapy nightmare.

Cintra will enter soon. She waits outside in the hall with her watch and a lingerie catalogue until the right moment to curl her lasso around his neck. She's Wonder Woman. She rushes in and beats him up in the last ten minutes of the session. He has to resist first. She pulls the lasso tight, until he's almost dead. Almost. "Robin, are you trying to get fresh with my boyfriend?" she screeches, hand on her hip.

The first time we did this, we could barely suppress our giggles. The look in his eye is ecstatic, like he's just got three cherries in a slot machine. Half gone. When the floor or my leg is stained with the evidence of a job well done, his eyes are muddy crucifixes. He averts them and packs quickly. He jogs out the door like he's in a relay race with the next client.

George pays us our cut with slick palms. He has a bloody nose. I picture my hands around his thick neck, my prints in his veins. His neck is scarred like someone slit it unsuccessfully in the 80s. That's the rumour, anyway.

In the cab home, I use my fingers to force my jaw to relax, circling around the bones in the shape of countries I want to visit. Cintra sings along with the radio under her breath. She's better than the original.

We're superheroes with heavy sandpaper lids. "Sober, sober up," Cintra says. The "brr" sounds funny. I stole the cape from the costume room. In case we ever really put our bank-robbing plan into action, we'll have the disguises. Payback.

Will we die if we rob the bank? The Ouija board says: Yes.

Lara watches the *PowerPuff Girls,* lying on the floor in front of the couch. She makes up songs about the characters. My husband is asleep. I kiss him on the forehead, because when he sleeps, he looks like a little boy and I remember when I used to adore him.

Cintra and I go back on the balcony. The sun is setting, softening against our sensitive skin.

Cintra and I are still in the last panel of a comic book, fading from bright colours to black and white, *to be continued* scrawled in the bottom corner. I put on the cape and stand on the edge of the balcony, feeling soft and furious.

CINEMATIC SUPERBABES ARE
BREAKIN' MY HEART

IT'S HARD TO GO ALL THE WAY WITH THE NEW BREED OF LADY
KILLERS WHEN THEY JUST WON'T LET GO OF THAT MAN

Lisa Rundle

With her fists flying, but never breaking a sweat, she not only unlocks the grasp of that strong man holding her down but reduces him and his (three? seven? twenty!) friends to blubbering rubble. Or, in one elegant, effortless gesture, drives a stake through his heart. It's the kind of X-treme Empowerment that's appearing with almost shocking regularity on movie screens nowadays. And after taking in one such film, I inevitably find myself kung-fu fighting out of the Cineplex and happily thwap-thwapping my way home.

Female-hero flicks are not only attractive to your average gal looking for action, they're downright addictive. From the mind-bending experience of seeing *Tank Girl* back in 1995 to the more recent *Lara Croft Tomb Raider* (I and II), *Charlie's Angels* (I and II) and the *X-Men* (I and II, which, despite the name, features some hefty heroines), things are looking up for superwomen-loving-women. The number of offerings in this vein, on screens small and large, is unprecedented.

Time to celebrate, right? After all, I'm not the only woman taking the adrenaline these ladies deliver home with me. You can see the delicious new script — women as fighters, not victims — being acted out on playgrounds and reverberating in the heads of grown women too, if my head is anything to judge by. (Walking alone at night, I now imagine perfectly executed high kicks, flips, and cut-him-down remarks in place of the futile squirms and wide-eyed silence of the sexualized, defenceless victim, a role so often reserved for women.) Amber Nasrulla in *The Globe and Mail* has noted that the new breed of female-led entertainment has inspired record numbers of women to take up martial arts.[1] Whoever still thinks that viewing audiences are mere passive containers has another thing coming — *kapow!*

There will always be a special place in my heart for all the girl-heroes I've loved before: Xena the Warrior Princess (and Gabrielle!), Buffy the Vampire Slayer (and Willow!). But I can't help noticing that the ranks of fans are not populated by feminist-friendlies alone, looking for good wholesome woman-positive entertainment. It seems the upshot of these vastly popular movies and TV shows isn't all girl power, all the time.

Like most of us, I've developed a healthy ability to suspend disbelief that allows me, on occasion, to guzzle pop culture gleefully and even find feminist heroes. But with the latest rash of lady killers onscreen (certainly in some ways a step up, for women actors if no one else), I've become all too aware, as I sit in the theatre full of, well, the general public, that what's generally being celebrated is a pretty damn traditional male watcher/female watched scenario. Superbabes are stereotypical heterosexual male sex fantasies writ large and as much as they kick ass, they wiggle it. Truly feminist characters these are not.

Did I just write that? I didn't think it possible I'd ever find myself proclaiming something "truly feminist" or not. In fact, I think there are multiple readings of almost anything and that they are all, in the most basic way, "true." But I'm also coming to accept that, whatever my preferred fantasy, there is without a doubt a hierarchy of readings (where the feminist one may not be the primary or, in many cases, even an intended one), and all readings need to be taken into consideration if we want to look honestly at what pop culture is feeding us. Besides, it's hard not to notice those "readings" that are being shoved in your face: like Lara Croft's giant, gravity-defying boobs.

It's no accident that Hollywood studios insist that strong women leads, in this case Angelina Jolie, must "remain feminine," as one of the *Tomb Raider* producers reassured in an interview. They know what they're selling and who they're selling it to. As long as the Alpha female is "still female" (read: counts heterosex-appeal among her most power-ful weapons), she safely remains an object of entertainment for the tra-ditional male viewer. The fantasy: dream fuck, not castration nightmare.

Think about any of the various *Charlie's Angels* threesomes, from Jill, Sabrina and Kelly to Dylan, Natalie and Alex. The distinction between their shows and soft porn is negligible. The action can feel like nothing more than a fun new scenario that requires the gals to run, jump and jiggle in their skimpy ensembles (though the most recent film did include a nod to the less fashion-conscious with a mullet-sporting Cameron Diaz, as well as some fancy, fully-clothed motorbike drivin'). And despite the opportunity for the mutant heroines of the *X-Men* to explore in depth things like marginalization, rejection by society for being different and the penalties for having unauthorized power(s), on top of everything else the gals are doing in the film (changing the weath-er, changing shape, etc.) they're wearing painted-on outfits and sacrific-ing themselves for their men. It's not that these characters aren't all strong, it's that they are also all good old-fashioned sex objects. In the end, it serves to remember that the lifeguards in *Babewatch,* I mean *Baywatch,* were heroes too.

It's the great talent of the high-powered, high-het babe that she can satisfy certain feminist desires — even ride to fame co-opting them — while staying open to absolute opposite readings. Could she be queer? Sure, she dabbles. Is she a feminist? She does what she wants. Is she the ultimate straight male fantasy, emerging as the product of the brains of the same? Oh yeah, definitely. Let's tally: the X-Men were created by Stan Lee and the movies were directed, written and (primarily) pro-duced by men, Lara Croft emerged from the mind of gamer Toby Gard, Charlie's angels were originally Aaron Spelling's creation, famous femi-nist that he is. Men are still the bosses of Hollywood and, at the risk of oversimplifying, it shows in what's being produced that not many women producers, directors or writers are getting a piece of the super-lady action behind the scenes. Or maybe more to the point, that not many women-positive productions, regardless of who they are created by, are seeing the dark of the theatre. In the last few years I've come to the crushing conclusion that most movies are by men, for men, and about men. Maybe that's not news. But it's so damn common, it's actually easy not to notice. And anyone who's not the main in the mainstream gets pretty used to inserting themselves into pop culture wherever they can, by identifying with the marginal characters, who may look like them, or with the heroes, who almost never do.

So now, when it feels almost as though this new breed of films is catering to feminist viewers, it's enough to make me weep tears of gratitude. But should I? It's the genius of mass culture that I can be sitting in the front row experiencing A while the wanker at the back is experiencing B, that it can be both an exhilarating, empowering experience *and* a degrading one that feminists have been pointing out for over thirty years. It bothers me that the biggest Neanderthal I know loves some of the same movies I do — because just as I'm filtering out the sexism to get to the feminism, he's filtering the other way around. And I suspect that the people who filter the way he does make up as much or more of the audience than the people who filter the way I do. After all, these blockbusters wouldn't be blockbusters if they were first and foremost feminist films. Surely, if they were, there would be slightly more variety amongst super-powered women, in their appearances if nothing else. They might even mirror, say, the luxurious variety of their human counterparts. And, for goddess's sake, we'd see a wee bit of armpit hair every now and again. It's only in the context of the utter lack of anything resembling feminism in the vast majority of pop culture that a little female strength is such a thrill.

OK. OK. About the eye-candy factor — I admit that women enjoy it too. We'd hardly be modern consumer humans if the shining stretches of skin weren't part of what gets us off. (The outfits! The hair!) And for those of us whose sexuality falls anywhere on the continuum other than "straight and narrow," we certainly get our share of viewing pleasure. The well-timed admissions of same-sex taste-testing by the stars themselves help feed this enjoyment. (Note that it also doesn't hurt the fantasy geared toward straight men either. Ah, that old movie magic.)

So women like to watch too. We want her. We want to be her. What's the problem? Couldn't one-size-fits-all pop culture be a good thing? Or at least an improvement? Maybe. But there's that nagging voice in my head that's asking: Shouldn't we want more? Shouldn't today's angels be rid of Charlie and be able to beat the bad guys (or gals) without having to spend so much time wiggling their barely bikinied bums? Cute as those bums are, I can't imagine missing them if I were getting some real feminist action. (I can see it now: Girls and women would go in droves to see superheroes who look like them, whose superpower glows from firmly rooted confidence within. These heroes would wield the kind of power that can be shared — not the power to crush things or beat things to a pulp or damage anything, but the power to be flexible, be steady, be yourself. It's the kind of power that, when you get close to it, makes you want to follow the person who's got it around until you figure out how to find the mysterious place inside that can give you the same.)

Of course, we are getting something *like* real feminist action, which is the confusing part. It's just been put through so many money-making mills that it's become a brainless clone of itself. That *is*, after all, what the mega-corp, mass-culture machine does best: it trolls for the new cool thing, finds (in this case) feminist empowerment for girls, takes away the political oomph, sexes it up and, presto! What ten years ago was about taking up space, screaming the realities of our lives, looking however we pleased, sleeping with whomever we chose, not being ashamed, and not standing for injustice, now, to the TV-watching world, means fun slogans that sell us tampons, music and, yes, $13-a-pop movies. Each new incarnation seems that much farther from the original — Riot Grrls are to *Buffy* as *Buffy* is to the vanilla witches of *Charmed*. The more watered-down the message of power and freedom for women and girls, the more palatable it is to the mainstream, capitalist world.

This isn't a surprise. We've recognized the distorted echoes of our own voices, but even this weaker, weirder version of feminism somehow feels better than nothing. It means we've had an impact. The world has changed because of us. It's just hard (as in painful and, therefore, as in difficult) to keep it at the front of our brains that the world hasn't changed enough. And that we're not sure how to make it change more. That sometimes we fear it never will, and that a small league of super-beauties, their power out of reach to us and out of touch with the kind of power that would really change this world, is the best we can hope for. It's the burden of having this kind of knowledge that makes us want these escapist fantasies, crave them. Give me the matrix! Plug me in!

Cultural writer and editor of this anthology Emily Pohl-Weary asks: "What is it about my real life that makes me want to crush my enemies?" The question ignites a flash of recognition: we know the answer. It's all the injustices and indignities we face in real life that make the fantasy of slaying our enemies so damn sweet. These larger-than-life ladies are fearless where we must stay fearful. That's why we love them.

Even when we suspect that we're not the ones who are really winning, and that, in a way, neither is the wanker in the back. After all, it's the billion-dollar industries that are making off with the dough.

Wait, am I saying my super babe crush days are over? Am I suggesting that a (ahem) *truly* feminist response would be to girlcott mass entertainment and its attendant merchandising industries? To rise above the allure of girl power, repackaged and sold back to girls? That we should refuse to take our girl power cut with sexism? Sorry, Great Ideal Feminist Angel in the House; I can't do it. I wouldn't ask myself or anyone else to give up that salve to real-life lack of power, as temporary as its effects may be.

What I *am* saying is this: sometimes, when the sugar buzz of a candy-coated viewing experience wears off and the fuzzy after-taste sets in, I just wanna brush my teeth and get on with the business of saving the world with the real-life super-powered gals I see all around me. I want to put my time and energy into stuff that breaks down the staring-me-up-and-down/shouting-lewd-comments-in-the-street status quo. And while I'll take the fantasy of power that's on offer now, I won't stop demanding better. It may be an uphill battle, but women know better than ever that they're up for the fight. Don't forget all those new, real-life, kung-fu fighting women now in training. We may get the last laugh after all.

*

NOTE

1. Amber Nasrulla, "Everybody is Kung-fu Fighting," *Globe and Mail*, May 17, 2003, L2.

KARATE GIRLS

Eliza Griffiths

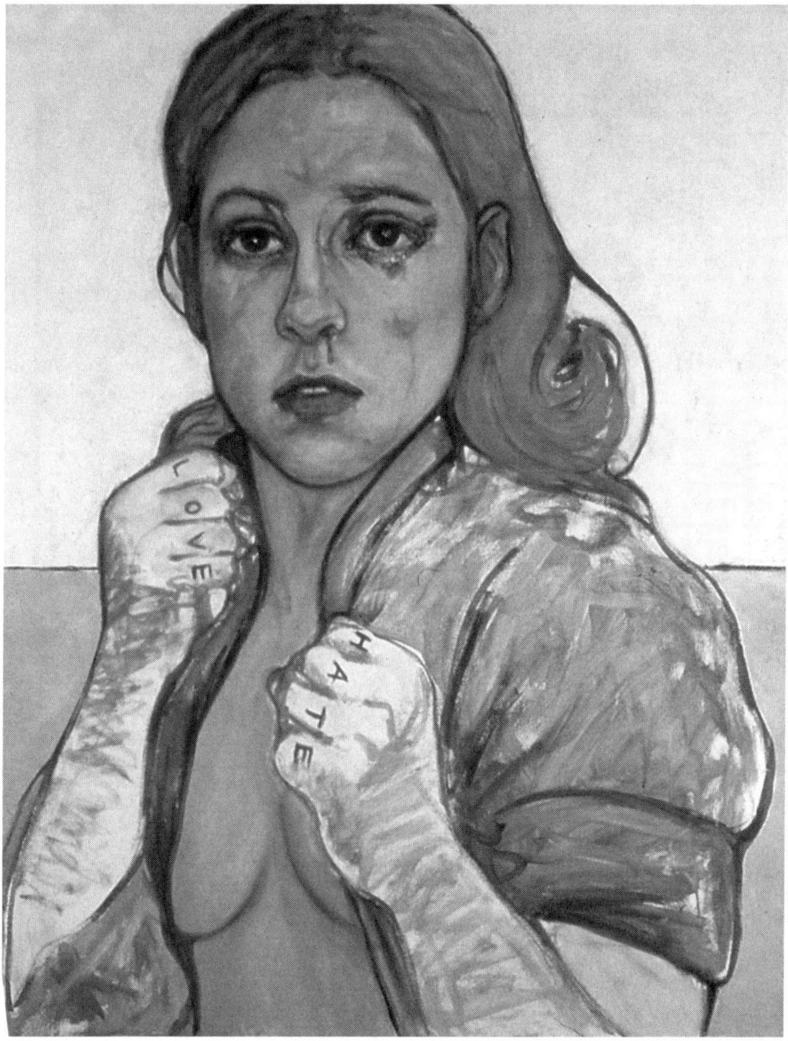
LOVE
HATE

BOND, JANE BOND

Halli Villegas

I am getting older. When I was young, Wonder Woman, Isis, and the first set of Charlie's Angels were on television. These were the female superheroes of my era: women so far from my actual experiences as a girl that they didn't inspire much in me except a lifelong penchant for red boots and big bracelets. Now, as a thirty-six-year-old woman, I am offered long-suffering wives on sitcoms like *Everybody Loves Raymond* or *About Jim*, neurotic sex kittens on *Sex and The City*, and the boringly realistic C. J. on *The West Wing*. Excuse me if I yawn. I do not see myself reflected in any of these women. There is nowhere in modern middle-age media scenarios for my heroic imagination to alight.

By necessity, I have become a detective, searching for bits and pieces to form a picture of what could be. Pam Grier in *Jackie Brown* and Rene Russo in *The Thomas Crown Affair* have some of the strengths I would like in a superwoman. Independence, brains, confidence and style. But they're a decade older than I am. These few women may offer a few good examples but the trail is growing cold. I get the feeling that, after thirty, a woman is supposed to put away dreams of power, become practical. Unlike the taut-tummied Buffy the Vampire Slayer, or the "new" Charlie's Angels, we are seen as no longer ripe enough to kick ass, and are instead supposed to settle for marriage and motherhood, and leave the ass-kicking for girls who can still dance around in boy's underwear and look sexy, not demented.

We have supergirls; now where are the superwomen?

During a recent bout of bronchitis, I was confined to bed, and watched the three newest James Bond movies. Formulaic and ridiculous as they were, I realized there was something compelling about the dapper, confident, unapologetic character. He's a relief from the endless neuroses of modern men and women.

A blueprint for a new kind of superwoman began to form in my mind: one who has all the qualities I would like to possess. She would fight for causes that interest me. She would have wit, strength and know how to dress. I believe the time has come for Jane Bond.

*

We are in a darkened theatre. After the ads for Dynamint gum featuring awkward teenage couples and a preview that has you sucking in your stomach and wondering about the virtues of sunless tanning, you hear the Jane Bond theme music sung by Angie Stone. Any woman who can sing about "that time of the month" with all the power of a gospel, warning "Don't even mess with me" the way that Stone does, is exactly the kind of woman who can sing Jane Bond's song.

On the screen we see a shot of a rumpled bed and Jane's long brown hair on a pillow. One olive-skinned, shapely plump leg hangs over her side of the bed. An alarm goes off on the bedside table. Jane's hand with short clean nails reaches out and turns it off. Jane sits up and reaches for her robe. We see that she is wearing a silk tank and boy's shorts. She is luscious, curvy, fit. Next to her, a young woman rises in the bed. The woman has spiky blond hair. She puts her hand on Jane's back.

WOMAN: Do you have to go so soon?
JANE (*turning back to the woman*): Sorry, darling, duty calls.
WOMAN: Jane, be careful, please.
JANE: I always am.

Jane bends the woman back over a pillow for a long goodbye kiss.

*

Since James Bond is portrayed as the ultimate man, a real man's man, if you will, using him as the basis for my new superwoman may seem like a mistake. However, I contend that James Bond is not quintessentially male. James is rather proud of dressing elegantly, likes his domestic comforts, knows how to use his sexual allure to his advantage and seems to prefer foreplay to sex. We never see James in graphic sex scenes. Instead he is popping a bottle of bubbly, kissing, making sexual puns or fitting a diamond neatly into the navel of his female friend. All that aside, however, he remains a one-dimensional character who represents some of the most insidious aspects of white male–dominated culture.

So my Jane differs from James in all but the most basic of ways.

James is almost ridiculously straight. He teeters on the edge of misogyny. Jane is bisexual. She is old enough to know that you never know in what form attraction will come. Jane enjoys herself with many sex partners and, like James, leaves them satisfied, safe and not feeling at all resentful that she won't drop everything to take care of their needs, or start a relationship.

James Bond is the ultimate WASP male, right down to the British accent. Despite England's years of colonizing other nations and the influx of immigrants of all nationalities, James is driven snow. Bi-racial, Jane carries the blood of many countries and cultures. She does not bemoan her round behind, soft belly or dark hair. She loves her body as it is. She stays fit but doesn't diet. She eats what she likes and likes what she eats. Jane Bond never refuses a glass of Dom Perignon because it will go straight to her thighs.

I have a sneaking suspicion James Bond uses a Soloflex or at the very least a Swedish Ball in the privacy of his own home to keep his six-pack popped. Jane belly dances.

*

The movie continues with a long shot of Jane driving down a crowded city street in a silver hybrid car. The car stops at a traffic light and behind it is a huge billboard for the new *Charlie's Angels* movie.

In a close-up of the car's interior, we see a small Buddha on the dashboard and Nina Simone is playing on the radio. Jane is wearing dark glasses and drinking a green power shake. She drives up to a sleek office tower and disappears into an underground parking garage.

The camera pans the garage's interior. Jane pulls sharply into a parking spot, but not before we see that it is very clearly marked Reserved for Jane Bond.

*

Some superheroes, like James Bond, are loners. They need to be unencumbered in order to put their lives on the line. If they had to worry about family, friends or lovers, they might think twice before taking risks, and hesitation can be fatal in the crime-fighting world. However, true superheroes need support, someone to take care of the details so that the world can be saved on a daily basis without them having to stop and pick up phone messages or fill out paperwork.

Jane is no different. She has her very own Moneypenny, named Dollar Bill. Dollar Bill is an intelligent assistant of the opposite sex who worries about her health and safety, longs to take care of her, but knows that Jane is her own woman and never so desirable as when she is free. Dollar Bill holds down the fort at the office. He takes calls, dispatches memos of great importance and yearns for Jane's return.

*

Back in the theatre, we watch Jane enter the reception area of her office, where a very handsome young man (Dollar Bill) is busy typing away at a computer keyboard. He looks up, sees Jane, picks up a pad from the desk and stands immediately.

DOLLAR: Jane, there are a bunch of messages for you this morning. Obviously you had your cell off. Again.
JANE: Yes, Sweetie, I had a very important meeting. (*She takes the pad from him.*) Anything interesting?
DOLLAR: No, but that's not the point. What the hell am I supposed to do if I have to get a hold of you?
JANE: I'd love it if you'd get a hold of me, but not today, Sweet Pea. We've got work to do.

*

Jane never sleeps with Dollar Bill — that would ruin the symbiotic relationship they have. However, there is always a frisson of sexual tension between them. In most of Jane's dealings with others there is a sexual undertone. For Jane, like James, sexuality is an integral part of her personality, one that people respond to.

Jane Bond knows what she wants and is not afraid to ask for it, whether it is a martini — shaken not stirred — or information regarding the nuclear weapons hidden in local caves. Jane does not deal exclusively with the concrete (diamonds, weapons, etc.) like James. She chooses to direct her considerable energies toward things like putting an end to sex slavery in Bangladesh.

In all James Bond movies, Q provides James with the gadgets he needs to be able to bring the bad guys down. Q is constantly admonishing James to return the technological wonders intact, which seldom happens. Q invents new aids in every movie, and James runs through them like water. The cost to his government must be staggering. On top of his other shortcomings, it's obvious James does not believe in recycling. Jane doesn't have a Q to invent lipstick-case weapons or invisible cars for her. There is no country to foot her bills if she blows up her hybrid. Like all women since time immemorial, she has to do it for herself.

James ultimately has to answer to M, the head of his organization. Often M asks him for sacrifices such as abandoning a partner or taking the back seat on a case. Although these orders don't sit right with James's conscience, he does it for the good of his country. Being a renegade, Jane does not have an M. There are no government affiliations to justify her forays into the underworld to right wrongs. She has her own agency and, consequently, her own conscience. Because of this, Jane is more humanitarian than James. She puts people before countries, suffering before nationality. There are more shades of grey in Jane's world.

*

The next scene opens with a wide shot of Jane dressed in a *salwar kameez* on a crowded street in Dhaka, Bangladesh. She hurries through the crowd of people of all ages and sizes. The camera closes in as she gives some coins to a beggar child who tugs at her hand. Then she hurries down a narrow alley and ducks into a dark doorway.

(*A man's voice with an East Indian accent is heard from the shadows*): Have you brought the goods?

JANE (*with a Bangledeshi accent*): Yes, I have her. But I believe that I should deliver her to the man myself. I have heard of your reputation. I don't trust you to pay me my share.

MAN (*laughter*): So you do not trust me. I am not the one who is selling my sister into slavery.

Jane: You know I had no choice. Since the drought our family has suffered, I have watched my brothers and sisters die one by one ...

MAN: Save your story, I don't care. I only care that she is a virgin. All right, here is the address of the brothel. Bring the girl this evening, late. I do not want the customers disturbed by any parting tears. Go, and you had better return, or I will arrange for you and your family to be killed, in a manner far more painful than any drought.

Close-up on Jane's eyes: they narrow in anger behind the scarf she has wrapped around her head. She bows slightly, turns and hurries out. A black curtain is pulled from a small window by an Indian woman in a sari, letting in a shaft of light that illuminates the speaker. It is a white man.

*

James Bond remains unfazed in any situation. We never know how he has come by this trait, whether it is arrogance, training or natural composure. When confronted by the enemy, James tends to go for the big show. There are huge explosions, lengthy car chases, drawn-out violent fights to the death, a lot of destruction and waste to achieve his goal.

Coming from a carefully cultivated place of central stillness, Jane is also imperturbable. She goes on a yearly retreat to a Buddhist monastery and meditates daily the rest of the year. When faced with evil, she is not caught unawares, but reacts in a measured way. She uses the appropriate amount of force for the situation, sometimes just a withering glance or a single blow aimed at the exact point of the enemy's weakness. Her Zen training has paid off.

Despite this, Jane does have her weaknesses. She is prey to a touch of vanity, the occasional foul mood where she lashes out at those closest to her. On occasion, the enemy is able to catch Jane in such a moment and take advantage of it. But not for long.

❋

Jane walks into an upscale lounge on the ground floor of the hotel. We hear the tinkle of crystal, music and low laughter. She is wearing a dress that shows her curves to advantage, but very little flesh is exposed, just her throat and décolletage. Jane seats herself on a bar stool and catches the bartender's eye.

The bartender makes his way over to her. A man at the bar stops him briefly, but Jane does not notice.

JANE: A Bombay gin martini with a twist. Shaken not stirred.

The bartender leaves and then returns with her drink. He sets it in front of her. He nods toward a man seated a few seats away, who raises his drink to her.

BARTENDER: With the gentleman's compliments. He said that dress is worth a dozen drinks.

Jane smiles, raises her drink to the man and can't help looking at herself in the mirror behind the bar to double-check what she already knows, that she is having a good hair day. In the mirror, she notices another man standing up in the booth behind her. He aims a gun at her head. She ducks as the first shot is fired. The bartender dives behind the bar. Other patrons begin to scream and crouch down in their booths.

Jane pulls a small gun from her garter and aims at the man, who is now running for the door. She shoots and hits him in the leg. The man collapses as two burly hotel security guards enter the lounge and run toward him, guns pulled.

BARTENDER (*rising from behind the bar, visibly shaken*): What the hell was that?

JANE (*laughing*): One of the few virtues of vanity.

She heads toward the exit where the guards have taken the man.

*

The allure of a good number of today's supergirls lies in the fact that they look and behave like sex kittens, but are actually intelligent, buff women. The sex-kitten ploy the superheroines adopt gives men a stereotype they are comfortable with. The men are then caught off guard when they discover the busty blonde has a bazooka. The girls are simply using that age-old female superpower: blatant sexuality.

It works if you are twenty and have perky breasts. By the time you're thirty-six, you better have something besides cleavage to distract the bad guy. Brains, strength and a good grounding in the martial arts all help immensely.

Jane eschews the "distract them with your gams" game. Not because she isn't sexy, but because she has a sense of integrity that demands that men see her as the intelligent, fierce woman she is from the first meeting. She carries herself with confidence and speaks with conviction. Perhaps this inability to play the typical sex-object role, even to her advantage, is part of Jane's vanity and therefore part of her weakness. For those of us who grew up believing the only way to get what you want was by appealing to men's sexuality, this "weakness" is part of her appeal.

The man who misreads Jane, gives her the wrong kind of attention when she is trying to talk business, or dismisses her as another hysterical female, might find himself with a black eye, broken nose or a shattered kneecap. Despite Jane's willingness to give a good swift kick when the situation warrants it, Jane prefers to use that most underrated of female superpowers, her intuition. Although Jane can size up a situation instantly, she has no problem pausing to check in with her gut. As often as possible she diffuses things before they get out of hand.

Jane Bond trusts herself; therefore she does not hesitate to take control. If she is wrong, she will apologize for the inconvenience caused but never for the original impulse. Like James, she never apologizes.

*

Onscreen, Jane is still dressed in her *salwar kameez*. She sits in a squalid room in Dhaka containing only a tiny bed and a light bulb hanging from a cord in the middle of the ceiling. There is a small window high up on the wall. She is about to dial a number on her cellphone when she hears a knock on the door.

Jane stuffs the phone under the mattress and slides out a small handgun, which she tucks into the waistband of her *salwar kameez*. The knock sounds again. Jane goes over to the door.

JANE: Who is it?
MAN'S VOICE WITH AN INDIAN ACCENT: A friend.
JANE: I have no friends in Dhaka.

She pulls the gun from her waistband and opens the door slowly. A handsome dark-skinned man in a white kurta is standing there. She puts the gun to his neck, glances behind him to see if anyone else is in the hall, pulls him into the room and shuts the door.

MAN (*calmly*): Please, can you take the gun away. My name is Santosh. I must talk to you.
JANE (*still pointing the gun at him*): Strip.
MAN: What?
JANE: You heard me, gorgeous; those kurtas can hide a multi tude of sins ... Let's see what you're hiding.
MAN (*speaking strongly, not pleadingly*): Nothing, I am hiding nothing ...

He sees that Jane is serious and begins to remove his clothing.

MAN: This is ridiculous.
JANE: Slowly, calmly, so I can see your hands ...
MAN: You must believe me.

He is now wearing only his pants. Jane motions for him to remove those. The man does so, saying: Your life, it is in danger, but I can help you ...

There's a close-up shot of totally gratuitous full-frontal nudity.

JANE (*still pointing the gun approximately at his groin area*): And why, dear friend, should I trust you?

Not only does James Bond seem to have been born with his sense of self, it also seems as if he had no mentors, no false starts. Jane Bond knows the reality that we all have to begin somewhere. She remembers the women who taught her how to shoot a gun, speak new languages, mix a good martini and meditate. She knows superwomen are always learning, always sharing with other women.

Although in real life sometimes women can be divided and conquered, Jane realizes there is super-strength that comes from women working together. Since Jane is a superwoman, she has time and energy to teach a self-defence class at a woman's shelter, mentor a teen girl and rescue women who are being exploited.

For Jane, rivalry with other women is a waste of time. Jane is comfortable with her place in the scheme of things. She knows she has the power to affect her life, and the myriad aspects of her nature are fully engaged on a daily basis. She knows there is no man, money or position worth a good woman in a tight spot.

*

There is a clear view onscreen of Jane and a woman in a sari (Sarita). They are crouched against a wall in an alleyway. There is shouting and gunfire nearby.

JANE: Thank God we got the girls out safely. Santosh had the truck waiting right where he promised.

She takes a small gun from her waistband and hands it to Sarita.

JANE: Here, take this.
SARITA (*horrified*): Oh, no, Jane, I couldn't.
JANE: You can't be afraid of a gun. For God's sake, you're helping to bring down the biggest sex-slave smuggling operation in East Asia. This may be the only way we're able to get out of here.
SARITA: Jane, it is against my religion to kill any living creature.
JANE: Mine too; I'm basically Buddhist. That's why you aim for the crotch. They don't call them the family jewels for nothing.

She hands the gun to Sarita, who takes it with a very reluctant hand and holds it limply.

JANE: When we get out of this, remind me to show you how to handle a gun. Don't worry, you shouldn't have to shoot; just a gesture in that direction makes men agree to anything. And for God's sake, show me how to wrap this damn sari correctly; it keeps coming undone. I'm afraid I'm going to trip and break my neck.

Sarita giggles and holds the gun with more confidence.

JANE (*grabbing her hand*): Let's go ...

They run toward the light at the end of the alley.

*

Jane and her cohorts will get out of every sticky situation they find themselves in. In the next movie she rescues a woman in Pakistan from an honour killing; in the previous one she helped a woman in the Ozarks, Arkansas, who was being threatened when she started a small loan company for women in her town to open their own businesses.

Just as James Bond's fight to save the world continues movie after movie, Jane's work to save humanity will never be finished, and that is what gives her victories such poignancy.

Jane Bond, the character, is invincible. She will be resurrected again and again. In each movie, she will experience her moment of defeat and be caught off guard, but she does not let her failures define her. She learns from them and carries on to finish what she started. The ultimate defeat would be for her to stop doing what she believes in, to let her power die.

Without the guns, exotic locations and limitless bankroll so thoughtfully provided by the movie studios, Jane still has the extraordinary powers all women have: those intimidating and exhilarating powers like strength, confidence, compassion, sexuality, intelligence and intuition.

＊

The final scene fills the screen. Jane is dressed in a white silk Indian nightshirt. She's sitting on a huge double bed that's draped with white netting. A fan turns overhead and there is a silver bucket with champagne sitting next to the bed. Jane is sipping from a flute. She puts it on the bedside table.

JANE: I am reminded of how we met.

Santosh, the handsome Indian man from Dhaka, lies on the pillow next to her. He raises himself on one arm. He is bare-chested.

SANTOSH (*looking at Jane adoringly*): How so?
JANE (*taking him in her arms*): I wasn't sure then whether you had a gun down your pants or you were just happy to see me.

Jane bends over him and her cellphone rings. As she starts to kiss him, she turns it off with one hand.

SANTOSH (*sighing beneath her*): Oh, Jane ...

＊

WHEN I WAS A GIRL, I WAS A BOY
MY QUEST FOR A FEMALE ACTION HERO

Esther Vincent

My mission: find the perfect woman. She has to be tough, smart and fun, have superpowers, and a cool cape. She should be four to six inches tall, made of plastic and able to rival all the plastic men her own size.

This search began when two friends who have a five-year-old son were concerned that his 95 percent-male action figure collection was leading him astray of a gender neutral view of the world. They heard I was going to be in Toronto shopping at some of the finest comic book and action figure stores within driving distance and asked that I bring home a female figure suitable for their boy.

I accepted the mission. I was happy to have the opportunity to scope out action figures while furthering the cause of confident and powerful women. Although some might suggest that worrying about gender equity in a five-year-old's toy collection is taking both feminism and parental influence a bit far, I believe kids take in information about whom they are expected to be from the first day. And through action figures and superheroes, we illustrate who we wish we were. They are our fantasy selves, exaggerated representations of our attitudes and beliefs.

When I was young, I learned a lot about what it meant to be a girl from TV, books and toys. My mother and grandmothers were the only women in my life. I had no sisters, aunts, nieces or female cousins. I had a father and brother at home and there were only boys in the neighbourhood. So I grew up doing "boy things" with them. We rode bikes, made tree forts, threw things at each other and play fought.

Even after encountering girls in school, I didn't go out of my way to spend time with them. I didn't know girls. I didn't know what girls were like. I had already internalized the message that — never mind blondes — boys had more fun.

I had one female friend, Colleen, who owned lots of pink clothes, a Lite-Brite, and Donny and Marie Osmond dolls (they weren't called "action" figures). She was very girlie. I liked her a lot but she was definitely not the same kind of girl as I was.

During my first days of kindergarten in 1973 the boys were allowed to drive the pedal car and play loud, active games like policeman and fireman. The girls were relegated to making pretend brownies in the play kitchen, which seemed to involve a lot of sitting around and stirring. I made such a fuss that I was allowed to play with the car.

That episode made it clear to me that if I was ever going to get ahead in the world I should learn how to stand up for myself. And because I was forced to make a choice — kitchen or peddle car — I also (maybe falsely) reasoned that it was also important to forsake all things pink and girlie. I had to avoid everything in that play kitchen and all it stood for. From that moment on I never looked back.

When I was a girl, I was a boy. I embodied boyhood with enthusiasm and single-mindedness (and it didn't hurt that I was, as my dad said, "built like a brick shit-house"). I wore only jeans, T-shirts and running shoes and did as little as possible with my hair, which although it was long from not being cut, was unkempt. When I was in grade three I had to wear a skirt for the class photo. The other kids pointed and laughed at me because they thought I was a boy in a dress. Eventually, one of them pointed out that I had a girl's name and therefore must actually be a girl. This elicited louder peels of laughter. I thought it was pretty funny, too.

Maybe because of my early male identification I tended to read and watch things about boys. My action figures were mostly male. I had no interest in dolls, mere mannequins that couldn't bend their arms and legs, or even stand up on their own. When I did encounter a female character, I seldom identified with her. I saw her the way the author, usually male, would; the way the other boys who read or watched did. She was an Other, someone outside of the natural order of things. Girls needed to be treated differently. Girls didn't like bugs or snakes. Girls didn't like roughhousing. Girls didn't like to do any of the *really* fun stuff. Girls were a pain in the ass.

When I was young, not only was I a boy, but I was misogynist. I was certainly not the first or only girl in the world for whom this was the case. "You wanted to be a boy?" a friend said to me recently. "Well, who the hell didn't?!?"

Many of us learned early that life for a girl had less potential than it did for a boy. And for centuries, girls and women have soaked up the message that they, and their female peers, are not as good as boys. Our mothers and grandmothers learned this lesson and then became our primary examples of behaviour and attitude. My own mother had a less than appreciative opinion of women. She also had few female relatives and very little contact with girls and women as a child. Her own mother was a dedicated homemaker who, as was common during the 1930s and 1940s, seldom went out and didn't have female friends. Like me, my mom didn't know how to be a girl. "I saw what women did as frivolous, unfulfilling, wasteful," my mom tells me. "I liked boys because I thought they were more intellectual. But that was coming entirely from a place of ignorance."

My mother recognizes her ignorance now, although she didn't at the time. Nor did I, as a young girl, have any reason to doubt my opinion that girls were no fun. Everywhere I looked there were images of active, capable men and inactive, helpless women, who were either dippy clotheshorses, diplomatic conversationalists or the caretakers of men. And when a woman did take action, her primary concern always seemed to be that she not muss her hair or break a nail.

Sure, there were a few choice feminine images. Superwoman, She-Hulk and The Bionic Woman come to mind, but they were all woefully inadequate attempts at gender equity. Even Wonder Woman, a fully developed character in her own right, suffered from gender tokenism in the otherwise entirely male Justice League of America. And don't get me started on Charlie's Angels. Not only were they helpless without the almighty word of some slimy jerk named Charlie, they, well, they ran like girls. That's just not cool.

Certainly, there was something to be said for the positive influence of the female characters who were peacemakers and diplomats, but when it comes to fighting super-criminals, eventually there comes a time for physical battle. No matter how smart your talk is, it's just talk. Maybe I was a female freak of nature, but I wanted to be where the action was. I wanted to be the one to leap tall buildings, throw boulders and set things ablaze with a glance. At the very least, I wanted to be able to swoop into battle, sword or sling-shot in hand, ready to slice through villains or pick off the enemy lines.

I liked the "man alone" characters, like Zorro. I wanted to be the single, self-sufficient, too-cool-for-school character who, with the trusted friendship of a horse or dog, went off in search of disasters to avert and evildoers to thwart. I loved Zorro for his quick mind and deadly swordsman's accuracy but also for his dark past, his apparent love for the people he defended, his desire to learn and expose the truth and, ultimately, his strident independence. There was just nothing like him for girls.

I looked for strength, independence, intelligence and courage, but would constantly be disappointed by women who resorted to the costume and accessory method of fighting evil. A magic tiara here, an alluring bust-line to "distract the enemy" there, putting on a pair of glasses to "look smart." These girls didn't truly kick ass. When pop culture sent the message that girls are weak, inactive fashion victims, I didn't think it applied to me because I didn't see myself as a girl. But many of the girls I grew up with took this message to heart. When they emulated their favourite superheroines by getting their outfits together, I knew they were falling for the myth that dressing for success is all that's needed to show power and ability.

I was not at all surprised when, with the onset of the eighties, I encountered the same phenomenon in *Vogue, Cosmo* and *Flare* — the adult woman's fantasy guides — which suggested that the red power-suit was the way to the top of the corporate ladder. No one mentioned that brains, perseverance and knowing yourself had anything at all to do with it. Although *GQ* would often suggest that a good suit could open doors, it never intimated that the right suit alone would make a man a CEO. And they never once suggested that a guy should show up to work in a head-to-toe red power-suit with matching handbag and shoes. Whose dumb idea was that? Someone who watched a little too much Wonder Woman if you ask me.

Some girls even believed they needed to present themselves as weak in order to be truly feminine. I remember a friend in Grade 8 trying to teach me to be a girl. "Boys like girls who are gullible," she said, and "Make sure you wiggle your bum when you walk." She didn't make this stuff up. But where did *she* hear it? Like me, she found many sources that suggested women's best weapons were seduction and manipulation.

Because of the influence of friends like this and, of course, the onset of puberty I became more conscious of my gender. I knew I wasn't a boy. I realized I didn't want to be one, either. Watch a couple of guys get bagged and you can see at least one obvious disadvantage. Instead I had to find out how to be myself, which, without surgery, was female.

I was briefly inspired by my friend's instruction and did my best for a few weeks to be as girlie as possible. I noticed this change was accompanied by a drop in respect from my male friends. I even brought it up in conversation with them and they defied me to contradict the girlie-girl stereotype. It had been proven by the course of the twentieth century, they argued, that men were smart and strong and women were foolish and dependent. It was human nature. I found myself, because of my burgeoning gender awareness, railing against this argument with just about every boy I met. If I was going to have to be a girl, I had to show that girls were valid and capable human beings.

I began to realize I was going to meet resistance at every turn. The boys were very difficult to convince. So I made it my own personal goal to prove them all wrong. I would be a strong, smart, witty, kind and confident woman who would bow to no man, who would achieve her own goals and who would do it without resorting to being conniving, needy or suggestive.

But where was I going to find a role-model? What superhero fit that bill? In my search for the perfect action heroine, I was facing the same question: what superhero would fit the bill for my young friend?

Looking for the "all woman" role model for my friends' son, I scoured the shelves in the stores expecting a rich treasury of obscure babes in arms (the military kind) with cult status. No such luck. While there were hundreds of male figures of every stripe, type and ability, there were just a few women. They tended toward the ridiculously busty and were often so scantily clad that I would have been embarrassed to hand them over to a five year old. They were the least articulated figures and were often formed in exaggerated stances with their chests thrust forward and their butts thrust back. Many also had strangely angry, bitchy or scornful looks on their faces and seemed more frightening than tough, even when they were supposed to be fighting for good, reinforcing the notion that tough women have to be "bitchy."

X-men II had just been released, but I found no Storm, Rogue or Mystique dolls. There were three different Wolverines, a Nightcrawler and a Cyclops readily available. When I asked at the counter, the clerk, who happened to be female, said she thought they were planning to make them, but she wasn't sure when. For the *Lord of the Rings,* which had been out for some time, there were figures of hobbits, humans, and elves, there were orcs, wraiths and horses, all of them male. But no sign of the only female characters, Arwen, Galdriel or Eowen. Even Lisa Simpson wasn't her usually feisty self. She was dressed in her pink "Easter Dress" and had a teddy bear as an accessory instead of her saxophone. In a frustrating flashback to my youth, I could find no female figure that rivalled the power, agility and talent of the males.

In my teens, once my world-view changed to embrace the idea of tough women, like myself, my response to this lack of representation was to abandon much of pop culture. I lost interest. I was unimpressed and felt left out. No character ever lived up to my ideal. So I resolved to function in the world autonomously. If no one would show me the way, I would carve it myself. I didn't follow any rules. I didn't take much advice. I tried to ignore how my gender influenced my path and tried to get away with doing what I wanted.

For years I still spent much of my time with guys. I didn't look like one, and I didn't act like one, but I was not particularly girlie either. I thought I was getting the best of both worlds and in many ways I was. I was usually able to get away with a lot because people were surprised by this tough, young chick who would just go ahead and get things done. People would tell me, "I've never met a girl like you."

I imagined this same phrase being repeated to women everywhere, but was never quite sure what it meant. Of course no one had ever met a girl like me, or like any girl they had ever met. But our portrayals of women are all too frequently rooted in stereotyping and uni-dimensional characterization. Like the Barbies and Strawberry Shortcake dolls that influence girl's perceptions, many of the adult women we see in popular culture do not reflect the vast diversity of attitudes, body types and strengths of the girls and women we meet in real life. So people, I think, come to expect that the women they meet should fit tidily into one of the half dozen pre-conceived female archetypes.

It took many years of retraining, but I eventually learned that women are not born weak and silly. I grew to realize that there had been a disparity between the women that I saw on TV and the girls and women I met in real life. From the girls who I had ignored in grade school, to the young women I met in high school, and the ultra tough punk-rock chicks I met (and chose to emulate) at gigs and parties, I saw different types of women everywhere. It wasn't that girls sucked, but that the way girls were represented sucked.

It has been argued to me by friends who are fans of the superhero genre that TV audiences of the past weren't interested in strong women. Ratings showed that tough chicks didn't rack up the viewers like a tough guy, or a half-naked, sexy chick. People didn't want to know about women who overcame adversity, who took over and told people what to do, or who had remarkable intelligence or technical ability. People wanted their fantasy bimbos, their scrawny, unbelievable "tough" girls and their cute, mousy bookworms. I never believed it.

It wasn't until long after I graduated from university that I discovered the fictional role model I had been looking for all my life. She was tough — brawny even. She was smart, confident and didn't have to wear high heels. Screaming with fury, she flew across the TV screen flailing weapons, magic and clever comebacks. She wore leather and chains and rode horses into battle. She was sexy, but she was no one's love slave. And she was on an inner journey that was all her own.

Xena. Long after I thought I didn't need to be saved, she swung out of the forest and proved to me that it *was* possible: a female character could be all that and still accepted by the teeming masses. I remember seeing the ads announcing her arrival and setting my schedule to watch the first episode. I was eager for something good but ready for the disappointment I had come to expect. I kept waiting for the catch. Where's the secret desire to be beautiful and popular instead of tough? Where's the condescending father figure? Where's the love interest whose needs take precedent over hers? He never showed. I just about cried.

Since Xena, there have been a number of female fantasy characters on TV and in movies who have broken out of the traditional mould — Agent Scully of *The X-Files*, Captain Janeway of *StarTrek: Voyager*. And of course, before Xena were her predecessors Lt. Riply in *Alien* and Sarah Connor in *Terminator* among others. Although many of today's heroines, from Buffy to the movie version X-Women, are tougher, smarter and more independent than they ever were, there are many more who still suffer terribly from stereotyping. They stumble into their good deeds instead of acting with confidence and self-awareness. Too often, they resort to using sex as a weapon. And most of them have some man to whom they must defer. In fact many of today's superheroines have expanded girlie capabilities, like the amazing ability to change costumes dozens of times per adventure. This may be terribly exciting to some, but really has nothing at all to do with developing depth of character or plot, and only serves to reinforce the stereotype that no matter how far a woman's life takes her, she is still a slave to her appearance, languishing in a world where her most dangerous foe is the bad hair day and her greatest fear is the horror that she might have a big butt.

In the face of these difficulties I continued my search for the right plastic figurine. I did my best to find a Xena figure, but none were available, and the one I have is not as able-bodied as her live action counterpart. She can only bend at the elbows and knees. She wouldn't present much of a challenge to a fully poseable Lex Luther or Magneto.

I finally settled on a well-designed and highly articulated figure from the sci-fi TV cartoon *Battle of the Planets*: one of the members of G-Force, a troupe of fearless young orphans who protected Earth by acting as one. I ignored the fact that she was wearing pink and that she was called "Princess." She fit all the other requirements: she looked tough and cool, but not mean, she had a great cape, could bend and move and do just as many actions as her male counterparts. She wasn't the perfect woman, but who is? At least she was going to be able to hold her own.

By the time I presented the gift, I had also acquired a hand-me-down figure of Batwoman with an incredibly cool motorcycle accessory. Once it was opened, the motorcycle took centre stage. Girl, boy, superhero or regular mortal — nothing beats a cool motorcycle. Maybe my young friend will be oblivious to gender issues and grow up frustrated by the lack of equal time given to machines and cyborgs. At least he'll have a more diverse world to play in while he gets there.

The argument is still occasionally made by collectors that action figures and the comics and movies from which they originate are the domain of boys. Product buyers say they don't stock female characters because their primarily male clientele won't buy them. That argument suggests that girls just don't naturally like to read or watch stories about themselves. I believe that girls don't usually go for this stuff because they must resort to choosing from a vast array of male characters or accept the limitations placed on their fantasy peers.

Fortunately, each season brings new and interesting female characters. We are slowly developing pop culture fiction that reflects the diverse and valuable capabilities of real women. It isn't presumptuous to say that this is happening at the same time as women are taking on greater challenges and more adventurous roles in real life. In politics, industry, business and science, women are starting to bring to life the stories which at one time were only fantasy. Of course, there are still many fantasies to bring to life and many more adventures to come.

Battle on, Warrior Princesses!

THE COMBING

Larissa Lai

In the beginning we were two, me and little Green Fish. Green Fish was smaller, but stronger. She thought she owned me. When I was there to kiss her and read to her and eat the delicious noodles she cooked with vegetables and pork in a steaming broth, she was happy and her smile alone was enough to light our little lakeside house.

She sang old opera arias with a deep, settled contentment as she flipped and flopped in her floral-scented bath. The arias were mournful, maudlin even, though Green Fish didn't seem to register this. There was one in particular I didn't like, about a Taoist priest who traps a woman under a bowl and buries her for a thousand years. But Green Fish seemed to derive such pleasure from singing it, and I didn't want to take that from her. She used half a bar of Shanghai milled soap each time and emerged ruddy and smelling sweet. I pressed my nose into the soft skin at the nape of her neck and breathed her in. She loved the bath, but mistrusted larger bodies of water. We called each other White Snake and Green Fish, but we were human.

I loved Green Fish but didn't want to belong to anyone. Once, when she was busy tending flowers in front of the house, I slipped down the back stairs and into the lake. I lay beneath its still surface and watched the sky, too lazy to breathe. It was very quiet under there, cool and still. I emerged at sunset, covered in mud and algae, and trudged, refreshed, up the back steps and into the kitchen that smelled of chicken soup and warm cake. Green Fish was angry. "You have no consideration for me," she said. "When I'm not around, you don't think about me at all."

I pulled pond weeds out of my hair, slicked mud off my arms and shoulders onto her shiny clean kitchen floor. "That's not true," I said. "I love you." But the words, though I thought I meant them, came out with a lack of conviction. This didn't seem to surprise her.

"You don't need to comfort me," she said, and burst into tears. I took her in my muddy arms and stroked her clean, thick hair. I kissed the top of her head. She smelled like expensive shampoo and chicken soup.

"I do love you," I said. This time it came out better.

She said, "I think you better take a bath."

Green Fish already had a large pan of water sitting on top of the stove. Perhaps she had put it there to soak up as much heat from the fast-burning wood as possible, but she was not the frugal type. More likely, she had placed it there in anticipation of my return. She hoisted it up and carried it to a dark corner at the back of the kitchen where we kept our big wooden tub. She poured the hot water in, then ladled in some cool from our water tank. She shook in a generous handful of her favourite bath salts. While she did this, I helped myself to a bowl of chicken soup. It smelled good, but it was too hot and burned my tongue.

The bath was too hot too, and the salts so heavily scented that I sneezed and scratched my nose in irritation. She sat on a little three-legged stool beside the tub and watched me bathe. "Isn't that nicer than the bottom of that nasty, slimy lake?" she said.

"So much nicer," I lied. She looked happy, and I didn't want to spoil it.

In the morning I woke early, restless and eager to leave our too-hot house, the cloying warmth of the bed. I opened the door quietly so as not to wake her and stepped out onto the cool street. I walked all the way to town, bought myself three steamed buns for breakfast, and three more to present to Green Fish when she woke. The King of Masks stood changing faces outside the Balanced Humours Apothecary. A crowd of people had gathered to watch. I found myself a comfortable spot and stood munching my breakfast while the King swapped a hero's face for a villain's, then a thief's face for a princess's. His hands moved so fast I couldn't even see a blur. Each painted opera face seemed real — as sudden and perfect as an unexpected rainshower.

I swallowed the last bite of my last bun just as he was peeling off his final face, that of a guileless scholar. The crowd folded in on the empty space they had encircled to create a makeshift stage. People moved randomly in different directions, scurrying to make up for time lost so early in the morning. A beggar pushed his way toward me and put out his hands. I had no money and told him so. He pointed at the warm packet of buns I dangled from a red string. I shook my head and began to walk away, but he followed me. He was handsome in a desperate sort of way, with a long face full of sorrow.

At Blue Willow Gate, he revealed himself as the King of Masks. "You helped yourself to what I had to offer," he said. I felt cornered. I handed him my package. Green Fish would understand. She was not uncharitable. I stepped through the gate, crossed the pretty bridge that arched over a narrow stream and hurried to the house without looking back.

Green Fish had made tea. She had cut two persimmons into four neat pieces each and laid them carefully on two leaf-patterned plates. She sat at the table in front of her tidy breakfast, a deep frown marring her pretty face. "Why did you leave me all alone?" she asked.

"I needed air," I said. "I bought you breakfast but I met a beggar who looked like he needed it more than you did ... " My voice trailed off. It sounded like a lie. I felt helpless.

Her face contorted unpleasantly. *You don't think about me*, said that look. *You don't love me. You are incapable of love.*

I wanted to go away, to find a place where I could pull my own truth close again. I felt thin. I longed for the bottom of the lake. But if I left now, things would only get worse. Steeling my nerve and willing a smile up from some distant place inside, I sat down at the table and took a sip of tea. It was lukewarm, and there were leaves floating on top that stuck unpleasantly to my lips.

I don't think Green Fish was blind to the contradictory emotions that drove me. When I had obediently finished my tea and eaten my persimmon, she suggested we go out into the garden. We spent the morning moving stones to make a stepping-stone bridge across the little stream that flowed through our property. "This one is nice because of its jagged edge along the side here," said Green Fish, "and I like the way this bit curves a little over the top. And see the colour? It seems grey, but when you hold it toward the light there is some pink in it. Look."

Engrossed in the beauty of the stone, she seemed lovely to me again. I kissed her ear softly. She turned and smiled at me, the corners of her mouth curling up ever so slightly. Then she moved away to find a place to lay the stone.

I didn't go to the market for a whole week, though I did steal off on a number of occasions to slip beneath the surface of the lake and watch the slow quiet sky. To the full extent of my ability to attend to anyone, I attended to Green Fish, and it seemed to be enough. She awoke on Sunday morning with an urge to make dumplings. "You go to the market," she said. "You know I'm not good with people." *Minced pork*, said her shopping list, *bamboo shoots, chives, dried mushrooms, rice flour, eggs* ... I stuffed it happily into my pocket and set out. I took my time chatting with the vendors, eyeing their goods for the freshest things and haggling firmly but politely for good prices. Pleased with my purchases and looking forward to witnessing Green Fish's pleasure in receiving them, I turned and headed straight for home.

Who should I see at the market's entrance but the King of Masks trying to cajole a pear from a farmer with a huge cartful. "I'll buy this man a pear," I said to the vendor, feeling generous. I gave him a coin and the farmer reluctantly handed the King the smallest and wormiest of the lot. The King accepted it with mock grace, holding it up to the light as though to suggest it had the power to bestow immortality. He bit into the dry thing with such relish that anyone who watched would have been quite convinced it was succulent and moist. He ate every last morsel, except the seeds, which he spat, brown and glossy, into his hand.

By now a small crowd had gathered. The king knelt at our feet, poked a small hole in the earth with his fingers and dropped the seeds in. Then he covered the hole back over and poured a few drops of water from his canteen onto the spot. In minutes, a seedling sprouted. We watched in amazement as it stretched and thickened into a pear tree, its crooked branches covered in shiny leaves, fingering the sky. Amongst the leaves flowers bloomed, then faded, scattering their fragrant petals at our feet. Their scent made me think of Green Fish. Miraculously, fruit swelled from the eyes of the flowers and grew into the fattest, juiciest pears any of us had ever seen. The King of Masks shimmied up the tree and tossed the fruit to his delighted audience. We gobbled the pears down, our chins running with juice. The King came down and joined

us. While we ate, the leaves of the tree yellowed. A wind blew up and
swept them all away. The King of Masks drew an axe from his bag and
chopped the tree down, hacked off the branches and pared away at the
trunk until it formed a straight yet supple walking stick. Then he turned
and, leaning on the stick, strolled away from us out of the market.
People began to disperse. I turned to the pear vendor, but he was looking at his cart. It lay in pieces on the ground, missing one handle. There
was not a pear in sight.

If I could have helped him I would have, but there was nothing I
could do, so I gathered up my parcels and walked away in the direction
of home. The King of Masks was waiting for me on the path. "I know
about you," he said. "We are creatures of the same kind." I didn't know
what he meant. He frightened me.

"Stay and talk to me," he said. "All I want to do is comb your hair."
I didn't trust him, but I didn't want the fate that had befallen the pear
grower either. I understood the King to be, like me, less than natural,
but that was all I understood. I weighed my options: I could refuse him
and risk baldness, or I could stay and keep his good will. I chose the latter. He sat on a stump and made me sit on the ground between his knees
with my back to him. There was something humiliating about the position, and I felt myself growing resentful. He unpinned my hair and it
tumbled, thick and black, down my shoulders. I was proud of my hair.
When I became human, much of my snake nature had entered it. It was
sinuous and coiled and vibrant with life. I worried about the effects of
his comb, which he drew from the depths of his bag. But his hands were
gentle. He moved the comb liquidly through the mass of my hair, with
slow even strokes. Its teeth raked ever so lightly against my scalp. There
was something hypnotic about the feeling.

Afterwards, he rebraided and pinned it for me. "I'll see you again,"
he said. My hair, as I walked toward Blue Billow Gate, did not feel any
less alive, but I did feel somehow changed, and this disconcerted me.

"What took you so long?" Green Fish asked when I returned. I told
her about the King of Masks and the pear vendor, but not about meeting him again in the woods. She said, "This King of Masks is not a good
person. I don't think you should be buying him pears."

I nodded. "You might be right," I said. "I won't do it again." I gave
her all the parcels I had bought, and she unwrapped each one with
delight.

"All this nice pork for so little?" she exclaimed. "So fresh, these bamboo shoots!" I beamed at her. "You sit here and keep me company," she said. She pulled a little stool up beside the counter where she worked so I could watch as she chopped and stirred, sloshed in a little of this sauce or that, sprinkled salt, a few flakes of chili. Periodically she left her chopping and mixing to add a few more sticks to the fire, though it would be a while before the dumplings were ready to cook. "I don't want you to be cold," she said. I wished she would be a little more careful. It was I who did the bulk of the fuel foraging, and it was hard work. But the kitchen was warm and bright and her contentment was infectious. From where I sat she seemed tall and healthy and supernaturally beautiful. I gazed up at her with full eyes and tried to forget about the wasted fuel.

I relaxed a little when she put the first batch of dumplings on to steam. Now not only was the stove being put to good use, but a delicious aroma that calmed and soothed me filled the air. Green Fish moved easily among her plates and knives, happy and industrious. When she judged the batch done, she lifted the lid. A huge cloud of aromatic steam billowed into the air. When it cleared I could see the dumplings in the pan, their white skins steamed translucent, hinting at the promise of pork, chives and mushrooms beneath. With precisely wielded chopsticks she picked them up and dropped them in a bowl for me, along with soy sauce, red vinegar and chili oil. The gesture with which she placed the bowl in my hands was at once distracted and full of care. Already she was thinking about the next batch. I loved her the most when she was like that; present, but content in her own world. My eyes followed her every movement. She seemed very soft in the fire's yellow-orange glow. That kitchen light was so warm and encompassing I felt no need to look beyond it — certainly not to the dark window through which the excess steam and smoke flooded. I don't know what made my gaze shift long enough to adjust to the darkness outside, but suddenly I saw a pair of eyes there, piercing and bright. I registered them for the length of a full breath before I screamed. The eyes vanished.

"Are you crazy?" said Green Fish. "What is wrong with you?"

"Eyes," I said. "In the window."

The slowness went out of her. She darted anxiously to the window and looked out into the gathering dark. "I don't see anything," she scowled. "Honestly. Why are you so nervous? Are you hiding something from me?"

I felt suddenly guilty for not telling her about the King, though I couldn't say why. "Of course not," I said. It came out sounding like a lie, and I knew it. And I knew that it was already too late to fix.

"You're frightening me," she said. "Why do I get the feeling that you hide things from me?"

"I don't know," I said. I dug into my bowl of dumplings. They tasted good, except that she had added too much vinegar.

The light inside had changed. It now seemed cheap and sharp. It highlighted the build-up of grease on our kitchen walls and ceiling. When we went to bed that night there was something that lay between us. It made me feel uneasy, but I could not name it. I rolled away from her toward the wall, careful that our skins should not touch.

In the morning, as soon as it was light, I got out of bed and went down the back stairs to the lake. Noiselessly I slipped into the water, let my breathing drop to an infinitely slower register. I watched the sky above slowly begin to brighten. In the distance came the sound of a boat. A dark shape pulled toward me. The face that leaned toward the water when the boat was directly overhead was sinister and lovely, but this time I was not surprised to see it. I lay at the bottom still as death. The boat passed overhead but its passenger didn't see me.

After the boat was gone I felt no longing. I felt clean again, as though some trouble that had been bothering me had finally been removed. I closed my eyes and dozed until the sun was low in the sky and the lake bottom grew chilly. I crawled back up out of the water. Dripping but happy, I squelched up the back stairs of our house and into the kitchen. Imagine my surprise to see the King of Masks, eyes wide with terror, tied firmly to one of the kitchen's supporting posts. Green Fish sat in the shadows at the back of the kitchen, her face tense with anger. "Where have you been all day?" she said. "And why was this man skulking about our garden? He says he knows you."

"It's the King of Masks," I squeaked.

"I don't know what has passed between the two of you," she said, "but I can tell you this: I don't like it. Not one bit."

I gaped at her in silence.

"Well?" she said. "Don't you have anything to say?"

"I ..." I said. "Not really."

"What have you been doing with him?"

"I ... I bought him a pear." I looked at the King. It was his fault. Why didn't he explain himself? I glared at him, but his expression did not change.

"He says all he wanted was to comb your hair," she said. "What does that mean?"

"I don't know."

"He said you let him do it before."

"I suppose I did."

"Why didn't you tell me about it?"

"I don't know."

"I wouldn't let a strange man comb my hair," she said. "I don't appreciate you playing stupid. I know you aren't."

The King remained silent.

"He's creepy," I said.

"Then why didn't you stay away from him? Why did you open yourself up to him?"

We argued like this well into the night, until we were so exhausted and despairing we could hardly stand. The King of Masks neither moved nor spoke, though his terrified stare got a little more glassy as the night wore on. I began to hate him for his strange and unarticulated desire that interfered so poisonously in my relationship with Green Fish. "How can I trust you?" she asked. "You don't love me ..." She looked drained. Her eyelids seemed very heavy. I wanted to say something to assuage the worry I had caused her, but her eyes fell shut before I could find the words. Feeling suddenly depleted myself, I lay down beside her on the kitchen floor at the feet of the King and fell asleep.

In the night, an owl hooted and I opened one eye. It hooted again and I opened the other. Moonlight streamed through the kitchen window. Green Fish lay where she had fallen, her exhausted face soft with sleep. On his post, the King dozed too. His face was not peaceful and still, though. It twitched every now and then, convulsing, it seemed, at having accomplished some clever trick at someone else's expense. In his sleep, he snorted. He laughed.

How desperately I hated him. I rose from the cold stone floor and moved toward the jar on the counter in which Green Fish kept her knives. I drew the sharpest one from the jar, and whipped around to face the King. Still he slept. My heart was full of a terrible wrath, a fury beyond fury. The anger rushed into my hands and I plunged it deep into his belly. His surprised liver and heart leapt out through the gash. As they did he awoke. His blood poured down the post and drenched the still sleeping form of Green Fish.

I could have hidden from the Taoist priest when he came for me, but in truth I wanted to be punished. Meek and exhausted, I crawled into the little white bowl that he held toward me. I don't know what happened to Green Fish. Absorbed in my own guilt I lost sight of her completely.

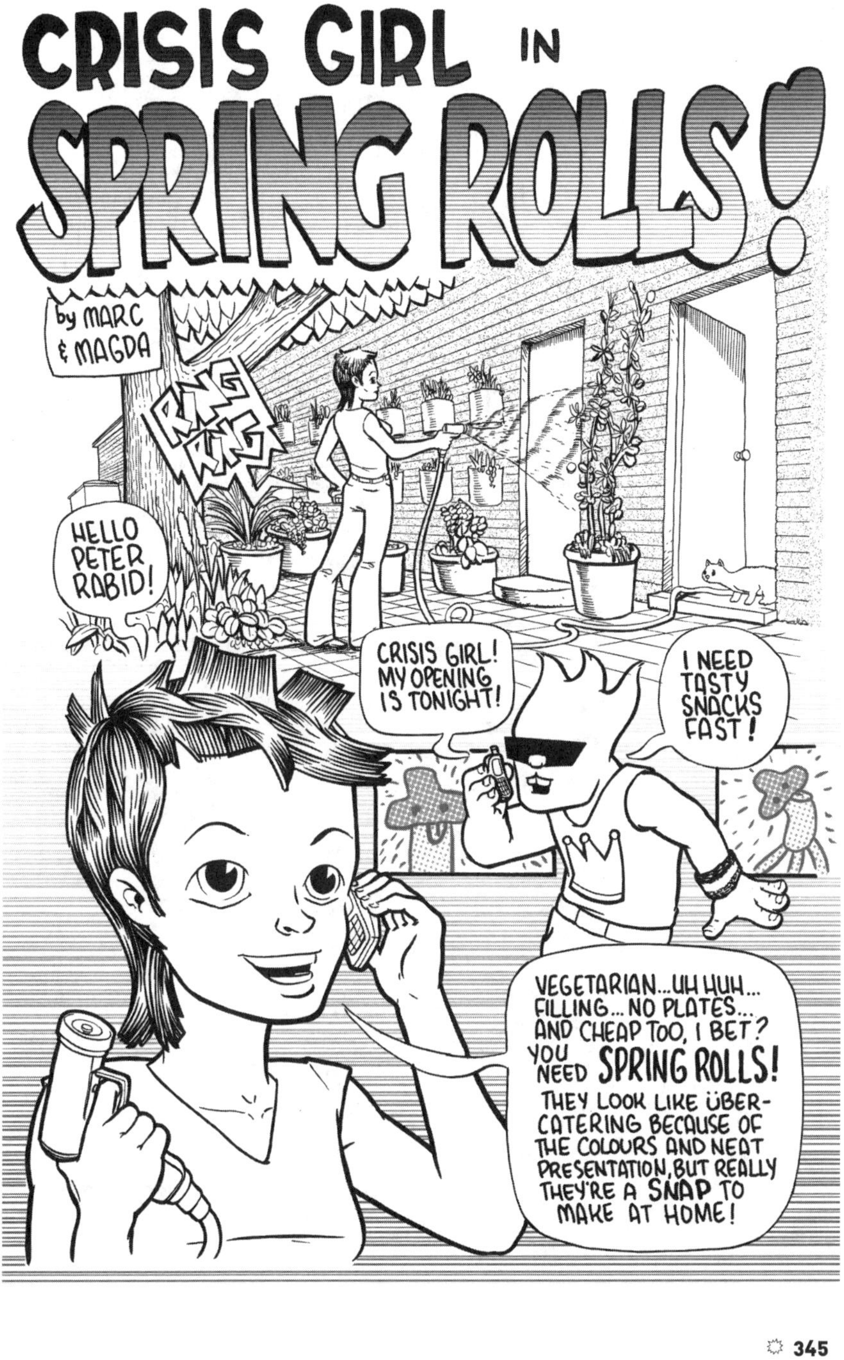
CRISIS GIRL IN
SPRING ROLLS!
by MARC & MAGDA
RING RING
HELLO PETER RABID!
CRISIS GIRL! MY OPENING IS TONIGHT!
I NEED TASTY SNACKS FAST!
VEGETARIAN... UH HUH... FILLING... NO PLATES... AND CHEAP TOO, I BET? YOU NEED SPRING ROLLS!
THEY LOOK LIKE ÜBER-CATERING BECAUSE OF THE COLOURS AND NEAT PRESENTATION, BUT REALLY THEY'RE A SNAP TO MAKE AT HOME!

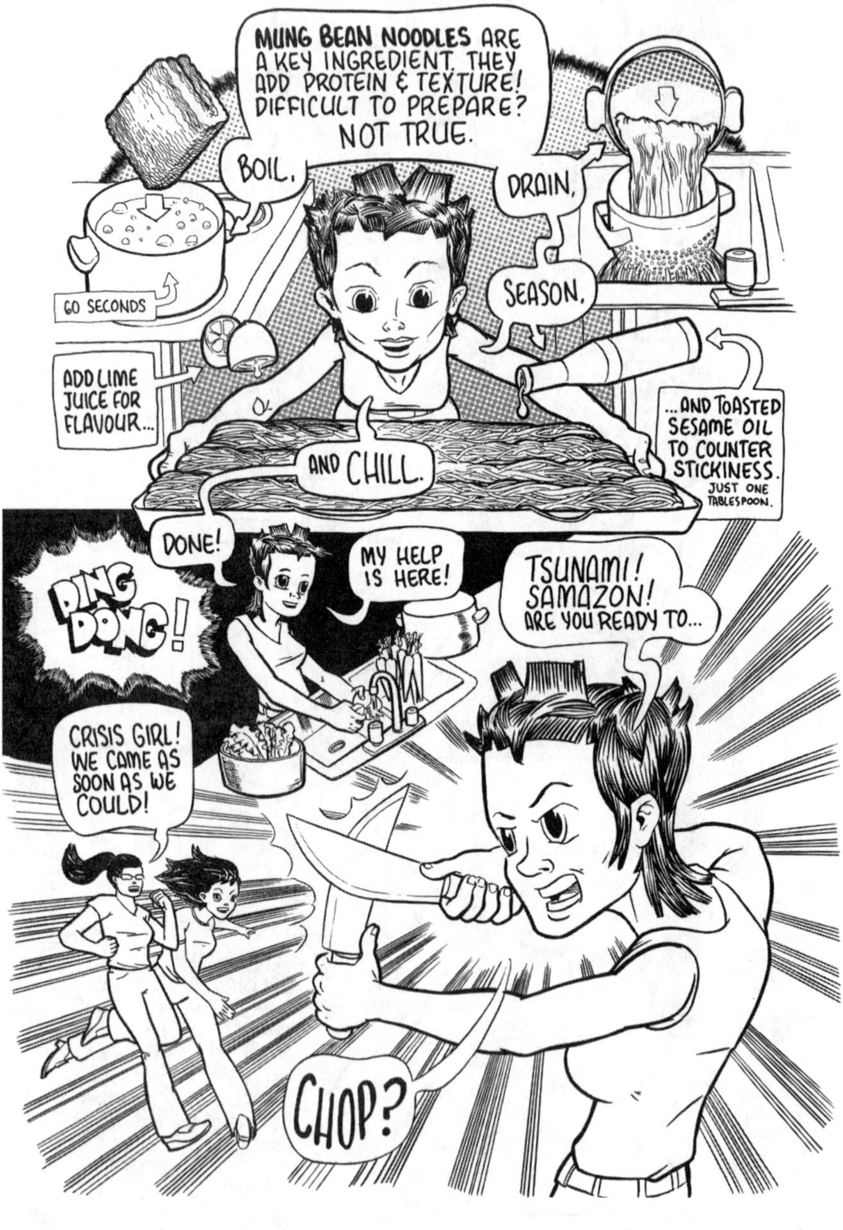
MUNG BEAN NOODLES ARE A KEY INGREDIENT. THEY ADD PROTEIN & TEXTURE! DIFFICULT TO PREPARE? NOT TRUE.
BOIL,
60 SECONDS
DRAIN,
SEASON,
ADD LIME JUICE FOR FLAVOUR...
...AND TOASTED SESAME OIL TO COUNTER STICKINESS.
JUST ONE TABLESPOON.
AND CHILL.
DONE!
MY HELP IS HERE!
DING DONG!
TSUNAMI! SAMAZON! ARE YOU READY TO...
CRISIS GIRL! WE CAME AS SOON AS WE COULD!
CHOP?

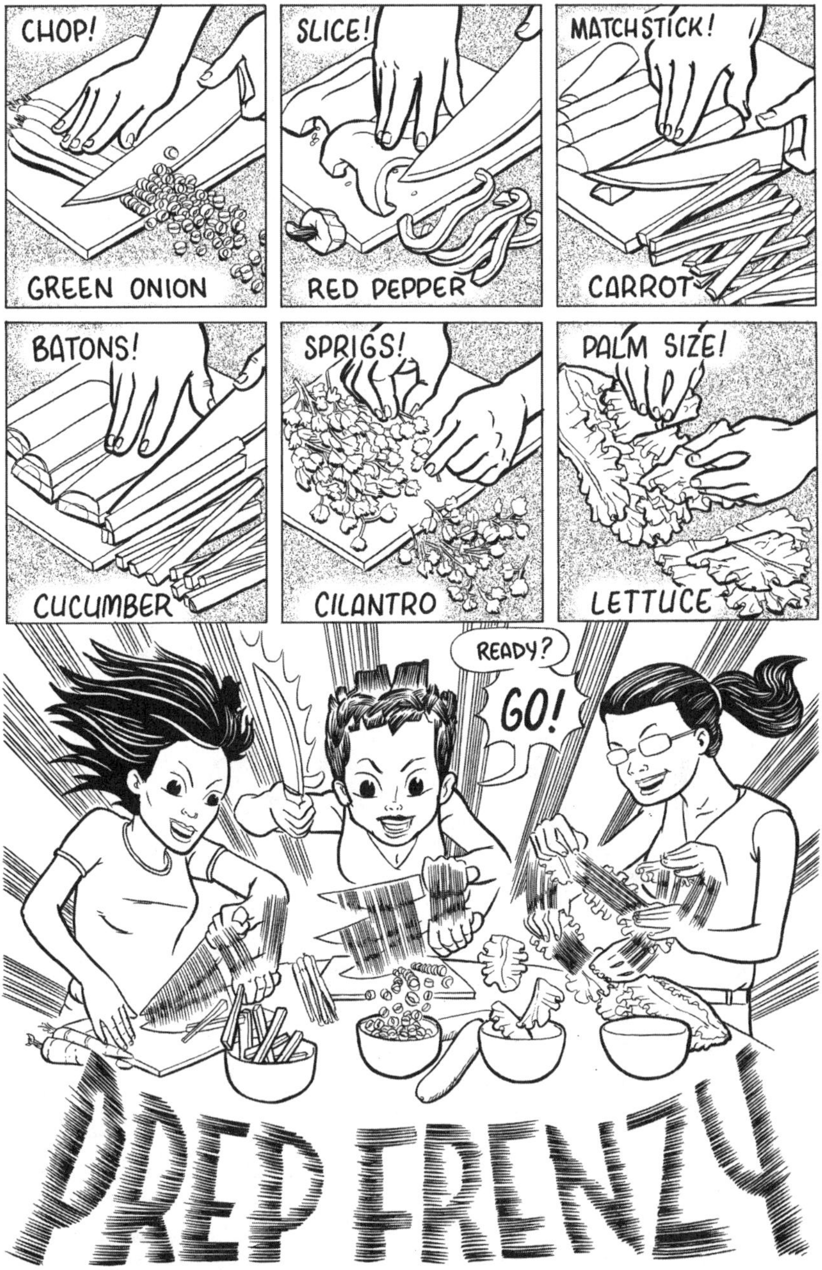
CHOP!
GREEN ONION
SLICE!
RED PEPPER
MATCHSTICK!
CARROT
BATONS!
CUCUMBER
SPRIGS!
CILANTRO
PALM SIZE!
LETTUCE
READY?
GO!
PREP FRENZY

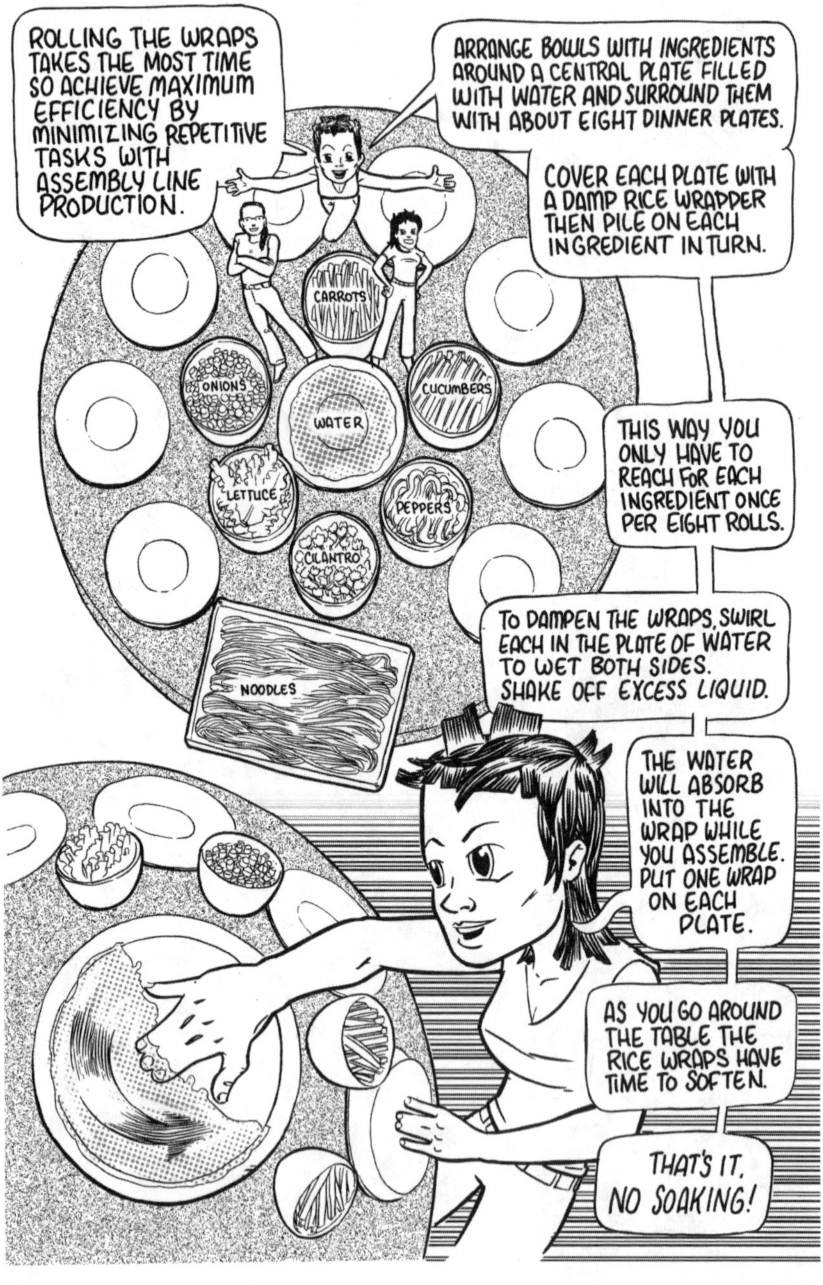
ROLLING THE WRAPS TAKES THE MOST TIME SO ACHIEVE MAXIMUM EFFICIENCY BY MINIMIZING REPETITIVE TASKS WITH ASSEMBLY LINE PRODUCTION.
ARRANGE BOWLS WITH INGREDIENTS AROUND A CENTRAL PLATE FILLED WITH WATER AND SURROUND THEM WITH ABOUT EIGHT DINNER PLATES.
COVER EACH PLATE WITH A DAMP RICE WRAPPER THEN PILE ON EACH INGREDIENT IN TURN.
CARROTS
ONIONS
CUCUMBERS
WATER
LETTUCE
PEPPERS
CILANTRO
NOODLES
THIS WAY YOU ONLY HAVE TO REACH FOR EACH INGREDIENT ONCE PER EIGHT ROLLS.
TO DAMPEN THE WRAPS, SWIRL EACH IN THE PLATE OF WATER TO WET BOTH SIDES. SHAKE OFF EXCESS LIQUID.
THE WATER WILL ABSORB INTO THE WRAP WHILE YOU ASSEMBLE. PUT ONE WRAP ON EACH PLATE.
AS YOU GO AROUND THE TABLE THE RICE WRAPS HAVE TIME TO SOFTEN.
THAT'S IT, NO SOAKING!

PACKING GUIDE

SPRINKLE OF ONIONS

SPRIG OF CILANTRO

LONG VEGGIES FOR RIGIDITY

NOODLES FOR CUSHIONING

LETTUCE FOR SUPPORT AND RICE WRAP REINFORCEMENT

DON'T OVERLOAD!

ROLLING GUIDE

1. ROLL FIRST THIRD. TUCK ALL INGREDIENTS INTO WRAP.

SQUEEZE DOWN!

2. FOLD OVER END FLAPS. SQUEEZE SOME MORE.

IF THE WRAP RIPS IN ① OR ② YOU CAN FIX IT IN ③

3. SQUEEZE AND CONTINUE ROLLING FOR MAXIMUM THINNESS.

4. FINISH THE ROLL WITH EVEN PRESSURE. GLUE DOWN THE END WITH A BIT OF WATER.

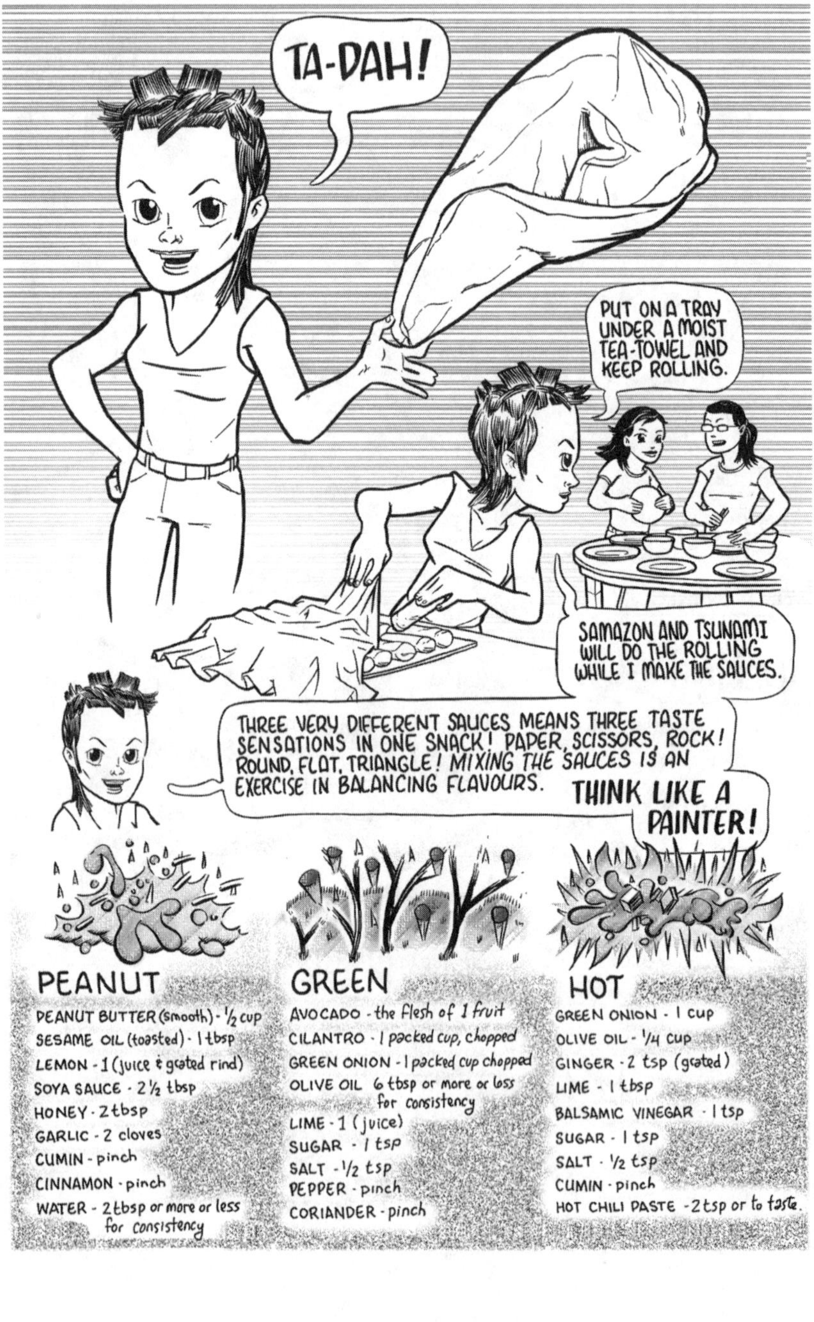
TA-DAH!
PUT ON A TRAY UNDER A MOIST TEA-TOWEL AND KEEP ROLLING.
SAMAZON AND TSUNAMI WILL DO THE ROLLING WHILE I MAKE THE SAUCES.
THREE VERY DIFFERENT SAUCES MEANS THREE TASTE SENSATIONS IN ONE SNACK! PAPER, SCISSORS, ROCK! ROUND, FLAT, TRIANGLE! MIXING THE SAUCES IS AN EXERCISE IN BALANCING FLAVOURS.
THINK LIKE A PAINTER!
PEANUT
PEANUT BUTTER (smooth) - 1/2 cup
SESAME OIL (toasted) - 1 tbsp
LEMON - 1 (juice & grated rind)
SOYA SAUCE - 2 1/2 tbsp
HONEY - 2 tbsp
GARLIC - 2 cloves
CUMIN - pinch
CINNAMON - pinch
WATER - 2 tbsp or more or less for consistency
GREEN
AVOCADO - the flesh of 1 fruit
CILANTRO - 1 packed cup, chopped
GREEN ONION - 1 packed cup chopped
OLIVE OIL 6 tbsp or more or less for consistency
LIME - 1 (juice)
SUGAR - 1 tsp
SALT - 1/2 tsp
PEPPER - pinch
CORIANDER - pinch
HOT
GREEN ONION - 1 cup
OLIVE OIL - 1/4 cup
GINGER - 2 tsp (grated)
LIME - 1 tbsp
BALSAMIC VINEGAR - 1 tsp
SUGAR - 1 tsp
SALT - 1/2 tsp
CUMIN - pinch
HOT CHILI PASTE - 2 tsp or to taste.

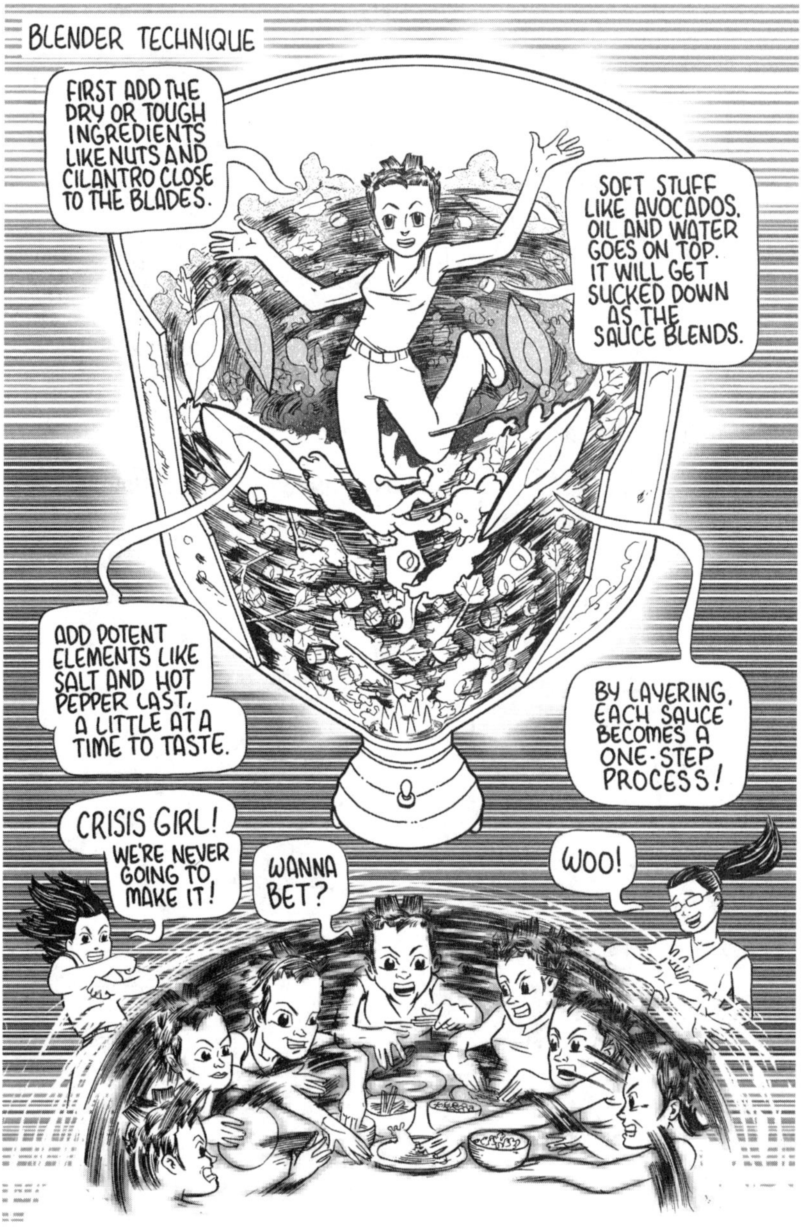
BLENDER TECHNIQUE
FIRST ADD THE DRY OR TOUGH INGREDIENTS LIKE NUTS AND CILANTRO CLOSE TO THE BLADES.
SOFT STUFF LIKE AVOCADOS, OIL AND WATER GOES ON TOP. IT WILL GET SUCKED DOWN AS THE SAUCE BLENDS.
ADD POTENT ELEMENTS LIKE SALT AND HOT PEPPER LAST, A LITTLE AT A TIME TO TASTE.
BY LAYERING, EACH SAUCE BECOMES A ONE-STEP PROCESS!
CRISIS GIRL! WE'RE NEVER GOING TO MAKE IT!
WANNA BET?
WOO!

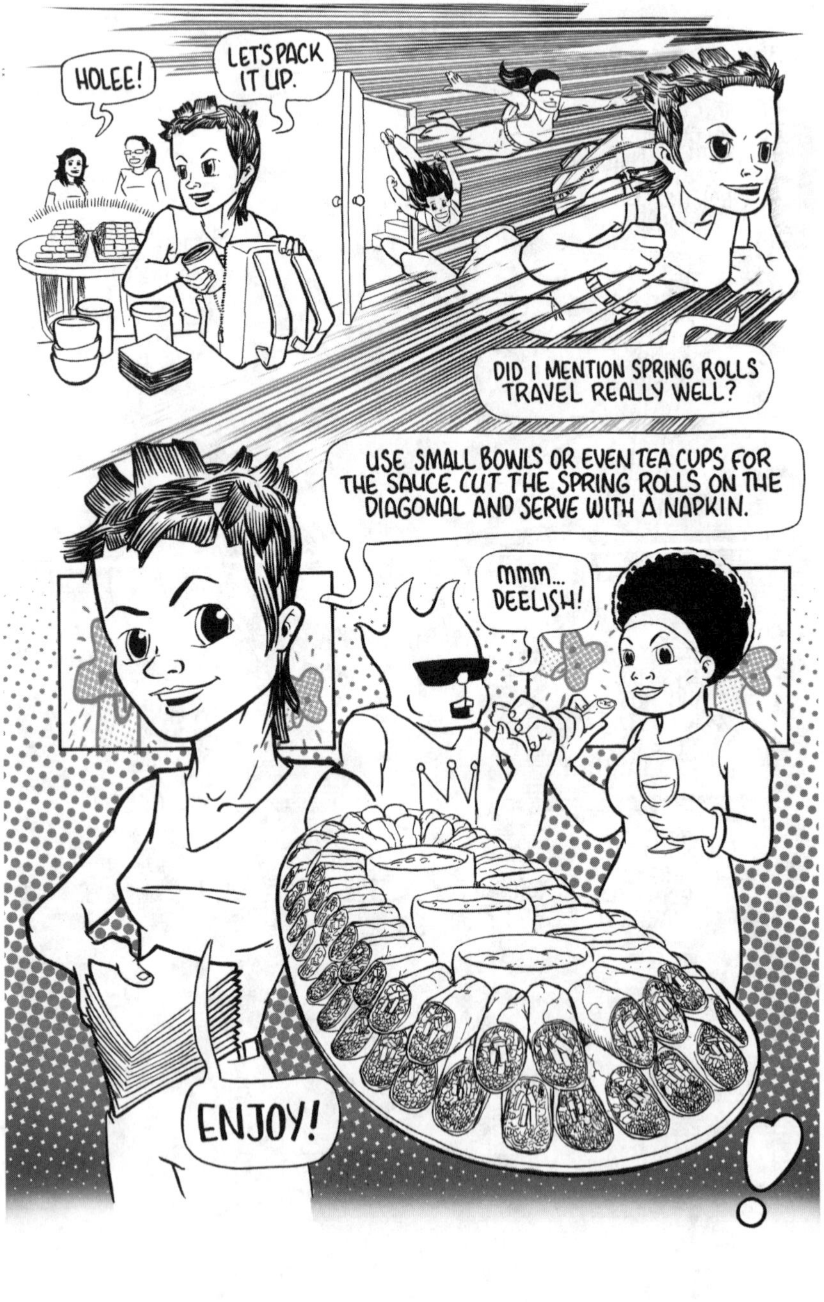
HOLEE!
LET'S PACK IT UP.
DID I MENTION SPRING ROLLS TRAVEL REALLY WELL?
USE SMALL BOWLS OR EVEN TEA CUPS FOR THE SAUCE. CUT THE SPRING ROLLS ON THE DIAGONAL AND SERVE WITH A NAPKIN.
mmm... DEELISH!
ENJOY!

CONTRIBUTORS

SONJA ELIZABETH AHLERS lives and works in Vancouver, BC. She just finished her new big book, *Fatal Distraction* — the five-years-in-the-works follow-up to *Temper, Temper* — which is due in the fall of 2004. She just toured for a month with the Bookmobile Project/*Projet Mobilivre* — the world's greatest project. She is about to turn off Missy Elliott's "Love Will Freak Us" and "Enter the Bitch" to go watch the movie *Foxes* (again) and sew a Siamese twin angora fierce bunny. It is Saturday night.

ROSE BIANCHINI has reincarnated many times as a youth worker, artist, editor, cultural creator, counsellor, writer and filmmaker. She believes that everything intersects if you look hard enough.

MATTHEW BLACKETT is the cartoonist of *m@b* and a freelance graphic artist.

SHARY BOYLE's practice is based in drawing and painting and extends into sculpture, performance and installation. She has exhibited and travelled internationally, setting up temporary studios from Avondale to Amsterdam. Her work has been published in magazines, comic anthologies and literary journals — most recently *The Walrus*, *The Story of Jane Doe*, *Shift*, *L.A Times Magazine*, *Canadian Art*, *Fireweed*, *J&L's Publications #2* and *Starship*. Boyle is currently working on porcelain figurines to be shown at Vancouver's Or Gallery in March 2004.

SUSAN BUSTOS is a graduate student in biochemistry at the University of Toronto where she researches the structure of mutant proteins. Her contribution to this anthology is her first scientific publication. She lives in the Annex neighbourhood with her husband.

SHEILA BUTLER is a visual artist and teacher. She has exhibited in both solo and group exhibitions in Canada and abroad, the most recent a small group exhibition at Stichting Kunst and Complex, Rotterdam, The Netherlands, in December 2002. Her work is included in Canadian collections such as the

National Gallery of Canada, the Art Gallery of Hamilton, The University of Toronto and the Winnipeg Art Gallery. Since 1989, she has been a member of the Visual Arts faculty at the University of Western Ontario, teaching undergraduate and graduate level courses in studio and contemporary theory and criticism.

MEAGAN CRUMP is a writer and the sole proprietor of Crump Industries.

WILLOW DAWSON is a texturally expressive artist who specializes in mixed media and illustration with a dark, edgy style. She is currently studying illustration at the Ontario College of Art and Design in Toronto. Published works include *Jezebelle*, a six-issue self-published zine series of art and poetry, and *Mother May I*, the first of a four-issue comic-book series on sexual assault written by Sarrah Young. Dawson has contributed art to Paul Sizer's *Little White Mouse, Open Space* #4, and John Greiner's *Wheelchair Riot.* She is currently developing a new book called "Gypsy" with writer Chaos McKenzie, and is illustrating her own autobiographical comic book/zine, *Not Yer Princess.*

A.M. DELLAMONICA had the kind of action-packed childhood that most people dream of, featuring actual plane crashes and the occasional long car trip. Her fiction first appeared in print in 1986 and — despite repeated washings — remains in circulation in a variety of locales, most recently *On-Spec* magazine. Her next anthology appearances will be in *Alternate Generals III: The Many Faces of Van Helsing* and *The Faery Reel.* Three other works can be found anytime at *Scifi.com.* Her 2002 *Asimov's Science Fiction* piece, "A Slow Day at the Gallery," is out in the *Year's Best Science Fiction #8.*

CANDRA K. GILL completed an MA in English literature and pedagogy from Northern Michigan University in December of 2002. She currently teaches college composition. Gill grew up in a home where speculative fiction novels, movies, television shows and magazines were regularly available, which resulted in her interest in the intersection between fandom and academia. She is a regular attendee of WisCon, the annual feminist SF convention for which she first wrote the piece that appears in this collection.

Originally from Windsor, Ontario, NANCY GOBATTO received her MA in English and Creative Writing from the University of Windsor and is currently working on a PhD in Women's Studies at York University (Toronto). Her writing has appeared in *Zygote, Guidance and Counselling, Kiss Machine, The Green Tricycle, XX Magazine, Word: Toronto's Literary Calendar,* and *Taddle Creek.* She clings desperately to Angel as her remaining connection to the Buffyverse and sees her therapist once a week, usually on Mondays.

HIROMI GOTO is the award-winning author of *The Kappa Child* and *Chorus of Mushrooms*. A collection of short stories, *Hopeful Monsters*, will be published in Spring 2004 with Arsenal Pulp Press. She also authored a children's fantasy novel, *The Water of Possibility*.

Ottawa-based ELIZA GRIFFITHS is a figurative painter whose work navigates a psycho-socio-sexual terrain through a framework of invented characters. She was born in London, England, in 1965 and emigrated to Canada in 1973. She received a BFA (studio) from Concordia and has had solo exhibitions across Canada and the United States.

NALO HOPKINSON of Toronto is a novelist, short-story writer and anthologist, and a chunky Black chick in a skinny blonde world. Don't even get her started on superhero women who seem to have high heels glued to their feet. Her new novel, *The Salt Roads*, visits with some kick-butt supernatural African women.

KIJ JOHNSON has sold several novels, including *The Fox Woman* and *Fudoki*, and dozens of short stories. She won the Theodore A. Sturgeon award for best short story, and the International Association for the Fantastic in the Art's Crawford Award for best new fantasy work of the year. She is currently at work on a new book, but she writes short fiction when she has the brain cells free. She lives in Kansas with writer Chris McKitterick.

DANIEL HEATH JUSTICE is an enrolled citizen of the Cherokee Nation and was raised in that part of the Mouache Ute territory known as Victor, Colorado. He now lives with his husband in the traditional lands of the Wendat Nation, where he is Assistant Professor of Aboriginal literatures at the University of Toronto.

SANDRA KASTURI is a poet, writer and editor. Her most recent project is the speculative poetry anthology, *The Stars As Seen from this Particular Angle of Night*, from The Bakka Collection/Red Deer Press. Her poetry has appeared in various magazines and anthologies, including several of the *Tesseracts* anthologies, *On Spec, Contemporary Verse 2, Prairie Fire* and *2001: A Science Fiction Poetry Anthology*. Kasturi has received four honourable mentions in *The Year's Best Fantasy & Horror* and runs her own imprint, Kelp Queen Press. She has also won a Bram Stoker Award for her editorial work at the on-line magazine, *ChiZine* (http://chizine.com).

LARISSA LAI was born in La Jolla, California to superhero immigrant parents, although she herself is, sadly, mortal. She grew up in St. John's, Newfoundland,

and lived in Vancouver for many years. This story was written during her MA studies at the University of East Anglia in England in 2000. She has written two novels, *When Fox Is a Thousand* and *Salt Fish Girl*, which was nominated for the Tiptree Award, the Sunburst Award and the W.O. Mitchell Award. She was the winner of the 1996 Astraea Foundation Emerging Writer's Award and the 2002 Xtra West Queer Heroes Award for Achievement in the Arts. Lai is currently working on her PhD in English at the University of Calgary.

SOPHIE LEVY is a writer, teacher, editor and all-purpose word-nerd. She has published a book of poetry, *Marsh Fear/Fen Tiger*, and a chapbook entitled *These Are the Licks* (cover art by SuperArtist Willow Dawson), both available at www.shebytches.com/sheshoppe.html. At Shebytches, you'll also find her alter ego, Pixie, casting a glitter-eyeshadowed eye over grrrl culture in T.O. Currently lounging in academia, she has no idea what she will be when she grows up, but her top three options are: International Woman of Mystery; Chair of Buffy Studies at the University of Somewhere with Good Weather; and, most likely, still an All-Purpose Word-Nerd.

CARMA LIVINGSTONE believes if you close your eyes and concentrate really hard, you will start to see beautiful coloured lights. In this plane of existence, Livingstone is a documentary producer at CBC Radio. "Madame Mouth's Little Get-Together" is her first published fiction.

JUDY MACDONALD is working on her second novel, "Solid." Her first book, *Jane*, is in development as a feature film. Felicity Grace would not have come to be without the inspiration of director Jerry Ciccoritti, the comic-book genius of connoisseur Steve Cope, and the cheerful enthusiasm of editor Emily Pohl-Weary.

MARC NGUI studied architecture at the University of Waterloo. He now spends his days doing illustration, comics, diagrams, storyboards, animation, multimedia installations and performances. His first graphic novel, *Enter Avariz*, was published in 2002. To see more of his work visit www.bumblenut.com.

PAOLA POLETTO is a mixed-media artist, arts administrator, poet and curator. She is co-curator of Digifest (2002–), an international digital media festival produced by the Design Exchange. Artist-curated projects include "Inflatable Museum" (on-line 2001–), "Girls and Guns" (Toronto-London, 2003) and "Robot Landscape" (Toronto, 2004). Exhibitions include "Rose Architecture" (Toronto-New York, 1999), "Moonscapes" (London-Toronto-Berlin, 2000),

"Rockit Girl" (London, ON-Toronto, 2000) and "Language Hotel" (Winnipeg, 2000). Poletto is also co-founder of the independent arts and literature magazine, *Kiss Machine.*

LISA RUNDLE is senior editor at *The Walrus* magazine and a columnist at *Herizons*. As a freelancer, she has written for *Saturday Night, This Magazine,* and *The Toronto Star.* She is a former editor of *rabble.ca.* She has her Masters in Women's Studies from York University and, with Allyson Mitchell and Lara Karaian, co-edited *Turbo Chicks: Talking Young Feminisms* (Sumach Press, 2001), an anthology filled with everyday superheroes. She is thrilled to have worked on this collection for Sumach with the supernatural Emily Pohl-Weary.

LISA SMOLKIN was born out of original sin in Williams Lake, BC. She makes art in the context of healing, expression and her own aesthetic correctness. Her influences include women and girls who have been silenced, the movie *White Nights,* heaven and delicious wholesome foods. She lives in a Toronto base-ment with her delightful son Jackie Elijah Dream.

NIKKI STAFFORD has written several books on sci-fi fandom and tough TV women, including *Lucy Lawless and Reneé O'Connor: Warrior Stars of Xena* (1998) and *Bite Me! An Unofficial Guide to the World of Buffy the Vampire Slayer* (2002). She has also edited two collections of fan stories, *How Xena Changed Our Lives* and *Trekkers: True Stories by Fans for Fans* (all published by ECW Press). She is working on two books for publication in 2004 on the television shows *Angel* and *Alias,* and lives in Toronto with her husband and two cats.

CARLY STASKO is a young grassroots activist, artist and educator who gives workshops in high schools and universities where she promotes critical think-ing, confidence and civics. A former producer at CBC Newsworld's *counterSpin,* Stasko is a facilitator of the Toronto Media Collective, a network of artists and activists who promote social justice. She publishes the zine *uncool* and is a contributor to *Turbo Chicks: Talking Young Feminisms.* She is also a board member for *THIS* magazine; her writing and art have been published in magazines such as *The Utne Reader, Canadian Dimensions, Fuse, Fireweed* and *THIS.*

By day, CATHERINE STINSON is a mild-mannered computer geek, book review-er for *Trade* magazine, organizer of the Toronto Church of Craft and tea drinker. By night, she plays a mean game of hockey, rides her bicycle at break-neck speed and likes to arm-wrestle in seedy bars.

MARIKO TAMAKI is a Toronto writer and performer currently kicking at the darkness till it bleeds daylight. Tamaki has published two books, *Cover Me* and *True Lies: The Book of Bad Advice,* and has appeared on stage with the likes of The Corporate Wet Nurse Association, Pretty Porky and Pissed Off, and TOA. Tamaki's third book, *Fake ID,* is due out in the spring of 2005.

SHERWIN TJIA is a poet, painter and illustrator, and author of *Pedigree Girls* and *Gentle Fictions* (Insomniac). His work has appeared in *Adbusters, Kiss Machine, Maisonneuve, dig, Geist, Trucker, Quarry, the Literary Review of Canada, Hive Magazine, Queen Street Quarterly, THIS Magazine, Crank,* and *Wegway.* He also appears in the anthologies *Career Suicide* (DC Books), *Geeks, Misfits and Outlaws* (McGilligan Books), *Sun Through the Blinds* (Shoreline), *Striking the Wok* (TSAR), and *The I.V. Lounge Reader* (Insomniac).

HALLI VILLEGAS divides her time between Toronto, Detroit and Woodville, Ontario. She has published two books of poetry, *Red Promises* (2001) and *In the Silence Absence Makes* (2004), both with Guernica Editions. Her work has appeared in *The Fiddlehead, The Annex Gleaner, Surface and Symbol, ATQ* and *Pagitica* in Toronto, among other publications. Villegas's work has recently been translated into Korean and will be appearing in the Korean/English language magazine *Variety Crossings.* She is currently working on a novel.

ESTHER VINCENT lives and writes in Peterborough. She tries to use her superpowers for good.

ELIZABETH WALKER's first crush was on a character from G-Force. She was five. Almost twenty-five years later, she lives and works in Toronto, where she is still a sucker for the dark hero in a cape.

ZOE WHITTALL is author of the book of poems titled *The Best 10 Minutes of Your Life* (McGilligan Books) and editor of *Geeks, Misfits & Outlaws,* an anthology of short fiction. She is writing a graphic novel with her partner Suzy Malik called "Self-Serve" and is finishing up a short-story collection titled "Bottle Rocket Hearts."

MAGDA WOJTYRA is a multidisciplinary artist and designer exploring the relationship between digital and traditional media, with a strong focus on colour. Her recent works include Web sites, digital art prints, textile art, custom colour jello sculptures, doll-making, furniture, interior design and theatrical backdrops. She has been published in *Domus, Shift, Strut* and *Digital Journal Magazines.* Wojtyra studied architecture at the University of Waterloo.

EMILY POHL-WEARY co-authored the Hugo Award-winning book about her grandmother's life, *Better to Have Loved: The Life of Judith Merril*. Merril, the "little mother of science fiction," wrote gender-bending science fiction in the 1950s. *Better to Have Loved* has been praised in *The Globe and Mail, Asimov's Science Fiction, The San Francisco Bay Guardian* and *The Village Voice*.

Pohl-Weary has been editing *Kiss Machine: A Conga Line of Arts and Culture* (www.kissmachine.org) since 2000, and is a regular writer for Toronto's entertainment weekly, *Now,* among other magazines. She's a former editor of *Broken Pencil: The Guide to Zine Culture and the Independent Arts* and is currently writing a silly novel.

More info about Pohl-Weary can be found at
http://emily.openflows.org

Have your say about female superheroes!
Visit the on-line *Girls Who Bite Back* discussion forum:
www.girlswhobiteback.com